Enforcement of the EU Public Procurement Rules

Steen Treumer & François Lichère (eds)

Enforcement of the EU Public Procurement Rules

DJØF Publishing Copenhagen
2011

Steen Treumer & François Lichère (eds)
Enforcement of the EU Public Procurement Rules
European Procurement Law Series vol. 3
First Edition 2011

DJØF Publishing is a company of the
Association of Danish Lawyers and Economists

Cover design: Bo Helsted
Print: Toptryk Grafisk, Gråsten

Printed in Denmark 2011
ISBN 978-87-574-2328-0

Sold and distributed in North America by:
International Specialized Book Services (ISBS)
Portland, OR 97213, USA
www.isbs.com

Sold in all other countries by:
DJØF Publishing Copenhagen
Denmark
www.djoef-forlag.dk

DJØF Publishing
17, Lyngbyvej
P.O.Box 2702
DK-2100 Copenhagen
Denmark

Phone: +45 39 13 55 00
Fax: +45 39 13 55 55
E-mail: forlag@djoef.dk
www.djoef-forlag.dk

Table of Contents

Foreword by the Editors of the European Procurement Law Series

This is the third volume in the Series where we tackle another core issue in EU public procurement law: Enforcement. An analysis of enforcement of the EU public procurement rules is of particular interest not only for those working in the field but also for those with a general interest in EU law or in enforcement of law. It is highly interesting from a general perspective because it is an area of law where the European legislator has made exceptional efforts in order to ensure effective enforcement at national level and has pushed the development forward. In this respect the state of the law in the field of public procurement deviates from the clear starting point in EU law. As a main rule remedies and procedural law concerning breaches of the law are considered matters for the national legislator according to the principle of national and remedial autonomy.

The European Commission showed early awareness of the fact that measures had to be taken in order to ensure fast and efficient enforcement of the public procurement rules at national level. This led to the adoption of the so-called Remedies Directives – Directive 89/665 and Directive 92/13 – applicable for the classic sector and the utilities sector respectively. These Directives are still the essential sources of law in the area even though these Directives recently were amended and developed with Remedies Directive 2007/66.

Another feature that makes this field particularly interesting is that the Court of Justice of the European Union also has been highly aware of the importance of effective enforcement in the field of public procurement. As a consequence the Court of Justice has interpreted the law in a very dynamic manner in a number of landmark cases leading to fundamental improvements of the enforcement system both at national and supranational level.

Public Procurement is also a field of law where you can find noteworthy examples of dynamic interpretation at national level. It is remarkable that the principle of effectiveness appears to have been used in some national jurisdictions as a lever for the creation of new law when national courts or review boards have deviated from their respective traditional laws i.e. on damages. Examples of this can be found in several Member States which is rather surprising as remedies and procedural law are in general to be considered as matters for the national legislator, cf. the principle of national and procedural autonomy mentioned above. However, this autonomy is subject to a number of limitations, namely the principles of equivalence and effectiveness. To establish the impact of these principles on the regulatory competence of the Member States is highly complex as it essentially concerns interpretation of a vague legal standard with unclear boundaries. These are therefore many possible interpretations and it is frequently very uncertain whether a given interpretation is correct.

Enforcement of the public procurement rules also takes place at supranational level as the European Commission supervises the compliance of Member States with their obligations under EU law. The Commission has used the procedure in numerous cases in the field of public procurement. Enforcement at supranational level is a very important part of the enforcement regime and can have major impact on the development of the substantive public procurement law in a Member State or in the Union as such. It should be borne in mind that there occasionally is interaction between the developments of the enforcement regime at supranational level and that at national level in the sense that developments at supranational level support or inspire national developments.

The analysis in this publication concentrates on national enforcement of the EU public procurement rules for various reasons. The main reasons are that enforcement mainly takes place at national level and that there is recent, important and unclear legislation (Remedies Directive 2007/66) not covered in much detail in existing legal literature. Furthermore, the comparative research agenda of the European Public Procurement Series makes it obvious and preferable to focus on the state of law in the Member States as there are remarkable variations and it is debatable whether they all are leading to effectiveness and compatible with the requirements of EU law.

The subject has already received scholarly attention. However, publications in this series are the result of the collaboration within a European research group made of academics specialized in procurement law who consider a comparative approach both valuable and necessary. Comparative knowledge may help to avoid mistakes and inspire to possibly different approaches to what are in the end the same principles and rules. Comparative information and analysis of procurement law and practice in the various Member States is therefore an important tool for the development of procurement regulation and practice in the EU.

More specifically, it is valuable for practitioners in the Member States to be aware of practices, regulation, case law, and interpretations of procurement law throughout the EU as this can assist them both in understanding the rules applicable and in developing best practices. As the Court of Justice reminds us on its official website, the courts of the Member States are the 'ordinary courts in matters of EU law'. National courts and review bodies may, and in some cases must, refer questions to the Court of Justice. With more and more Member States leading to increased delays in the preliminary reference procedures, national courts and review bodies will more often have to look for answers elsewhere. Precedents from other national courts or review bodies giving application to the common European rules and principles are a precious source of inspiration.

Finally, it should no be overlooked that the Court of Justice too is aware of the value of the comparative approach and its rulings are from time to time influenced by a development or a trend in regulation or practice at national level. Increased comparative knowledge of the case law of different Member States may alert the Court of justice to the difficulties national courts and review bodies are facing in giving full effect to European law. In some cases, it may make EU institutions aware of common trends developing at national level, a spontaneous *jus commune* which it is better to follow than just to oppose or even worse: to ignore.

It is our hope that the European Procurement Law Series will contribute to a strengthened dialogue between the various legal cultures in the field of procurement and that it will become a well-known source of inspiration.

The next volume of the Series will consider contracts below the thresholds of the Public Procurement Directives and services contracts partially covered by the Directives (Annex II B Services).

We would like to thank Professor François Lichère for co-editing the current volume and our most helpful publisher, Vivi Antonsen, always ready to forgive our many shortcomings.

ROBERTO CARANTA
PROFESSOR
UNIVERSITY OF TURIN

STEEN TREUMER
PROFESSOR
UNIVERSITY OF COPENHAGEN

1 Enforcement of the EU Public Procurement Rules: The State of Law and Current Issues

By Steen Treumer

1 Introduction

An analysis of enforcement of the EU public procurement rules is of particular interest not only for those working in the field but also for those with a general interest in EU law or in enforcement of law. It is highly interesting from a general perspective because it is an area of law where the European legislator has made exceptional efforts in order to ensure effective enforcement at national level and has pushed the development forward. In this respect the state of the law in the field of public procurement deviates from the clear starting point in EU law. As a main rule remedies and procedural law concerning breaches of the law are considered matters for the national legislator according to the principle of national and remedial autonomy.

The European Commission showed early awareness of the fact that measures had to be taken in order to ensure fast and efficient enforcement of the public procurement rules at national level. This led to the adoption of the so-called Remedies – Directives Directive 89/665 and Directive 92/13 –applicable for the classic sector and the utilities sector respectively. These Directives are still the essential sources of law in the area even though these Directives recently were amended and developed with Remedies Directive 2007/66.

Another feature that makes this field particularly interesting is that the Court of Justice of the European Union (hereafter the Court of Justice) also has been highly aware of the importance of effective enforcement in the field of public procurement. As a consequence the Court of Justice has interpreted the law in a very dynamic manner in a number of landmark cases leading to fundamental improvements of the enforcement system both at national and supranational level.[1] Public Procurement is also a field of law where you can find noteworthy examples of dynamic interpretation at *national* level. It is remarkable that the principle of effectiveness appears to have been used in some national jurisdictions as a lever for the creation of new law when national courts or complaints Boards have deviated from their respective traditional laws i.e. on damages.[2] Examples of this can be found in several Member States which is rather surprising as remedies and procedural law are in general to be considered as matters for the national legislator, cf. the principle of national and procedural autonomy mentioned above. However, this autonomy is subject to a number of limitations, namely the principles of equivalence and effectiveness.[3] To establish the impact of these principles on the regulatory competence of the Member States is highly complex as it essentially concerns interpretation of a vague legal standard with unclear boundaries. There are therefore many possible interpretations and it is frequently highly uncertain whether a given interpretation is correct.[4]

Enforcement of the public procurement rules also takes place at supranational level as the European Commission supervises the compliance of Member States with their obligations under EU law. Contrary to what many believe the European Commission has limited resources and can only follow up on a fairly limited number of cases a year. It follows from Art.258 of the Treaty on the Functioning of the European Union (hereafter TEUF) which was formerly Art.226 of the EC Treaty that the Commission can bring a Member State before the Court of Justice if it considers that it has failed to fulfil an obligation under the Treaty including compliance with specific Directives. The Commission has used the procedure in numerous cases in the field of public procurement.

The analysis in this publication and chapter will concentrate on national enforcement of the EU public procurement rules for various reasons. The

1. For instance in C-503/04, *Commission v Germany*, C-81/98, *Alcatel* and C-406/08, *Uniplex*.
2. See section IV in the article of S. Treumer in in D. Fairgrieve and F. Lichère (eds.), 'Damages as an effective remedy', Hart, (forthcoming in 2011).
3. It follows from the principle of equivalence that the substantive and procedural conditions for a remedy for breach of EU law must not be less favourable than those relating to similar domestic claims. From the principle of effectiveness follows that the conditions for a remedy must not make it virtually impossible or excessively difficult to obtain reparation, cf. the formulation in the Joined Cases C-6/90 & 9/90, *Francovich* at parapraph 43.
4. In this sense the complexity resembles the interpretations of the well-know principles of equal treatment of tenderers and of transparency.

main reasons are that enforcement mainly takes place at national level and that there is recent, important and unclear legislation (Remedies Directive 2007/66) not covered in much detail in existing legal literature. Furthermore, the comparative research agenda of the European Public Procurement Series makes it obvious and preferable to focus on the state of law in the Member States as there are remarkable variations.

Nevertheless, enforcement at supranational level is also a very important part of the enforcement regime and can have major impact on the development of the substantive public procurement law in a Member State or in the Union as such.[5] It should also be borne in mind that occasionally there is interaction between the developments of the enforcement regime at supranational level and that at national level in the sense that developments at supranational level support or inspire national developments.[6]

The analysis in the following is intended to give an overview of the state of law and of some major developments in the area. However, the present chapter will also to a wide extent cover several current and complex questions of interpretations that have not been analyzed in much detail in legal literature including advanced works on public procurement.[7]

Section 2 considers enforcement at supranational level and section 3 provides an analysis of national enforcement of the Public Procurement Directives regulated by the Remedies Directives. Section 4 considers remedies for infringements of the public procurement rules outside the scope of the Public Procurement Directives and section 5 is the conclusion.

5. The case C-243/89, *Commission v Denmark*, is an example of a case that has influenced the approach in a Member State to a very high degree. After this case the Danish legislator has clearly prioritized the field of public procurement law and taken enforcement in this field much further than what is required from EU public procurement law. See the chapter of S. Treumer on Danish enforcement in the present publication.
6. See for instance the motivation of the German court making the reference in C-91/08, *Wall*, on ineffectiveness and the ruling of the Danish Complaints Board for Public Procurement in ruling of 16 October 2007, *Kuwait Petrolium A/S v Sønderborg Kommune*, where the Board adopted the conditions for grant of interim measures developed in the case law of the Court of Justice. The latter ruling is commented in section 2.2 of the chapter on Denmark in the present publication. C-91/08, *Wall*, is considered in section 4.2 of the present chapter.
7. Examples of works with an in-dept analysis of the issue of enforcement are S. Arrowsmith, *The Law of Public and Utilities Procurement*, 2nd edn. 2005, chapter 21 where the reader will find elaborate references to other works in the field, P. Trepte, *Public Procurement in the EU. A Practitioner's Guide*, chapter 9, 2nd ed., 2007 and C. Bovis, *EU Public Procurement Law*, 2007, chapter 16.

2 Enforcement at supranational level

The competences that will be covered in this section are in several instances of a general nature. These remedies can therefore be applied in all instances where the conditions are fulfilled and are not specifically linked to the procurement context. The following will concentrate on the enforcement in the field of public procurement after a brief introduction of the relevant measures.

The Court of Justice can grant interim measures, it can establish that the rules have been breached and it has also recently established that a Member State that had not terminated a contract concluded in breach of the public procurement rules should have done so in order to comply with Art.260 of the TFEU (formerly Art.228 of the EC Treaty). The latter development is very important and linked to the new remedy ineffectiveness introduced by Remedies Directive 2007/66 considered in further detail in section 3.4 of this chapter.

2.1 Interim measures

It follows from Art.279 of TFEU (formerly Art.243 of the EC Treaty) that the Court of Justice has the general power to grant interim measures in cases before it. The Rules of Procedure of the Court of Justice spell out the conditions for the grant of interim relief and that the application for interim measures must be made by a party to the case before the Court. In the current context a case would be based on Art.258 of TFEU and a tenderer who has complained to the European Commission is not a party to the proceedings brought by the Commission.

There have been relatively few cases concerning interim measures before the Court of Justice in the field of public procurement.[8] In this respect there is a clear difference from the pattern in national enforcement of the public procurement law. It is very common to apply for interim measures in national case law even though it is very difficult to obtain at least in some Member States.

The Rules of Procedure contain specific conditions for the grant of interim relief and these conditions have been developed in the case law of the Court

8. See C-45/97 R, *Commission v Ireland (Dundalk)*, C-194/88 R, *Commission v Italy (Lottomatica)* and C-87/94 R, *Commission v Belgium (Wallon Buses)*. The Commission had also applied for interim measures in C-243/89, *Commission v Denmark (Great Belt Bridge)* but as Denmark acknowledged the breaches the Commission withdrew the application.

of Justice. The first condition is that the party applying for interim measures establishes that he has a prima facie case. The second condition is urgency which usually[9] implies that the applicant has to show that it will suffer serious and irreparable harm if interim measures are not granted. It appears that the condition of urgency is satisfied whenever there is a threat of a breach of EU law and this constitutes a serious breach. The breach must also be 'irreparable' which in the procurement case law appears to have been applied in the sense of 'irreversible'.[10] The Court of Justice has in the few procurement cases emphasized the need to prevent a breach and to avoid presenting the Court with a fait accompli and has even granted interim measures where a contract has been concluded.[11] Finally, there is a balance of interest tests. Interim measures will be granted if the two first conditions are fulfilled unless the contracting authority can show that it also would suffer serious and irreparable harm.

2.2 Enforcement proceedings against Member States according to Art.258 TFEU

This procedure has been used in several cases in the field of public procurement. The procedure can be initiated by the Commission on its own initiative but can also be the result of a complaint by an individual. Some of these cases have been striking examples of success[12] but as mentioned above the Commission has only resources to bring a few cases a year in the field of public procurement. If the Court of Justice finds that the Member State has failed to fulfil an obligation under the Treaty, the State shall take the necessary measure to comply with the judgment of the Court of Justice, cf. Art.260 TFEU (formerly Art.228 of the EC Treaty).

9. This is the usual approach even though the Court of Justice not always explicitly or consistently assesses the condition this way, cf. P. Trepte, *Public Procurement in the EU. A Practitioner's Guide*, chapter 9, 2nd ed., 2007, p. 586.
10. Cf. P. Trepte, *Public Procurement in the EU. A Practitioner's Guide*, chapter 9, 2nd ed., 2007, p. 587.
11. Cf. C-194/88 R, *Commission v Italy (Lottomatica)*.
12. P. Trepte, *Public Procurement in the EU. A Practitioner's Guide*, 2nd ed., 2007 p. 579 mentions C-243/89, *Commission v Denmark*, as an example. Another example is C-503/04, *Commission v Germany*, concering the duty to set aside a contract concluded in breach of the EU public procurement rules.

2.3 Enforcement proceedings against Member States according to Art.260 TFEU

If the Commission considers that the Member State concerned has not taken such measures it can, after following certain procedural steps, bring the case before the Court of Justice and the Court may impose a lump sum and/or penalty payment on the Member State, cf. Art.260 TFEU. This procedure has not been used on many occasions but was applied in C-503/04, *Commission v Germany*, with far-reaching implications.

This case was a follow up to the judgment in the joint cases C-20/01 and C-28/01, *Commission v Germany*. It concerned 30 years service contracts awarded without notice and the point of view of the Commission was that the contracts should be terminated which they originally were not. The argument of the Commission was that the duty to terminate the contracts followed from the Court's establishment of the breach and Art.228 EC (now Art.260 TFEU). From the later provision, it follows that a Member State is required 'to take the necessary measures to comply with the judgment'.

In order to motivate Germany to comply with its point of view the Commission requested the Court to impose a daily payment of €126.720 with regard to one of the contracts and €31.680 with regard to the other contract until compliance. Not surprisingly Germany saw to it that the local authorities in question terminated the contracts. Interesting enough it took more than half a year from the time the action in C-503/04 was brought until the contract that potentially could cost €126.720 in daily payments was terminated.[13] Germany then thought the matter settled but the Commission insisted that the case continued before the Court of Justice. Because of the terminations of the German contracts before the judgment, the Court had only to consider the possible breach of EU law with regard to one of the contracts, cf. para 20 of the judgment.[14] This resulted in the landmark judgement of 18 July 2007, C-503/04, *Commission v Germany*, where the Court established that a breach of the EC

13. The action was brought 7 December 2004 and the city of Brunswick and BKB agreed to cancel the contract on 4-5 July 2005, cf. M. Niestedt, 'Penalties Despite Compliance? A Note on Case C-503/04, Commission v Germany', Public Procurement Law Review 2005 NA 164 (NA 165). The slow termination of this contract was eventually decisive for the admissibility of the action.

14. Germany supported by The Netherlands argued that the action had become void of purpose and thereby inadmissible because of the termination of the contracts prior to the judgment, cf. para 17 of the judgment. This argument was set aside as the contract concluded by the City of Brunswick had not been terminated 1 June 2004 which was the date of the expiry of the period prescribed in the reasoned opinion issued under Art.228 EC.

public procurement rules in the concrete case led to a duty to terminate the public contract in question.

However, readers should also be aware of a parallel development in the recent amendment of the Remedies Directives, cf. Remedies Directive 2007/66. It follows from this Directive that concluded contracts in specific circumstances can become ineffective, cf. Art.2d. These circumstances also cover the situation that the contracting authority illegally has awarded a contract without prior publication of a contract notice in the Official Journal of the European Union in violation of Directive 2004/18/EC. This change is analyzed in further detail in section 3.4 of this chapter.

The first important issue to consider is whether there is a duty to terminate the contract as a main rule. It is striking that the Court of Justice in C-503/04, *Commission v Germany*, does not waste many words on the justification for imposition of a duty to terminate the contract and that it does not come up with many references to the particularities of the breach of the public procurement rules in the concrete case even though they are special. Nevertheless, the Court of Justice stresses that without termination of the contract in question the failure to fulfil obligations would continue for decades, cf. para 29 as it was a 30 years service contract. The Advocate General also stressed the length of the contract and that this circumstance made termination of the contract a proportionate measure, cf. consideration 78 of her opinion.

One possibility would be to interpret the judgment as implying that the contract as a main rule has to be terminated once the Court has established under Art.258 TFEU that the public procurement rules have been violated. However, it is submitted that this would not be a correct interpretation of the judgment.[15] It is instead submitted that the judgment must be interpreted more narrowly in the light of the particularities of the concrete case. The case concerned what is considered the most serious violation of the public procurement rules by the Court, cf. case C-26/03, *Stadt Halle*, at para 37, as the contract was awarded without notice and thereby without consideration of the EC public procurement rules. As pointed out by the undersigned[16] it would be a paradox if there, in such a situation, would not be an obligation to terminate

15. It can be added that it would also not be a legal situation to be wished for as it would not take into account the need for basic legal certainty with regard to contracts concluded on the basis of the EU public procurement rules.
16. See S. Treumer, 'The Discretionary Powers of Contracting Entities – Towards a Flexible Approach in the Recent Case Law of the Court of Justice?' Public Procurement Law Review 2006 p. 71 (at p. 81).

the contract. This would have constituted a lacuna in the legal protection[17] as competitors could have forgotten all about the contract as it per se would be 'protected' due to its conclusion and the possibility of obtaining damages where there has been no tender is close to impossible. The judgment has to be read bearing this in mind combined with the fact that the disputed contract was a particularly long-running contract.

Nevertheless, the laconic formulations of the Court seem to indicate that a duty to terminate contracts is not only limited to situations where there has been no tender and thus to be an obligation with a broader scope.[18] The Court would surely have taken care to specify otherwise if the opposite had been intended. It is submitted that it will take a careful examination of the concrete circumstances in each individual case to establish whether there is an obligation to terminate a contract concluded in breach of the EC public procurement rules and that it will not be the main rule that a breach leads to such an obligation.

It is possible to identify various situations where an obligation to terminate the contract appears to be particularly relevant. It is evident that the duty to terminate the contract can frequently materialize where the breach consists in direct illegal award like in C-503/04, *Commission v Germany*. The same applies where the contract has been concluded with a tenderer who should have been excluded, e.g. because of illegal state aid or because of technical dialogue prior to the submission of bids. Termination also appears to be highly relevant where the contract has been concluded with a tenderer whose bid should have been rejected because it did not comply with the tender conditions. This scenario is seen in practice, and quite often competitors argue that

17. Compare with L. Hummelshøj and H. Bang Schmidt, 'EU-udbud: Retsvirkningen af at undlade udbud' (EC public procurement: The legal effect of lack of tenders) Ugeskrift for Retsvæsen 2006 B 80. These authors also pointed out the lacuna but argued in favour of legislative action on the issue in Denmark and not that there was a Treaty based obligation to terminate contracts concluded in breach of the EC public procurement rules.
18. It should be mentioned that Danish courts have been willing to a wide interpretation of C-503/04, *Commission v Germany*. The Court of Appeal has accepted that a duty to terminate the contract follows from the case law of the Court of Justice in cases of very gross and serious violations of the EU public procurement rules. Nevertheless, the Court of Appeal did not consider the mistakes in the concrete case to be sufficiently serious. According to the interpretation of the Court of Appeal the duty to terminate based on other legal sources than the Remedies Directives is not only limited to situations of direct illegal procurement, cf. also what has been submitted by the undersigned. See in further detail the chapter of S. Treumer on Danish enforcement of the EU public procurement rules in the present publication.

the winning bid should have been rejected because it did not comply with the tender conditions. Breaches like the above-mentioned could frequently lead to the annulment of the relevant decision of the contracting authority.[19] The breaches in the above-mentioned situations are substantial because they have or are likely to have influenced the outcome of the competition for the award of the public contract.

As follows from above it is to be presumed that it is necessary to make an individual assessment of the circumstances in the case in question and that no breach per se leads to the obligation to terminate the contract.[20] A number of circumstances that are likely to be relevant in the assessment of whether there is a duty to terminate the concluded contract is a) whether the breach is sufficiently serious b) the impact on the internal market if the contract is not terminated c) the degree of completion of the contract and d) the public interest and the interest of the contract party of the contracting authority.[21]

Another interesting and also controversial question is whether the contracting authorities have the right or the obligation to terminate public contracts in a situation where breaches have not been established by a court or review board.[22]A contracting authority or a Member State will frequently deny that there has been a breach of the public procurement rules which subsequently leads to a public procurement dispute at centralized or decentralized level. However, a contract authority will also in some situations willingly admit a breach or might on rare occasions become aware of a breach on its own.

It is submitted that it is the substantial breach as such which infers the right or obligation to terminate the contract and that it is not a condition that

19. See section 3.3. of this chapter on annulment of illegal decisions.
20. Compare with Joined Cases C-21/03 & 34/03, *Fabricom*. It clearly follows from this case that it is mandatory to make a concrete assessment of whether a firm previously engaged in technical dialogue may or shall be excluded from the tender procedure based on this ground and that the firm in question can not be excluded per se. See further on this S. Treumer, 'Technical Dialogue and the Principle of Equal Treatment-Dealing with Conflicts of Interests after Fabricom', Public Procurement Law Review 2007, p. 99.
21. See S. Treumer, 'Towards an Obligation to Terminate Contracts Concluded in Breach of the EC Public Procurement Rules: the End of the Status of Concluded Public Contracts as Sacred Cows', Public Procurement Law Review 2007, p. 371, section 4 (pp. 378-382) for an analysis on this.
22. It is presupposed that the duty to terminate the contract can also be a consequence of national enforcement as submitted by the undersigned in the article mentioned in footnote 21 and confirmed in Danish practice from the Court of Appeal.

the breach has been established by a Court or review board in enforcement proceedings or admitted/realized by the contracting authority itself. Whether the breach only leads to a right and not a duty to terminate the contract is an open question but depending on the circumstances of the case it is likely that both of these options are likely to appear. The distinction between situations where the contracting authority has either a right or a duty to act is well known in EU public procurement law.[23]

That the breach as such is sufficient to establish a right or duty to terminate the concluded contract would seem to be a consequence of the obligation to give effect to EU law. C-503/04, *Commission v Germany*, was based on Art.228 EC of the EC Treaty (now Art.260 TEUF) which is just a special formulation of the general principle on the obligation to give effect to EU law also formulated in more general terms in Art.4 of the Treaty on the European Union (formerly Art.10 of the EC Treaty). It follows from the latter provision that Member States shall take all appropriate measures whether general or particular to ensure the fulfilment of the obligations out of this Treaty or resulting from action taken by the institutions of the Community.

It is hard to see why you should not be able to entrust the contracting authority with the discretion to decide on whether it should terminate the contract or not.[24] Based on the experiences in the Member States so far it is to be expected that most likely contract authorities will be extremely reluctant to terminate concluded contracts due to breaches of the EU public procurement rules. More importantly the contract party of the contracting authority would presumably be entitled to challenge the termination of the contract[25] before a

23. This is for example seen with regard to the question of exclusion of tenderers from the public procurement procedure. In C-94/99, *Arge Gewässerschutz*, concerning exclusion based on illegal aid the Court of Justice explicitly comments on the distinction.
24. C-91/08, *Wall*, relates to the possible duty to terminate the contract but does not consider and thereby exclude such a right. However, in Norway the legislator in 2005 estimated it as unfortunate if an administrative body (the contracting authority) should be able to declare contracts invalid as this is normally the competence of the courts. This point of view was expressed with regard to the recommendation of a provision establishing a duty to cancel contracts illegally concluded without a tender. See further on this Kai Krüger, 'Paradise Lost-Is the law adequate in combating corruption in public procurements? A Norwegian approach in *Festskrift til Helge Johan Thue*, 2007, p. 624.
25. There exits as mentioned a German example of such a challenge. See section 1 of the article of S. Treumer, 'Towards an Obligation to Terminate Contracts Concluded in Breach of the EC Public Procurement Rules: the End of the Status of Concluded Public Contracts as Sacred Cows', Public Procurement Law Review 2007, p. 371 at foot-

national court just like the competitors are entitled to challenge the lack of termination of the contract concluded in breach of the EU public procurement rules.

If a contracting authority decides to terminate the contract in order to comply with the public procurement rules it is most likely going to be difficult to have this decision set aside by national courts or review boards. The Court of Justice has in general chosen a path that emphasises flexibility as it has in several cases adopted an interpretation which grants the contracting authorities a wide margin of discretion directly or indirectly.[26] This also applies to the contracting authorities' termination of the tender procedures without an award – precontractual termination – which can take place after the submission of bids where it can be evident who is the likely winner of the competition was even though the contract has not yet been awarded.[27]

C-503/04, *Commission v Germany*, is a very important step forward for the efficient enforcement of the EC public procurement rules and is likely to lead to increased compliance with the rules just as the changes of the Remedies Directives and the new remedy of ineffectiveness in this Directive which is considered in section 3 of this article. The case gives rise to numerous questions and uncertainties even though it clarifies that a breach of the public procurement rules can lead to an obligation to terminate a concluded contract.

Finally, it should be added that the judgment in C-503/04, *Commission v Germany*, concerned a violation of the public procurement directives but as many will know the Court of Justice has in reality developed a secondary public procurement regime in its recent case law, cf. C-324/98, *Telaustria* and subsequent case law. The Court of Justice has here imposed a duty to act – including a transparency obligation – based on primary law and general principles with a very unclear content[28] which subsequently has led to many other cases on the issue. One could ask whether a breach of this secondary

note 9. The German court found that the contracting authority was entitled to terminate the contract.

26. See S. Treumer, 'The Discretionary Powers of Contracting Entities – Towards a Flexible Approach in the Recent Case Law of the Court of Justice?', Public Procurement Law Review 2006, p. 71.

27. The leading case in the area is C-27/98, *Metalmeccanica Fracasso SpA*, where the Court allowed termination in a situation where four tenderers submitted a bid. After the examination of the bids only one tenderer remained.

28. This has been covered in several publications during the last decade. See for example the recent article by A. Brown, 'EU Primary Requirements in Practice: Advertising, Procedures and Remedies for Public Contracts Outside the Procurement Directives', Public Procurement Law Review 2010, p. 169.

public procurement regime could equally entail a duty to terminate the contract in question. The Court of Justice considered the issue recently in the preliminary ruling in C-91/08, *Wall*, with regard to *national* enforcement and clarified that this is not so 'in every case', cf. para 65 of the judgment. This case is further commented in section 4.2 of the present chapter.

3 Enforcement at national level according to the Remedies Directives

As mentioned in the introduction to this chapter the European legislator has regulated the enforcement in the field of public procurement commonly referred to as the Remedies Directives. These Remedies Directives apply only to tender procedures falling within their scope. The Remedies Directive 89/665 applies to contracts falling within the scope of the Public Sector Directive whereas Remedies Directive 92/13 applies to contracts falling within the scope of the Utilities Directive. The approach is similar in the two Remedies Directives and the minor material differences that do exist will not be considered here. Both Directives have recently been amended by Directive 2007/66 which introduced a number of important changes including the new remedy ineffectiveness which is considered below in section 3.4 in further detail. The Remedies Directives are intended only to establish a minimum level of protection of the rights and obligations in the public procurement Directives.

The fact that a contract is not falling within the scope does not imply that the rights of the tenderers in question right are not protected. Their rights are instead protected by the common principles and in particular the principles of equivalence and effectiveness. This issue is touched upon in section 4 of this chapter. The analysis in this section addresses the enforcement regime created by the Remedies Directives.

The first generation of the Remedies Directives adopted around 1990 essentially sought to ensure that decisions taken by the contracting authorities could be reviewed effectively and as rapidly as possible and that specific remedies for breach of the public procurement Directives were available at national level. It follows from Art.2(1) of the Remedies Directives that Member States shall ensure that aggrieved tenderers[29] can apply for interim meas-

29. Persons having or having had an interest in obtaining a particular contract and who has been or risks being harmed by an alleged infringement, cf. Art.2(3) of the Remedies Directives.

ures, annulment of illegal decisions taken by a contracting entity and for damages.

The recent changes of the Remedies Directives introduced the new remedy ineffectiveness, alternative penalties depending on the chosen approach to the remedy ineffectiveness,[30] preclusive time-limits for review and a complex set of stand-still provisions which all are topics dealt with previously in the case law of the Court of Justice. Art.2a(2) of the Remedies Directives introduced a basic standstill provision according to which a contract may not be concluded following the decision to award a contract before the expiry of 10 or 15 calendar days depending on the chosen means of communication of the award decision. Remedies Directive 2007/66 also introduced new rules on automatic suspension for review of the standstill period further commented upon below in section 3.1.

A few Member States have created new bodies responsible for the enforcement of the EU public procurement rules but this has not been mandatory even though this would probably have made the enforcement system more efficient. There are several advantages compared to bringing a case before a national court. The Complaints Boards will typically be able to ensure a fast assessment, the costs of the case are lower and the complaints boards have a deeper insight into the complex field of public procurement than an ordinary court or tribunal. Until recently aggrieved tenderers had a free choice in Denmark between bringing a case before the Complaints Board for Public Procurement or the ordinary courts. Hardly anybody brought a case directly before the ordinary courts so in reality the courts have only considered public procurement cases on appeal after previous consideration by the Complaints Board in the first instance.

In the following a number of selected issues related to the remedies above will be considered.

3.1 Interim measures

Access to interim measures is crucial in order to ensure an efficient enforcement of the public procurement rules especially since it is very difficult to challenge a concluded public contract. It is stated in Art.2(4) of the Remedies Directives[31] that review procedures need not automatically have an automatic suspensive effect on the contract award procedures to which they related except where provided for in Art.2(3) and Art.1(5) of the Directive. These ex-

30. See Art.2e(1) of the Remedies Directive.
31. Compare with the former version of Art. 2(3) of the Remedies Directives.

ceptions are worth noticing. An important automatic suspension rule was introduced with Remedies Directive 2007/66 with Art.2(3) concerning review of contract award decisions. If the application for review of the award decision was made in the standstill period the Member States shall ensure that a contracting authority cannot conclude the contract before the review body has made a decision on the application either for interim measures or for review.

It follows from Art. 1(5) of the Remedies Directives that Member States may require that the person concerned first seek review within the contracting authority. In that case Member States shall ensure that the submission of such an application for review results in immediate suspension of the possibility to conclude the contract.

As mentioned previously it follows from Art.2(1) that Member States shall ensure that interim measures can be granted in the review procedures. Member States may provide that the body responsible for review procedures may take into account the probable consequences of interim measures for all interests to potentially be harmed, as well as the public interest, and may decide not to grant such measures when their negative consequences could exceed their benefits, cf. Art.2(5). The criteria suggested in this article are heavily inspired by the case law of the Court of Justice on interim measures, cf. section 2.1 of this chapter. However, the latter article does not establish the criteria for the assessment of whether interim measures should be granted or not. As a consequence the national legislator has a wide frame to regulate within and the criteria and procedures established in national legislation on interim measures vary to a considerable degree as can be seen in the other chapters of the present publication. It is typical difficult to obtain interim relief at national level[32] and has in Denmark been so difficult that it has been questioned whether the requirements following from the principle of effectiveness have been met.[33]

32. A. Brown, 'Effectiveness of Remedies at National Level in the Field of Public Procurement' Public Procurement Law Review 1998, p. 89. See also section 3 in the article of S. Treumer, National håndhævelse af EU's udbudsregler – er håndhævelsessystemet effektivt på EU-udbudsområdet? p.99 in J. Fejø and S. Treumer (eds.), EU's Udbudsregler – implementering og håndhævelse i Norden (The EC Public Procurement Rules-Implementation and Enforcement in the Nordic Countries), 2006.

33. See S.T. Poulsen, P.S. Jakobsen and S.E. Kalsmose-Hjelmborg, *EU Udbudsretten*, 2nd ed. 2011, p. 543 and the article of S. Treumer, fn. 32 above. See also section 2.2. of the chapter of S. Treumer on the enforcement in Denmark of the EU public procurement rules in the present publication.

3.2 Establishment of a breach

A ruling of illegality is the basic and most common form of sanctioning applied by the national courts and Complaints Boards in the field of public procurement.

The purpose of an application for review could be to establish a breach of the public procurement rules in order to have the illegal decisions of the contracting entity set aside, allowing the complainant to be taken into consideration for the award of the contract. The purpose of the application for review could also be to establish that the public procurement rules have been breached in order to pave the way for a subsequent claim for damages or to facilitate a settlement of the dispute outside of the court/complaints board. However, the plaintiff or complainant will in some cases limit the case to a claim for a ruling on the illegality of the decisions of a contracting authority. In several of these cases the purpose with the complaint is to get an overruling of a specific procedural approach applied by the contracting authority or occasionally to the get an overruling of common procurement practice.

The national courts and complaints boards will typically allow the contracting authorities a wide margin of discretion when they assess whether the public procurement rules have been breached or not. The same approach has been adopted by the Court of Justice of the European Union in its case law on public procurement.[34]

3.3 Annulment of illegal decisions

It follows from the Remedies Directives that Member States shall ensure that annulment of illegal decisions is a part of the available remedies at national level, cf. the Remedies Directives Art. 2(1)(b). Prior to the implementation of Remedies Directive 2007/66 the absolute majority[35] of Member States had

34. See S. Treumer, 'The Discretionary Powers of Contracting Entities – Towards a Flexible Approach in the Recent Case Law of the Court of Justice?', Public Procurement Law Review 2006, p. 71.

35. Cf. also C. Bovis, *EU Public Procurement Law*, 2007, chapter 16 p. 413. The approach in Denmark deviates from this approach as it has been possible to annul the decision *to conclude* the contract from the first implementation of the Remedies Directives. However, as follows from section 4 of the chapter by S. Treumer on the Danish enforcement system in the present publication this widening of the competences appears not to have had any importance in practice. In France it has also been established practice for more than 100 years based on Supreme Court practice that a contract can be declared null and void after an annulment of relevant decisions of the contracting authority. However, numerous annulments of the French authorities have only had 'Platonic effect', cf. L. Richer in *Droit des contracts administratifs*, 5th ed

limited the powers of their review bodies to the award of damages after the conclusion of the contract, cf. Art. 2(7) of the Remedies Directives (Art.2(6) in the original version of the Remedies Directives). Set aside orders would therefore traditionally aim at nullifying a decision of a contracting entity prior to the conclusion of the contract and the set aside or annulment order would typically not make the contract as such invalid.

The annulment of the award decision is of particular interest. The legal implications of an annulment of the award decision are not specified in the Directives. However, it is submitted that the effect of an annulment of an *award decision* must be that the contracting authority cannot base its decisions on the annulled decision. The contracting authority would therefore presumably have to make a new award decision or recommence the tender procedures depending on the circumstances behind the annulment. In some situations the tender procedures are so flawed that the contracting authorities have to terminate the tender procedures and retender if they still wish to contract ex-house. This could for instance be the case in a situation where the award criteria are illegal.

The new remedy of ineffectiveness that is analysed in section 3.4 below is very important as it effectively will ensure termination or shortening of contract concluded in breach of the EU public procurement rules. This has not been the normal consequence of the application of the above-mentioned remedy 'annulment' in the field of EU public procurement law.

3.4 Ineffectiveness

The remedy of ineffectiveness is a very important remedy introduced with Remedies Directive 2007/66 that essentially secures that qualified breaches of the EU public procurement rules can lead to the termination of the contract and thereby imply that the concluded public contracts no longer has the status as sacred cows.

As previously mentioned most Member States had limited the powers of their review bodies to the award of damages after the conclusion of the contract until the implementation of Remedies Directive 2007/66, cf. Art.2(6) of the Remedies Directives (now Art.2(7)). It was also the traditional and common perception in legal theory[36] that there was no duty based on EU law to

(2006) at p. 189. In other words the contracts have usually remained in force and have been completed as originally foreseen.

36. See S. Treumer, 'Towards an Obligation to Terminate Contracts Concluded in Breach of the EC Public Procurement Rules: the End of the Status of Concluded Public Contracts as Sacred Cows', Public Procurement Law Review 2007, p. 371 with refer-

terminate a public contract concluded in breach of the EU public procurement rules, regardless of the number of breaches or their character. European public procurement practice was in accordance with legal theory and consequently breaches of the EU public procurement rules did normally never lead to the termination of the public contract.[37] The state of law has now fundamentally changed with 1) the ruling in C-503/04, *Commission v Germany*, cf, section 2.3 establishing that there can be a duty to terminate the contract due to breaches of EU procurement law and with 2) the introduction of the remedy ineffectiveness.

Ineffectiveness is in particular a remedy against direct illegal award of contracts. Direct illegal awards have been considered the most serious violation of the public procurement rules by the Court of Justice, cf. case C-26/03, *Stadt Halle*, at para 37. However, effective remedies against direct illegal awards were not present until the above-mentioned changes. Public contracts were 'protected' due to their conclusion and it is in reality impossible to be granted damages where there has been no tender. It was indeed a paradox that the available remedies against the most serious violation were manifestly ineffective until recently.

It follows from Art.2d(2) that the consequences of a contract being considered ineffective shall be provided for by national law. However, it follows from the same provision that national law may provide for the retroactive cancellation of all contractual obligations or limit it to obligations which still have to be performed. Furthermore, recital 13 makes clear that ineffectiveness essentially implies that 'the rights and obligations of the parties under the contract should cease to be enforced and performed'.

The Member States shall ensure that a contract is considered ineffective by a review body independent of the contracting authority or that its ineffectiveness is the result of a decision of such a review body in circumstances outlined in that provision, cf. Art.2d(1) of the Remedies Directives, including direct illegal award. Art.2d(1) concerns in principle a duty to consider the contract ineffective. Art.2e(1) of the Remedies Directives requires less as it establishes that the review bodies should have competence to provide for ineffectiveness or to impose alternative sanctions in certain situations.

ences to literature. See also the proposal for Remedies Directive 2007/66, COM (2006) 195. It was written in section 1 of the Explanatory Referendum to this proposal that, 'Furthermore, in the case of an illegal direct award of contract the injured enterprises can in fact only seek review for damages, but such review does not allow an illegally awarded contract to be opened again for competition.

37. See S. Treumer, fn. 36 above at p. 372.

3.4.1 Exceptions to ineffectiveness

Contracting entities can avoid the sanction ineffectiveness by following a specific procedure outlined in the new provisions of the Remedies Directives. The Remedies Directives stipulate in Art.2(d)(4) that Member States shall provide that ineffectiveness in the case of direct illegal award does not apply where the contracting authority considers that the award of the contract without prior notice in the Official Journal of the European Union is permissible and has published a notice as described in Art.3a of the Remedies Directives expressing its intention to conclude the contract. It is an additional condition that the contract has not been concluded before the expiry of at least 10 calendar days with effect from the day following the date of the publication of the notice for voluntary ex ante transparency. These provisions of the Remedies Directive are implemented by §4 of the Danish Act on the Enforcement of the Procurement Rules. §4(2) of the Act specifies the requirements to the notice, cf. Art.3a of the Remedies Directives.[38]

However, the remarks in the preparatory works regarding §4 are interesting as they create doubts as to the range of the protection against ineffectiveness for those that comply with the procedure outlined in §4. It is stipulated in the preparatory works that the Danish Complaints Board for Public Procurement (and thereby surely also the ordinary courts) can declare the contract ineffective even though the conditions outlined in §4 of the Act corresponding to Art.2(d)(4) of the Remedies Directives are fulfilled. It is specified that this is the case when the Complaints Board later rules that a contract could not legally be concluded without a notice in the Official Journal of the European Union and finds that the contracting authority has made an apparent incorrect assessment of whether a notice was needed. It is specified in the preparatory works that the assessment of the Complaints Board shall be based on an objective consideration of the character of the violation of the EU public procurement rules where the clarity of the rules should be taken into consideration. This limitation of the range of the exception in §4 is remarkable as it does not seem to follow from or to be clearly supported by the wording of Art.2(d)(4) of the Remedies Directives.[39]

38. However, the reference in Art 3(a)(e) regarding 'any other information deemed useful by the contracting authority' is 'implemented' with a remark in the preparatory works to §2(2).
39. The use of the word 'considers' in Art.2d(5) clearly gives the impression that the contracting authorities are allowed a wide discretion just like the use of the word in Art.29 on competitive dialogue. This is not the case with regard to competitive dia-

The Danish interpretation appears to be sound and appropriate even though the Danish legislator seems to adopt a stricter approach than required by the EU public procurement rules. This approach is not excluded as specified by consideration 20 of the Preamble to Remedies Directive 2007/66. It follows from this consideration that 'this Directive should not exclude the application of stricter sanctions in accordance with national law.' However, it cannot be excluded that a contracting authority would challenge the narrow interpretation suggested in the Danish preparatory works as it could be argued that this is a limitation of a right granted by the Remedies Directive to contracting authorities as such.

An approach similar to the Danish one was suggested by a law firm in connection with the Swedish implementation of Remedies Directive 2007/66. However, the Swedish legislator did not adjust the law on this point as it did not limit the scope of the immunity granted to those that follow the procedure of voluntary ex ante transparency.[40] The UK Government appears to share the idea that abuse of the procedure outlined in Art.3a of the Remedies Directives does not protect against ineffectiveness.[41] It is very important that contracting authorities are aware of this interpretation and of the risk that they are not granted immunity from ineffectiveness even though they formally complied with the procedure of voluntary ex ante transparency.

Art.2(d)(3) of the Remedies Directive opens up for another important exception to ineffectiveness as a main rule. This exception applies to the situations covered in Art.2(d)(1). It follows from this provision that Member States may allow review bodies not to consider a contract ineffective where overriding reasons relating to the general interest require that the effects of the contract should be maintained. Member States will surely be inclined to create such a legal basis in their national regulation as consideration of the general interest in such cases is considered highly relevant. However, the European legislator has in a remarkable way limited the possibilities of taking into consideration *economic* reasons relating to the general interest as they

logue but presumably the contracting authorities enjoy a much wider discretion in the current context.

40. Prop. 2009/10:180, p. 142.

41. See Implementation of the Remedies Directive: OGC Guidance on the 2009 amending regulations (Part 3: The new remedies rules), p 36. It is stated that 'An overly brief or vague explanation may not therefore be sufficient, and failure to include the right information could have the same effect as having published no VEAT [Voluntary Ex-Ante Transparency Notice] notice if a court was to find that the information published was insufficient.

may only be considered if in exceptional circumstances ineffectiveness would lead to disproportionate consequences. It is furthermore specified that economic interests directly linked to the contract concerned shall not constitute overriding reasons relating to a general interest and that they include, inter alia, the cost resulting from the delay in the execution of the contract, the costs resulting from the launching of a new procurement procedure, the costs resulting from the change of the economic operator performing the contract and the costs of legal obligations resulting from the ineffectiveness,[42]cf. Art.2(d)(3). It is submitted that all of these costs would traditionally have been considered by national courts and complaints boards had it not been for this explicit provision that excludes consideration of these costs. The exception provided for in Art. 2)(1) would therefore typically not rule out the application of the sanction ineffectiveness. It is actually rather difficult to come up with many examples of consideration that could fall under the scope of the exception. The preparatory works to 17(3) of the Danish Act on Enforcement of the Procurement Rules specifies that such overriding reasons in the general interest could be present when ineffectiveness makes it impossible for the contracting authority to comply with its duty to deliver services or goods to the citizens or endangers the life or health of human beings or animals.

Preclusive time limits can also be introduced by the Member States according to the Remedies Directive. The most interesting provision with regard to ineffectiveness is Art.2(f)(1)(a) that allows the stipulation of a time limit of 30 calendar days relating to review of ineffectiveness in accordance with Art.2(d)(1) either from the contract award notice or from the date on which the contracting authority informed the tenderers and candidates concerned of the conclusion of the contract.

The Remedies Directive also ensures that the Member States can stipulate that a complaint concerning ineffectiveness based on Art.2(d)(1) in any case must be made before the expiry of a period of 6 months with effect from the day following the date of the conclusion of the contract. Most Member States probably have ensured or will ensure that complaints or law suits are cut off after 6 months' time in this situation.

A new type of claims for damages will materialize due to the introduction of the remedy ineffectiveness and the establishment of the principle that there can be a duty to terminate contract concluded in breach of the EU public procurement rules. The contracting party is likely to claim damages from the

42. This could be damages to the contract party losing the contract due to its ineffectiveness. See section 3.5.2 of this chapter for an analysis of this.

contracting entity in case the contract is terminated due to a breach of the EU public procurement rules. These claims are considered in further detail in section 3.5.2. below.

3.5 Damages[43]

In the middle of the 1990s it was rightly stated[44] that a striking feature of the case law in the field of enforcement of the public procurement rules was the almost[45] total absence of successful actions for damages. This feature has changed as there now are several examples in various Member States including cases where damages for loss of profit have been granted.[46]

It follows from the Remedies Directives that the review bodies must be able to award damages to persons injured by the infringement of the rules. However, the details of the issues concerning damages are not regulated and the wording in the Remedies Directives does not contribute much to the creation of a clear legal situation and generates doubt on some points. It is not even clear from these directives whether they require the award of lost profit or not which is of crucial importance for the efficiency of the remedy of damages. A high percentage of aggrieved tenderers do not consider it worth the effort to initiate an action seeking to recover the costs of preparing a bid or participation in the procurement procedure. However, it is normally presumed in both theory and frequently in the case law of the Member States that tenderers under certain conditions can require the award of lost profit for breach of the EU public procurement rules although this has been unclear from the outset.

43. See in particular S. Treumer, 'Damages for Breach of the EC Public Procurement Rules-Changes in European Regulation and Practice', Public Procurement Law Review, 2006 p. 159 and the subsequent articles pp. 171-240 written by various experts on the state of law on damages in France, Germany, United Kingdom, Sweden and Norway. See also the broader and updated analysis in D. Fairgrieve and F. Lichère (eds.), 'Damages as an effective remedy', Hart, (forthcoming in 2011).
44. See A. Brown, 'Effectiveness of Remedies at National Level in the field of Public Procurement', Public Procurement Law Review 1998 p. 89 (at p.93). This article is of particular interest as some of the information in the article of Adrian Brown was derived from a study, which his employer, Herbert Smith law firm, co-ordinated for the European Commission in 1996, involving a comparative assessment of procurement remedies in all of the Member States (15 at that time).
45. A. Brown, fn. 44 cited above, mentions that an isolated example occurred after the ruling in the Storebaelt case (C-243/89, *Commission v. Denmark*, [1993] E.C.R: I-3353) where a number of unsuccessful tenderers were awarded damages to cover wasted bid costs, rather than loss of potential profit.
46. See S. Treumer, fn. 43 cited above.

It is not clear from the wording of the Remedies Directives whether damages are available for all violations of the EU public procurement rules or whether other conditions apply. This issue is considered in further detail in section 3.5.1. in the light of recent case law from the Court of Justice.[47] Section 3.5.2. is an analysis of claims for damages from the contracting party when a contract becomes ineffective or terminated on. This type of claims is essentially new and not considered in the case law of most Member States.[48] These claims will be a consequence of the recent changes of the enforcement system with the introduction of the remedy ineffectiveness and the establishment of the principle that there can be a duty to terminate a contract concluded in breach of the EU public procurement rules.

3.5.1 Conditions for damages

Art.2(1)(c) of the Remedies Directives indicates only that the Member States are obliged to award damages to persons harmed by an infringement. However, it is clear from the ruling of the Court of Justice in C-275/03, *Commission v Portugal*, that it violates the Remedies Directive to make damages conditional on proof of intentional or negligent breach. Very recent case law from the Court of Justice has addressed the conditions of damages, cf. the cases C-314/09, *Strabag*, and C-568/08, *Spijker*. However, this case law appears to cause more confusion than clarity.

In C-314/09, *Strabag*, the Court of Justice ruled that the Remedies Directive 89/665 precludes national legislation which makes the right to damages for an infringement of public procurement law conditional on that infringement being culpable. This result was surprising as the issue in principle comes under the procedural autonomy of the Member States. Furthermore, the national legislation in question even rests on the presumption that the contracting authority is at fault which normally would make it very easy to satisfy this condition. The Court of Justice based this dynamic and far-reaching interpretation on the principle of effectiveness and the objective of the Direc-

47. See section 3 of the article of S. Treumer, 'Damages for Breach of the EC Public Procurement Rules-Changes in European Regulation and Practice', Public Procurement Law Review, 2006 p. 159 for an analysis of this issue prior to the cases C-314/09, *Stadt Graz* and C-568/08, *Spijker*. The analysis includes arguments based on the regulation and case law on the conditions in a number of Member States and Norway.

48. It is not entirely new as there is at least one case in Germany. There are to my knowledge no case of this type in Denmark so far even though the issue of termination due to breaches of the EU public procurement law has been pursued with success in a few cases.

tive, cf. para 39 and 43 of the judgment. The approach in the Strabag case appears indirectly to rule out that a Member State make damages for breaches of EU public procurement law conditional of a 'sufficiently serious' breach or 'substantial' breaches. Thus, it would appear from this ruling that any breach of the EU public procurement rules in principle is sufficient ground for damages.

It can be added that the reasoning of the Court in the *Strabag* case is not beyond criticism. It is for instance far from obvious that the legislation as such entails that the tenderer runs a risk of only 'belatedly being able to obtain damages', cf. para 42 of the judgment. It would be more appropriate to consider such a risk a simple consequence of having to bring the case before the judiciary. It is more the rule than the exception that court procedures on damages takes years in the national courts of the European Union.

The subsequent ruling from the Court of Justice in C-568/08, *Spijker,* takes a fundamentally different approach. In this ruling the Court emphasized the procedural autonomy of the Member States in an answer to a preliminary question on the conditions for damages. The Court concluded that it is for the Member States to establish the relevant criteria under observance of the principles of effectiveness and equivalence, cf. para 92. The ruling does not appear to be in compliance with the ruling in the *Strabag* case as it does not clarify that another Chamber of the Court had developed the law far beyond the starting point of national procedural autonomy, cf. the *Strabag* case. The ruling in the Spijker case could be interpreted as an implicit overruling of the approach in the Strabag case. It is noteworthy that the Court only refers to para 33 of the later judgment and not paragraphs 39 and 43 which are the essential paragraphs of the *Strabag* case. Consequently the state of law remains blurred after the two recent judgments from the Court of Justice. Presumably, the Member States will uphold their different national approaches until the EU law limitations have been clarified in the case law of the Court of Justice. It should be noted that the above-mentioned judgments both are from Chambers composed of 5 judges. The next time the issue arises it would be relevant to address it before a Grand Chamber of the Court.

3.5.2 Claims for damages when a contract becomes ineffective

Until recently it was very difficult to come up with examples of cases in the Member States where a contracting authority had terminated a contract covered by the EU public procurement rules due to a breach of the procurement rules.[49] However, this situation is likely to change in future practice. This is a consequence of the new rules on ineffectiveness combined with the recent case law from Court of Justice on the duty to terminate tender procedures after breach of the EU public procurement rules.[50]

It follows from Art.2(d)(2) of the Remedies Directive that the consequences of a contract being considered ineffective shall be provided for by national law. The grant of damages to the contracting party when a contract becomes ineffective is typically not addressed in the national legislation implementing Remedies Directive 2007/66. Nevertheless, some Member States have considered the issue when they implemented the Directive.

The approach of the Danish legislator is an example. The provisions of the new Danish Act on the Enforcement of the Public Procurement Rules do not address the issue as such. However, the question is considered in the preparatory works[51] to the Act. The reader with a common law background must be aware that the preparatory works according to Danish legal tradition are of utmost importance and often decisive for a given interpretation. It is stated in the preparatory works that damages are not excluded provided that the ordinary conditions for damages is fulfilled. The assumption is therefore that the contracting party can claim damages. The preparatory works do not address whether the contracting party can obtain compensation for the loss of profit. This question is difficult to answer with certainty and the interpretations on this issue are likely to be divided until the issue is settled in the Danish case law.

One approach would be to draw an analogy from the approach in cases where a contract is invalid. In such a case it would according to Danish law be excluded to obtain compensation for loss of profit as this is reserved to valid contracts where you seek to maintain the economic consequences of the contract to the benefit of the contracting party. At first sight this would appear to be a relevant approach as this would be in accordance with the aim of the introduction of the new remedy ineffectiveness.[52] The latter is specified in

49. Some Danish examples are mentioned in section 5.1 of the chapter of S. Treumer on Danish enforcement in the present publication and in section 1 of the article of S. Treumer, 'Towards an Obligation to Terminate Contracts Concluded in Breach of the EC Public Procurement Rules: the End of the Status of Concluded Public Contracts as Sacred Cows', Public Procurement Law Review 2007 pp. 371-386.
50. C-503/04, *Commission v Germany* and C-91/08, *Wall.*
51. See the remarks regarding §18 of 27 January 2010.
52. This was the preferred approach in the Norwegian preparatory works on enforcement in the field of public procurement, NOU 2010:2, p. 175.

consideration 21 of the Preamble to Remedies Directive 2007/66 where it is stated that 'The objective to be achieved … is that the rights and obligations of the parties under the contract should cease to be enforced and performed.

Another approach could be to emphasize that the new remedy is invalidity sui generis – a close relative of invalidity but with characteristics and legal implications that on some points deviate from the well-known features of invalidity. The public procurement context is special and it is the duty of the contracting authority to comply with the EU public procurement rules. Ineffectiveness is ultimately a consequence of a fundamental failure of the contracting authority and one could question whether it is reasonable that a tenderer in good faith should be excluded from claiming damages for the loss of profit. It would appear appropriate to let the contracting authority carry the financial risk of a contract's possible ineffectiveness as it is the addressee of the public procurement rules and a tenderer should as a matter of principle be able to rely on its observance of the public procurement rules. This approach could also have a positive effect on the observance of the public procurement regime as it would be a clear incentive for compliance.

A consequence of this is that the contracting authority at least theoretically could face a double claim for damages for loss of profit: A claim from one or more of the tenderers that did not win the competition for the contract and a claim from the contracting party losing the contract because it becomes ineffective.[53] For obvious reasons the contracting authority would in practice never be obliged to cover the loss of profit twice as only one tenderer in principle can document that it would have won the competition for the contract[54] if the public procurement rules had been observed.

It can be added that the Swedish legislator also considered the issue of damages in case of ineffectiveness. It follows explicitly from the preparatory works to the implementation of Remedies Directive 2007/66[55] that the con-

53. If the contracting party wins the competition for the contract again in a subsequent tender procedure the consequence is presumably that a claim for damages for loss of profit is without legal basis as this would lead to an unjustified enrichment of the contracting party. The law suit for damages would normally be considered after the conclusion of the contract in the second tender procedure.
54. It is usual to require that the claimant has documented that it would (certainly) have won the contract had it not been for the violation of the EU public procurement rules. The requirement to the degree of certainty probably varies from Member State to Member State.
55. The changes of the Swedish public procurement laws LOU (classic sectors) and LUF (utilities) entered into force 15 July 2010. The issue of damages in cases of ineffec-

tracting party can claim damages. There is a reference to case law[56] concerning damages for loss of profit in the preparatory works and it would therefore appear implicitly to follow from these that the contracting party can make a claim for loss of profit in Sweden. The Swedish Government stressed in the preparatory works that damages to the contracting party was considered to be reasonable and that the preventive effect supports this solution.[57]

The above-mentioned approach with a theoretical acceptance of a claim for damages for loss of profit from the contract party will without doubt be questioned by many. However, the reader should bear in mind that it would be highly unlikely that a contracting authority has to pay damages for loss of profit to a contracting party. There are several reasons for this and it suffices to stress three of them. Firstly, the tenderer has to be in 'good faith' which will frequently not be the case. In most cases the contracting authority can undermine the claim by challenging the good faith of the tenderer as the tenderer has been or ought to have been aware that the contract should have been tendered out or of the other violations that lead to ineffectiveness. National courts and complaints boards will presumably emphasize that the tenderer is a professional and it will therefore be very difficult to be considered in 'good faith' regardless of the undisputed complexity of EU public procurement law.

Secondly, the contracting party has to fulfil the ordinary conditions for damages and consequently has to establish a casual link. The contracting party must therefore establish that it would have won the contract had the public procurement rules been complied with. This will be almost impossible in cases where there has been no tender but also very difficult when the ineffectiveness is caused by other breaches.[58]

Thirdly, it is highly likely that the ordinary courts or a complaints board will hesitate to grant damages for loss of profit to the contracting party and therefore will be inclined to interpret the facts of each individual case to the disadvantage of the contracting party claiming damages for loss of profit. It is still a clear exception that tenderers receive compensation for loss of profit in the traditional scenario where a losing competitor claims damages for breach

tiveness is considered in K. Pedersen, *Upphandlingens grunder – en introduktion til offentlig upphandling och upphandling i försörjningssektorerna*, 201, p.167.

56. NJA 2000 p. 712 and NJA 2007 p. 349.
57. Prop. 2009/10:180, pp. 225-226.
58. The contracting authorities enjoy a wide margin of discretion and typically use the award criteria the economically most advantageous tender.

of the EU public procurement rules.[59] If the above-mentioned approach is accepted it will probably be even rarer that the contracting party makes a successful claim for loss of profit in cases where the contract has been terminated.

Finally, it should be noted that many contracting authorities have started to insert contract clauses in their public contracts limiting or cutting of the responsibility of the contracting authority in case the contract is declared ineffective or terminated due to breach of the public procurement rules. These clauses could subsequently be challenged on the basis of contract law principles. It could for instance be argued that the contracting entity as a professional and the addressee of the public procurement legislation cannot cut off its responsibility for acting in compliance with the law. These clauses might also be challenged on the basis of EU public procurement rules as it could be argued that they undermine the effect of the remedy ineffectiveness.

3.6 Alternative penalties

The 'alternative penalty' is an alternative to ineffectiveness of the contract (ineffectiveness ex tunc of the full contract) and will therefore become relevant in several and fundamentally different situations, cf. Art.2d(2) of the Remedies Directive. It becomes relevant when the review board decides not to declare the contract ineffective on the basis of overriding reasons relating to the general interest, cf. Art.2d(3). It also becomes relevant when only a part of the contract is declared ineffective including the situations where the ineffectiveness has been limited to those obligations which still have to be performed, cf. Art. 2d(2) and when the contract is not declared ineffective in spite of contracting in the standstill period or in breach of suspension of the tender procedures, cf. 2e(1).

The level of and criteria for the measurement of the economic sanctions are not specified in the Remedies Directives but it follows from Art.2e(2) that alternative penalties must be effective, proportionate and dissuasive and that the award of damages does not constitute an appropriate penalty for the purposes of this paragraph.

59. See S. Treumer, 'Damages for Breach of the EC Public Procurement Rules-Changes in European Regulation and Practice', Public Procurement Law Review, 2006 p. 159 for an overview of trends in European practice. A striking feature of the case law in the field was the almost total absence of successful actions for damages. However, this feature has rapidly changed, as there are now several examples of successful actions in various Member States.

The Danish legislator appears to have established a priority between the application of ineffectiveness and alternative penalties in the preparatory works to the Act on the Enforcement of the Public Procurement rules. The preparatory works must be interpreted as giving preference to alternative penalties. This prioritization is probably the most balanced taking into consideration the entirety of involved interests. However, it seems inappropriate that the legislators' reasoning on this point is linked to the preferred choice of remedies of the contracting authorities.[60] Obviously this should not be decisive for an important choice between remedies.

It is highly interesting that there are also indications of a similar approach and confusion in the United Kingdom where the 'UK stakeholders' strongly favoured ineffectiveness to be limited to future obligations instead of retroactive ineffectiveness. The approach was subsequently to limit ineffectiveness to those which have yet to be performed at the time of the legal action and it appears that the choice was mainly made by the stakeholders or at least that their opinion was a decisive factor. This is criticized in the chapter on United Kingdom in the present publication.[61] As pointed out in the chapter on United Kingdom it is doubtful whether the details of an instrument devised to punish extreme violations of the law should be decided by the stakeholders that the new instrument is directed against. Prospective ineffectiveness (ineffectivness ex nunc) is 'ineffectiveness light' and is less of a deterrent.[62]

4 Remedies for infringements of the public procurement rules outside the scope of the Public Procurement Directives

It is well-known to specialists working in the field of public procurement that the Court of Justice has started to develop a secondary public procurement regime covering contracts falling outside of or only partially covered by the Public Procurement Directives, cf. C-324/98, *Telaustria* and subsequent case law.[63] This implies that the contracting authorities are obliged to ensure some

60. See section 6 of the chapter of S. Treumer on Danish enforcement in the present publication for further details.
61. See the chapter of M. Trybus, 'An Overview of the United Kingdom Public Procurement Review and Remedies System with an Emphasis on England and Wales', section 6 on ineffectiveness.
62. See M. Trybus, fn. 61 above.
63. This issue has been covered in several publications in the last decade. See for instance the recent article of A. Brown, 'EU Primary Law Requirements in Practice: Advertis-

degree of transparency and to take certain actions mirroring the essentials of some of the detailed provisions in the Directives even though the contracts are falling outside or not fully covered by the standard regime outlined in the Public Procurement Directives. This secondary public procurement regime applies under certain conditions to contracts falling below the threshold values and to service concessions. It is certain that far from all the duties to act outlined in the Public Procurement Directives apply when a contract is outside or partially covered but it is very uncertain and controversial to establish which duties have to be observed according to the secondary public procurement regime. This has to be established on a case by case basis as pointed out by Advocate General Mengozzi in C-226/09, *Commission v Ireland.*

It is to a large extent unclear whether it follows from *EU law* that the provisions and principles from the Remedies Directives can be applied where the secondary public procurement regime has been violated. This issue is rarely addressed in national case law and in the case law of the Court of Justice of the European Union. One reason for this is that the development of the secondary procurement regime is fairly recent and that national courts and Complaints Boards presumably will be reluctant to rule that analogue remedies apply outside the scope of the Public Procurement Directives. Another reason is that it often will not be needed to invoke EU law as the legal basis for a given remedy because it clearly follows from national law whether the remedy is available or not. The contracts falling outside the scope of the Public Procurement Directives are often covered by a national public procurement regime. It can then clearly follow from this regime that the 'standard' remedies introduced by the Remedies Directives equally apply to contracts falling outside of the Public Procurement Directives. In such a case the complainant will normally not need to invoke EU law as the legal basis for a given remedy even though a similar legal protection could be derived from EU law.

The following analysis will briefly consider selected aspects of the question of enforcement of the public procurement regime outside of the Public Procurement Directives which to a large extent has been neglected in legal literature.[64]

ing, Procedures and Remedies for Public Contracts Outside the Procurement Directives', Public Procurement Law Review 2010, p. 169.

64. The forthcoming Ph.D.-dissertation of Carina Risvig Hansen, Copenhagen Business School will consider these issues in further detail.

4.1 Damages

It would not be difficult to find violations of the public procurement regime outside of the Public Procurement Directives. However, this does not at all imply that it is easy to identify cases where a plaintiff or complainant has claimed damages for a breach of the secondary public procurement regime. This regime is not very developed at present and the essential obligation consists in a requirement for transparency typically in the form of advertisement of the contract. A claim for damages for breach of the transparency obligation would be the exception. Firstly, the legal basis for such a claim is uncertain and the contract value will often not justify the efforts and risks allocated to a damages claim. Secondly, the prospect of success would be very poor. As the contract has not been advertised there has not been a competition and the plaintiff has therefore not had tender costs. The chances of obtaining damages for loss of profit are extremely low as it normally required in national procurement law on damages that the tenderer proves that it would have obtained the contract. The situation corresponds to claims for damages where contracts covered by the Public Procurement Directives are awared directly and illegally. A few have claimed damages in this situation but it appears that all have been unsuccessful. Nevertheless, it is of relevance to consider the possible legal basis for a damages claim in this context.

It is submitted[65] that the relevant conditions for a damages claim is the standard conditions established with regard to the liability of the Member States for violation of EU law and therefore that the breach must be 'sufficiently serious'.[66] It should be noted that this most likely is a stricter requirement than what follows from a damages claim in situations covered by the Remedies Directives, cf. C-314/09, *Strabag*.[67] From this ruling based on a dynamic and far-reaching interpretation on the principle of effectiveness and

65. See also S. Arrowsmith, *The Law of Public and Utilities Procurement*, 2nd ed., Sweet & Maxwell, London 2005 in particular p. 1421 with footnote 87.
66. The factors which the competent court may take into consideration include the clarity and the precision of the rule breached, the measure of discretion left by the rule to the national or Community authorities, whether the infringement and the damage caused was intentional or involuntary, whether any error of law was excusable or inexcusable, the fact that the position taken by a Community institution may have contributed towards the omission, and the adoption or retention of national measures or practices contrary to Community law, cf. Cases C-46 &48/93, *Brasserie de Pêcheur and Factortame III.*
67. The approach in this case appears to deviate from a subsequent case from another Chamber in the Court of Justice. See C-568/08, *Spijker* and section 3.5.1 of this chapter.

the purpose of the Remedies Directives appears to follow that any breach of the Public Procurement Directives in principle is sufficient ground for damages. It can be added that the Court of Justice in C-91/08, *Wall*, concerning the duty to terminate a contract due to breaches of the secondary public procurement regime demonstrated that it is not necessarily willing to establish the same standard for remedies outside of the scope of the Public Procurement Directives as inside the scope of the Directives. The *Wall* case is considered in further detail in section 4.2 below.

4.2 Ineffectiveness and the duty to terminate the concluded contract

As previously outlined in section 2.3 above the Court of Justice established in C-503/04, *Commission v Germany*, that there can be a duty to terminate a concluded contract where the provisions of the Public Procurement Directives have been violated. The judgment in this case was unusually laconic and the Court limited its remarks on the 'new' obligation to terminate contracts concluded in breach of the EU procurement rules. This is not surprising as it stretched the interpretation of the obligations arising from the Treaty rather far in this case. A similar and rather cautious approach can be seen in C-324/98, *Telaustria*, and subsequent case law on the creation of the secondary public procurement regime.

The preliminary ruling in C-91/08, *Wall*, was a very fast follow-up to the case in C-503/04, *Commission v Germany*, and the national court posed to the Court of Justice a very logical but also extremely delicate question: Does a breach of the secondary public procurement regime, cf. C-324/98, *Telaustria*, and subsequent case law, entail a duty to terminate the contract in question in a case concerning *national* enforcement of the public procurement rules? This appeared to be the overlooked but logical consequence of the development of the secondary public procurement regime. The referring national court apparently presumed this to be the case and based itself on the rationale behind the new provisions in the Remedies Directives on ineffectiveness[68] and C-503/04, *Commission v Germany*. The Court of Justice basically rejected the idea of applying the rationale from C-503/04, *Commission v Germany*, and clarified that there was not a duty to declare a contract ineffective or to terminate it in 'in every case' of an alleged breach, cf. para 65 of the judgment.

However, it still remains unsettled whether the Court of Justice – that is to say in a case concerning *supranational* enforcement – would consider itself

68. Referred to as the principles in Art.2 of Directive 89/665, cf. consideration 138 in the opinion of the Advocate General Bot.

competent to finding that a contract should have been terminated in a case where the secondary public procurement regime as developed in its own case law has been violated. It is submitted that the Court most likely would consider itself competent to do so. It can be added that it is probably a question of the span of a few years before the Court of Justice will apply the rationale from C-503/04, *Commission v Germany*, on breaches of the secondary procurement regime. As the latter gradually becomes more and more developed and the new sanction ineffectiveness based on the Remedies Directives becomes firmly grounded in national law and practice, it will become less controversial to draw consequences corresponding to those applicable to the contracts covered by the Public Procurement Directives.

4.3 Standstill

It is an important element of Remedies Directive 2007/66 that the contracting entity must observe a standstill period of at least 10 or 15 calendar days following the decision to award of the contract, cf. Art. 2a. The period is 10 days if the notification of the reasons behind the decisions has been forwarded by electronic means of communication and 15 days from the dispatch by mail. The standstill period should give the tenderers concerned sufficient time to examine the contract award decision and to assess whether it is appropriate to initiate a review procedure, cf. consideration 6 of the Preamble to the Directive. This rule is based on a principle developed in the case law of the Court of Justice and is of utmost importance for the effective enforcement of the public procurement rules. It is therefore relevant to consider whether a similar principle apply for contracts outside of the scope of the Public Procurement Directives. This issue has not been considered in the case law of the Court of Justice but it has been addressed in national case law and in the legislation of at least a few Member States.

As an example it is explicitly stated in the preparatory works to the Danish Act on the Enforcement of the Public Procurement Rules that it is not obligatory to observe the above-mentioned rules on standstill if the contract in question is excluded from the Public Sector Directive or the Utilities Directive.[69] However, French lower courts have ruled that a standstill period must be observed for contracts outside the scope of the Public Procurement Directives.

69. A similar approach appears to have been taken in the United Kingdom, cf. the chapter of M. Trybus in the present publication. The latter considers that the limitations of the Crown Proceedings Act 1947 on the remedies system for contracts below the thresholds are not in compliance with EU law.

Very recent case law from the French Supreme Court appears to have overrules this practice[70]

It can be argued that a standstill period is also mandatory outside of the scope of the Public Procurement Directives.[71] Individuals are entitled to effective judicial protection of the rights they derive from the Community legal order and the standstill period is a very important element in the creation of an effective remedies system. It would therefore appear that it would be necessary to ensure the observance of the standstill period also outside of the scope of the Public Procurement Rules and the Court of Justice is highly likely to rule to this effect once the issue is brought before it.

5 Conclusion

The regime for enforcement of the EU public procurement rules is highly interesting because it is an area of law where the European legislator has made exceptional efforts in order to ensure effective enforcement at national level and has pushed the development forward. In this respect the state of the law in the field of public procurement deviates from the clear starting point in EU law. As a main rule remedies and procedural law concerning breaches of the law are considered matters for the national legislator according to the principle of national and remedial autonomy.

Another feature that makes this field particularly interesting is that the Court of Justice repeatedly has demonstrated awareness of the importance of effective enforcement in the field of public procurement. As a consequence the Court has interpreted the law in a very dynamic manner in a number of landmark cases leading to fundamental improvements of the enforcement system both at national and supranational level.

Public Procurement is also a field of law where you can find noteworthy examples of dynamic interpretation at *national* level. It is remarkable that the principle of effectiveness appears to have been used in some national jurisdictions as a lever for the creation of new law when national courts or complaints Boards have deviated from their respective traditional laws i.e. on damages, cf. section 1. Examples of this can be found in several Member States which is rather surprising as remedies and procedural law are in gen-

70. See the chapter of F. Lichère and N. Gabayet on France in the present publication.
71. See Carina Risvig Hansen, 'Pligt til annoncering af offentlige kontrakter – uden effektiv håndhævelse af reglerne?', Ugeskrift for Retsvæsen, 2011 B101.

eral to be considered as matters for the national legislator, cf. the principle of national procedural autonomy.

It is going to be extremely interesting to follow the future developments in the field and in particular the regulation and case law on the new remedy ineffectiveness. This new remedy will surely motivate the contracting entities to observe the public procurement rules to a higher degree in the future. However, it is unlikely that it will be frequently applied by national courts and complaints boards. Many tenderers will most likely hesitate to invoke the remedy and the conditions for the application of the new remedy are narrowly construed in Remedies Directive 2007/66. Furthermore, Member States have typically provided for the various exceptions outlined in the Directive and the exceptions will undoubtedly frequently be relied upon by contracting entities and in the last instance by national courts and complaints boards.

Until now attention has been focused on national enforcement of the Public Procurement Directives according to the requirements outlined in the Remedies. It can be expected that much more attention will be given to the remedies concerning contracts falling outside the scope of the Public Procurement Directives, cf. section 4 of this chapter. Surely the secondary public procurement regime introduced with the ruling in C-324/98, *Telaustria* will be further developed in the coming years in the case law of the Court of Justice. As a consequence there will be a need and a push for the creation of effective remedies for infringements of this part of the substantive EU public procurement rules in the years to come. As it follows from section 4 of this chapter and from the chapters on the various national systems in the present publication effective remedies appear currently *not* to be in place in all the Member States in this respect.

It will be fascinating to see whether the national courts and complaints boards will be willing to interpret national law in a dynamic manner when it comes to the enforcement of the secondary public procurement regime. It is my prediction – based on prior trends in the case law at national level in the field – that national courts and complaints boards typically will not be willing to do so even though there certainly will be exceptions.[72] Even so, it is unlikely that the European Commission will overlook this challenge and it

72. Just as in the previous case law. See for example the remarks on standstill in section 4.3 of this chapter (French Courts), damages in section 1 and 3.5 (courts and complaints boards from various Member States) and ineffectiveness/establishment of a duty to terminate contracts concluded in breach of the EU public procurement rules (Danish courts) in section 5.1 in the chapter written by S. Treumer on the Danish enforcement regime in the present publication.

must be expected that the Commission will initiate law suits based on the argument that certain Member States have not ensured effective judicial protection for the contracts falling outside the scope of the Public Procurement Directives.[73]

The Court of Justice might initially hesitate to develop a secondary public procurement enforcement regime because the legal basis for such a development is vague and because it generates considerable legal uncertainty. Nevertheless, as the secondary public procurement regime becomes more and more developed and firmly grounded in national case law, literature and regulation it will become less controversial to draw the logical and inevitable consequence: To create an effective remedies regime covering also the contracts falling outside the scope of the public procurement Directives.

Selected Bibliography

S. Arrowsmith, *The Law of Public and Utilities Procurement*, 2nd edn. 2005, chapter 21

C. Bovis, *EU Public Procurement Law*, 2007, chapter 16

S.E. Hjelmborg, P.S. Jacobsen and S.T. Poulsen, *Public Procurement Law – the EU directive on public contracts*, 1. edition 2006, chapter 8 (second edition is forthcoming)

D. Fairgrieve and F. Lichère (eds.), 'Damages as an effective remedy', Hart, (forthcoming in 2011)

J. Fejø and S. Treumer (eds.), *EU's Udbudsregler – implementering og håndhævelse i Norden* (The EC Public Procurement Rules-Implementation and Enforcement in the Nordic Countries), 2006.

K. Krüger, 'Kontraktsrettlige retsvirkninger av anbudsfeil ved offentlige anskaffelser (upphandling–udbud), En sammenligning mellom nye svenske, danske og norske anbudsregler med hovedvekt på kontrakter innen bygg og anlegg', *Festskrift till Torgny Håstad*, 2011

P. Trepte, *Public Procurement in the EU. A Practitioner's Guide*, chapter 9, 2nd ed., 2007

S. Treumer, 'National håndhævelse af EU's udbudsregler – er håndhævelsessystemet effektivt på EU-udbudsområdet?', p. 99 in J. Fejø and S. Treumer (eds.), *EU's Udbudsregler – implementering og håndhævelse i Norden*, 2006

S. Treumer, 'Damages for Breach of the EC Public Procurement Rules-Changes in European Regulation and Practice', Public Procurement Law Review, 2006 p. 159 and the subsequent articles pp. 171-240 written by various experts on the state of law on damages in France, Germany, United Kingdom, Sweden and Norway

73. See section 2.3.3. of the Commission Interpretative Communication on the Community law applicable to contracts awards not or not fully subject to the provisions of the Public Procurement Directives, C179/2 of 1 August 2006.

S. Treumer, 'Towards an Obligation to Terminate Contracts Concluded in Breach of the EC Public Procurement Rules: the End of the Status of Concluded Public Contracts as Sacred Cows', Public Procurement Law Review 2007 p. 371

2 Many Different Paths, but Are They All Leading to Effectiveness?

By Roberto Caranta

1 Foreword

It has been some times since the stipulated deadline for the implementation of Directive 2007/66/EC elapsed.[1] Pursuing accrued effectiveness in the application of EU procurement law,[2] the Directive revised the previous legislation mainly introducing two new remedies, standstill and ineffectiveness (with the ancillary remedy of alternative penalties).[3]

All the Member States covered in this book have now implemented Directive 2007/66/EC, a few of them having had time for second thoughts and amendments to the implementing legislation. Judgements in the first few cases have been handed down in some of the jurisdictions analysed here. The resulting picture is quite differentiated. This is unsurprising. Remedies are not any niche triviality in the overall legislation, easily amended without affecting other segments of the legal order considered. Quite on the contrary, remedies lie at the core of any legal order, and tampering with them is sure to produce shockwaves.[4]

It is to be added that even after Directive 2007/66/EC entered into force the remedies in public procurement have been harmonised to a limited extent only. As the Court of justice held in *Santex*, Directive 89/665/EEC 'lays down the minimum conditions to be satisfied by the review procedures estab-

1. Directive 2007/66/EC of the European Parliament and of the Council of 11 December 2007 amending Council Directives 89/665/EEC and 92/13/EEC with regard to improving the effectiveness of review procedures concerning the award of public contracts.
2. See Recitals 3 ff of Directive 2007/66/EC, referring to weaknesses to be remedied.
3. S. Treumer 'Enforcement (EU)' above.
4. In a similar vein M. Burgi 'Enforcement of EU Public Procurement Rules'§ 1.2.

lished in the national legal systems, so as to ensure compliance with the requirements of Community law concerning public contracts'.[5]

What is not covered by the Directive is left to the residual procedural autonomy of the Member States.[6] This was very much stressed in the recent *Spijker* judgement concerning different facets of judicial protection, including damages claims.[7] The Court held that 'In the absence of EU provisions in that area, it is for the legal order of each Member State to determine the criteria on the basis of which damage arising from an infringement of EU law on the award of public contracts must be determined and estimated'.[8] Moreover, in *GAT* the Court of justice held that national law could well give review bodies the powers to raise legality issues of their own motion. Even if this is not provided for in the remedies directives, it indeed enhances the effectiveness of the review system.[9]

Inevitably Member States have approached the implementation of Directive 2007/66/EC differently. At times, rules on remedies in public procurement have been rewritten almost from scrap. Other times, the new remedies have been grafted into the existing legislation. In both cases, the peculiar legal traditions of each Member State are deemed to influence the way remedies are not just implemented but applied. Harmonisation by EU law is partial at best here, and calls for comparative analysis.[10]

This chapter will endeavour to map these differences – and the similarities –having in mind whether or not – and if so to which extent – they impact the effectiveness of the review of public procurement decisions and contracts.

5. Case C-327/00 *Santex* [2003] ECR I-1877, paragraph 47; see also Case C-315/01 *GAT* [2003] ECR I-6351, paragraph 45, and more recently Case C-314/09 *Strabag* [2010] ECR I-0000, paragraph 33.
6. Case C-315/01 *GAT* [2003] ECR I-6351, paragraph 46. See also M. Burgi 'Enforcement of EU Public Procurement Rules'§ 1.2. This is so even if the procedural autonomy of Member States in public procurements is more limited than in other areas due to the remedies directives having partially harmonized the matter: see S. Treumer 'Enforcement (EU)' above, §§ 1, 3 (writing of 'a minimum level of protection'), and 5.
7. Case C-568/08 *Combinatie Spijker Infrabouw* [2010] ECR I-0000; see also Case C-91/08 *Wall* [2010] ECR I-0000, paragraphs 63 f.
8. Paragraph 90.
9. Case C-315/01 *GAT* [2003] ECR I-6351, paragraphs 48 ff.
10. See R. Caranta 'Pleading for European Comparative Administrative Law: What is the Place for Comparative Law in Europe?' in K.J. de graaf, J.H. Jans, a. prechal, R.J.G.M. Widdershoven (eds.) *European Administrative Law: Top-Down and Bottom-Up* (Groningen, Europa Law Publishing, 2009) 155.

2 Private law or Public law? Civil or Administrative Courts?

Public contracts – or, and possibly more correctly at this stage, contracts to which a public administration is a party – lie somewhere on the border between private and public law. How much at one or the other side of the border has long been decided by national legislation and legal traditions.

Putting it in a somewhat simplistic way, it can be said that in France contracts to which a public administration is a party are in principle ruled by public law.[11] This basically means that the public administration retains some of its exorbitant powers and is not bound by the contract the same way as any private contactor. In other jurisdiction, belonging to both the civil law (Germany) and the common law (England) traditions, the same contracts are in principle ruled by private law (or by a mix where private law might be seen as prevailing).[12]

The distinction historically focused on the contract performance or contract implementation phase, and essentially boiled down to the question whether or not the public administration could change its mind after passing a contract because of changed circumstances and more specifically because of a different appreciation of the general interest having determined it to look for a contractor. From answers to this question which at times were different more in principle than their actual consequences, a further difference arose.[13]

Having grounded in public law what may now safely be called public contracts, France was ready to afford protection to potential bidders claiming that the rules passed for choosing the contractors had been breached. Those claims were and are in the end part and parcel of the standards for judicial review of administrative action, the only possible question being what to do

11. F. Lichère and N. Gabayet 'Enforcement of EU Public Procurement Rules in France' § 1.
12. See M. Burgi 'Enforcement of EU Public Procurement Rules'§ 1.1 and 7; see also M. Trybus 'An Overview of the UK' esp. § 8. The same is true of the situation in the Netherlands as it is described in Case C-568/08 *Combinatie Spijker Infrabouw* [2010] ECR I-0000, paragraph 11: 'the award of public contracts is a matter for private law, the award of a public contract constitutes an act of private law, and decisions preliminary to the award of a public contract taken by administrative bodies are regarded as preparatory acts of private law. The civil courts have jurisdiction to hear disputes on the award of public contracts as regards both the adoption of protective measures and the procedure on the substance'.
13. R. Noguellou U. Stelkens 'Propos introductifs/Introduction' in R. Noguellou U. Stelkens (eds.) *Droit comparé des contrats publics. Comparative Law on Public Contracts* (Bruylant, Brussels 2010) 1.

when a contract has already been entered into? Not an intractable problem, and one being soon mostly solved with reference to the theory of the *acte détachable*.[14]

Having kept contracts to which a public administration is a party within the realm of private law, other jurisdictions had more problems in affording remedies to third parties. The same happened when those contracts were considered as part of budgetary law (*Fiscus*) rather than administrative law. Private contract law is for the parties to the contract, and does not go into any depth as to the procedures to choose one's partner.[15] Outside the limited grounds afforded by pre-contractual liability (mainly, bad faith on the part of the public purchaser), potential bidders had no ground in private law for complaining about not being the chosen one.[16]

In a way, it is not so much that in France there existed an extensive body of rules on how the public administration should choose its partners where none existed for instance in Germany. The difference laid on whether breaches to these rules were actionable in court by potential bidders or not, in the latter case being considered as internal working rules for the public administration whose breach could be relevant for accounting or auditing purposes.

Then EEC law was obviously attracted by the French model. What is now the EU cannot rely only on the Commission acting as a watchdog to police compliance with the rules it edicts. This is even more so in the field of public contracts, Member States being at the same time the public purchasers and easily tempted to buy national to foster domestic firms and protect local products.[17] To establish and police the internal market, the EU needs to enlist the help of disaffected potential bidders and this means giving them enforceable rights along the French model.[18]

The above goes a long way towards explaining not just how EU public procurement law is, but also why given jurisdictions find it easier than others

14. F. Lichère and N. Gabayet 'Enforcement of EU Public Procurement Rules in France' § 5.1.
15. See for instance M. Trybus 'An Overview of the UK' § 1.1.
16. U. Stelkens et H. Schröder 'Les droit de contrats publics en Allemagne' in R. Noguellou U. Stelkens (eds.) *Droit comparé des contrats publics* above nt 13, point 3.2.1.
17. On the resource limits placed on the Commission when enforcing EU law see S. Treumer 'Enforcement (EU)' §§ 1, 2 and 2.2; generally on the use of infringement procedures in public procurement cases P. Trepte *Public Procurement in the EU* 2nd (Oxford, Oxford University Press, 2007) 578 ff, and C. Bovis *EC Public Procurement: Case Law and Regulation* (Oxford, Oxford University Press, 2006) 50 ff.
18. C. Bovis *EC Public Procurement* above fn 17, 67.

to adopt and adapt to its rules and principles. Inevitably those legal systems – like Germany – which adhere to a private law systematization of public procurement contracts face more difficulties in accommodating the rules on non-discrimination and transparency in the award of the same contracts.[19] On the contrary France has no problem in extending the procurement remedies to all public contracts. In the end, they are quite in line with the pre-existing administrative law traditions already developed there.[20]
The possible existence of a specialized administrative jurisdiction is relevant mainly in so far as it may have contributed to and strengthened the public law character of contracts to which a public administration is a party.

3 The Province of Effective Remedies

A sharp divergence between Member States occurs as to the scope of application for the remedies provided under EU law. This reflects a divergent approach to the relationships between EU and national public procurement law. On the one hand, we have Member Countries acting as if the scope of EU procurement were strictly limited to the contracts covered in the substantive directives (presently Directives 2004/17/EC and Directives 2004/18/EC).[21] Contrasting with this minimalist approach, other Member States are happy to have the same rules originating from the EU – or at least some of them – applied to all procurement.[22]

The first attitude is grounded on what appears to be an outmoded approach to EU law which is still based on international law concepts. This basically intergovernmentalist attitude pretends that the scope of EU law is confined to what the Member States – the *Herren des Vertrags* – have expressly agreed upon in the Council when passing the directives. At a general level, this attitude was defeated already fifty years ago in the seminal constitutional rulings *van Gend & Loos* which dispelled the initial reconstruction of the (then) EEC

19. See J. Germain 'Les recours juridictionnels ouverts au concurrent évincé contre un marché public communautaire après sa conclusion en France et en Allemagne' [2009] *Rev. Fr. Dr. Adm.* 58, and U. Stelkens et H. Schröder 'Les droit de contrats publics en Allemagne' above nt 16, point 3.2.1.
20. F. Lichère and N. Gabayet 'Enforcement of EU Public Procurement Rules in France' § 1.
21. E.g. M. Trybus 'An Overview of the UK' § 1.2.
22. E.g F. Lichère and N. Gabayet 'Enforcement of EU Public Procurement Rules in France' §§ 1, 3 and 6.2.

as one more instance of intergovernmental cooperation.[23] It is hard to argue why this attitude should hold sway in public procurements. Indeed, some of the most interesting cases of the past decade made abundantly clear that the general principles of non-discrimination and equal treatment flowing from the provisions of what has become the TfEU Treaty, along with the corollary obligation – or principle[24] – of transparency apply beyond the boundaries drawn in the 2004 directives.[25] Therefore, while contracts below the thresholds, list B services, and service concessions may not be covered, or may be only partially covered, by the said directives, EU general principles still apply.[26]

The ill-timed reaction by many Member States led by Germany against the Commission's Communication on the rules applicable to public contracts not covered or only partially covered by the 2004 directives[27] inevitably foundered.[28] In the essence, the scope of application of general principles

23. Case 26/62 [1963] ECR 1; see A. J. Menéndez 'The European Democratic Challenge: The Forging of a Supranational *Volonté Générale*' 15 (2009) *Eur. Public Law* 281; on the meaning of *Van Gend & Loos* from a constitutional perspective M. DANI 'Constitutionalism and Dissonances: Has Europe Paid Off its Debt to Functionalism?' 15 (2009) *Eur. Public Law* 329 ff.
24. In general EU law transparency is rather seen as a principle: e.g. S. Prechal and M. de Leeuw 'Dimensions of Transparency: The Building Blocks of a New Legal Principle?' [2007] *REALaw – Rev. Eur. Adm. Law* 51, et D.U. Galetta 'Trasparenza e governance amministrativa nel diritto europeo' [2006] *Riv. it. dir. pubbl. comunitario* 265. In procurement law it is argued otherwise: see P. Craig and M. Trybus, *Public Contracts: England and Wales*, in R. Noguellou U. Stelkens (eds.) *Droit comparé des contrats publics* above fn 13, 3.2 'transparency is perhaps more a means to an end than an end in itself. In other words transparency is a vehicle for other principles such as competition, value for money, and non-discrimination rather than a principle in itself'.
25. The leading case is Case C-324/98 *Telaustria Verlags GmbH* [2000] ECR I-10745; it developed an indication found in Case C-275/98 [1999] *Unitron Scandinavia et 3-S* ECR I-8291, paragrah 31.
26. See U. Neergaard 'Public Service Concessions and Related Concepts – the Increased Pressure from Community Law on Member States' Use of Concessions' [2007] *PPLR* 387; A. Brown 'Seeing Through Transparency: the Requirement to Advertise Public Contracts and Concessions Under the EC Treaty' [2007] PPLR 1; S. Treumer 'The Discretionary Power of Contracting Entities – Towards a Flexible Approach in the Recent Case Law of the Court of Justice?' [2006] PPLR 82.
27. [2006] OJ C 179/02.
28. Case T-258/06 *Commission* v *Germany* [2010] ECR II-0000; see Z. Petersen 'Below-threshold Contract Awards under EU Primary Law: Federal Republic of Germany v Commission (T-258/06) [2010] *PPLR* NA215.

based on the Treaty cannot be restricted by secondary legislation.[29] These days the case law on the requirements following from the principles of non-discrimination and equal treatment and the ensuing obligation of transparency is expanding, covering cases where the award criteria were tampered with without informing potential bidders[30] as well as cases where the contracting authority allowed a relevant subcontractor to be changed.[31]

If the general principles of non-discrimination and equal treatment and the obligation of transparency apply to any award procedure for contracts of trans-boundary interest, the situation with remedies cannot be dramatically different.[32] There cannot be any no go area for the principle of effective judicial protection. This is even more so since the principle of effective judicial protection of rights granted by EU law is a most general principle having been developed quite independently from public procurement.[33] In the context of the substantive provisions of EU procurement law, the TfEU principles don't demand the full application of the very detailed provisions to public contracts not covered or not fully covered by the 2004 directives.[34]

In the remedies area, considering that the requirements laid down in Directives 89/665/EEC, 92/13/EEC and 2007/66/EC, are not very detailed, it may be argued that Member States could hardly satisfy the principle of effective judicial protection by providing remedies more limited in scope and strength.

29. See also A. Brown 'EU Primary Law Requirements in Practice: Advertising, Procedures and Remedies for Public Contracts Outside the Procurement Directives' [2010] PPLR 169.
30. Case C-226/09 *Commission* v *Ireland* [2010] ECR I-0000.
31. Case C-91/08 *Wall* [2010] ECR I-0000; see A. Brown 'Changing a Sub-contractor Under a Public Service Concession: *Wall AG v Stadt Frankfurt am Main* [2010] *PPLR* NA160.
32. See M. Trybus 'An Overview of the UK' § 1.2; this even if the above mentioned Communication does not deal much with remedies: see A. Brown 'EU Primary Law Requirements in Practice' above fn, 178.
33. See M. Trybus 'An Overview of the UK' § 1.2. On the principle of effective judicial protection see R. Caranta 'Judicial Protection Against Member States: A New Jus commune takes shape' [1996] CMLRev. 703, and more recently (and for complete references) M. Eliantonio *Europeanisation of Administrative Justice?* (Groningen, Europa Law Publishing, 2008).
34. E.g. Case Case C-324/98 *Telaustria Verlags GmbH* [2000] ECR I-10745, paragraphs 60 f.

Moreover, some of the 'new remedies' such has the standstill and ineffectiveness have been dynamically developed by the case law of the Court of justice well before making their way into the remedies directives.[35]

The recent *Wall* case, decided by the Grand chamber of the Court of justice could be read as disproving the above considerations.[36] The case concerned subsequent amendments to a service concession, that is a contract excluded from the coverage of the 2004 directives. The Court held that the change of a highly qualified subcontractor could be considered to be a substantial alteration to the contract, so much that 'If need be, a new award procedure should be organised'.[37] However, and somewhat contradictorily, when asked whether the national court was under a duty to terminate the contract, the Court of justice held that 'the principles of equal treatment and non-discrimination on grounds of nationality enshrined in Articles 43 EC and 49 EC and the consequent obligation of transparency do not require the national authorities to terminate a contract or the national courts to grant a restraining order in every case of an alleged breach of that obligation in connection with the award of service concessions'.[38]

This judgement is in no way contributing in clarifying a potentially contention issue (so much so that a number of Member States intervened in the proceedings). At no point of the reasoning the Court refers to the infringement judgement against Germany which – as it will be shown – led to the establishment of the duty to terminate long-term concession contracts directly awarded.[39]

An alternative take on this judgement could be to suggest that in the end it only decided that ineffectiveness does not follow from all and every breach.[40] This is not mind-bloggling. Even after the modifications introduced in 2007, the remedies directives stopped short of making ineffectiveness the general rule. If the Court of justice had held that the general principles of the Treaty require ineffectiveness to follow from all and every breach of procurement rules the limits found in the remedies directives would no longer have made sense.[41]

35. See S. Treumer 'Enforcement (EU)' §§ 2.3 and 4, and, with reference to standstill, A. Brown 'EU Primary Law Requirements in Practice' above fn 29, 180 f.
36. Case C-91/08 *Wall* [2010] ECR I-0000. See S. Treumer 'Enforcement (EU)' § 4.2.
37. Paragraph 43.
38. Paragraph 65.
39. Case C-503/04 *Commission/Germany* [2007] ECR I-6153.
40. A. Brown 'EU Primary Law Requirements in Practice' above fn 29, 180.
41. See also S. Treumer 'Enforcement (EU)' § 4.2.

This said, the Court should have taken the opportunity presented by *Wall* to clarify the situation. This very much so because the approach followed in some of the Member States such as the UK is one to avoid providing effective remedies in connection to award procedures concerning contracts not covered by the 2004 directives.[42] The same happens in Germany concerning contracts below the EU threshold.[43] In other jurisdictions, even if the attitude is less structured, bidders to contracts falling outside the scope of the substantive directives are afforded a more limited protection. In Denmark, for instance, the application of the new standstill provisions has been excluded for those contracts not covered by the substantive directives.[44] It is fair to say that other jurisdictions – such as Italy and France – don't suffer from this problem, having extended the remedies to the breaches affecting the procedures leading to the conclusion of all and any public contracts.[45] In turn, however, this might be seen as a problem when heavy and remedial procedural requirements are imposed with reference to contracts whose value might be very modest.[46]

4 The Question of Standing

While under a private law context it could make sense to deny potential bidders any standing to challenge the choice of a contractor, in a public law environment anyone having a 'sufficient' interest in the matter should be able to go to court. A sufficient interest immediately identifies those competitors potentially interested to be chosen as partners for the contract at stake because the subject matter of the given contract falls within the scope of their business.[47]

42. See critically M. Trybus 'An Overview of the UK' §§ 1 f.
43. M. Burgi 'Enforcement of EU Public Procurement Rules'§ 1.1.
44. See critically S. Treumer 'Enforcement' (Denmark), § 2.1.
45. F. Lichère and N. Gabayet 'Enforcement of EU Public Procurement Rules in France' §§ 1, 3 and 6.2 (the latter references concerning the standstill period, concerning which it was for the case law rather than the legislation to decide the spill-over of EU remedies to any contract).
46. D.C. Dragoş, B. Neamţu and R. Velişcu 'Remedies in Public Procurement in Romania' § 2.1.2.
47. This is the case in Italy M. Comba 'Enforcement of EU Procurement Rules' § 1, and France, even if the situation might slightly change according to the specific judicial procedure followed: F. Lichère and N. Gabayet 'Enforcement of EU Public Procurement Rules in France' § 2, 1.1.1, with reference to the SMIRGEOMES case.

This approach is followed by Article 1(3) Directive 89/665/EEC, under which the remedies provided in the directive are to be made available 'at least to any person having or having had an interest in obtaining a particular public supply or public works contract and who has been or risks being harmed by an alleged infringement'.

Most Member States are quite generous on standing. It is to be remembered that not just fair competition but also taxpayers money are best served by allowing challenges to procurement decisions. While the former might explain the remedies system at EU level, both are relevant and reinforce each other at national level.[48] So for instance in the UK standing is granted following a very flexible and liberal test not just to competitors but to representative trade organisations. Only taxpayers and the general public are excluded.[49] In some other jurisdiction too standing is extended beyond the circle of competitors and potential competitors, to include, as in the case of Denmark, public bodies such as the Competition and Consumer Authority,[50] or the Prefect in France.[51]

Germany only faced challenges in recognising standing to competitors and needed *ad hoc* legislative interventions.[52] This is probably due to a certain private law fundamentalist approach, failing to take into account that as a minimum public fiscal interests are involved in contracting by public authorities. These interests may as well benefit from the protection afforded by giving standing to watchful competitors. Italy may provide for an interesting instance. Somewhat independently from the remedies directives but anyway because of the influence of what was then EEC law, courts started to relax standing rules from the moment they accepted that even when choosing to award a contract directly, public authorities were not using their private law capacity. In all such cases contracting authorities were making a choice ruled – and limited – by the general principles of public law, such as non-discrimination and equal opportunities for all bidders.[53]

48. R. Caranta 'Transparence et concurrence' in R. Noguellou U. Stelkens (eds.) *Droit comparé des contrats publics* above nt 13, 154 ff.
49. M. Trybus 'An Overview of the UK' § 1.3.
50. See above S. Treumer 'Enforcement (Denmark)', § 1 and, describing how this has lost relevance, § 9.
51. F. Lichère and N. Gabayet 'Enforcement of EU Public Procurement Rules in France' §§ 2.1.1.1 and 5.2.
52. See J. Germain 'Les recours juridictionnels ouverts au concurrent évincé' above fn 19, 53.
53. Const. St., Sez. V, 22 marzo 1995, n. 454, in *Giur. it.*, 1996, III, 1, 34, note C. Vivani.

Another question is the standing of those benefiting from the challenged procurement decision to oppose judicial action. This seems to be an issue only in Romania, and should be solved for the positive under the ECHR.[54]

5 The 'Old' Remedies

Directive 89/665/EEC required Member States to afford disaffected competitors three basic remedies, that is interim relief, annulment and damages. These are still very much relevant today. Directive 89/665/EEC however did not go very far in detailing the conditions for granting the remedy awarded. The potential for divergence at national level was therefore – and still is – quite relevant.

5.1 Interim Measures

Interim measures are measures taken to avoid having the consequences of the lamented breach consolidated during the time necessary to courts in order to come at a final decision. In public procurement, these are mainly measures aimed at suspending the procedure pending judicial action, and especially so to avoid the contract being concluded, making effective judicial review more difficult (but not impossible, as it will be shown).[55] In France, however, the *référé* judge has much wider powers, including giving directions to the contracting authority and deleting clauses which infringe the applicable legal requirements.[56]

Under Art. 2(4) of Directive 89/665/EEC, review procedures provided at national level did not have to lead to immediate and necessary suspension of the award procedure. The rule still stands but it has been carved and hollowed inside by Directive 2007/66/EC. Under new Art. 1(5), if review with the same contracting authority is a condition precedent for judicial protection, administrative recourse suspends the possibility to conclude the contract. Moreover, under new Art. 2(3), the contract cannot be concluded before the review body has been given the time to decide on the interim measures asked for or on the merits.

54. D.C. Dragoş, B. Neamţu and R. Velişcu 'Remedies in Public Procurement in Romania' § 5.
55. S. Treumer 'Enforcement (EU)' § 3.1.
56. F. Lichère and N. Gabayet 'Enforcement of EU Public Procurement Rules in France' § 2.1.1.3; as the Authors point out, however, the *référé* procedure is somewhat a mix between an interim and definitive measure.

The conditions for granting interim relief are more or less the same all over Europe. In the substance, they are the same applying in procedures in front of EU Courts.[57] Firstly, if the remedy is not provided, the claimant might suffer an irrecoverable loss. A variation of this condition – at times seen as an autonomous one – focuses not just on the claimant's position, but on the interests of all parties involved, the general interests served by the contract at stake included therein. Secondly, the claimant must show a strong *prima facie* case.[58]

These conditions strengthen the discretion of national courts rather than limiting it.[59] Unsurprisingly, the chances of being granted an interim measures vary very much from jurisdiction to jurisdiction. Basically, on the one hand there is the risk of halting the conclusion of contracts which may serve to satisfy very relevant general interests. This is a widespread concern in many jurisdictions and very much so in Romania, the necessity to comply with the deadlines for spending grants from the EU structural funds being one of the reasons for this[60] On the other hand, if no interim measure is taken, the contracting authority risks ending paying twice, once to the contractor and the other to a successful claimant for damages. The picture presented by different jurisdictions is therefore quite a varied one. Italy is possibly the only country where courts are quite generous in granting interim measures.[61] This is so very much so that the Parliament tried to limit the courts' power in case of contracts for major infrastructure projects.[62] This peculiar attitude may be explained with a marked judicial preference for those which in Germany are called primary remedies to the detriment of damages actions.[63] French courts are reluctant at holding that the (mainly economic) interests of the claimant

57. S. Treumer 'Enforcement (EU)', § 2; on those rules see P. Trepte *Public Procurement in the EU* above fn 17, 588 ff.
58. E.g. concerning Denmark, S. Treumer 'Enforcement' (Denmark), § 2.2; see also on Germany M. Burgi 'Enforcement of EU Public Procurement Rules'§ 2.2.b.
59. See D.C. Dragoş, B. Neamţu and R. Velişcu 'Remedies in Public Procurement in Romania' § 8.
60. D.C. Dragoş, B. Neamţu and R. Velişcu 'Remedies in Public Procurement in Romania' § 8.
61. See M. Comba 'Enforcement of EU Procurement Rules' § 3.
62. This was clearly inconsistent with EU law and was rectified in the recently enacted Code of administrative judicial procedure: see R. Caranta 'Le contentieux des contrats publics en Italie' in *Rev. fr. Dr. Adm.* 2011, 57, and V. Parisio, F. Gambato Spisani and G. Pagliari 'I riti speciali' in R. Caranta (dir.) *Il nuovo processo amministrativo* (Torino, Zanichelli, 2011) 724 ff.
63. R. Caranta Le controversie risarcitorie' in R. Caranta (dir.) *Il nuovo processo amministrativo*, above fn 62, 635 ff.

might be harmed beyond remedy if no interim relief were granted.[64] Danish courts too are very prudish about granting interim relief (one possible reason being the theoretical availability of a remedy in damages for the successful claimant).[65] Finally, in Germany the position of the best bidder is specifically protected through the grant of a right to demand the preliminary award of the contract.[66]

Concerning the procedure, in *Spijker* the Court of justice held that 'Directive 89/665 leaves Member States a discretion in the choice of the procedural guarantees for which it provides, and the formalities relating thereto'.[67] More specifically, 'Directive 89/665 does not preclude a system in which, in order to obtain a rapid decision, the only procedure available is characterised by the fact that it is geared to a rapid mandatory measure, that lawyers have no right to exchange views, that no evidence is, as a rule, presented other than in written form and that statutory rules on evidence are not applicable'.[68]

In an infringement procedure brought against Greece, the Court of justice held that it must be possible to adopt interim measures, independently of any prior action brought on the merits of the procurement decision.[69] The ruling was affirmed in a successive proceeding brought against Spain. The Court of justice moved from the consideration that 'the short duration of the procedures for the award of public contracts means that infringements of the relevant rules of Community law or national rules transposing that law which mar those procedures need to be dealt with urgently'.[70] For that purpose, according to the Court, 'Article 2(1)(a) of that directive requires Member States to empower the review bodies to take, at the earliest opportunity and by way of interlocutory procedures, interim measures with the aim of correcting the alleged infringement or preventing further damage to the interests concerned, including measures to suspend or to ensure the suspension of the procedure for the award of a public contract or the implementation of any decision taken by the contracting authorities'.[71] Therefore, following what it had already

64. F. Lichère and N. Gabayet 'Enforcement of EU Public Procurement Rules in France' § 2.2.2.1.
65. S. Treumer 'Enforcement (Denmark)', §§ 2.2 and 8; a similar consideration may play in the UK.
66. M. Burgi 'Enforcement of EU Public Procurement Rules'§ 2.2.a.
67. Case C-568/08 *Combinatie Spijker Infrabouw* [2010] ECR I-0000, paragraph 57.
68. Paragraph 59.
69. Case C-236/95 *Commission* v *Greece* [1996] ECR I-4459, paragraph 11.
70. Case C-214/00, *Commission v Spain* [2003] ECR I-4667, paragraph 96, referring to recital 5 of the Directive.
71. Paragraph 97.

held in the case brought against Greece, it reiterated that 'the Member States are under a duty more generally to empower their review bodies to take, independently of any prior action, any interim measures, including measures to suspend or to ensure the suspension of the procedure for the award of the public contract in question'.[72]

These cases brought about the need to change the legislation in Italy too.[73] German law, instead, was already in line with the requirement later developed by the Court of justice.[74]

National implementing measures and judicial attitudes diverge as to the possible content and effect of interim measures. In Denmark, interim measures bring the award procedure to a halt,[75] while in France the procedure goes on, only the contract cannot be signed.[76]

Directive 2007/66/EC has strengthened interim relief by providing for an automatic suspension pending the standstill period. This has led to a number of different attempts at implementation in Romania.[77] In Germany a contract concluded in breach of the automatic suspension will be considered null and void.[78] Automatic suspension will be particularly relevant in those jurisdictions not too keen to grant interim relief. In case the contract has been concluded anyway, review bodies can still award interim measures. In principle,

72. Paragraph 98.
73. See M. Comba 'Enforcement of EU Procurement Rules' § 3; the judgments by the Court of justice gave vent to an unusually hot debate: see M.P. Chiti, *La tutela cautelare* ante causam *nel processo amministrativo: uno sviluppo davvero ineluttabile?*, in *Giorn. dir. amm.*, 2003, 898; E. Barbieri, *Diritto comunitario, processo amministrativo e tutela 'ante causam'*, in *Riv. it. dir. pubbl. comunitario*, 2003, 1267; R. Caranta, *La tutela cautelare* ante causam *contro gli atti adottati dalle amministrazioni aggiudicatrici*, in *Urbanistica e appalti* 2003, 885, and L. Stevenato, *La Corte di giustizia ancora come il Benvenuto Cellini dei diritti processuali nazionali: tutela cautelare e processo amministrativo spagnolo (o europeo?)*, in *Dir. proc. amm.*, 2004, 266.
74. M. Burgi 'Enforcement of EU Public Procurement Rules'§ 2.2.
75. S. Treumer 'Enforcement (Denmark)', § 2.2.
76. F. Lichère and N. Gabayet 'Enforcement of EU Public Procurement Rules in France' § 2.1.1.2; see also the changes to this effect in Romania: D.C. Dragoş, B. Neamţu and R. Velişcu 'Remedies in Public Procurement in Romania' § 8
77. D.C. Dragoş, B. Neamţu and R. Velişcu 'Remedies in Public Procurement in Romania' § 8.
78. M. Burgi 'Enforcement of EU Public Procurement Rules'§ 2.2.1.

these measures would anticipate ineffectiveness, meaning that implementation of the contract will be stopped.[79]

5.2 Annulment and Beyond

The fact that the remedies directives stopped well short of full harmonisation is nowhere more evident than when we consider the standard of review against which the compliance to substantive procurement rules is assessed.

Art. 2(1)(b) of Directive 89/665/EEC was not affected by Directive 2007/66/EEC. It provides that review bodies must be given the power 'either set aside or ensure the setting aside of decisions taken unlawfully'. The grounds of illegality are not really clarified. The only specification found in Art. 2(1)(b) is that 'discriminatory technical, economic or financial specifications in the invitation to tender, the contract documents or in any other document relating to the contract award procedure' must be removed. This implies that discriminatory specifications are illegal, but of course a number of quite different illegal decisions may be envisaged. Suffice it to think of recourse to a negotiated procedure outside the situations for which this is allowed[80] or of the exclusion of what appears to be an abnormally low offer without providing the opportunity for explaining the problem away.[81]

It is of course clear that direct award outside the exceptional cases where it is allowed is among the gravest breaches of EU law.[82] However in the main the remedies directives are mostly silent as to the grounds of review. This opens the door to the question of which breaches are relevant.[83] The question is inescapably linked to the margin of unreviewable and unreviewed discretion – or margin of appreciation – left to contracting authorities.[84] A few instances may clarify the problem. Some breaches are just patent and reviewing them does not mean to go very deep into the choices made by the contracting

79. S. Treumer 'Enforcement (Denmark)', § 2.2; D.C. Dragoş, B. Neamţu and R. Velişcu 'Remedies in Public Procurement in Romania' § 9.
80. Among the many cases which could be quoted here see Case C-157/06 *Commission* v *Italy* [2008] ECR I-7313.
81. Joined Cases C-147/06 and C-148/06 *SECAP and Santorso* [2008] ECR I-3565.
82. Case C-26/03 *Stadt Halle* [2005] ECR I-1, paragraph 37.
83. A number of instances are listed by P. Trepte *Public Procurement in the EU* above fn, 556.
84. The issues around the definition of discretion and margin of appreciation are quite numerous and complicated: see R. Caranta 'On Discretion' in S. Prechal and B. van Roermund (eds.), *The Coherence of EU Law. The Search for Unity in Divergent Concepts* (Oxford, Oxford University Press, 2008) 185, and a number of articles in the same collection.

authority. This is the case with direct awards when this is not allowed by EU law. These cases might imply difficult questions of interpretation as for instance as to the limits of in-house under EU law.[85] They, however, can be fully reviewed by courts, all questions focusing on the interpretation of legal provisions. Other cases, such as whether a bidder qualifies for a given contract, what weight to give to award criteria, how to rank different bids against non-quantitative award criteria, or whether a given bid is abnormally law may involve wide margins of appreciation. Whether and to what extent the latter decisions are reviewed very much depends on choices made at national level.[86]

The Member States have applied to procurement review the same national standards they apply to judicial review generally. This means that a great variety of approaches are to be found.[87] French courts are used to give a hard look to procurement decisions, and in principle they will look into possible violations to any and every procurement rule.[88] Italian courts are quite keen to detect formal breaches, and while showing some deference to the margin of appreciation of contracting authorities, can go as far as to check the proportionality of admission criteria.[89] In Germany too, while a number of cases concern illegal direct awards, different breaches might be reviewed, for instance the wrong decision to use a negotiated procedure rather than a more competitive procedure.[90] In Romania the hard look by the National Council for Solving Legal Disputes – an independent quasi-jurisdictional body competent to hear procurement cases at first instance – may be contrasted with the more deferential stance taken by the courts.[91] Review is quite limited and pe-

85. See M. Comba and S. Treumer (edds.) *The In-House Providing in European Law* (Copenhagen, DJØF, 2010).
86. See below § 8.
87. Because traditions of judicial review vary a lot: see the papers in R. Caranta and A. Gerbrandy (eds.) *Tradition and Change in Administrative Law* (Groningen, Europa Law Publishing, 2011), and in O. Essens, A. Gerbrandy and S. Lavrijssen (eds.) *National Courts and the Standard of Review in Competition Law and Economic Regulation* (Groningen, Europa Law Publishing, 2009).
88. See the very articulated list provided by F. Lichère and N. Gabayet 'Enforcement of EU Public Procurement Rules in France' § 4.
89. See M. Comba 'Enforcement of EU Procurement Rules' § 4, and R. Caranta 'Le contentieux des contrats publics en Italie' above fn 62, 58.
90. M. Burgi 'Enforcement of EU Public Procurement Rules'§ 2.4; see also §4.
91. See D.C. Dragoş, B. Neamţu and R. Velişcu 'Remedies in Public Procurement in Romania' § 6, listing the potential grounds for review and listing some statistics as to success rate of the claims.

ripheral in the UK, with courts focusing on major formal violations.[92] Somewhat in the middle, the Danish Complaints Board, has shown a certain deference towards the margin of appreciation granted to contracting authority, often focusing on illegal technical dialogue prior to the submission of bids and more recently on the legality of the award criteria chosen by the contracting authority.[93]

A specific question is whether annulment might be used to protect best bidders from abusive – and normally discriminatory – termination either of the procedure or of the contract. Only exceptionally the Danish Complaints Board was ready to strike down decisions to terminate the procedure because of insufficient reasons given.[94] In Italy a remedy is normally available either in tort if the decision to terminate the contract is illegal or in pre-contractual liability if the contracting authority was not careful enough to foresee and make known in advance the possible reasons for changing its mind.[95]

The remedies directives are silent as well as to the question of what are the scope and effects of annulment.[96] The scope may very much vary depending on which decision is suspected to be illegal. If the award criteria published in the notice were discriminatory, then the whole procedure will have to be annulled.[97] In case perfectly legal criteria were wrongly applied, only the award decision will have to be annulled.[98]

Concerning the effects of the annulment, they will normally play retroactively. A specific question is whether or not the annulment of the procedure, including up to the decision to conclude the contract, might affect a contract concluded in the meantime. This question is now addressed by the rules on effectiveness which will be examined at a later stage, but France had already somewhat solved the problem through the theory of the *acte détachable du contrat*.[99]

92. M. Trybus 'An Overview of the UK' § 4.
93. S. Treumer 'Enforcement (Denmark)', § 3.
94. S. Treumer 'Enforcement (Denmark)', § 3.
95. S. Ponzio 'State Liability in the Field of Public Procurement. The Case of Italy' in D. Fairgrieve and F. Lichère (eds) 'Public Procurement Law. Damages as an Effective Remedy' (Oxford, Hart, 2011).
96. S. Treumer 'Enforcement (EU)' § 3.3.
97. See S. Treumer 'Enforcement (Denmark)' § 4.
98. For more cases see German courts seem to enjoy some margin to raise legality issues of their own motion: see M. Burgi 'Enforcement of EU Public Procurement Rules'§ 5.
99. F. Lichère and N. Gabayet 'Enforcement of EU Public Procurement Rules in France' § 5.1.

A more limited effect to the finding of illegality is at times applied to in the UK and in Denmark, where it is not unusual for a complainant to ask for a declaratory judgment of illegality instead of outright annulment with a view for a future action for damages and a possible settlement out of court.[100]

Conforming to a tradition of strong judicial intervention, German courts may instead go well beyond annulment (or, seen otherwise, they can remedy the breach by substituting the illegal decisions rather than quashing them). To a point they can direct the activity of the contracting authority following a finding of illegality so that it complies with the procurement rules, the limit being that courts cannot choose the best bid.[101] At the same time, a deeply rooted respect for the sanctity of contract stops German courts from annulling contract award decisions, which could be seen as an infringement of EU law.[102] In Romania the National Council for Solving Legal Disputes can request the contracting authority to issue an act, or it can adopt any other necessary measure for remedies against illegal decisions taken by the contracting authority short of awarding the contract itself.[103]

5.3 Damages

The provisions on damages have not been directly affected by the amendments brought about by Directive 2007/66/EC. Under Art. 2(1)(c) Member States are asked to empower review bodies to 'award damages to persons harmed by an infringement'. Here too harmonisation is very 'light' and lot of uncertainty remains as to what is required from Member States.[104]

The case law has addressed the issue whether Member States may require fault as a requirement for damages actions. In a couple of infringement pro-

100. M. Trybus 'An Overview of the UK' § 5; S. Treumer 'Enforcement (Denmark)' § 3.
101. See the discussion by M. Burgi 'Enforcement of EU Public Procurement Rules'§ 4 and 5; similar powers are enjoyed by *référé* judges in France: F. Lichère and N. Gabayet 'Enforcement of EU Public Procurement Rules in France' § 2.1.1.3.
102. See the discussion and the negative reply to the question by M. Burgi 'Enforcement of EU Public Procurement Rules'§ V; apparently infringement is avoided by serving a pre-award notice after the decision as to the best bid has been taken; in other jurisdictions the same would be considered an award notice (see *ibidem* § VI.2), and of course by allowing ineffectiveness when EU law so mandates. The whole construction could be seen as a contortion to square the circle between pre-existing dogmatic construction and the need to comply with EU law.
103. D.C. Dragoş, B. Neamţu and R. Velişcu 'Remedies in Public Procurement in Romania' § 2.1.2.
104. S. Treumer 'Enforcement (EU)', § 3.5; M. Burgi 'Enforcement of EU Public Procurement Rules'§ 7; see also P. Trepte *Public Procurement in the EU* above fn 17, 558.

cedures brought against Portugal, the Court of justice held that liability could not be conditioned on the proof of fault on the part of the contracting authority.[105]

The issue resurfaced again in *Strabag*.[106] An Austrian court asked whether domestic rules providing for a rebuttable presumption of fault were consistent with Art. 2(1)(c) of Directive 89/665/EEC. The Court, having paid lip-service to the procedural autonomy of Member,[107] reasoned on the basis of the need for effective and rapid remedies and the systemic relations between annulment and damages.[108] More into the details, the Court stressed that, under what has become Art. 2(7) of the directive, Member States may choose to rule out annulment once the contract is concluded and ineffectiveness does not apply, damages becoming the only remedy available. This being so, the court held that 'the remedy of damages provided for in Article 2(1)(c) of Directive 89/665 can constitute, where appropriate, a procedural alternative which is compatible with the principle of effectiveness underlying the objective pursued by that directive of ensuring effective review procedures [...] only where the possibility of damages being awarded in the event of infringement of the public procurement rules is no more dependent than the other legal remedies provided for in Article 2(1) of Directive 89/665 on a finding that the contracting authority is at fault'.[109]

This can be read as if illegality were a sufficient condition for liability.[110] This means that the case law on damages for breach of procurement rules is more demanding than the general rule on liability for breaches of EU law. Since the well-known *Brasserie du pêcheur and Factortame* cases, the Court of justice conditions Member States liability on the existence of a manifest and serious breach.[111] While this does not mean that fault may be required, it allows defendants to escape liability by showing an excusable mistake.[112]

An alternative reading of the judgment would therefore be to focus on the fact that excusable mistakes are possible only when either the rules are uncer-

105. Case C-275/03 *Commission* v *Portugal* [2004] and Case C-70/06 *Commission* v *Portugal* [2008] ECR I-1.
106. Case C-314/09 *Strabag* [2010] ECR I-0000.
107. Paragraph 33.
108. Paragraphs 36 ff.
109. Paragraph 39.
110. See S. Treumer 'Enforcement (EU)', § 3.5.1.
111. Joined Cases C-46/93 and C-48/93 *Brasserie du Pêcheur and Factortame* [1996] ECR I-1029
112. As shown by the relatively old case C-392/93 *British Telecommunications Plc* [1996] ECR I-1631.

tain or the decision-maker enjoys wide discretion. The latter should be normally ruled out in public procurement,[113] while the former might well be the case, and probably – given the contradictory judgments handed down by Austrian courts – was the case in *Strabag*.[114] This would have the merit of going some way towards avoiding imposing such a strict standard on contracting authorities when EU institutions walk away quite easily from liability for breaches of procurement rules, and a better coordination of the case law would anyway make the law clearer on this point.[115]

Apart from the issue of whether fault may be required, where the answer is not, EU law and case law fail to provide answers on two fundamental conditions for tort claims, namely whether loss of profit has to be recoverable and what standard of proof on causation may be imposed to the claimants.[116]

Holding that the referring court had no power to decide on claims for damages, in *GAP* the Court of justice did not address the question whether Art. 2(1)(c) of Directive 89/665, is 'to be interpreted as meaning that if the breach committed by the contracting authority consists in imposing an unlawful award criterion, the tenderer will be entitled to damages only if he can actually prove that, but for the unlawful award criterion, he would have submitted the best tender?'.[117]

A more auspicious chance was left to fall dead in *Spijker*, a Dutch case concerning works for two bascule bridges.[118] At interim relief stage the court upheld the award, and the contract was concluded. The measure was then reversed, and since the national court held that the contract could no more be challenged, the claimant sued for damages. The national court basically asked what are the rules applicable to actions for damages. While referring to procedural autonomy Advocate general Cruz Villalón was anyway ready to provide some guidance. He remembered that the Court had indeed provided guidance based on the principles of equivalence and effectiveness. On the basis of the case law in competition law matters, he suggested that also causation could be presumed.[119]

113. But see below on the case law on procurements by EU institutions.
114. See paragraphs 15 ff.
115. E.g. Case T-4/01 *Renco* [2003] ECR II-171.
116. See S. Treumer 'Enforcement (EU)' § 3.5.1.
117. Case C-315/01 *GAT* [2003] ECR I-6351, paragraph 39.
118. Case C-568/08 *Combinatie Spijker Infrabouw* [2010] ECR I-0000.
119. See paragraph 104: 'on the basis of Directive 89/665, by means of the rule on the limits of procedural autonomy, the Court has, in the *Commission* v *Portugal* cases, inferred that a national rule on the attribution of liability, one which requires proof of fault or fraud, is unlawful, and therefore, from that perspective, I can see no obstacle

The Court of justice, however, would have none of this. It admitted that neither the directive nor the case law address 'the conditions under which an awarding authority may be held liable or as to the determination of the amount of the damages which it may be ordered to pay'.[120] It held that the scant provision found in Article 2(1)(c) is the 'concrete expression to the principle of State liability for loss and damage caused to individuals as a result of breaches of EU law' and recalled the three conditions first spelt out in *Francovich* and *Brasserie du pêcheur and Factortame* (namely that 'the rule of EU law infringed must be intended to confer rights on them; the breach of that rule must be sufficiently serious; and there must be a direct causal link between the breach and the loss or damage sustained by the individuals').[121] This being said, the Court was content with summoning the principles of equivalence and effectiveness, without any further ado.[122]

The Court, which had been quite bold in *Strabag*, here refuses to elaborate more on the conditions for liability.[123] Apart for the possible divergent policies of the two panels involved in the two cases, one reason could be that the Dutch court was asking a totally open question, actually wanting the Court to lay down the requirements for liability which have been left undecided in the previous case law. It remains to be seen whether the Court of justice is ready or not to decline the principle of effective judicial protection when more precise questions – like the one in *Strabag* – will be asked in the future.

In the meantime, national courts and review bodies are left to fend for themselves. This has lead to divergent solutions in different Member States.[124] A big issue is causation.[125] The more liberal solution, followed in France and albeit more timidly in Italy, place on the plaintiff the burden to

to extending that idea to other national rules, such as, generally, those concerning evidence or determination of damage'.

120. Paragraph 86; see also, with reference to the case law, paragraph 88.
121. Paragraph 86; the leading cases are Joined Cases C-6/90 and C-9/90 *Francovich and Others* [1991] ECR I-5357, paragraph 35, and Joined Cases C-46/93 and C-48/93 *Brasserie du Pêcheur and Factortame* [1996] ECR I-1029, paragraphs 31 and 51.
122. Paragraphs 90 f.
123. S. Treumer 'Enforcement (EU)' § 3.5.2.
124. The topic is now thoroughly investigated by the papers collected in D. Fairgrieve and F. Lichère (eds) 'Public Procurement Law. Damages as an Effective Remedy' above fn 95.
125. See R. Caranta 'Damages for Breaches of EU Public Procurement Law: Issues of Causation and Recoverable Losses' in D. Fairgrieve and F. Lichère (eds) 'Public Procurement Law' above fn 95; see also, distinguishing different procurement situations affecting the availability of a redress in damages, C. Bovis *EC Public Procurement* above fn 17, 87 ff.

show it had some – or serious – chances to win the contract if the procurement rules had been complied with.[126] The French system is indeed the more advanced. If the claimant can show that he had at least a chance to be awarded the contract, he will recover the costs shouldered for taking part into the procedure. If he can prove he has a serious chance of being awarded the contract, the lost profit will be compensated. Other jurisdiction are showing signs of gradually shifting to a middle ground. In the UK courts have applied the loss of chance theory to procurement cases, a lighter standard than the balance of probabilities normally applied to tort claims. Even the loss of chance standards however does not help much in case no tender was submitted.[127] A few recent cases in Denmark testify to an attempt by the Complaints Board to lessen or even reverse the burden of proof on causation issues, while other cases are more on the line of a traditional strict approach.[128]

Another question focuses on the recoverable losses.[129] A few jurisdictions are ready to award lost profits, again maybe following a chance-based approach.[130] Other would award either costs for participating in the procedure or lost profits. A few would also consider damages to the professional standing of the firm which was affected by the unlawful management of the procurement procedure (loss of future business chances).[131]

Ineffectiveness has brought about a new issue for damages, namely whether the chosen contractor who sees the contract to which he was a part terminated has a right to compensation. The directives are silent on this, meaning that the Member States will have to choose.[132] In general it can be said that a relevant consideration will be whether or not the private contractor may be said to be in good faith. This means not only that he must not have caused the illegality (e.g. by submitting incorrect information during the award procedure); also he must not have been aware of the breach of pro-

126. F. Lichère and N. Gabayet 'Enforcement of EU Public Procurement Rules in France' § 7; see also the discussion in Germany as analysed by M. BURGI 'Enforcement of EU Public Procurement Rules'§ 7.1; see also S. Ponzio 'State Liability in the Field of Public Procurement. The Case of Italy' above fn.
127. M. Trybus 'An Overview of the UK' § 8.1.
128. For references S. Treumer 'Enforcement (Denmark)' § 7.
129. See R. Caranta 'Damages for Breaches of EU Public Procurement Law' above fn.
130. See M. Burgi 'Enforcement of EU Public Procurement Rules'§ VII.1.
131. This is excluded in Germany: M. Burgi 'Enforcement of EU Public Procurement Rules'§ 7.1, and in Romania D.C. Dragoş, B. Neamţu and R. Velişcu 'Remedies in Public Procurement in Romania' § 13.
132. In most jurisdictions the debate is only starting now: e.g. M. Burgi 'Enforcement of EU Public Procurement Rules'§ 7.3.

curement rules prior to the conclusion of the contract.[133] In Romania, compensation could be afforded in such a case,[134] but an attempt to prevent the ineffectiveness question from arising in the first place has been cut short by the courts.[135] The problem could also be discussed under a less 'private law' perspective, reasoning of legitimate expectation and referring by analogy to the withdrawal of illegal State aids. Given the restrictive case law on this topic, this approach would further limit the chances for successful claims.

6 The 'New' Remedies

6.1 Standstill

Under Art. 2(a) of Directive 89/665/EEC, as added by Directive 2007/66/EC, contracts cannot be concluded before a set period running from the date a notice of the award decision was served to concerned bidders. The provision codifies the case law of the Court of justice, according to which 'Complete legal protection also requires that it be possible for the unsuccessful tenderer to examine in sufficient time the validity of the award decision. Given the requirement that the Directive must have practical effect, a reasonable period must elapse between the time when the award decision is communicated to unsuccessful tenderers and the conclusion of the contract in order, in particular, to allow an application to be made for interim measures prior to the conclusion of the contract'.[136]

The standstill period foreseen by Directive 2007/66/EC is quite short (minimum 10 or 15 days, depending on the communication mean used). In the main, the Member States have stuck to the minimum periods,[137] but Italy

133. See the discussion in S. Treumer 'Enforcement (EU)' § 3.5.2 and S. Treumer 'Enforcement (Denmark)' § 7.1, and F. Lichère and N. Gabayet 'Enforcement of EU Public Procurement Rules in France' § 6.1.
134. D.C. Dragoş, B. Neamţu and R. Velişcu 'Remedies in Public Procurement in Romania' § 11.
135. D.C. Dragoş, B. Neamţu and R. Velişcu 'Remedies in Public Procurement in Romania' § 5.
136. Case C-212/02, *Commission v Austria*, paragraph 23.
137. E.g. on Germany see M. Burgi 'Enforcement of EU Public Procurement Rules'§§ 3.3 and 6.2; this is the case also in France, even if apparently a one day longer term could be read into the law: see the discussion by F. Lichère and N. Gabayet 'Enforcement of EU Public Procurement Rules in France' § 3.

has opted for a longer period, thereby making sure that the standstill expires after the expiring of the term to bring judicial review.[138]

Even if short, the standstill is enough to allow prospective complainants to seize the courts or other review boards,[139] thus triggering the automatic suspension discussed above.[140]

The Court of justice clarified some aspects of the rules on standstill following an infringement action brought by the Commission against Ireland.[141] Irish legislation provided for a standstill period, but it started from the moment the unsuccessful bidder was informed of the award decision, not from the moment when, on his request, he was informed of the reasons for choosing another tender. The Court of justice held that 'the reasons for the decision to reject the tender must be communicated at the time of the notification of that decision to the tenderers concerned and, in all cases, in sufficient time before the conclusion of the contract, in order to allow the unsuccessful tenderers to bring, in particular, an application for interim measures until such conclusion'.[142]

The Member States have taken notice that the standstill letter must provide unsuccessful bidders with the reasons for the award decision.[143] The problem is still that of the level of detail required. German law is very protective of the bidders, providing that all the reasons for the decision have to be disclosed.[144] French law less so.[145] In Romania, the simple incompleteness of the notices will normally not lead to ineffectiveness.[146]

138. M. Comba 'Enforcement of EU Procurement Rules: the Italian system of remedies' §§ 1 and 2.
139. See M. Trybus 'An Overview of the UK' § 3; M. Burgi 'Enforcement of EU Public Procurement Rules'§ 3.3.
140. Above 5.1.
141. Case C-455/08, *Commission v Ireland*, paragraph 28; see also Case C444/06, *Commission v Spain*, paragraph 39, and Case C-327/08, *Commission v France*, paragraphs 41 and 58; the latter case is commented by A. Brown 'A French Provision Breaches Directives 89/665 and 92/13' in PPLR 2009, NA222.
142. Paragraph 31; see also paragraph 34.
143. E.g. M. Trybus 'An Overview of the UK' § 3.
144. See M. Burgi 'Enforcement of EU Public Procurement Rules'§ 6.
145. F. Lichère and N. Gabayet 'Enforcement of EU Public Procurement Rules in France' § 3.
146. D.C. Dragoş, B. Neamţu and R. Velişcu 'Remedies in Public Procurement in Romania' § 11.

6.2 Ineffectiveness

Ineffectiveness is one of the big new remedies introduced by Directive 2007/66/EC. The novelty was anticipated by a well known case arising from a breach of Directive 92/50/EEC which was protracted even after a first infringement decision by the Court of justice.[147]

Directive 2007/66/EC can be seen as a codification of the case law. The directive lays down quite precise conditions for the standstill. Art. 2(d)(1) and 2(e)(1) list different cases in which contracts are to be considered ineffective. In a nutshell, they are direct illegal award, breach of the standstill period, derogation from the standstill period for contracts based on a framework agreement and a dynamic purchasing system.[148]

The judgement against Germany and the adoption of Directive 2007/66/EC have induced courts in Italy, France, and, albeit not without some wavering, Denmark to evolve their case law and allow annulment judgements to affect the contract concluded in the meantime, at times under more generous conditions than the ones laid down in the Directive.[149]

Other jurisdictions, and particularly those, such as Germany and the UK, which tended to follow the private law paradigm, were less ready – and less enthusiast – at what was a real novelty going against the sanctity of contract.[150]

The conditions for ineffectiveness laid down by Directive 2007/66/EC might be seen as restrictive when the already mentioned infringement judgement against Germany is considered.[151] As was remarked, however, the case then decided concerned an illegal direct award, namely one of the gravest

147. Case C-503/04 *Commission/Germany* [2007] ECR I-6153; see also M-J. Clifton 'Ineffectiveness – The New Deterrent: Will the New Remedies Directive Ensure Greater Compliance with the Substantive Procurement in the Classical Sector?' [2009] *PPLR* 167.
148. See S. Treumer 'Enforcement (EU)' § 3.4.; on the specific issues concerning framework agreements see G.M. Racca 'Derogations from the standstill period' § 2.
149. See S. Treumer 'Enforcement (EU)' §§ 4; M. Comba 'Enforcement of EU Procurement Rules' § 6; F. Lichère and N. Gabayet 'Enforcement of EU Public Procurement Rules in France' § 6.1, and 5.2, and S. Treumer 'Enforcement (Denmark)', § 6.
150. See M. Trybus 'An Overview of the UK' § 1.1, and, referring to the 'immunity of the concluded contract' M. Burgi 'Enforcement of EU Public Procurement Rules' § 4.
151. Case C-503/04 *Commission/Germany* [2007] ECR I-6153.

possible infringements of EU procurement law, so it cannot be taken as imposing ineffectiveness for all and every violation of procurement rules.[152]

Most Member States had been happy to limit the possible cases of ineffectiveness to those listed by Directive 2007/66/EC. In the pursuit of accrued effectiveness of judicial protection, Romania has added a few more instances, tellingly including the case of breaches of the rules against conflict of interests in the award procedure.[153] In Italy administrative courts might be seen as having a quite general power to declare a contract concluded in breach of award procedure rules ineffective.[154]

In case of direct award, ineffectiveness may be avoided if the contracting authority has previously published a notice for voluntary transparency under Art. 2(b)(4). Under Art. 2(b)(5) a similar provision applies in the case of awards under framework agreements.

Art. 2(d)(3) provides for an important exception to the ineffectiveness in case of overriding reasons relating to the general interest militates against depriving the contracts of their effects. This must be distinguished from a merely economical one, but the difference is not self-evident, and the exception could easily morph into a loophole.[155] This is rightly taken as to cover the duty to deliver essential services to the people.[156] The Danish legislation failed to replicate the exclusion for purely economic interests, while the German one omitted to incorporate them all. In both countries this has lead to uncertainties as to whether or not they might be invoked.[157]

The directive allows Member States to choose whether the ineffectiveness operates retroactively or for the future only, and this both accommodates potential different approaches and leads to legal taxonomy discussions at national level.[158] In principle, the choice needs to be made at the stage of legislative implementation. Member States may however decide to leave the

152. S. Treumer 'Enforcement (EU)' § 2.3; moreover, the contract at issue was a long duration one, meaning that the effects of the direct illegal award were to extend themselves for decades after the judgment handed down by the Court.
153. D.C. Dragoş, B. Neamţu and R. Velişcu 'Remedies in Public Procurement in Romania' § 12.
154. M. Comba 'Enforcement of EU Procurement Rules' § 6, and R. Caranta 'Le contentieux des contrats publics en Italie' in *Rev. fr. Dr. Adm.* 2011, 58.
155. M. Trybus 'An Overview of the UK' § 6.
156. S. Treumer 'Enforcement (EU)' § 3.4.
157. S. Treumer 'Enforcement' (Denmark) § 5.2, abd M. Burgi 'Enforcement of EU Public Procurement Rules'§ 6.3.2.
158. E.g. D.C. Dragoş, B. Neamţu and R. Velişcu 'Remedies in Public Procurement in Romania' § 11.

choice with courts. This allows for both a combination of or a 'shopping' among some of the other possible limits to ineffectiveness, such as the overriding reasons of general interest, to be played on a case by case basis. For instance, taking into account economic expediency reasons (which are expressly excluded from the range of relevant overriding reasons of general interest), a court so empowered by the national rules could decide to provide for prospective ineffectiveness only. In another case, it could be held that the overriding reasons of general interest are satisfied not just ruling out retroactive ineffectiveness, but shifting the 'effects of the ineffectiveness' some time in the future to allow for retendering.[159]

The national legislative choice between retroactive or proactive ineffectiveness does not entail a duty to give reasons, while invoking in court overriding reasons of general interest does. However, if the choice is delegated to courts it will normally come assorted with a duty to give reasons flowing from national law. If a contract whose performance already started is declared to be retroactively ineffective a problem of restitution might arise.[160] This will either be solved under private law rules or, as is the case in France, through the application of specific public law rules on unjust enrichment.[161]

Unsurprisingly given the novelty of the remedy, a number of Member States rather preferred to limit ineffectiveness to the prospecitive effects, even if this impacts the effectiveness of the remedy (the so called 'ineffectiveness light').[162] In Denmark non-retroactive effects are the rule,[163] and the same is the case in the UK.[164] In other jurisdictions, however, ineffectiveness operates retroactively. This is the case for instance in France, Romania. and in Germany.[165]

159. One such case is recalled by S. Treumer 'Enforcement' (Denmark) § 6.
160. M. Burgi 'Enforcement of EU Public Procurement Rules'§ 6.3.1; the situation in France is more nuanced, the retroactive or prospecitive effects of remedies affecting concluded contracts depending on different remedies: F. Lichère and N. Gabayet 'Enforcement of EU Public Procurement Rules in France' §§ 6.1 and 6.2.
161. F. Lichère and N. Gabayet 'Enforcement of EU Public Procurement Rules in France' § 7.3.
162. M. Trybus 'An Overview of the UK' § 6.
163. S. Treumer 'Enforcement (EU)' § 5.2.
164. M. Trybus 'An Overview of the UK' § 6.
165. F. Lichère and N. Gabayet 'Enforcement of EU Public Procurement Rules in France' § 6.1; D.C. Dragoş, B. Neamţu and R. Velişcu 'Remedies in Public Procurement in Romania' § 12, and M. Burgi 'Enforcement of EU Public Procurement Rules'§ 6.3.2.

In most Member States where ineffectiveness may be declared only if it is sought by the claimant,[166] but in Italy it is up to the courts to decide the remedy provided (or at least claimants are strongly pushed to ask for ineffectiveness).[167]

6.3 Alternative Penalties

Directive 89/665/EEC as amended by Directive 2007/66/EC provides for alternatives penalties in cases where in principle ineffectiveness should be declared, but either it is not or it is limited. These are for instance the case of overriding reasons relating to a general interest (Art. 2d(3)), and the case ineffectiveness was declared *pro futuro* only (Art. 2d(2)).

Art. 2e(2) lays down a number of guidelines to be followed by national courts when exercising their discretion – expressly qualified as broad – when imposing alternative penalties. A number of factors which might be considered are listed in the same provision. These are the seriousness of the infringement, the behaviour of the contracting authority and the extent to which the contract remains in force in case of ineffectiveness is declared prospectively only. Alternative penalties must anyway be 'effective, proportionate and dissuasive'.

Alternative sanctions are either the imposition of fines on the contracting authority or the shortening of the duration of the contract. The award of damages does not constitute an appropriate penalty, meaning that a contracting authority may find itself paying both damages and the alternative penalty. This means that the alternative penalty is not aimed at redressing the harmful consequences of a tortious act. Its nature is rather one of an administrative sanction or fine striking the breach of procurement rules.

It is up to the Member States to provide for detailed rules and parameters to calculate the penalties as well as naming the payee institution.[168] Concerning the first profile, the Member States have provided for penalties which may exceed one million Euros.[169]

166. See for Germany M. Burgi 'Enforcement of EU Public Procurement Rules'§ 6.3.1; the same is apparently the case in the UK M. Trybus 'An Overview of the UK' § 7
167. M. Comba 'Enforcement of EU Procurement Rules' § 6; this is again due to a strong preference of the administrative courts case law for primary remedies.
168. Which in case a State contracting authority has committed the breach ends up being nothing else but the another branch of the same State: F. Lichère and N. Gabayet 'Enforcement of EU Public Procurement Rules in France' § 6.2.
169. E.g. S. Treumer 'Enforcement (Denmark)' § 6; see also D.C. Dragoş, B. Neamţu and R. Velişcu 'Remedies in Public Procurement in Romania' § 12.

The remedies provisions in the Directive convey the impression that alternative penalties should be an exception in cases when ineffectiveness should be pronounced. A number of jurisdictions such as the UK and Denmark, where the sanctity of contract is more deeply rooted, seems however ready to develop a marked preference for alternative penalties.[170]

7 Of some Miscellaneous Matters Affecting the Effectiveness of Judicial Review

Going beyond the remedies available, a number of other issues affect the effectiveness of review of public procurement decisions. In principle, as was already remarked with reference to the choice of the competent jurisdiction, they might fall under the residual procedural autonomy of Member States.

One such issue is whether review bodies may raise of their own motion some grounds of illegality of the procurement decisions not raised by the claimant. As already recalled, in *GAP* the Court of justice considered this as falling within the procedural autonomy of the Member States.[171] However, the Court also held that this power cannot be used to deny the right to claim damages for the harm caused by the decision challenged on the ground that the award procedure was in any event defective owing to the unlawfulness, raised *ex proprio motu*, of another (possibly previous) decision of the contracting authority.[172]

Costs of procedure and legal expenses are another issue affecting the effectiveness of remedies. In case they are high, such as in England, they contribute to discourage litigation.[173] The same effect is played by rules provid-

170. S. Treumer 'Enforcement (EU)' § 3.6., and S. Treumer 'Enforcement (Denmark)' § 6; the same will be probably the case in the UK M. Trybus 'An Overview of the UK' § 6.
171. German courts seem to enjoy some margin to raise legality issues of their own motion: see M. Burgi 'Enforcement of EU Public Procurement Rules'§ 4; French courts can do this in *référé* procedures: F. Lichère and N. Gabayet 'Enforcement of EU Public Procurement Rules in France' §§ 2.1.1.3 and 6.2.
172. Case C-315/01 *GAT* [2003] ECR I-6351, paragraph 54; one could wonder this also apply to illegal decisions which should have been challenged and were not, but the case is far from clear.
173. M. Trybus 'An Overview of the UK' § 11; consider also the effects played by recent changes affecting costs in Romania in the light of the data provided by D.C. Dragoş, B. Neamţu and R. Velişcu 'Remedies in Public Procurement in Romania' § 7; the situation may be similar in Italy: M. Comba 'Enforcement of EU Procurement Rules'

ing for penalties in case actions brought against award decisions are rejected.[174] When on the contrary costs and/or expenses are low, possibly because, as it is now the case in Denmark, the contracting authority cannot recover its costs in front of the Complaints Board even if it wins the case,[175] competitors are prodded to challenge unfavorable decisions.[176]

Time limits are a different issue, with a more complicated interplay between procedural autonomy, the application of the general principles of non-discrimination and effectiveness, and harmonisation. The Court of justice has held that 'that Directive 89/665 does not preclude national legislation which provides that any application for review of a contracting authority's decision must be commenced within a period laid down to that effect and that any irregularity in the award procedure relied upon in support of such application must be raised within the same period, if it is not to be out of time, with the result that, when that period has passed, it is no longer possible to challenge such a decision or to raise such an irregularity, provided that the period in question is reasonable'.[177] However, it has criticized national arrangements for failing to meet the reasonableness and legal certainty standards.[178] Moreover, while introducing the innovative remedy of ineffectiveness, Directive 2007/66/EC has somewhat reduced its impact providing for time limits. Most Member States have enacted the same time limits,[179] but both Denmark and Romania have been less strict, in some cases allowing for more generous timelimits.[180]

§ 1; the cost factor seems to be less relevant in Germany: see M. Burgi 'Enforcement of EU Public Procurement Rules'§ 1.3.3.

174. This was the intent behind some rules recently passed in Romania whose consistency with both EU and domestic constitutional law may be questioned: D.C. Dragoş, B. Neamţu and R. Velişcu 'Remedies in Public Procurement in Romania' § 2.2.
175. S. Treumer 'Enforcement (Denmark)' § 1; rather unsurprisingly, the Danish government is minded to change the situation.
176. F. Lichère and N. Gabayet 'Enforcement of EU Public Procurement Rules in France' § 1.
177. E.g. Case C-241/06 *Lämmerzahl* [2007] ECR I-8415, paragraph 50.
178. E.g. Case C-456/08 *Commission* v *Ireland* [2010] ECR I-0000; see also Case C-406/08 *Uniplex* [2010] ECR I-0000; see the discussion by G.M. Racca 'Derogations from the standstill period and framework agreements remedies in Italy' § 3; for the consequences the latter case had in the UK see M. Trybus 'An Overview of the UK' § 1.4.
179. E.g. concerning Germany M. Burgi 'Enforcement of EU Public Procurement Rules'§ 6.3.2.
180. S. Treumer 'Enforcement (Denmark)' § 1; D.C. Dragoş, B. Neamţu and R. Velişcu 'Remedies in Public Procurement in Romania' § 12; the choice in Romania could

Articles 1(4) and 1(5) of Directive 89/665/EEC allow the Member States both to require the complainant to notify the contracting authority of the alleged infringement and of his intention to seek review and to first seek review with the contracting authority. Germany has used this possibility, in particularly asking claimants to object without undue delay. It is debated whether the latter requirement is in line with the *Uniplex* case.[181]

A final relevant aspect is possible recourse to non- or quasi-judicial bodies as a first stop shop for redressing breaches to procurement rules. When implementing of Directive 2007/66/EC a few Member States have thought it fit to make compulsory recourse to these bodies.[182] This is so in Romania with the National Council for Solving Legal Disputes.[183] This has also been the case in Denmark, where affected bidders must seize the Complaint Board for Public Procurement, whose competencies have been expanding to include the power to award damages and whose decisions might then be appealed with ordinary courts.[184] The situation is similar in Germany, but the jurisdiction of the review chambers normally working within the Federal Cartel Office is limited to the primary protection (therefore excluding the award of damages).[185]

Generally speaking, these boards are seen as an efficient solution, combining speed, lower costs, and expertise.[186] It is fair to say that a good deal of the former and more of the latter are also provided by administrative courts in countries like France and Italy, where special procedural devices are used, such as giving competence to one judge instead than to a panel the power to

have been due to a desire to lay the ground for terminating the contract in the case the EU Commission brings an infringement procedure which is then adjudicating upon a long time after the conclusion of the contract.

181. Case C-406/08 *Uniplex* [2010] ECR I-0000; see the discussion by M. Burgi 'Enforcement of EU Public Procurement Rules'§ 1.3.2.
182. Italian legislation instead opted for excluding an alternative remedy to judicial review: M. Comba 'Enforcement of EU Procurement Rules' § 1.
183. D.C. Dragoş, B. Neamţu and R. Velişcu 'Remedies in Public Procurement in Romania' § 2.1.
184. See S. Treumer 'Enforcement (Denmark)' §§ 1, 5.2 and 7.
185. M. Burgi 'Enforcement of EU Public Procurement Rules'§ 1.3.1.
186. S. Treumer 'Enforcement (EU)' § 12; a degree of informality might be an additional bonus: see D.C. Dragoş, B. Neamţu and R. Velişcu 'Remedies in Public Procurement in Romania' § 2.1.

decide on *référé* actions,[187] or providing for accelerated decision-making procedures.[188]

On the contrary, arbitration is nowhere used. This is hardly surprising, since arbitration is not appropriate to polycentric disputes like the one arising from award procedures.[189] A different assessment could be made for systems setting up a first stop cost-free venue for claimants providing them with an independent assessment as to the legality of the measures and decisions taken by the contracting authority.[190]

Of course, non-legal factors may influence the propensity to seek judicial protection, the financial crisies having often being remembered as one of these factors.[191]

8 The Gaping Black Hole: Which Standard for Review?

As already remarked, a major point of divergence between different national enforcement standards is to be found in the standard of review applied to procurement cases. Harmonisation is here partial to say the least, and each Member States naturally follows its own traditions and inclinations. Which are quite different.[192]

If any guidance is to be drawn from the case law from EU courts when reviewing procurement decisions by EU institutions, it points in the direction that marginal review is fine.[193] Here it is sufficient to recall the *Renco* case.[194] Renco had taken part in the procurement for general renovation and maintenance works in the Council's buildings in Brussels; the contract was to be

187. F. Lichère and N. Gabayet 'Enforcement of EU Public Procurement Rules in France' § 2.
188. V. Parisio, F. Gambato Spisani and G. Pagliari 'I riti speciali' above fn 62, 698 ff.
189. E.g. F. Lichère and N. Gabayet 'Enforcement of EU Public Procurement Rules in France' § 8.3.2.3. The situation is in principle different at the performance stage: see M. Trybus 'An Overview of the UK' § 10; even there, however, fear of auditing systems may play a chilling effect: D.C. Dragoş, B. Neamţu and R. Velişcu 'Remedies in Public Procurement in Romania' § 15.
190. This used to be the case with the Danish Antistrust Authority: see S. Treumer 'Enforcement (Denmark)' § 10.
191. E.g. S. Treumer 'Enforcement (Denmark)' § 1.
192. See, with reference to another topic, the works collected by O. Essens, A. Gerbrandy and S. Lavrijssen (eds.) *National Courts and the Standard of Review in Competition Law and Economic Regulation* above fn 87.
193. See for more references S. Treumer 'Enforcement (EU)' § 3.3.
194. Case T-4/01 *Renco* [2003] ECR II-171.

awarded according to the criterion of the most advantageous economic offer. Renco's offer was held to be abnormally low and excluded after being discussed at some length. The firm sued the Council asking for compensation for the harm suffered as a result of the allegedly unlawful conduct of the Council in the procedure to award the contract in question; the plaintiff claimed that the contract documents referred to very vague selection criteria allowing the procuring entity a discretion too wide; it also lamented that criteria not specified in the contract documents had been referred to, thus frustrating its legitimate expectations, and that the defendant institutions had failed to state the reasons for rejecting its tender. The Court of First Instance held that 'according to settled case-law, the Council has a broad discretion in assessing the factors to be taken into account for the purpose of deciding to award a contract following an invitation to tender'.[195] Of course it is debatable whether the situation in *Renco* was really one of broad discretion. All the procuring entity had to do was to choose the best bid. The Court very much emphasised the difficulties of the procurement, but it was just a somewhat complex contractual arrangement, as complex as many procurements are.[196]

The same can be claimed on the basis of the case law on effective judicial protection. The Court of justice has been quite reserved here. The more relevant case is *Upjohn*. A UK court asked the Court of justice what was needed to meet the requirements of the principle of effective judicial protection in the review of decisions revoking national marketing authorisation taken following complex assessments in the medico-pharmacological field. More specifically, the referring court wondered whether national courts and tribunals needed to be empowered to substitute their assessment of the facts and, in

195. Paragraph 62.
196. Para 64: 'First, the contract was to be awarded not to the tender with the lowest price but to the most economically advantageous tender, which necessitates the application of various criteria which vary according to the contract in question (see, in particular, paragraph 65 below). Secondly, the procedure was to lead to the conclusion of a framework agreement for a term of five years renewable for 12-month periods. Thirdly, the contract was mixed and consisted of three different types of work for which the methods of determining the price varied. Furthermore, part B of the contract consisted of a large number of jobs to be defined and remunerated only during the execution of the contract. In the light of the specific characteristics of the contract in question, the comparative assessment of the tenders which the Council had to carry out necessarily meant that it not only had to check the accuracy and reliability of the unit prices given in the tenders but also had to estimate the total cost of the types of job covered by the contract over a five-year period on the basis of the contract terms and the prices stated in the tenders'.

particular, of the scientific evidence relied upon by the national authorities. The Court of justice first of all recalled the principle of procedural autonomy. It then recalled its case law to the effect that Community institutions called upon to make complex assessments are considered enjoying 'a wide measure of discretion, the exercise of which is subject to a limited judicial review in the course of which the Community judicature may not substitute its assessment of the facts for the assessment made by the authority concerned'.[197] The conclusion was that 'Community law does not require the Member States to establish a procedure for judicial review of national decisions revoking marketing authorisations, taken [...] in the exercise of complex assessments, which involves a more extensive review than that carried out by the Court in similar cases'.[198] The same principle has been reaffirmed recently, even if it was somewhat qualified by stressing the need for the competent authority to 'to examine carefully and impartially all the relevant aspects of the individual case'.[199]

This line of cases points to the facts that national courts could hardly be asked to be tougher that EU courts when reviewing procurement decisions. It goes without saying that the EU case law could well evolve. In the field of review of competition measures the EU courts seem to have ditched marginal review for good in the well-known *Tetra Laval* case.[200]

If this were so, the requirements of effective judicial protection could be strengthened. In the meantime, it is submitted that the different degree of deference shown to procurement decisions by national courts goes a long way in showing the diverging litigation patterns observed in Member States. Otherwise said, it is not due to chance that procurement is litigated a lot in countries like France and Italy and much less so in the UK (even if litigation is on the increase there).[201]

197. Case C-120/97 *Upjohn* [1999] ECR I-223, paragraph 34.
198. Paragraph 35.
199. Joined Cases C-379/08 and C-380/08 *ERG and Others* [2010] ECR I-0000, paragraph 60.
200. Case C-12/03 P *Commission v Tetra Laval BV* [2005] ECR I-987, affirming Case T-5/02 *Tetra Laval BV* [2002] ECR II-4381; see the discussion by see the discussion by A. Gerbrandy, S. Lavrijssen and O. Essens 'European and National Standards of Review' in O. Essens, A. Gerbrandy and S. Lavrijssen (eds.) *National Courts and the Standard of Review* above fn 87, 269 ff.
201. Of course, other factors may contribute to the picture: see M. Trybus 'An Overview of the UK' §§ 1 and 11, and M. Burgi 'Enforcement of EU Public Procurement Rules'§ 1.3.3.

9 The Dance of Remedies

Other elements contribute into explaining the different litigation pattern. Directives 89/665/EEC and 92/13/EEC as amended by Directive 2007/66/EC provide for a rich panoply of remedies. The new directive added standstill, ineffectiveness and alternative sanctions to interim relief, annulment and damages.

The ways these remedies interact depend on many different considerations. Both Directive 2007/66/EC and the judgements by the Court of justice against Germany point out at the importance of remedying the breach in kind, by either not having the contract concluded or by having it declared ineffective. In this perspective, the logical sequence would be standstill, interim relief and annulment of the award decision and/or of the decisions taken during the award procedure (e.g. the notice, the decision to exclude one bidder or an abnormally low offer, and so on). While standstill is automatic, being directly provided by the law, interim relief is to be crucial if conclusion of the contact is to be avoided in the first place.[202]

Ineffectiveness should be resorted to if the above sequence is for some reason insufficient to remedy the breach of procurement rules (e.g. because the standstill period was not complied with, or because interim relief was not granted). Alternative sanctions and damages should be the last resort option.[203] Ineffectiveness could lead to damages claims from the disenfranchised private contractor.[204]

Reasons for following this logic would be many. A few have been mentioned in the national reports: successful damage claims are rare,[205] and this is especially so for the gravest violations, such as direct awards.[206] Bidders do prefer to be awarded the contract rather than damages because the former is better for their business.[207]

It is, however, easy to list countervailing arguments, the main being that the contracting authority might use its margins of appreciation to avoid

202. S. Treumer 'Enforcement (EU)' § 3.1.
203. This seems to be the case for damages in Romania: D.C. Dragoş, B. Neamţu and R. Velişcu 'Remedies in Public Procurement in Romania' §§ 14 and (also referring to suspension) 16.
204. S. Treumer 'Enforcement (EU)' § 3.5.2.
205. This might be the case also in France, where courts are more ready to award damages for illegal award than in other jurisdictions F. Lichère and N. Gabayet 'Enforcement of EU Public Procurement Rules in France' § 8.3.2.3.
206. S. Treumer 'Enforcement (EU)' § 3.4 and more generally 3.5.
207. M. Burgi 'Enforcement of EU Public Procurement Rules'§ 7.

awarding the contract to the firm having seized the courts and that anyway in many cases it will just be impossible to conclude anew the procedure challenged. The delays brought about by judicial review will indeed often make the original technical specifications and the tenders submitted outdated if no more realistic considering the market conditions.

Add to this that, as it is the case in both the UK and in Denmark, some courts are still very restive to grant interim relief,[208] which adversely impact the time for completing possibly important public projects, and anyway, as in Denmark, the implementing legislation as a rule provides for ineffectiveness having effects for the future only.[209] The costs of the claims may be another consideration.[210] The countervailing considerations may be so strong to that, even after the introduction of a remedy like ineffectiveness, damages actions might be seen growing.[211]

National legislation may try and more or less corral the preferences of complainants. This is especially the case for the relationship between what in Germany are called primary (annulment and ineffectiveness) and secondary remedies (damages).[212] In Italy the recently enacted legislation strongly pushes the successful claimant to ask to be awarded the contract, otherwise severely curtailing his right to damages.[213] The UK stops short of building a hierarchy of remedies, but courts are ready to consider whether annulment or ineffectiveness have restored the chances of the claimant to try and have the contract awarded and thus making groundless a damage action based on the loss of chance theory.[214] The more liberal approach is followed in France through the theory of 'parallel remedies'. It is up to the complainant to choose which remedies to activate. If some remedies are in a relation of ex-

208. M. Trybus 'An Overview of the UK' § 2.
209. S. Treumer 'Enforcement (EU)' § 3.1, and works referred in nt 28 therein.
210. The relevance played by both costs and the availability of interim relief is vividly emerging from 2.
211. See S. Treumer 'Enforcement (Denmark)' § 1, pointing out that now the Complaints Board has been given jurisdiction to award damages and it is ready to compensate even lost profit; as to the effects of ineffectiveness see § 5.2.
212. See M. Burgi 'Enforcement of EU Public Procurement Rules'§ 1.1; it is worth remarking that the French too distinguish between two kinds of *recours*, but they don't establish a hierarchy between them: F. Lichère and N. Gabayet 'Enforcement of EU Public Procurement Rules in France' § 7.
213. M. Comba 'Enforcement of EU Procurement Rules' § 8, and R. Caranta 'Le contentieux des contrats publics en Italie' in *Rev. fr. Dr. Adm.* 2011, 60 f.
214. M. Trybus 'An Overview of the UK' § 9.

clusivity, this is only because there are presently so many of them.[215] Even the time limits for bringing an action are differentiated, tort actions having to be lodged within the usual long four years deadline starting from the moment the claimant became aware of the loss.[216]

The reasons for these contrasting approaches have both their relative merits. Making annulment (and now ineffectiveness) a condition precedent to damages means somewhat limiting the risk for the taxpayer to pay both the unduly chosen contractor and the successful claimant for damages.[217] Of course since the parties to ineffective contracts are not easily capable of claiming damages, this reason loses much of its force.[218] The parallel remedies approach, besides strengthening the legal protection of claimants allowing them to choose the remedy or combination of remedies they think optimal,[219] reduces the risk of a successful plaintiff getting neither the contract – maybe because the contracting authority in retendering was not too keen in awarding it to the undertaking having challenged its previous choice – nor damages.[220]

10 Conclusions

Inevitably given the partial harmonisation brought about by the remedies directives, judicial protection of actual or potential bidders is still differentiated in the Member States.

215. F. Lichère and N. Gabayet 'Enforcement of EU Public Procurement Rules in France' § 8.
216. F. Lichère and N. Gabayet 'Enforcement of EU Public Procurement Rules in France' § 7.1.
217. Unsurprisingly the law-makers may be very sensible to these arguments: see concerning the preparatory work for the Danish legislation S. Treumer 'Enforcement (Denmark)' § 9.
218. See above § 5.3.
219. M. Burgi 'Enforcement of EU Public Procurement Rules'§ 8; it is worth remarking that in administrative law matters § 839 BGB strongly subordinates secondary protection; however, given the private law characterisation of public contracts in Germany, § 839 BGB plays a very minor role in the liability system (*ibidem* VII) and is not referred to solve this problem. In general see now Case C-118/08 *Transportes Urbanos y Servicios Generales SAL* [2010] ECR I-; see J. Martín y Pérez de Nanclares 47 [2010] *Common Market L. Rev.* 1861
220. On the risks of retendering for successful claimants see S. Treumer 'Enforcement (Denmark)' § 8.

This is due to a number of reasons, some of which pertain to the path followed when implementing the directives. A relevant one has to do with the different techniques followed. Some Member States, such the UK have been reacting to the remedies directives and to the judgments handed down by the Court of justice by changing the national legislation as little as possible.[221] Of course, the assessment by a Member State of the minimum requirement for correct implementation may or may not be shared by EU institutions (including the Court of justice). The latter might be true with Romania, where newly introduced remedies were almost immediately amended trying to bring them in line with EU law.[222] A variation to this approach might be the German one, where the concern not to change too much was focused on the existing dogmatic constructions more than on preserving as much as possible the legal texts already in force at the time of the implementation of Directive 2007/66/EC.[223] In France, on the contrary, EU law remedies have been generously implemented. Only they were piled on top of the existing one, leading to a somewhat complicated picture.[224] By contrast, in Italy the occasion provided by the implementation of the directive has been taken to recast the entire system of remedies for breaches of public contract rules.[225]

A partially different aspect is the scope of application given to the rules taken in implementing the EU directives. This aspect was already discussed. Here it is enough to recall that many Member States such as the UK favor a narrow implementation not going beyond the express requirements of EU law,[226] while others, such as France and Italy don't think it fit to have diverging legal protection systems based on whether the 2004 directives apply or not.

Putting together these differences one does not find the traditional comparative law opposition between civil law and common law. The picture is

221. Concerning for instance the UK reactions to Case C-406/08 *Uniplex* [2010] ECR I-0000 see M. Trybus 'An Overview of the UK' § 1.4.
222. D.C. Dragoş, B. Neamţu and R. Velişcu 'Remedies in Public Procurement in Romania' § 1 (recalling how the first implementation instrument left ineffectiveness out).
223. Just consider the treatment of pre-award notice by M. Burgi 'Enforcement of EU Public Procurement Rules'§ 6.2.
224. F. Lichère and N. Gabayet 'Enforcement of EU Public Procurement Rules in France' § 8.3.2.3.
225. M. Comba 'Enforcement of EU Procurement Rules' § 1; in turn the specific provisions on public contracts were then made a chapter of the new *Codice del processo amministrativo*: see V. Parisio, F. Gambato Spisani and G. Pagliari 'I riti speciali' above fn 62, 717 ff.
226. M. Trybus 'An Overview of the UK' § 1.

one characterised by the divergence between jurisdictions traditionally considering contracts passed by public authorities as one of the partitions of public law, such as France, and jurisdictions classing them under private (or budgetary) law, such as Germany, the UK, and to some extent Denmark. Those Member States in the first group did not need more than a little technical fine-tuning to their legislation and case law to accommodate the new remedies provided by Directive 2007/66/EC. To the other jurisdictions the new remedies – and even some of the old – are rather novel and foreign, and implementation normally does not go beyond what is expressly required by EU law. Italy is somewhat of a touchstone. Traditionally public law ruled the award of the contract but private law ruled its conclusion and performance. Directive 2007/66/EC has strengthened a tendency already present to link more closely award and conclusion under the empire of public law, avoiding a situation where contracts passed in breach of public law are still applying their effects.

Differences in approach are still quite present. However, the quite dramatic original divergences among the Member States – some of which, such as Germany, were not even providing remedies for disaffected competitors – have been considerably reduced. This is not only the result of harmonization. National courts are often looking into the case law of the EU courts to design the conditions under which different remedies are to be granted. This has been the case for instance in Denmark concerning interim relief.[227] Better knowledge of the national case law would probably further contribute towards spontaneous convergence.[228]

At the same time, the same basic limits in the harmonization process, coupled with a very hands-off approach to review by EU courts, inevitably hinder convergence. This is notably the case with the grounds for annulment of illegal procurement decisions, both the legislation and the case law being both limited and quite deferential to the choices of contracting authorities. The same can be said as to damages, and of course the two are linked, since illegality is one requisite of liability and self-restraint in finding illegality brings along fewer possibilities to successfully sue in tort.

The overall impression from the comparative law research on remedies in public procurement following implementation of Directive 2007/66/EC is that remedies are strong where they have always been, in France particularly but also in Italy. They remain less 'effective' in jurisdictions where they have

227. S. Treumer 'Enforcement (Denmark)' § 2.2.
228. See R. Caranta 'Pleading for European Comparative Administrative Law' above fn.

traditionally been so, such as England and to a certain extent Denmark. It is probably fair to say that the remedies directives (the old and the new ones) have changed the situation for better in some jurisdictions, such as in Germany and – but not without problems – in Romania. One could, however, even question whether the lamented 'certain number of weaknesses in the review mechanisms in the Member States' which prompted the adoption of Directive 2007/66/EC could not have been addressed by strengthening the old remedies – annulment and damages in particular – rather than by introducing new ones.[229]

Be it as it might be, to seek accrued convergence would more probably than not mean going deeper and deeper into the residual procedural autonomy of the Member States. The remedies directives having been revised not long ago, it will fall on the shoulder of the Court of justice to decide for the future the pace of the evolution – if any – of the remedies for breaches of EU public procurement and concession law.

At present, anyway, duly implemented remedies directives provide for what is considered by many a quite effective mechanism for judicial protection. Somewhat paradoxically, some consider the ensuing system even too efficient when seen from the delay or freeze effect it can place on the implementation of important projects approved by the competent national or subnational authorities in the pursuance of the general interest.[230] Needless to say, this opinion is heard louder in times of crisis as the present one.

11 Bibliography

This work relies mainly on the contributions collected in this volume. To those add:

C. Bovis *EC Public Procurement: Case Law and Regulation* (Oxford, Oxford University Press, 2006).

A. Brown 'EU Primary Law Requirements in Practice: Advertising, Procedures and Remedies for Public Contracts Outside the Procurement Directives' [2010] PPLR 169.

R. Caranta and A. Gerbrandy (eds.) *Tradition and Change in Administrative Law* (Groningen, Europa Law Publishing, 2011).

229. Recital 3.
230. See S. Treumer 'Enforcement (Denmark)' § 1.

R. Caranta 'Damages for Breaches of EU Public Procurement Law: Issues of Causation and Recoverable Losses' in D. Fairgrieve and F. Lichère (eds) 'Public Procurement Law. Damages as an Effective Remedy' (Oxford, Hart, 2011).

R. Caranta 'Le contentieux des contrats publics en Italie' in *Rev. fr. Dr. Adm.* 2011, 54.

R. Caranta 'Transparence et concurrence' in R. Noguellou U. Stelkens (eds.) *Droit comparé des contrats publics. Comparative Law on Public Contracts* (Bruylant, Brussels 2010), 145.

M-J. Clifton 'Ineffectiveness – The New Deterrent: Will the New Remedies Directive Ensure Greater Compliance with the Substantive Procurement in the Classical Sector?' [2009] *PPLR* 167.

M. Comba and S. Treumer (eds.) *The In-House Providing in European Law* (Copenhagen, DJØF, 2010).

O. Essens, A. Gerbrandy and S. Lavrijssen (eds.) *National Courts and the Standard of Review in Competition Law and Economic Regulation* (Groningen, Europa Law Publishing, 2009).

D. Fairgrieve and F. Lichère (eds) 'Public Procurement Law. Damages as an Effective Remedy' (Oxford, Hart, 2011).

J. Germain 'Les recours juridictionnels ouverts au concurrent évincé contre un marché public communautaire après sa conclusion en France et en Allemagne' [2009] *Rev. Fr. Dr. Adm.* 58.

R. Noguellou U. Stelkens (eds.) Droit comparé des contrats publics. Comparative Law on Public Contracts (Bruylant, Brussels 2010).

V. Parisio, F. Gambato Spisani and G. Pagliari 'I riti speciali' in R. Caranta (dir.) *Il nuovo processo amministrativo* (Torino, Zanichelli, 2011).

Z. Petersen 'Below-threshold Contract Awards under EU Primary Law: Federal Republic of Germany v Commission (T-258/06) [2010] *PPLR* NA215.

S. Ponzio 'State Liability in the Field of Public Procurement. The Case of Italy' in D. Fairgrieve and F. Lichère (eds) 'Public Procurement Law. Damages as an Effective Remedy' (Oxford, Hart, 2011).

U. Stelkens et H. Schröder 'Les droit de contrats publics en Allemagne' in R. Noguellou U. Stelkens (eds.) *Droit comparé des contrats publics. Comparative Law on Public Contracts* (Bruylant, Brussels 2010), 307.

P. Trepte *Public Procurement in the EU* 2nd (Oxford, Oxford University Press, 2007).

S. Treumer 'The Discretionary Power of Contracting Entities – Towards a Flexible Approach in the Recent Case Law of the Court of Justice?' [2006] PPLR 82.

3 Derogations from standstill period, ineffectiveness and remedies in the new tendering procedures: efficiency gains vs. risks of increasing litigation

By Gabriella M. Racca

1 Derogations from the standstill period in the European provisions with regard to new tendering procedures

A possibility of derogation from the standstill period is contemplated 'in the case of a contract based on a framework agreement as provided for in Article 32 of Directive 2004/18/EC and in the case of a specific contract based on a dynamic purchasing system as provided for in Article 33 of that Directive'.[1] Such derogation is not mandatory and Member States have the discretionary choice to invoke it, with the aim of ensuring the efficiency gains linked to these new tendering procedures. If the said derogation is invoked, the national law must provide for the ineffectiveness[2] of the individual contracts, above European thresholds, in case of infringements of the award procedure. More specifically, this applies to infringements[3] occurring in the second call for competition among economic operators already part of the framework agreement. The same applies in case of dynamic purchasing systems in which the invitation to tender for a specific contract is addressed to all the economic operators previously admitted to the system.[4] The *ratio* of such a wide provision of ineffectiveness is probably due to the fear – clearly expressed in Directive 18/04/EC – of an improper use of this tool 'in such a way as to

1. Art. 2b par. 1(c), dir. 66/07/EC.
2. Art. 2,d, 2, dir. 66/07/EC.
3. Infringements of the 'second indent of the second subparagraph of Article 32(4) or of Article 33(5) or (6) of Directive 2004/18/EC'.
4. Ar. 33, par.5 e 6 dir. 2004/18/EC.

prevent, restrict or distort competition'.[5] Nonetheless, the risk of making these procedures too cumbersome, as underlined also in the recent Green paper[6] is considerable.

To-date, most Member States opted for the implementation of such derogation to the standstill period in compliance with the European provision.[7] Interesting specifications can be found in EU Member States implementations. In France, for example, the derogation from the standstill period seems to be linked to the respect of a delay (16 days or 11 days in case of electronic communication) between the second call for competition and the award of an individual contract based on a framework agreement or a dynamic purchasing system.[8] Nonetheless, it is not yet possible to foresee whether the benefits of proceeding quickly to the signature of the contract will be thwarted by the ensuing possible increase of litigation linked to the wider provision of ineffectiveness entailed. The present situation is also due to Member States' scarce use of these new tendering procedures.

5. Art.32 par. 2. dir 18/04/EC.
6. Green Paper on the modernisation of EU public procurement policy. Towards a more efficient European Procurement Market, Brussels, COM(2011) 15/4.
7. Summary results on the survey on the draft transposition of the directive 2007/66/EC into Member States law, in www.publicprocurementnetwork.org, reporting the full compliance with the EU Directive of Denmark, Poland, Romania, while for Germany and Italy the implementation seems partial. For the UK implementation: Public Contracts Regulations (Amendment) Regulations 2009 SI 2009 No. 2992, art. 32, (7), 'where a contracting authority awards a contract under a framework agreement or a dynamic purchasing system, that contracting authority need not comply with paragraph (1)'.
8. Ordonnance no 2009-515 du 7 mai 2009, L. 551-15.-Le recours régi par la présente section ne peut être exercé ni à l'égard des contrats dont la passation n'est pas soumise à une obligation de publicité préalable lorsque le pouvoir adjudicateur ou l'entité adjudicatrice a, avant la conclusion du contrat, rendu publique son intention de le conclure et observé un délai de onze jours après cette publication, ni à l'égard des contrats soumis à publicité préalable auxquels ne s'applique pas l'obligation de communiquer la décision d'attribution aux candidats non retenus lorsque le pouvoir adjudicateur ou l'entité adjudicatrice a accompli la même formalité. La même exclusion s'applique aux contrats fondés sur un accord-cadre ou un système d'acquisition dynamique lorsque le pouvoir adjudicateur ou l'entité adjudicatrice a envoyé aux titulaires la décision d'attribution du contrat et observé un délai de seize jours entre cet envoi et la conclusion du contrat, délai réduit à onze jours si la décision a été communiquée à tous les titulaires par voie électronique.

2 The Italian implementation of the derogation from standstill period in case of contracts based on framework agreements

As already pointed out, derogation from the standstill period can be foreseen in the case of individual contracts awarded on the basis of a previous framework agreement (the so-called master contract) or after the admission in a dynamic purchasing system.[9]

A general standstill provision was provided for in the former Italian regulatory system, but the consequences of its derogations were not defined.[10] Furthermore, the standstill period could be waived whenever the public administration invoked reasons of urgency. At first, in the delegated law, the Italian Parlament transposed the EU directive not including the provision of derogation to the standstill for framework agreements procedure, thus implying a critical implementation of the legislative decree that finally provided for it. In fact, the EU Directive does not impose a mandatory avoidance of the standstill period but foresees the possibilility of derogation so as not to make the procedure too cumbersome. Nonetheless, in the preparatory works for the legislative decree and in the opionion of the Parliamentary commission, the inclusion of the derogation of the standstill period in framework contracts[11] was suggested by the joint Justice and Environment, Territory and Public Works Commissions and it was finally included in the legislative decree, implementing the remedies directive. Such provision is now included in art. 11, para. 10 bis[12] of the Italian Public Contracts Code. Yet, the implementation presents a criticality: the Government law decree that provided for this dero-

9. Directive 2007/66/EC of European Parliament and Council of 11 December 2007 [2007] O.J. L 335, art. 2b, (c).
10. Italian public contracts code, d.lgs April 12, 2006, n. 163, art. 10, c. 7 (before the implementation of Directive 2007/66, occurred by Legislative Decree March 20, 2010, n. 53. See also R. Caponigro 'Annullamento dell'aggiudicazione ed effetti sul contratto' (2009) *Il Foro Amministrativo – C.d.S.* 2423 et seq.
11. Italy's Camera dei Deputati, Commission II (Justice) and VIII (Environment, Public Works), March 3, 2010: 'b) art.11, par. 10-bis, law decree, come introdotto dall'articolo 2, comma 1, lettera c), valuti il Governo l'opportunità di estendere le deroghe ivi previste per l'applicazione dello *standstill period* anche nei casi di appalti basati su un accordo quadro di cui all'articolo 59 del codice e nei casi di appalti specifici basati su un sistema dinamico di acquisizione di cui all'articolo 60 del codice'.
12. Italian Public Contracts Code, d.lgs April 12, 2006, n. 163, art. 11, c. 10 *bis*, 'Il termine dilatorio di cui al comma 10 non si applica nei seguenti casi: ... b) nel caso di un appalto basato su un accordo quadro di cui all'articolo 59 e in caso di appalti specifici basati su un sistema dinamico di acquisizione di cui all'articolo 60'.

gation of the standstill period exceeded the limits of the Parliament's delegation attributed to it, thus possibly leading to a recourse to the Italian Constitutional Court.

The Directive also provided that if this derogation is invoked, Member States shall ensure that the contract concluded after the second step of competition, provided in the framework agreement will be ineffective[13] whenever the essential rules regulating this second step of competition are violated.[14] This straightforward provision for ineffectiveness has not been included in the Italian implementation.[15] This may consequently lead to some problems with regard to compliance with the EU provisions, and it could induce Italian procuring entities to prefer a 'voluntary' application of the standstill period before signing the individual contract, thus forgoing the efficiency gains ensuing from framework agreement procedures. This choice could be detrimental considering the peculiar Italian implementation of such a long standstill period of 35 days. On the contrary, the derogation from the standstill period could become an incentive for public entities to adhere to framework agreements, thus awarding a contract with a simple call for competition in a short time, particularly thanks to the use of electronic tools.[16]

As well known, the master contract can include more economic operators and it involves the opening of a second step of competition for the awarding of single 'contracts'[17] The so-called 'mini competition' – among at least three

13. In accordance with Articles 2d and 2f of Directive 2007/66/EC.
14. There is an infringement of the second indent of the second subparagraph of Article 32(4) or of Article 33(5) or (6) of Directive 2004/18/EC of the European Parliament and of the Council of 31 March 2004, on the coordination of procedures for the award of public works contracts, public supply contracts and public service contracts.
15. R. De Nictolis 'Il recepimento della direttiva ricorsi nel codice appalti e nel nuovo codice del processo amministrativo' (2010) in *www.giustizia-amministrativa.it*, last visited on September, 2010.
16. ECJ, in case C-455/08, *EU Commission* v *Ireland*, [2010], declares that, by adopting Article 49 of Statutory Instrument No 329 of 2006 and Article 51 of Statutory Instrument No 50 of 2007, Ireland established the rules governing the notification of contracting authorities' and entities' award decisions and their reasoning to tenderers in such a way that by the time that tenderers are fully informed of the reasons for the rejection of their offer, the standstill period preceding the conclusion of the contract may already have expired.
17. G. M. Racca – R. Cavallo Perin – G. L. Albano 'The safeguard of competition in the execution phase of public procurement: framework agreements as flexible competitive tools' (2010) VI *Quaderni Consip*; G. L. Albano – M. Sparro 'A simple model of framework agreements: competition and efficiency' (2008) *J.P.P.* 356.

economic operators – is ruled by much simpler provisions.[18] The procedure for the award must define, if necessary, more precise terms than the ones already defined in the framework agreement. Furthermore, the procuring entity must consult in writing the economic operators capable of performing the contract, an adequate time limit to allow tenders to participate must be set, and confidentiality of the tenders until the stipulated time limit for reply has expired must be assured. The contract must be awarded to the tenderer who submitted the best tender on the basis of the award criteria set out in the specifications of the framework agreement. Any violation of such rules, according to the EU provisions, can determine the ineffectiveness of the contract whenever the standstill period has not been applied. This may lead economic operators being harmed by such violations to file claims against the Italian implementation of the EU Directive and thus requesting a direct application of the same.

3 The criticalities arising from the safeguard of participants in framework agreement procedures and the evolution of remedies

The main risk involved in the new remedies Directive consists in a wider provision for ineffectiveness that can limit and discourage the use of framework agreements and could lead to a significant increase of bid protests. Some criticalities are emerging with regard to the application of framework agreements. A specific focus on remedies is needed. Evidence of the risks involved in such procedure could be traced in the lack of tenderers' protests and the provision of specific remedies against ensuing risks. More specifically, a comparison with the U.S experience in this regard, allows us to trace the difficulties deriving from the lack of adequate remedies designed for harmed bidders.[19] It thus seems encouraging that the new remedies directive has foreseen specific provisions for such a tool. It is significant that some cases of violations in this regard have recently emerged, specifically considering the constant increase of the use of such a tool in Europe. This should prevent its

18. Directive 2004/18/EC of the European Parliament and of the Council of 31 March 2004, cit., art. 32, §4, II c., ii. For Italian implementation see the Italian public contracts code, d.lgs April 12, 2006, n. 163, art. 59, c. 8.
19. C. Yukins 'Integrating Integrity and Procurement: The United Nations Convention Against Corruption and The Uncitral Model Procurement Law' (2007) *P.C.L.J.* 307; C. Yukins 'Are IDIQs inefficient? sharing lessons with European framework contracting' (2008) *P.C.L.J.*565 et seq.

widespread use without the necessary means and limits to ensure compliance with EU provisions on public procurement. Until now the main Italian case law was related to the possible restriction of competition and of business opportunities due to framework contracts.[20] This tender procedure can lead to infringements when the contracting authority chooses the negotiated procedure[21] to select the economic operator with whom to sign the framework agreement. Case law includes claims by economic operators (previous suppliers) challenging the choice of the contracting entity to adhere to a framework agreement; economic operators challenging the value for money resulting from the performance agreed upon in the framework agreement when the contracting entity is non obliged to adhere to such agreement;[22] or else, economic operators part of the framework agreement disputing the choice of terminating the contract. Other interesting examples of case law refer to the 'congruence assessment' (valutazione di congruità, prescribed by Italian law)[23] in order to avoid to get conditions worse than the ones set in the framework agreement (when the adherence to the framework agreement is not mandatory). For example, a private supplier challenged an Italian health agency's evaluation of 'incongruence' of its offer in a single award procedure, in comparison with the ones set in the framework agreement, and the court agreed with the procuring entity assessment.[24]

A significant European case is the dispute concerning the conclusion of a framework agreement for the supply of haemostats[25] of a UK Central Pur-

20. State Council, Sect. V – November 23, 10 – n. 8158; T.A.R. Lombardia – Brescia sez. II, November 5, 2009 – n. 1920. T.A.R. Puglia – Lecce, sez. III, March 11, 2010, n. 700, T.A.R. Lazio – Rome sez. III, 23 June 2009, n. 6031.
21. State Council, Sect. V – November 14, 08 – n. 5693.
22. Regional Administrative Court of Puglia – Sect. I, May 6, 2009, n. 1038.
23. Art. 26, clause III, law 488 of 1999, in replacement, first, of art. 3, clause 166, of *Law no. 350 of December 24, 2003,* and later of art. 1, *L.D. no. 168 of July 12, 2004*, as amended by the relative law of conversion no. 191 of 30.7.2004: the conditions set in the framework agreement define a sort of benchmark that must be complied with by all procuring entities, even when they decide to have recourse to their own awarding procedure with a view to try and obtain better conditions.
24. State Council, Sect. V – November 23, 10-n. 8158; State Council, Sect. V – February 2, 09-n. 557, S. Ponzio, 'La verifica di congruità delle offerte rispetto alle convenzioni Consip negli appalti pubblici di forniture e servizi?' (2009) *Foro amm. – C.d. S.*, 2355. G. M. Racca 'Aggregate Models of Public Procurement and Secondary Consideration: An Italian Perspective', in R. Caranta and M. Trybus (eds.), *The law of green and social procurement in Europe*, Copenhagen, 2010, 175.
25. Directive 2004/18/EC of the European Parliament and of the Council of 31 March 2004, cit., art. 9, concerning the Methods for calculating the estimated value of public

chasing Body[26] (NHS Business Services Authority) through a restricted tendering procedure. One of the unsuccessful tenderers filed a claim against the supposed violation of the equal treatment and non-discrimination principle, disputing before that the application of the standstill period and of the deadline to file claims. The UK provision for prompt claims left a discretionary power to the judge on the interpretation of the prompt claim, thus limiting the possibilities of bringing proceedings by aggrieved undertakings. The ECJ further clarifies that the term cannot start from the notice of non-awarding of the contract and the deadline must be defined and adequate. This is an example of how the inadequacy of remedies does not prevent the emergence of serious violations of the principles of equal treatment and non discrimination. Surprisilingly enough, the reasons for the refusal to award the framework agreement were based on a score of zero for price and other cost effectiveness factors, because the tenderer had submitted its list prices while all the other tenderers had offered discounts on their list prices. Secondly, with regard to the delivery performance and capability criterion, all tenderers which were new to the relevant market in the United Kingdom received a score of zero for the sub-criterion relating to customer base in the United Kingdom. Central Purchasing bodies should develop good practices and fully comply with the European directives, providing the comunication of a 'correct award decision' to each tenderer, accompanied by a summary of the relevant informations. Otherwise the derogation from the standstill period will become a serious obstacle to effective judicial protection. The aim of the new remedies directive 66/07/EC is precisely to fully clarify the reasons of the choice of the best tender also in order to assure transparency and encourage transborder participation.

contracts, framework agreements and dynamic purchasing systems, § 9, 'With regard to framework agreements and dynamic purchasing systems, the value to be taken into consideration shall be the maximum estimated value net of VAT of all the contracts envisaged for the total term of the framework agreement or the dynamic purchasing system'. ECJ, in case C-406/08, *Uniplex (UK) Ltd* v *NHS Business Services Authority*, [2010] E.C.R. 11. The award criteria, with the relevant weighting to be given to each, set out in the tendering documentation sent to the tenderers, were as follows: price and other cost effectiveness factors (30%); quality and clinical acceptability (30%); product support and training (20%); delivery performance and capability (10%); product range/development (5%); and environmental/sustainability (5%).

26. ECJ, in case C-406/08, *Uniplex (UK) Ltd* v *NHS Business Services Authority*, [2010] E.C.R. I-11.

4 Conclusions as to the effect of the remedies directive on the new tendering procedures

The *ratio* of the new remedies directive 66/07/EC provides for a correction of infringement occured during the awarding procedure before the signing of the contract. Nevetheless, the Directive allows derogation from the standstill period when a master contract is in place so as to ensure efficiency gains in the subsequent award of the individual contracts. On the other hand, the price to pay for such efficiency is a wider provision for ineffectiveness for any infringment occurred in the mini-competition. It is becoming evident that framework agreements and dynamic purchasing systems are not suitable for small procuring entities, but they are ideal for complex awarding organizations such as Central purchasing bodies that can aggregate public demand and achieve savings in procedure costs and scale economies in the costs of works, services and supplies.[27] Cental purchasing bodies' professionalism in using framework agreements and dynamic purchasing systems should guarantee the correctness in carrying out such more complex procedures, also with the use of platforms and IT tools. The ratio of the Remedies Directive, in compliance with this perspective recognizes that these professional organizations need to guarantee efficiency, and thus the derogation from the standstill period. On the other hand, they must guarantee full transparency and communication with all tenderers on the reasons of their rejection of their offer. The professional skills necessary to elaborate such more complex tendering documents should assure full compliance to all European and national provisions, so as to not be too affected by the wide provision for ineffectiveness that the Directive entails.

Future case law will provide us with further data for a comprehensive evaluation of the outcomes of the implementation of the provisions of the Remedies Directive, whether the efficient development of competition and improvement of the quality of the performance has been attained or if it resulted in the limitation and infringement of free competition among European economic operators.

27. Green Paper on the modernisation of EU public procurement policy. Towards a more efficient European Procurement Market, Brussels, COM(2011) 15/4; G. M. Racca 'Collaborative procurement and contract performance in the Italian healthcare sector: illustration of a common problem in European procurement' (2010) 8 P.P.L.R. 119-133.

Bibliography

S. Arrowsmith 'Framework Purchasing and Qualification Lists under the European Procurement Directives' (1999) 8 P.P.L.R. 115-146 and 168-186.

C. H. Bovis *EU Public Procurement Law* (Cheltenam, Edward Elgar Publishing Limited, 2008) 97-98, 259-261.

R. Caranta 'L'accordo quadro' in M. A. Sandulli – R. De Nictolis – R. Garofoli (edited by) *Trattato sui contratti pubblici*, (Milano, Giuffrè, 2008) III 1942 et seq.

R. Caranta 'Le centrali di committenza', in M. A. Sandulli – R. De Nictolis – R. Garofoli (edited by) *Trattato sui contratti pubblici*, (Milano, Giuffrè, 2008) II, 607-622.

J. Chard – G. Duhs – J. Houlden 'Body beautiful or vile bodies? Central purchasing in the UK' (2008) 1 P.P.L.R. NA26.

R. Di Pace 'L'accordo quadro' in C. Franchini (edited by) *I contratti di appalto pubblico*, (Torino, UTET, 2008) 628.

G. Della Cananea, 'Le alternative all'evidenza pubblica' in P. Rescigno – E. Gabrielli (edited by) *Trattato dei contratti* (Torino, UTET, 2007), I, 381 et seq.

N. Dimitri – G. Piga – G. Spagnolo, *Handbook of Procurement*, (Cambridge, Cambridge University Press, 2006).

J. Edler – L. Georghiou 'Public procurement and innovation – Resurrecting the demand side' (2007) Research Policy 949-963.

R. H. Garcia (eds.) *International public procurement: a guide to best practice*, (London, Globe Law and Business, 2009).

L. Knight – C. Harland – J. Telgen – K. V. Thai – G. Callender – K. McKen *Public Procurement. International Cases and Commentary*, (Routledge, 2007).

R. Noguellou – U. Stelkens (edited by) Droit comparè des Contrats Publics – Comparative Law on Public Contracts (Bruxelles, Bruylant, 2010).

G. M. Racca – R. Cavallo Perin – G. L. Albano 'The safeguard of competition in the execution phase of public procurement: framework agreements as flexible competitive tools' (2010) VI Quaderni Consip

G. M. Racca 'Professional Buying Organisations, Sustainability and Competition in Public Procurement' (2010) paper presented on 4th International Public Procurement Conference (IPPC 2010) – Seoul (Korea), 26-28 August 2010.

G. M. Racca 'Collaborative procurement and contract performance in the Italian healthcare sector: illustration of a common problem in European procurement' (2010) 8 P.P.L.R. 119-133.

O. Soudry *A Principal-Agent Analysis of Accountability in Public Procurement* (International Public Procurement Book 2008) 433.

P. Trepte, *Public Procurement in the EU* (Oxford, Oxford University Press, 2007).

J.-J. Verdeaux 'Public Procurement in the European Union and in the United States: a Comparative Study' (2003) P.C.L.J. 713.

L. Vogel *Macroeconomic effects of cost savings in public procurement* (Brussels, Economic papers, 2009).

C. Yukins 'Are IDIQs inefficient? sharing lessons with European framework contracting' (2008) P.C.L.J. 546.

C. Yukins 'Integrating Integrity and Procurement: The United Nations Convention Against Corruption and The Uncitral Model Procurement Law' (2007) P.C.L.J. 307.

4 EU Procurement Rules – A Report about the German Remedies System

By Martin Burgi

1 Introduction

This report is not only meant to lay down the specifics of the German remedies system but is also dictated by the concern to spark the reader`s interest in the importance of review measures. The provisions in the field of public procurement law confer individual rights to bidders and candidates, but these are, beyond doubt, only of value if effective enforcement in front of judicial bodies is guaranteed. The protection of bidder's rights is said to be the most important political goal in public procurement law, which is why the decisions of contracting authorities and judicial bodies alike can be challenged by bidders.

Highly appreciated, the German law on public procurement offers a potpourri of various review mechanisms.

1.1 An overview of the German Remedies System

It is widely known that German Public Procurement Law is a discipline markedly influenced by European law, especially by the procurement directives.

Traditionally, the German legislator in public procurement law has always found its own and special way regarding the establishment of a public procurement system and the adoption of the European Remedies. Regarding Directives 2004/18/EC and 2004/17/EC, Germany opted for a rather complicated procurement law on the basis of three different legal acts (GWB,[1] VgV[2] and Procurement Regulations),[3] constituting the so-called *cascade variant*. Another basic feature of German procurement law is the dichotomy between

1. Act against the Restraints on Competition.
2. Public Procurement Regulation.
3. Contracting rules for the award of public service contracts, public work contracts and contracts for professional services (VOL/A, VOB/A, VOF).

public procurement law applicable for public contracts above and below the thresholds. In line with this complicated German way regarding substantive law, comparable peculiarities can be detected in the German Remedies System:

For a long time, the German remedy mechanisms in public procurement law have been integrated in a two-stage system: *primary legal protection-mechanisms*, mainly dealing with questions of judicial inquiry on the one hand and a fully-developed *secondary remedies system* on the other hand. The latter concentrates on damages and will be discussed at the very end of this article. The other category of legal protection focuses on review measures such as interim measures, annulment or ineffectiveness. Not surprisingly, and bearing in mind that bidders are nearly exclusively interested in obtaining the award, the primary legal protection system is gaining much more attention in legal practice when compared to its only rudimentarily regulated antagonist (damages system). Generally speaking, the German review system provides for primary legal review mechanisms only if the award decision has not yet been made, whereas secondary remedies in the shape of damages claims are made available only in the aftermath of the procurement procedure, e.g. when the award has already been granted to the most economically advantageous tender.

Recalling the remarks made above, distinction must be drawn between provisions governing public contract awards above and those below the thresholds.[4] Given that, legal protection is only granted in case of award procedures for public contracts falling within the scope of Directives 2004/18/EC and 2004/17/EC.

Contrary to the procedure set out in the Directives and the laws of other Member States, the award of the public contract coincides with its conclusion. The award itself is nothing other than the acceptance of the contract offered (§ 145 BGB)[5] which directly leads to its conclusion. This is why the procurement stages 'award' and 'conclusion' cannot be reasonably distinguished from one another[6] – at any event in Germany. Consequently, applica-

4. The current values are 4, 845 million Euro for public works contracts, 193,000 Euro for public service and supply contracts. These value thresholds apply directly and without transformation since the adoption of Regulation 1177/2009. All in all, the thresholds have been slightly reduced.
5. German Civil Code (BGB).
6. Dreher, in: Immenga, Ulrich/Mestmäcker, Ernst-Joachim (eds.), *Wettbewerbsrecht,* 4th edn., C.H. Beck, München 2007, § 114 GWB para 26; Stickler, in: Kapellmann, Klaus/Messerschmidt, Burkhardt, *VOB Teile A und B*, 3th edn., C.H. Beck,

tions for primary remedies can only be filed in court if the contract has neither been awarded nor concluded.[7]

This German solution is not in itself incompatible with European law. Given that the Directives do not oblige Member States to install mechanisms to annul contracts[8] and only basically call for effectiveness, the latter also may be comparably guaranteed by installing a system providing measures to correct infringements as soon as possible.[9]

The most surprising and yet characteristic feature of the German Remedies procedure system is its contradictory character. On the one hand, the regime is indeed equipped with public law features but also obvious civil law elements: First, the review body`s final decision constitutes an administrative act according to § 114 GWB and clearly is a measure originating from public law. Second, the procurement review system of the Federal Republic has been traditionally marked by its obvious affinity to administrative law as well (automatic suspensive effect § 115 I GWB resembling § 80 VWGO,[10] official investigation § 110 GWB).

Nevertheless, the review framework alongside with the entire set of public procurement law rules were integrated into civil law with §§ 97-129 GWB entering into force in 1998. Single references to German Civil Procedure Law (ZPO[11] is applicable e.g. due to § 120 II GWB), the applicability of the Ger-

München 2010, § 18 VOB/A para 6; Pietzcker, in: Grabitz, Eberhard/Hilf, Meinhard (eds), *Das Recht der europäischen Union*, Band IV, Öffentliches Auftragswesen, C.H. Beck, München 2009, B 18 para 42; contract is concluded with the award decision: VK Bremen, 16.7.2003, VK 12/03; VK Münster, 14.10.1999, VK 1/99; OLG Naumburg, 23.12.2004, 4 U 162/04; OLG Thüringen, 29.5.2006, 6 Verg 2/02; BGH, 19.12.2000, X ZB 14/00.

7. Dreher, in: Immenga, Ulrich/Mestmäcker, Ernst-Joachim (eds.), *Wettbewerbsrecht*, 4th edn., C.H. Beck, München 2007, § 114 GWB Rn. 27; Other European Member States may therefore provide for primary review mechanisms between the award decision and the conclusion of the public contract.
8. ECJ, Case 87/94-Walloon Buses, ECR 1994, I-1398, 1405 para 33; Stickler, in: Kapellmann, Klaus/Messerschmidt, Burkhardt, *VOB Teile A und B*, 3th edn., München 2010, § 18 VOB/A para 20; Martin-Ehlers, Andrés, 'Das Verfahren vor dem Vergabesenat', EuZW 2000, pp. 101, 105.
9. Pietzcker, in: Grabitz, Eberhard/Hilf, Meinhard (eds.), *Das Recht der europäischen Union*, Band IV, Öffentliches Auftragswesen, B 18 para 46; Dreher, in: Immenga, Ulrich/Mestmäcker (eds,), Ernst-Joachim, *Wettbewerbsrecht*, 4th edn., C.H. Beck, München 2007, § 114 GWB Rn. 32; Dreher, 'Rechtsschutz nach Zuschlag', NZBau 2001, p. 245.
10. Rules of the Administrative Courts (VwGO).
11. Code of the German Civil Procedure (ZPO).

man Civil Code (BGB) regarding public contracts awarded in breach of the automatic suspensive effect (§ 134 BGB) or the request for damages (§§ 280 ff., 823 BGB) and, not to be forgotten, the assimilation of award and conclusion, are important indicators of a civil law origin.

Furthermore, the decision of the review body of first instance (procurement tribunal) is to be challenged in front of a review senate installed at one of the competent higher regional courts and therefore lies within the competence of genuinely civil law courts.

1.2 An European incentive for Remedies Directives

The supremacy of European law should in no way be underestimated, especially as far as public procurement law and the review procedures provided therein are concerned. In fact, the European legislature influenced German procurement law and the respective procedural procurement law immensely when introducing the first generation of Procurement Directives flanked by the two Remedies Directives 89/665/EEC[12] and 92/13/EEC.[13] The adoption of these two specific directives was designed to ensure the rights bidders enjoyed under the Directives.

Member States are obliged to fulfill the obligations arising from the Treaty and secondary European law alike. Directives are – by definition – not directly applicable, but need to be transposed into national law before producing effects. In other words, the German legislature had to pay heed to the objectives of the Directives and refrain from releasing differing legislative acts in the course of transposition. An exact copy was, of course, not obligatory in view of Art. 288 II TfEU (former Art. 249 II EC).[14] This article is based upon the fact that flagrant disparities between Member States cannot be fully abandoned, so that it has been advisable for the rule setters to fix only the minimum standards and structures which should be complied with by every Member State.

12. Council Directive 89/665/EEC of 21 December 1989 on the coordination of the laws, regulations and administrative provisions relating to the application of review procedures to the award of public supply and public works contracts.
13. Council Directive 92/13/EEC of 25 February 1992 coordinating the laws, regulations and administrative provisions relating to the application of Community rules on the procurement procedures of entities operating in the water, energy, transport and telecommunications sectors.
14. Art. 288 II TfEU saying that a directive is binding only regarding the aim to be achieved.

Back then (prior to 1998), German Public Procurement law and its review system have been exclusively part of budgetary law with the two stringent consequences that subjective rights were nowhere to be found, neither were private entities granted legal protection. On the contrary, the review mechanisms offered were matters *ex officio and* bidders and candidates were denied the right to invoke a review procedure on their own motion.

As a consequence, the European Commission, having revealed and frequently criticized Germany`s noncompliance with European law, initiated a treaty violation procedure against the Federal Republic of Germany pursuant to then Art. 234 EC (Art. 267 TfEU). *The Second Act amending Public Procurement Law* (Vergaberechtsänderungsgesetz) in 1998, finally led to the implementation of §§ 97-129 into the GWB. These rules introduced procurement provisions granting subjective and enforceable rights and finally offered review measures largely meeting the requirements formulated by the European Directives. Plus, they were at long last considered to be in line with the rulings of the European Court of Justice.

Up until today, the set of review mechanisms is only available for contract awards exceeding the European threshold values. Hence, the so-called budgetary solution[15] still applies below the thresholds, albeit a revolutionary change in that regard is controversially discussed in Germany at the moment. This tendency is mainly due to reiterating rulings of the ECJ concerning the importance of fundamental procurement principles as enshrined in the Treaty and Directive 2004/18/EC. All in all, the rulings tend to declare the direct applicability of fundamental procurement rules, namely competition, transparency and non-discrimination, even for public award contracts falling short of the thresholds. Given the above, further basic changes to the remedies system below the threshold values are likely to happen in the future on the European and the national level.

Even in the aftermath of the enactment of the legislative package and Directives 2004/18/EC and 2004/17/EC entering into force, European experts on procurement law detected numerous weaknesses within the heterogeneous review regimes of the Member states. During that time, the review measures made available in most Member States were still not sufficiently compliant with the extent and importance of the subjective rights granted by the Directives. The weaknesses revealed were the reason why bidders refrained from tendering. Nevertheless, the European legislature was not inclined to create harmonization by way of a uniform European review procedure knowing that

15. Governed by Federal and State Budgetary Regulations (BHO and LHO`s).

the law of each Member state is a product of different historical, social developments and experiences. In absence of European rules and in compliance with the doctrine of procedural autonomy, Member States are mainly free to choose the appropriate measures. In particular, the conditions and the set of review mechanisms available fall exclusively under national law, whereas the European Directives only provide for a minimum framework which should be complied with.

Keeping the commonly accepted European goal of installing effectiveness and rapidness in review procedures in mind, the new Remedies Directive 2007/66/EC was adopted in 2007. Today, Member States are explicitly asked to ensure effective and rapid review mechanisms, meaning that diverse and adequate means in order to prevent, correct or set aside unlawfully taken award decisions and rules to safeguard the bidder`s rights flowing from the Directives and the Treaty respectively, should be provided for. Consequently, another comprehensive reform took place in Germany, beginning with the implementation of the German law on the modernization of Public Procurement Law[16] entering into force in April 2009.

In fact, the recent transposing acts – transposing the requirements flowing from the Directive on time – have led to a nearly exemplary, modern German Remedies system. Without doubt, uncertainties and questions relating to practice still remain and years to come, courts will be occupied with interpreting and explaining as well as laying down rules and administering justice. The rules on damages, in particular, are lacking legal clarity.

Despite these fractional gaps, the German legislature worked out a dendritic system equipped with different means of legal correction. It should not go unnoticed that the rules broadly allow for the consideration of both the interests of the public entity in awarding the contract as soon as possible in order to fulfill public tasks[17] and the interests of potentially aggrieved private enterprises in obtaining legal relief.[18] Summing up, the GWB is designed to be very protective of the bidder's rights while the concerns of the contracting authority are not completely disregarded either.

16. Law on the Modernization of Public Procurement Law (2009) of 20.4.2009, BGBl. I, 790.
17. Preliminary decision about the award (§ 121 GWB) or permission to award the contract in advance (§ 115 II GWB).
18. Claim for damages (§§ 125, 126 GWB, §§ 280ff BGB, § 823 BGB), automatic suspensive effect (§ 115 I GWB), declaration of ineffectiveness or voidance.

1.3 Main characteristics of the German Remedies System

The following section is dedicated to singular main characteristics of the German Remedies system. Questions relating to competence, locus standi and costs are briefly discussed.

1.3.1 Review bodies

With view to the principle of procedural autonomy, the European procurement Directives refrain from creating much too detailed procedural rules. As a matter of fact, the European legislator focuses only on the *essentialia*, which is to make available sufficiently effective relief within each Member State.

According to the minimum standards set out by Art. 2 II of European Directive 2004/18/EC, different legal bodies may share the competence regarding varying review measures. It is up to domestic law to designate the courts and tribunals having jurisdiction. In transposition, Germany created a system forked into multiple ways regarding matters of competency. As a rule, the ordinary courts are asked in case of applications for compensation (§ 104 II GWB)[19] whereas questions of primary legal review are dealt with in front of the review chambers or the so-called procurement tribunals unless an immediate complaint is brought before one of the higher regional courts, also known as appellate courts (§ 102 GWB). It is important to accentuate that the review chambers are not considered 'courts' senso strictu in national law. Nonetheless, they are 'courts' in the European law language.[20]

Briefly noted, review chambers work independently and judge solely on the basis of the currently existing law provisions (§ 105 I GWB). Its members are selected for the duration of five years and – with Germany being a constitutional state – they are free and supposed to act independently (§ 105 IV GWB). The exact number of review chambers, commonly situated at the Federal Cartel Office, rests in the competence of the Bund.

In addition to the share of competence between different review chambers, the German regime provides rules of competency regarding the distinction between federal and state law. According to § 106 a and § 104 GWB, federal review chambers are to decide about federal procurement law review issues while public contract procedures on the State level are consequently dealt

19. Nevertheless with regard to infringements in cartel law, the cartel law offices remain competent according to §104 II GWB in connection with §§ 19, 20 GWB.
20. Müller-Wrede, in: Müller-Wrede, Malte (ed.), *Kompendium des Vergaberechts*, Bundesanzeiger Verlag, Köln 2008, Chapter 26 para 15; ECJ, Case C-54/96-*Dorsch Consult* [1997] NJW 1997, 3365.

with by locally installed review chambers. The installation itself along with questions of organization and allocation is governed by the respective State (§ 106 II GWB). Pursuant to this norm, the *Länder* are due to constitute common review chambers (principle of efficiency). In case the competence cannot be definitely decided about, § 106 a III 1 GWB envisions that the registered office of the contracting authority should be applied as a decision-making aid. In the past, award review agencies in the sense of non-judicial bodies have also been mentioned in the GWB, but with the implementation of the latest reform, this provision has been removed in order to foster effectiveness and decrease complexity.

Irrespective of the competent body, all decisions are effectively enforceable (§ 114 III GWB). Clearly, this is because the decision appears in the form of an administrative act.

1.3.2 Locus standi and admissibility

The issue of competence being settled, the admissibility requirements as featured in § 107 GWB are subject to the following remarks. Presenting this provision in a nutshell, it can be noted that a bidder or candidate interested in applying for review has to fulfill detailed but not inadequately difficult requirements.

1.3.3 Locus Standi

Beginning with the locus standi, the right to file an application is granted to every undertaking having an interest in the particular contract and claiming that rights under section § 97 VII GWB have been violated because the contracting authority acted in non-compliance with fundamental procurement provisions. A successful application, however, requires that the claiming bidder has either already suffered a loss or is about to suffer such. The well known causation-principle of *sine qua non* (tort law) stipulates that the loss is suffered in consequence of the breach with procurement rules. Thereby, the German legislature set up quite detailed conditions which have to be satisfied cumulatively prior to obtaining legal review.

Nonetheless, compliance with the European demands as enshrined inter alia in Art. 1 III of Directive 2007/66/EC is given. Its Art. 1 III declares that Member States enjoy the autonomy to establish detailed rules as long as '*at least any person having or having had an interest in obtaining a particular contract and who has been or risks being harmed by an alleged infringement*' is offered access to legal review. Obviously, the German equivalent is designed to be a bit more detailed and stricter than its European pendant, yet the main requirements of the said Directive are met (in addition see further remarks below), so that Germany cannot be said to have adapted an overly narrow provision.

1.3.4 Obligation to object

Other important admissibility rules flanking the locus standi question are dealt with in § 107 GWB as well. § 107 III GWB entails the applicant`s obligation to raise an objection prior to the initiation of the real review procedure. According to § 107 III No. 1 the objection should be filed without undue delay. A bidder wishing to use a review procedure (except for applications relating to the claim of ineffectiveness) is meant to notify the contracting authority of the alleged infringement and his intention to seek review as soon as he becomes aware of the infringement. Clearly, this provision was enacted not only as a 'door-opener' for a review procedure. Functioning as a rule of foreclosure, it is primarily supposed to reduce unnecessary review procedures and thereby serve the aim of procedural efficiency. An applicant is denied the right to initiate a review proceeding the moment he does not object, but knows about the infringement of procurement law. On the other hand, the contracting authority supposedly in breach of procurement provisions is given the possibility to correct the violation prior to an official body`s decision. Thereby the award procedure process can continue and review chambers are not unnecessarily called upon, which helps to tighten effectiveness in the longer term.

Notwithstanding this legitimate process-effective argument, the requirement of a rapid objection is suspected of not being backed by Art. 1 IV, V of Directive 2007/66/EC or any other rule stemming from European law.[21] Strictly following the view the European Court of Justice maintained in its preliminary ruling in the Uniplex Case in 2010,[22] a rejection of an application on the basis of an untimely objection is incompatible with European law. In light of the objective of rapidity, Directive 2007/66/EC allows Member States to set up (preclusive) time limits or other requirements for the application of review measures (see Art. 1 IV, V). Hence, national law may prevail an aggrieved bidder to challenge a decision of a contracting authority shortly after the violating event became known or ought to have become known by the

21. Krohn, Wolfram, '„Unzulässigkeit" einer unverzüglichen Rügepflicht – Uniplex' NZBau 2010, 188; Jaeger, NZBau 2009, 558; Kühnen, Jürgen, 'Die Rügeobligenheit' NZBau 2004, 427.
22. ECJ, Case C-406/08-*Uniplex* [2010] ECR I-406/08.

tenderer. Nevertheless, such requirements of domestic law must compromise the principle of effectiveness in no way.[23]

Clearly, the Uniplex-judgement has raised numerous questions and led to fierce discussions relating to the compatibility of § 107 III No. 1 GWB with the demands of the Directive.

Ostensibly, the German legislature used its margin of discretion because § 107 III No. 1 requires that an objection should be raised immediately after the event became known.

A special definition on 'immediate objections' can neither be found in the Directive nor in the entire framework set up by German public procurement law. Applying § 121 BGB, the term 'immediately' can be interpreted in the sense of 'without undue delay'. Still, the timeliness of the objection is said to be strongly dependent on the opinion of the competent court dealing with the procedure at issue.[24] To clarify, regarding an award with a complicated technical or financial background, more problems are evoked and this is why an objecting bidder clearly needs more time to consider his chances of success. The procurement of a standardized product certainly creates fewer problems which is why the time limit for an objection should not be assessed too generously. Owing to the fact that every award procedure is coined by its own characteristics, it is nearly impossible to set up and fix objective time limits the review chambers could work with in every case. Some courts – trying to find a solution in compliance with EU law – fight for a limitation period of one to two weeks,[25] others reduce the limit to 1-5 days.[26] These different interpretations mirror the existing legal rag rug concerning the exact time limit for initiating a review request. Some courts hold that the time-limit criteria can only be appraised in a discretionary manner. Following these opinions, only the competent judge is to decide what undue delay means. This point exactly is supposed to create legal uncertainty and is incompatible with the requirement of sufficiently precise, clear and forseeable[27] national transforming acts. Individuals should be able to calculate the exact time limit *ex ante,*

23. ECJ, Case C-406/08-*Uniplex* [2010] ECR I-406/08, para 39.
24. Krohn, Wolfram, '„Unzulässigkeit" einer unverzüglichen Rügepflicht – Uniplex' NZBau 2010, p. 186, 187; Hübner, Alexander, 'Das Ende der „unverzüglichen" und uneingeschränkten Rügeobliegenheit (Paragraph 107 Abs. 3 Satz 1 GWB)' VergabeR 2010, p. 414.
25. OLG Düsseldorf, 13.4.1999; OLG Dresden, 7.5.2010, W Verg 6/10.
26. OLG Naumburg, 30.7.2004, 1 Verg 10/04.
27. ECJ, Case C-361/188-*Commission-Germany* [1991], ECR I-2567; ECJ, Case 406/09-*Uniplex*, NZBau 2010, p. 183, 185 para 39, 42.

which is not possible if the duration of the time limit is solely dependent on the judge`s decision in the respective case. In consequence of and in accordance with the ECJ`s ruling, the German norm is considered incompatible with the European objective of a rapid and effective review procedure.[28] In consequence, national courts shall refrain from applying the relevant norm with regard to the supremacy of European law.[29]

Other opinions, however, fight for the compatibility of the § 107 III GWB. In contrast to the constellation given in the Uniplex-case, the word 'immediate' could be interpreted in a way installing adherence to European law. The justifications offered are mainly based on two assumptions: first, § 107 III GWB is a rule of foreclosure and hinders a bidder to initiate a review procedure only if he is already informed and knows about the breach of procurement law. Second, the word 'immediate' has been interpreted for about hundreds of years in civil law jurisdiction, so that it is relatively clear that anything beyond two weeks cannot be justifiably regarded as immediate in the sense of §§ 121 BGB, 107 III GWB.[30]

Given that the German courts are still arguing about the compatibility of § 107 III GWB with European law, it is advisable for the national legislator to enact a new, clearer rule, capable of being applied in practice and establishing legal certainty to a sufficient degree. Until now, a bill has not been designed, however.

According to § 107 III No. 2 and 3 GWB, an application is inadmissible if obvious violations (identifiable on the basis of the notification or the tender documents) are not objected to within a certain time limit, whereas § 107 III No. 4 GWB stipulates an objection to be filed at least 15 days with effect from the day following the date on which the contracting authority has sent a reply rejecting the objection. The only question remaining is which criteria apply in ascertaining whether the bidder could have detected the infringement. There are two possibilities: some experts dwell on the subjective view of the bidder affected, others stipulate that the objective view of an average

28. Krohn, Wolfram, '„Unzulässigkeit" einer unverzüglichen Rügeobliegenheit' NZBau 2010, p. 183; Hübner, Alexander, 'Das Ende der „unverzüglichen" und uneingeschränkten Rügeobliegenheit (Paragraph 107 Abs. 3 Satz 1 GWB)' VergabeR 2010, p. 414.
29. Krohn, Wolfram, '„Unzulässigkeit" einer unverzüglichen Rügeobliegenheit' NZBau 2010, p. 188; ECJ, Case 406/08-*Uniplex*, NZBau 2010, p. 186 para 49; VK Hamburg, 7.4.2010; VK Rheinland-Pfalz, 20.4.2010, VK 2-7/10.
30. Fighting for the compatibility with European law: OLG Dresden, 7.5.2010, W Verg 6/10; BKartA, 5.3.2010, VK 1-16/10.

bidder or the knowledge of an expert in public procurement law constitute the relevant parameters.

Pursuant to § 108 GWB, the application should be directed in written form and should contain the main reasons for the application.

Closing with a short overview of § 113 GWB, the competent review chamber itself is obliged to rule within a time limit of five weeks. Due to the fundamental procurement principle of transparency, all important facts and reasons underlying the court`s decision should be mentioned in written form as well. Not surprisingly, the applicant himself is meant to assist in order to strengthen efficiency and effectiveness.

As already mentioned above, decisions of the review chambers can be challenged in front of a review senate, exclusively installed at one of the higher regional courts and acting as Court of Appeal by means of the immediate complaint (§ 116 GWB). The Court of Appeal has the competence to either replace the judicial decision or recommit it under the condition that the reasons given by the review senate are sufficiently considered when re-deciding.

1.3.5 Costs

For his own merits, a bidder seeking review will be expected to look at the costs resulting from an application. These costs arise due to the administrative body`s efforts and expenses in preparing, documenting and finally making a decision (§ 128 I GWB).

Clearly, costs should not refrain aggrieved bidders from initiating a review procedure. Anyway, bidders are empirically afraid to take legal steps against the contracting authority. Bringing such legal action is considered the least favored alternative (compared to informal settlement, for instance). From the bidders` perspectives it is tantamount to 'biting the hand that feeds them'.[31]

In Germany, the costs (procedural fees and expenses)[32] amount to a sum of at least 2,500 Euro and should not exceed the threshold of 50,000 Euro (§ 128 II GWB). In extraordinary cases, e.g. if the economic importance of the contract award requires so,[33] the costs can go far beyond these generally ac-

31. Trepte, Peter, *Public Procurement in the EU*, Oxford University Press, New York 2007, p. 553.
32. E.g. copying expenses, costs of notification and communication, Niebuhr, in: Niebuhr, Frank/Kulartz, Hans-Peter/Kus, Alexander/Portz, Norbert (eds.), *Kommentar zum Vergaberecht*, Luchterland, Neuwied 2000, § 128 GWB para 2.
33. Niebuhr, Niebuhr, Frank/Kulartz, Hans-Peter/Kus, Alexander/Portz, Norbert (eds.), *Kommentar zum Vergaberecht*, Luchterland, Neuwied 2000, § 128 GWB para 3, 4;

cepted values (principle of equity). § 128 III GWB establishes the duty of the loosing party to cover the costs. Again, slight derogations from this rule are possible due to the provision offering room for decisions of equity.

Since German procurement law is considered one of the most complex fields of law, the inclusion of a legal expert (lawyer) is highly advisable to bidders, sometimes even indispensable, though still not obligatory in front of the procurement tribunal.[34] By contrast, the conditions under which a contracting authority is allowed to seek legal advice are much stricter.[35] Regarding the procedure in front of the review senate, the parties should legally represent themselves (§ 120 I 1 GWB).

Focusing on the fees due to the enlistment of a lawyer, § 128 IV S. 2 GWB lays down, that the forfeited party should also cover the costs of the procedural opponent regarding prosecution and expenses on defending counsel. The usual lawyers` fees are dependent on the jurisdictional amount, which mostly corresponds to 5 % of the purchase value.[36]

1.4 Most important breaches

Due to the comparative research agenda of this draft, information about which breaches are most frequently brought to court or the number of successful cases per year should be given, too. It appears worthwhile to focus on the tendency and inclination of the courts to grant primary or secondary legal review mechanisms.

Owing to the fact that primary legal review procedures do not focus on the general examination of the contract being lawful, applications for review are only admitted in case of a breach of public procurement provisions with a

Brauer, in: Kulartz, Hans-Peter/Kus, Alexander/Portz, Norbert, *Kommentar zum GWB-Vergaberecht*, Werner Verlag, Köln 2006, § 128 GWB para 5; Weyand, Rudolf, *Praxiskommentar Vergaberecht*, 2nd ed., Werner Verlag, Köln 2008, § 128 GWB para 1776.

34. Brauer, in: Kulartz, Hans-Peter/Kus, Alexander/Portz, Norbert, *Kommentar zum GWB-Vergaberecht*, Werner Verlag, Köln 2006, § 128 GWB para 30; Niebuhr, in: Niebuhr, Frank/Kulartz, Hans-Peter/Kus, Alexander/Portz, Norbert (eds.), Kommentar zum Vergaberecht, Luchterland, Neuwied 2000, § 128 GWB para 15.
35. C.f. the rulings of VK Bund, 14.12.2004, VK 2-208/04, VERIS, p. 18; OLG Düsseldorf, 20.7.2000, Verg 1/00.
36. Gatawis, Siegbert, 'Anwalts- und Verwaltungskosten im Verfahren vor der Vergabekammer' NZBau 2004, p. 381; Lausen, Irene, 'Kosten im Nachprüfungsverfahren' NZBau 2005, p. 441; Mertens, in: Franke, Horst/Kemper, Ralf/Zanner, Christian/Grünhagen, Matthias, *VOB-Kommentar*, 4th edn., Werner Verlag, Köln 2010, § 21a VOB/A para 42 ff.; the calculation of the lawyer's expenses is governed by detailed rules in the RVG (German Lawyer's Fees Act).

protective character as enshrined in § 97 VII GWB. Direct awards constitute the most serious and common breach provoking legal review procedures. Contracting entities, aware of litigants, make specific efforts to award the contract as soon as possible. This way, they reduce remedial possibilities, because after the conclusion of a contract a claim for compensation is the only relief possible. In most cases, the direct award does not happen intentionally (see the controversy about inhouse-cases); it is mostly because contracting entities either do not know that procurement law is applicable and they do not know how to interpret the provisions. Or, they are misinformed (e.g. by lawyers or other agencies providing information) about the fact that procurement law is indeed to be applied. Thus, direct awards are mainly a consequence of the complexity of procurement law itself.

The fact, that direct awards constitute the most serious of all breaches, is in line with the findings of the European Court of Justice[37] and the European legislator`s estimation in this regard, which was – according to its recital No. 13 – one of the driving incentives for the adoption of the New Remedies Directive. Another very problematic procurement breach, nearly as frequent and grave as the direct award, is that German contract awards are sometimes being granted in the course of the wrong procedure.[38] Contracting authorities try hard to avoid the application of the complicated German procurement law landscape either by awarding a contract directly or by unlawfully using more flexible and open procedural mechanisms such as the negotiations procedure (e.g. by way of interpreting its conditions widely). Likewise, both policies violate the subjective rights of bidders under § 97 VII GWB.[39] Sometimes, bidders initiate a claim even if they have been lawfully excluded but other bidders in a comparable situation have not.

In contrast to that, damages are indeed the least preferred remedy due to difficulties of proof and quantum.

1.5 Review practice (statistical information)

Recalling the principle of procedural autonomy and the Member State`s discretion regarding the organization and installation of review chambers, it

37. ECJ, Case C-26/03- *Stadt Halle* [2005] I-1.
38. In that case, German courts consider the contracting authority to have breached bidder's rights, c.f. Portz, in: Kulartz, Hans-Peter/Marx, Fridhelm/Portz, Norbert/Prieß, Hans-Joachim, *Kommentar zur VOB/A*, Werner Verlag, Köln 2010, § 17 VOB/A para 57; OLG Celle, VergabeR 2009, pp. 898 ff. affirming this decision BGH, NZBau 2010, pp. 124 ff.
39. BGH, NZBau 2010, p. 124.

should be noted that currently 24 review chambers are installed within Germany. Analyzing the statistical report issued by the Federal Ministry of Economics (BMWi)[40] about primary legal review procedures dealt with in front of the review chambers in the year 2009, 1,275 applications have been directed and about 1,200 of them have been completed. Interestingly, the vast majority of the applications were of national origin, only 13 applications were filed by international tenderers. Surprisingly, in only 236 of 1,200 cases, the review chambers decided in favor of the applying bidder. Therefore, a success rate of poor 16.16 % can be ascertained. Nevertheless, the success rate of the contracting authority is in no way different, which is why 472, that is to say 37.02 %, cases have been completed because the complainant dropped the case.

Remembering the fact that a review chamber is generally obliged to rule within a period of 5 weeks, it should be briefly noted, that this time limit has been extended in 37.96 % of the contract award procedures.

The contracting authority`s application for the allowance to award a public contract in advance rests in the competence of the review chambers as well. In about 47 cases (3.69 %), the contracting entity asked for this form of interim relief. Only two decisions have been made in aid of the contracting entity, which plainly demonstrates the reluctancy of the review chambers to empower the contracting authority to award the contract if a tenderer has started a review procedure.

About 212 cases were qualified as immediate appeals, arousing the competence of the 16 Review senates at the Court of Appeal. The statistic reveals that only nine applications have been successful while 69 were subject to abandonment and 49 have been rejected. For the moment, 57 cases have not yet been decided about at all.

Not only the immediate complaint against the Review chamber`s decision lies in the competence of the higher regional courts. Pursuant to § 118 I 3 GWB the procedure to apply for a prolongation of the suspensive effect, equally constituting a measure of interim relief in favor of the bidder, is dealt with in front of the special review senates. 32 of the 84 submitted applications have been positively ruled while a rejection occurred in 25 cases. The application for a contract award in advance (§ 121 GWB) is obviously a very rarely used procedure, judging by the fact that only four applications have been filed in the year 2009 and only one review senate empowered the apply-

40. The annual report can be looked at under http://www.bmwi.de/BMWi/Navigation/-Wirtschaft/Wirtschaftspolitik/oeffentliche-auftraege,did=191022.html (downloads).

ing authority to award the contract in advance. Furthermore, only two cases (out of 212) were brought to the Federal High Court of Justice (BGH), whereas only one application has been transferred to the ECJ.

In the year 2008 however, 1,158 primary legal review procedures have been initiated in front of the Review chambers and 227 applications have been filed with the Review Senate of the Higher Regional courts which demonstrates that the number of review cases remains roughly the same.

All in all, the opportunities offered by the rules on primary legal review procedures are used quite frequently. The national system is equipped with a more or less effective remedies system on the first stage (primary legal remedies). Effectiveness does, of course, not mean that applying bidders have to be successful in every case. The most important requirement is that review mechanisms (at best when infringements can still be corrected) are actually available at an early stage. This fact helps understanding why only 10% of the enterprises involved in awards file a damages claim.[41] Owing to the fact that full compensation is very difficult to obtain (see following remarks in the chapter), the bidder`s affinity towards a damages claim appears even less distinctive.

This short overview dealing with the specifics of the German remedies system in general has already demonstrated its compliance with European law as enshrined in the Remedies Directives or in the Treaty (regarding most obligations of transposition). All the same, it appears worthwhile to have a closer examining look at the single German review measures and whether they also comply with their European pendant.

2 Interim Measures

Comparing legal relief to all other forms of relief in the medical context, similarities and differences can be detected at the same time. In both areas, relief is meant to be applied after either the breach of law or the illness started. Normally, relief means that something, which already happened, has to be cured. In the legal context, however, the word 'relief' is also used to describe preventive actions (interim measures or standstill period). In comparison, preventive measures gain more attention in law life than in the day-to-day life of a doctor, whose main work consists in healing and not in preventing.

41. European Business Test Panel, *Monatsinfo 10/2004 des forum vergabe e.V.*, p. 162.

Therefore, the interim measures, available prior to the conclusion of the contract should therefore be presented before the 'healing' measures (ineffectiveness, annulment and damages) and the newly implemented relief of ineffectiveness which are all outlined separately.

2.1 Interim Measures – what it is all about

Apart from the general criticism raised against the relief-solutions in the Member States, the European legislature's main focus concentrated on the immensely important interim relief procedures. Due to the irreversibility of the contract award decision, the procurement legislature has needed to introduce measures whereby infringements can still be rectified. Thus, opportunities for relief should be installed at the earliest time possible.

Above all, the combat against illegal direct awards (see recital 13 of Directive 2007/66/EC) lay in the focus of the European institutions and does until now. Therefore, Art. 2 I a of the Remedies Directive envisions that interim measures, such as the suspension of the contract, should be offered. Ideally, the procedure itself or any decision by the contracting authority should be equipped with a suspensive effect.

The establishment of detailed conditions and requirements, however, falls exclusively under the national regime so that Member States are autonomous to work out specific rules for the interim relief procedure. Art. 2 III of the Directive, for example, explicitly allows for discretion on the installation of the suspensive effect being automatic. Nevertheless, it should be guaranteed that fundamental European requirements are not virtually impossible or excessively difficult to be complied with.

Without measures like the ones already mentioned (suspensive effect), an aggrieved tenderer would be left without comparably effective mechanisms, resulting in the fact that the contracting authority would be able to set the scene completely. Not only would the contract be concluded, the tenderer or candidate would not have another chance to contest the legality of the respective award decision nor would they be granted the award. Consequently, interim measures should ideally take effect from the earliest moment possible in order to either eliminate existing violations or prevent further damage. The installation of effective and available interlocutory procedures may also have a psychological effect which should not go unnoticed. To all intents and purposes, interim measures can encourage the concerned to make greater use of preliminary proceedings instead of starting a main procedure straight away or asking for compensating actions after the contract has already been concluded. By way of reinforcing interim forms of relief, infringements of European law on the award of public contracts or the national rules transposing it could be corrected as soon as possible and without causing further damage to the entire contract award procedure. If the parties were to wait until the final review decision, the procedure is likely to be considered unlawful and the entire process would have to start afresh. Seen with the eyes of an economically thinking aggrieved bidder, taking interim measures is not as costly as waiting until the outcome of a time and money-consuming review procedure. Besides interim measures establish an ideal opportunity to bring in line the contradicting interests of first, the contracting authority, second the general public and third and most important, private entities.

Beyond doubt, Germany was anxious to improve the existent legal framework on interim measures by way of amending the GWB correspondingly and abandoning any obstacle to effective review. The latest reform culminated in a dendritic and apparently complex interim relief system. Both parties are equipped with interlocutory actions. Due to § 115 I, § 115 II 5 and § 118 I 3 GWB, the aggrieved *bidder* (who is not ranked among those likely to win the contract) is enabled to seek interim relief while § 115 II 1-4, § 115 II 6 and § 121 GWB are applicable in favor of the *contracting authority* or, since very recently, the *bidder who is supposedly awarded the contract.*

2.2 German Provisions on interim measures

2.2.1 §§ 115 GWB, 118 GWB: legally required suspensive effect

Starting with the measures available for the aggrieved bidder, § 115 I GWB constitutes by far the most important provision in the field of interlocutory relief[42] as the bidder`s official request for review is endowed with an automatic suspensive effect. According to this rule, the contracting authority should award the contract no earlier than the procurement tribunal's decision is made and the expiry of the period for the complaint. Any award made nonetheless is null and void pursuant to § 134 BGB.[43] The interdiction of the award only applies if the contracting authority has been notified in writing about the application for legal review by the review chamber.

The commencement of an interim review procedure is not dependent on the initiation of a main proceeding, as such a requirement would clearly have an influence on the availability or the speed of interim measures. This would

42. Kus, in: Kulartz, Hans-Peter/Kus, Alexander/Portz, Norbert, *Kommentar zum GWB-Vergaberecht*, Luchterland, Neuwied 2000, § 115 GWB para 1.
43. Kus, in: Kulartz, Hans-Peter/Kus, Alexander/Portz, Norbert, *Kommentar zum GWB-Vergaberecht*, Luchterland, Neuwied 2000, § 115 GWB para 18.

contradict the principle of effectiveness. As a rule, interim relief is not designed to foreshadow the outcome of the main procedure.[44]

The suspensive effect should only end if its deadline fully complies with the standstill period and does not comprise the bidder`s right to effectively introduce a main procedure.

§ 115 II 5 GWB, however, allows for an application directed at the reinstatement of the suspensive effect provided that the latter ended or the contracting entity has been officially allowed to award the contract by virtue of § 115 II 1-4 GWB. The relief set out in § 115 II 5 GWB is strictly dependent on an application, which is not dealt with in front of the procurement tribunal this time, but falls in the review senate`s (appelate court's) competence.[45]

Finally, § 118 I 3 GWB constitutes the third form of interlocutory action. Remembering the different jurisdictional instances involved, decisions of review chambers are challenged in front of the review senates. The immediate complaint generally has a suspensive effect upon the decision of the review tribunal of first instance (§ 118 I 1 GWB) and lapses two weeks after the expiry of the time limit for the complaint. Assuming that the review chamber has rejected the application for review, the review senate finds itself competent to prolongate the suspensive effect on request of the aggrieved bidder. The prolongation can extend up to the time of the final decision.

In the past, interim relief measures have been exclusively granted to either the contracting authority or the aggrieved bidder who was not ranked high enough to obtain the procured contract or who has not been considered unlawfully. Whereas the aggrieved bidder is interested in having the contract suspended and infringements rectified, the contracting authority is eager to award the public contract and fulfill its administrative public tasks. The best bidder is supposed to share the interest of the contracting authority in a rapid award procedure as well which is the reason why last-year`s amendment of the GWB brought about the best bidder`s right to claim for the preliminary award of the contract, too. Of course, their interest collides with the respective concern of the competing bidders or the interest of the general public in the integrity and lawfulness of public award procedures. These opposing interests in particular are subject to a comprehensive balance check regarding

44. ECJ, Case C-296/95-*Commission-Greece* [1996] ECR I-4467 para 11; Prieß, Hans-Joachim (ed.), *Handbuch des europäischen Vergaberechts*, 5th edn., Carl Heymanns Verlag, Köln 2007, 3 15; ECJ, Case C 214/00-*Commission-Spain* [2003] ECR I-97-99.

45. Kus, in: Kulartz, Hans-Peter/Kus, Alexander/Portz, Norbert, *Kommentar zum GWB-Vergaberecht*, Luchterland, Neuwied 2000, § 115 GWB para 39 ff.

the interlocutory measures applicable, which corresponds fully with Art. 2 V of Directive 2007/66/EC, ruling that the probable consequences of interim measures should be taken into account.

2.2.2 §§ 115 II 1-4, 121 GWB: Preliminary decision by the review bodies

Before a detailed description is given, it should be mentioned that § 115 II 1-4 GWB offer the opportunity to apply for a preliminary decision regarding the award and thereby provide for a derogation of the generally automatic suspensive effect. The awarding agency or the private entity entitled to be the most economically advantageous tenderer, can apply for the review body's official allowance to award the contract without adhering to special formal requirements or time limits.[46] The procurement tribunal is meant to decide on the basis of a probability check, taking into account the probable consequences for all interests likely to be harmed, thus covering the interest of the general public in a cost-effective award procedure without unnecessary time lag, the success chances of the applying entity to obtain the contract or the success chances regarding the application for review. The applying contracting purchaser is only empowered to award the contract prior to the pending decision in the main proceeding, if the interests and benefits tied to an early award outweigh the negative impacts. If the review chamber does not allow for the preliminary award, the review senate may decide on the same matter, but this time only upon application of the contracting entity (§ 115 II 6 GWB). Noteworthy, this instrument is very rarely used in practice.

§ 121 I GWB deals with a similar procedure. Either the contracting authority or the bidder ranked highest can apply for the preliminary award of the contract. A synopsis of these two procedures (§ 121 I, § 115 II 1-4 GWB) shows that the last form of application is filed to the review senate (an immediate complaint has been handed in) whereas the other arouses the competence of the review chamber. Irrespective of this distinction, the procedures are comparable in many ways, especially as a probability check considering the different interests involved forms the centre of examination in both procedures.

2.3 Summary

Closing this section, it should be reiterated that the German system provides an excellent and comprehensive review regime regarding interim measures,

46. Byok, in: Byok, Jan/Jaeger, Wofgang, *Kommentar zum Vergaberecht*, Verlag Recht und Wirtschaft GmbH, 2nd ed., Frankfurt a.M. 2005, § 115 GWB para 1101.

bearing in mind that Germany – going beyond the Art. 2 IV of the Directive – chose the automatic suspensive effect as one of the most effective and elegant solutions, offers legal actions for both parties and includes two different instances of review.

With the exclusion of § 121 III GWB, the majority of the said provisions do not contain specific rules for the time zone in which the contracting body should decide.[47] § 121 III GWB, however, requires the procurement tribunal to decide no later than five weeks after the application has been forwarded. As far as the other interim measures are concerned, the end of the suspensive effect mostly determines the time limit for the judge's decision. More precisely, in case of an application relating to §§ 115 II 1-4 GWB, it is only logical, that the suspensive effect can only be exempted from, if it has not already expired. Basically speaking, § 113 GWB embodying the principle of acceleration and the spirit and purpose of interim relief[48] should be kept in mind as well. In case of legal or virtual difficulties, a judge may ask for prolongation, of course.

Altogether, the characteristics establish a high degree of legal certainty and integrity. In view of the practical consequences, only few proceedings were started in 2009. The conditions for a contracting authority to preliminarily award the contract might indeed be considered elaborate, which is why only two of 47 applications on the basis of § 115 II 1-4 GWB and only one of four by virtue of § 121 I GWB have been heard successfully by the competent review bodies.

On the other hand, the law on public award contracts is generally designed to vouchsafe the bidders` rights as they traditionally find themselves in an inferior position compared to the public purchaser. Therefore, interim measures in favor of the contracting authority should not gain too much attention compared to enforceable rights of the bidder. Interim measures offered by German procurement law are mostly in aid of the latter, the more so as the automatic suspensive effect remains the rule. Thereby, the contract is prevented from being concluded, so that (the) other interlocutory mechanisms are not asked for that often. If an application on the basis of § 118 is introduced, in about 32 of 84 cases, the applying bidder ends up with a prolongation of the suspensive effect.

47. Byok, in: Byok, Jan/Jaeger, Wolfgang, *Kommentar zum Vergaberecht*, 2nd ed., Verlag Recht und Wirtschaft, Frankfurt a.M. 2005, § 115 GWB para 1102.
48. Byok, in: Byok, Jan/Jaeger, Wolfgang, *Kommentar zum Vergaberecht*, 2nd ed., Verlag Recht und Wirtschaft, Frankfurt a.M. 2005, § 115 GWB para 1102.

3 Standstill Period (legally required)

In comparision to the interim measures outlined above, the provisions relating to the standstill period belong to the same category of review mechanisms, as both set of norms seek to install relief *before* the conclusion of the contract.

By definition, the standstill period means that the contracting authority should refrain from actually setting the scene (by the conclusion of the contract) in order to enable effective review procedures.[49] Directive 2007/66/EC stipulates explicitly that Member States are asked to adopt a provision respecting the minimum conditions set up in Art. 2 a- 2c, because the absence of such a period has been considered one of the most bemoaned weaknesses of the Remedies Directives in existence. In particular, an adequate period should elapse between the decision to award a contract and its conclusion. It is for multiple reasons that a certain period should apply before the conclusion of the contract finally takes places. First, the award of the contract or at least its conclusion is *irreversible* which is why legal action should be taken as early as possible in order to prevent a probably illegal conclusion of a contract.[50] The contract cannot be concluded unless this period has elapsed. Secondly, the applying bidder or candidate is given sufficient time to *think thoroughly* about his chances, intentions and risks of initiating a review procedure which is time consuming and costly.

In Germany, § 101 a I 3-5 GWB, largely gearing to the wording of the respective provisions of Directive 2007/66/EC, govern the standstill period. The duration of the standstill period lies in the Member State`s discretion. Germany enjoys the freedom to exceed or maintain the minimum standstill period as envisioned in Art. 2 a II. Additional orientation is given by the requirement that 'the standstill period should give the tenderers concerned sufficient time to examine the contract award decision and to assess whether it is appropriate to initiate a review procedure' (recital 6 of Directive 2007/66/EC).

In transposition of Art. 2 a II and the idea anchored in recital 5 of the New Remedies Directive, the duration of the standstill period is dependent on the chosen means of communication. In order to clarify: A contract may not be concluded before the expiry of a period of 15 calendar days with effect from

49. ECJ, Case 81/98-Alcatel [2000], ECR I-7671, NZBau 2000, p. 33.
50. Hertwig, Stefan, *Praxis der öffentlichen Auftragsvergabe*, 4th edn., München 2010, p. 151; Brauer, Eva, 'Das Verfahren vor der Vergabekammer' NZBau 2009, p. 297.

the day following the date on which the information falling in the scope of § 101 a I 1-3 GWB has been sent to the tenderer or candidate. If fax or electronic means are used, a 10-day period applies, again, taking effect from the day following the date on which the information (contract award decision) has been sent. According to § 101 a I 4 GWB, the receipt of the information is not relevant, but the dispatch is.[51] By virtue of this provision, deadlines can be calculated relatively easily.

Bidders who have not yet been lawfully excluded and candidates in the sense of § 107 II GWB are deemed to be concerned. Presuming that the contracting authority awards the contract without adhering to the standstill obligation, bidders are entitled to initiate a review procedure for ineffectiveness (§ 101 b I No. 1 GWB), too. If the standstill period elapses, the contract can officially be awarded, implicating legal clarity and legal certainty.[52]

Art. 2 b of Directive 2007/66/EC allows for certain derogations from the generally binding standstill period. Germany does not cover this topic explicitly. Notwithstanding, the analysis of § 101 a II GWB contains valuable hints that the standstill period must not be complied with in exceptional circumstances. As information is not required in case of a negotiations procedure without prior negotiation (extreme urgency), the duty of preliminary information does not apply. And if the information is not sent, the standstill period cannot begin to run. Thus, the rules of the standstill period do not apply in case of extreme urgency.

All in all, the German rules transposing are fully compatible with European law.

4 Establishment of a breach by the review body (§ 114 I 1, clause 1 GWB)

According to § 114 I GWB, the *procurement tribunals* find themselves in the competence to decide on the infringement of bidder's rights enjoyed under § 97 VII GWB. Besides, the review bodies are due to choose appropriate means to firstly remedy the infringement and secondly prevent further harm.

51. Dreher, Meinrad/Hoffmann, Jens, 'Die Informations- und Wartepflicht sowie die Unwirksamkeitsfolge nach den neuen §§ 101 a und 101 b GWB' NZBau 2009, p. 218.
52. Dreher, Meinrad/Hoffmann, Jens, 'Die Informations- und Wartepflicht sowie die Unwirksamkeitsfolge nach den neuen §§ 101 a und 101 b GWB' NZBau 2009, p. 218.

Clearly, this provision is known to be one of the most important and frequently used procedures provided by the German remedies system. The significance of it increases markedly whenever a breach could not be prevented from happening or healed with the help of one of the interim measures quoted above.

As a matter of fact, the establishment of the breach is considered *the* fundamental requirement for all legal steps and consequences that are to follow. The decision of the review chamber is endowed with binding force, which is why procurement tribunals very much resemble courts.[53]

Notwithstanding, the tribunal's decision on the infringement of bidder's rights pursuant to § 97 VII GWB is not explicitly declared at all[54] – the ascertainment of the breach is made implicitly when the review chamber issues the administrative act[55] and announces the measures considered appropriate to rectify the infringement and prevent further damage to the interests of the bidders involved. The latter guarantee that the procurement procedure in question is either ended or – if continued – from now on in conformity with public procurement law. The affirmation itself is of no use unless concrete guidance is given by the tribunals. As § 114 I 1, 1.clause must be regarded as a non-independent procedure, the tenor of the judgment does not expressly include the establishment of the breach, either.[56]

The whole procedure starts with the examination of the application.[57] At this stage, the review body probes whether the formal requirements dealt with in § 107 GWB (time limits, locus standi or earlier objection) are fully complied with. If this is the case, the body will take a closer look on the substantial part of the application, namely examining whether the subjective rights of claiming bidder have actually been infringed in. In the affirmative, the procurement tribunals are enabled to actively exert influence on the procurement procedure. It is to say that they enjoy a far-reaching freedom concerning

53. Maier, in: Kulartz, Hans-Peter/Kus, Alexander/Portz, Norbert, *Kommentar zum GWB-Vergaberecht*, Werner Verlag, Köln 2006, § 114 GWB para 3.
54. Maier, in: Kulartz, Hans-Peter/Kus, Alexander/Portz, Norbert, *Kommentar zum GWB-Vergaberecht*, Werner Verlag, Köln 2006, § 114 GWB para 11.
55. Mertens, in: Franke, Horst/Kemper, Ralf/Zanner, Christian/Grünhagen, Matthias, *VOB Kommentar*, 4th edn., Werner Verlag, Köln 2010, § 21a VOB/A para 42.
56. Kus, in: Niebuhr, Frank/Kulartz, Hans-Peter/Kus, Alexander/Portz, Norbert, *Kommentar zum Vergaberecht*, Luchterhand, Neuwied 2000, § 114 GWB para 24.
57. Kus, in: Niebuhr, Frank/Kulartz, Hans-Peter/Kus, Alexander/Portz, Norbert, *Kommentar zum Vergaberecht*, Luchterhand, Neuwied 2000, § 114 GWB para 2.

which legal paths could best be taken.[58] Therefore, a procurement tribunal may decide to issue commands or give advice as which procedural steps should be taken by the contracting authority. A tribunal might, for example, propose that a certain bidder or bid should better be included, that the authority should catch up with its notification duties, better start the whole procedure afresh or simply bring the procedure to an end by adhering to the law.[59] But it is impossible for the tribunal to recommend the inclusion of other award criteria or the purchase of a different service, as it is not competent to voice concern about the rationality of the purchase. And since the contracting authority is known as 'the boss of the procedure' and an obligation to contract is unknown to procurement law,[60] the review body cannot proactively govern the conclusion of the contract in the sense that it commands which bid should be granted the contract.[61] Another restriction stems from the immunity of the concluded contract. Once concluded, a contract award decision cannot be set aside, § 114 II 1 GWB. Among the possibilities to utter recommendations, the procurement body might also impact the procurement procedure by announcing the direct annulment of the procedure due to failure.

Concluding, the reviewing body is basically free to choose between different measures to install legality and prevent further damage to the bidder's interests. Still, the decision has to be made within the boundaries set by the procurement principles flanked by the principle of proportionality.[62]

Contrary to the flexibility the system offers relating to the decision of which measures are appropriate once the infringement is proven,[63] the intensity of control regarding the establishment of the breach itself is not quite as vast. This is mainly due to the contracting entity enjoying a margin of discre-

58. Grabitz, Eberhard/Hilf, Meinhard, *Das Recht der europäischen Union*, Band IV, Öffentliches Auftragswesen, E 18 para. 40.
59. Mertens, in: Franke, Horst/Kemper, Ralf/Zanner, Christian/Grünhagen, Matthias, *VOB Kommentar*, 4th edn., Werner Verlag, Köln 2010, § 21a VOB/A para 42.
60. Portz, in: Kulartz, Hans-Peter/Marx, Fridhelm/Portz, Norbert/Prieß, *Hans-Joachim, Kommentar zur VOB/A*, Werner Verlag, Köln 2010, § 17 VOB/A para 58.
61. Portz, Kulartz, Hans-Peter/Marx, Fridhelm/Portz, Norbert/Prieß, *Hans-Joachim, Kommentar zur VOB/A*, Werner Verlag, Köln 2010, § 17 VOB/A para 58.
62. Byok, Jan/Jaeger, Wolfgang, *Kommentar zum GWB Vergaberecht*, 2nd ed., Verlag Recht und Wirtschaft, Frankfurt a.M. 2005, § 114 GWB para 1071; Maier, in: Kulartz/Kus/Portz, Kommentar zum GWB-Vergaberecht, § 114 GWB para 13.
63. Kus, in: Niebuhr, Frank/Kulartz, Hans-Peter/Kus, Alexander/Portz, Norbert, *Kommentar zum Vergaberecht*, Luchterhand, Neuwied 2000, § 114 GWB para 34; Grabitz, Eberhard/Hilf, Meinhard, *Das Recht der europäischen Union*, Band IV, Öffentliches Auftragswesen, E 18 para. 40.

tion in the procedure. In consequence, tribunals can only examine whether the contracting authority acted arbitrarily, made an obviously wrong decision, based its decision on false and improperly investigated facts, made off-topic considerations or use of invalid assessment factors or standards.[64]

Completing, the procurement tribunal is in general not bound by the contents of the application. Nevertheless, it is not given the authority to enter into a comprehensive examination of the whole procedure. Finding relief irrespective of the infringement claimed (§ 114 I S. 2GWB) is not allowed.[65] The decision should be made within five weeks after the application has been filed (§§ 113, 114 GWB). If it be the case, a prolongation may be granted, but this extra-time should not spread over more than two weeks.[66]

In case of an application for review in the sense of § 114 I 1. clause GWB being settled due to either the grant of the award, cancellation/cessation of the award or otherwise, the tribunal in competence may only declare whether a breach has happened and bidder's rights (§ 97 VII GWB) have been actually infringed,[67] § 114 II 2 GWB. Thereby, the illegality of a finished procedure can be positively affirmed while concrete healing measures cannot be instructed any more.[68]

64. Byok, in: Byok, Jan/Jaeger, Wolfgang, *Kommentar zum GWB Vergaberecht*, 2nd ed., Verlag Recht und Wirtschaft, Frankfurt a.M. 2005, § 114 GWB para 1071.
65. Maier, in: Kulartz, Hans-Peter/Kus, Alexander/Portz, Norbert, *Kommentar zum GWB-Vergaberecht*, Werner Verlag, Köln 2006, § 114 GWB para 12; Kus, in: Niebuhr, Frank/Kulartz, Hans-Peter/Kus, Alexander/Portz, Norbert, *Kommentar zum Vergaberecht*, Luchterhand, Neuwied 2000, § 114 GWB para 34.
66. Mertens, in: Franke, Horst/Kemper, Ralf/Zanner, Christian/Grünhagen, Matthias, *VOB Kommentar*, 4th ed., Werner Verlag, Köln 2010, § 21a VOB/A para 41.
67. See Portz, in: Kulartz, Hans-Peter/Marx, Fridhelm/Portz, Norbert/Prieß, Hans-Joachim, *Kommentar zur VOB/A*, Werner Verlag, Köln 2010, § 17 VOB/A para 56; Mertens, in: Franke, Horst/Kemper, Ralf/Zanner, Christian/Grünhagen, Matthias, *VOB Kommentar*, 4th ed., Werner Verlag, Köln 2010, § 21a VOB/A para 90 ff. and Conrad, Sebastian, 'Der Rechtsschutz gegen die Aufhebung eines Vergabeverfahrens bei Fortfall des Vergabewillens' NZBau 2007, pp. 287 ff. for more detailed information.
68. Byok, in: Byok, Jan/Jaeger, Wolfgang, *Kommentar zum GWB Vergaberecht*, 2nd. ed., Verlag Recht und Wirtschaft, Frankfurt a.M. 2005, f§ 114 GWB para 1077 ff.; Kus, in: Niebuhr, Frank/Kulartz, Hans-Peter/Kus, Alexander/Portz, Norbert, *Kommentar zum Vergaberecht*, Luchterhand, Neuwied 2000, § 114 GWB para 43.

5 Annulment by the review body

The aforesaid outlined that a procurement tribunal is empowered to take the appropriate means to end the infringement and prevent further damage once the breach of § 97 VII GWB has been officially affirmed. This being so, annulment lies in the competence of the examining body as well. Notwithstanding its general importance, the main features of this review instrument will only be discussed in brief.

Annulment or setting aside of unlawful decisions is not only a dictate evolving from the Directive, it is a necessity stemming from the fundamental public procurement principles (transparency, competition and non-discrimination) and, of course, the imperative of effectiveness. The reviewing body can either opt for the removal of single discriminating specifications irrespective of their content (e.g. financial, technical or economical) or their importance (substantial influence on the award process), or the discriminating or unlawful decisions can be set aside (see Art. 2 I b of Directive 2007/66/EC). The word 'decision' has a wider meaning than in current usage: there are not many restrictions regarding nature or content. Due to its extensive meaning, multiple stages of the award procedure can be affected and a wide range of determinations (either final or interlocutory) is amenable to judicial review. This means that even the decision to initiate an award can be dealt with in front of a judicial review body.[69] Furthermore, the termination of an award procedure, its illegal cessation,[70] the rejection of a single tender,[71] the decision about the bidder`s suitability or exclusion or every other decision infringing a protective law norm (§ 97 VII GWB) can be examined. Market survey studies, internal considerations or any other kind of solely preparing

69. Niestedt, Marian/Prieß, Hans-Joachim, *Rechtsschutz im Vergaberecht*, Carl Heymanns Verlag, Köln 2006, p. 15.
70. The question whether the contracting authority's decision to cease the procedure could be reviewed has been controversially discussed in Germany. At the beginning, the courts mainly held that review was not possible as the other way of terminating a procedure (conclusion of the contract) could not be examined either. Due to a decision of the ECJ, the German courts, including the BGH changed their opinion. Nowadays, the illegal cessation of the procedure can be annulled, too. C.f. Portz, in: Kulartz, Hans-Peter/Marx, Fridhelm/Portz, Norbert/Prieß, Hans-Joachim, *Kommentar zur VOB/A*, Werner Verlag, Köln 2010, § 17 VOB/A para 51; ECJ, VergabeR 2002, pp. 361 ff.; BGH, VergabeR 2003, pp. 40 ff.
71. Kus, in: Niebuhr, Frank/Kulartz, Hans-Peter/Kus, Alexander/Portz, Norbert, *Kommentar zum Vergaberecht*, Luchterland, Neuwied 2000, § 114 GWB para 36.

character are not amenable, however,[72] Most importantly, changes and decisions *after* the conclusion of the contract cannot be set aside,[73] too.

Besides, the only restrictions concerning annulment derive from the principle of proportionality.[74] As the setting aside of important award decisions affects interests of the general public and the interest in a fast award procedure, annulment should only be chosen '*ultima ratio*',[75] meaning that annulment is the appropriate means only if the duration, gravity, intensity of the infringement and the importance of the bidder's interests involved require so.[76]

It is worth noticing that the European rules of setting aside have not been fully adapted in Germany. This is mainly due to fact that the differentiation between the contract award decision and the conclusion of the contract is unknown to the German procurement system. In reiteration, the contract award decision and the conclusion of the contract coincide. Keeping the 'pacta-sunt-servanda'-rule and the interests of the contract partners involved in mind, a contract award decision cannot be set aside.[77] Strictly speaking, this means that even an unlawfully awarded contract remains effective,[78] which is emphasized by § 114 II 1 GWB in particular.

Actually, once the contract award decision has been made, the decision at issue is immune to any other remedy than that of damages. But immunity follows only if the award decision is effective. In case of an infringement against § 101a I GWB or § 101b I No. 1, 2 GWB, the contract award decision can still be reviewed.[79]

72. ECJ, Case 26/03-*Stadt Halle* [2005] ECR I-33-39.
73. Jennert, in: Müller-Wrede, Malte (ed.), *Kompaktkommentar Vergaberecht*, Bundesanzeiger Verlag, Köln 2008, p. 610.
74. Diemon-Wies, in: Maibaum, Oliver/Hattig, Thomas, *Praxiskommentar Kartellvergaberecht*, Bundesanzeiger Verlag, Köln 2010, § 114 GWB para 18 f.; Weyand, Rudolf, *Praxiskommentar Vergaberecht*, 2nd ed., Werner Verlag, Köln 2007, § 114 GWB para 2175.
75. Maier, in: Kulartz, Hans-Peter/Kus, Alexander/Portz, Norbert, *Kommentar zum GWB-Vergaberecht*, Werner Verlag, Köln 2006, § 114 GWB para 12; Byok, in: Byok, Jan/Jaeger, Wolfgang, *Kommentar zum Vergaberecht*, 2nd. ed., Verlag Recht und Wirtschaft, Frankfurt a.M. 2005, § 114 GWB para 1071.
76. Byok, in: Byok, Jan/Jaeger, Wolfgang, *Kommentar zum Vergaberecht*, 2nd. ed., Verlag Recht und Wirtschaft, Frankfurt a.M. 2005, § 114 GWB para 1071.
77. Grabitz, Eberhard/ Hilf, Meinhard, *Das Recht der europäischen Union*, Band IV, Öffentliches Auftragswesen, E 18 para 45.
78. Of course, effectiveness can only be given if a procedure according to § 101 b GWB has not taken place.
79. Diemon-Wies, in: Maibaum, Oliver/Hattig, Thomas, *Praxiskommentar Kartellvergaberecht*, Bundesanzeiger Verlag, Köln 2010, § 114 GWB para 35.

All the same, this German construction is suspected of not being compatible with European law. But as Germany is known for its ample and fully developed interlocutory relief system (as shown above), the principle of effectiveness has *not* been violated. Softly spoken, the German approach is probably even the better one, because it appears to be more effective as infringements should primarily be eliminated and corrected at the earliest stage possible. Setting aside is an effective means as well, but takes effect much later. In the latter case, it is likely that a costly and time-consuming award process has to be re-started again provided that the contracting authority is still determined to procure. Interim measures are always the better way to 'sanction' a breach. But this does not prevent a bidder from initiating both review procedures. It just means that it is advisable to initiate a review procedure at the earliest time possible instead of risking the conclusion of the contract leading to immunity of the decision.

Taking everything into account, the German regime regarding setting aside conforms with European law and is effective.

6 Ineffectiveness

6.1 Overview

Measures taking effect before the contract is finally concluded, are of the utmost importance. Nevertheless, not every breach can be corrected at the earliest moment possible, because it might happen that bidders get aware of an infringement too late or the conditions of the review measures available were not fulfilled. Therefore, an effective remedies system requires additional review mechanisms, something like a *back up* in case interim measures, preliminary information or the standstill period is not effective enough. In Germany, there are two ways of review measures ex post: the newly installed remedy of ineffectiveness and the 'well established' remedy of damages. As its scope of application bears relation to § 101 a GWB, enshrining the rule about preliminary information, this provision will be reported before the conditions and main features of ineffectiveness are outlined more closely.

6.2 Preliminary information: the contracting authority's duty

The following section focuses on the specifics of the contracting authority`s obligation of *preliminary information*. The norm governing preliminary information belongs to the rules applying before the conclusion of the contract, as they intend to correct infringements as soon as possible. By means of preliminary information, the legislature tried to find the best way to prevent a contract from being concluded so that bidders do not have the chance to file an application for review and are solely left with the chance to get compensated.

In the past, Germany maintained a specific provision about preliminary information, which is not expressly required by European law. What has been § 13 VgV in the past, is now § 101 a GWB.

This provision is of crucial relevance: § 101 a GWB decides about the exact date of the standstill period taking effect. In turn, an infringement of the latter indicates ineffectiveness according to § 101 b I No. 1 GWB.

In compliance with the constraints following from Art. 2 a I of the Remedies Directive, § 101 a I 1 GWB requires the contracting authority to keep tenderers and candidates equally informed. That is to say that the name of the winning entity, all[80] the reasons why the person concerned has not been considered and the earliest date possible for the conclusion of the contract[81] have to be announced (Art. 2 a II (4)). If the contract award procedure is very complex, the information given should be more detailed. In any case, the mere information that the bidder has not been the best bidder is not sufficient.

The communication should be given in writing and should embrace all reasons alongside a comprehensive comment about the decisive circumstances.[82] *Tenderers* are deemed to be concerned if they have not been definitely excluded yet (cf. § 101 a I 1 GWB; Art. 2 a II (1) Dir. 2007/66/EC) whereas *candidates* are considered to be concerned if the contracting authority failed to make available the information about the rejection of their application before the notification of the contract award decision to the tenderers concerned (§ 101 a I 2 GWB; Art. 2 a II (3) Dir. 2006/77/EC).

As mentioned earlier, the effect of the standstill period is strictly dependent on the notification of the preliminary information. Even the form of communication has an impact on it in the sense that the awarded contract should not be concluded before the expiry of a period of ten calendar days following the date on which the contract award decision has been sent via fax

80. Egidy, Stefanie, 'Das GWB-Vergaberecht nach der Novelle 2009; Flexibel, europarechtskonform und endlich von Dauer?' DÖV 2009, p. 840; Kratzenberger, Rüdiger, 'Der Begriff des „Öffentlichen Auftraggeber" und der Entwurf des Gesetzes zur Modernisierung des Vergaberecht' NZBau 2009, pp. 119, 120.
81. The contract can be concluded if the standstill period elapses, this constitutes the earliest time possible.
82. Dreher, Meinrad/Hoffmann, Jens, 'Die Informations- und Wartepflicht sowie die Unwirksamkeitsfolge nach den neuen § 101 a und § 101 b GWB' NZBau 2009, p. 216.

or by other electronic means. If other mediums of communications are used, the standstill period elapses no earlier than a period of at least 15 calendar days. In consequence, the standstill period does not start supposing that the notice of the contract award decision fails to be sent.[83]

Pursuant to § 101 a II GWB, the obligation to keep tenderers and candidates equally informed about the award decision and all the decisive reasons does not apply in a negotiations procedure without prior publication due to urgency.

The main rationale underlying the provision of § 101 a GWB is that the parties interested in the contract award are endowed with sufficient time and all information necessary to consider lodging an action for ineffectiveness and weighing up their chances of success within a review procedure. Therefore, German experts in public procurement law comprehensively suggest that the contracting entity should also give a precise statement about the bidder`s rank in the award procedure, revealing further information about success chances.[84]

It is of interest to know that German procuring entities showed compliance and indeed vigilant behavior regarding the adherence to the preliminary information-rule. In the past, only few cases have been discussed in front of judicial bodies which is not tantamount to the absence of problems and legal insecurities in this field. As problems of interpretation are not specifically invoked by the adoption of Directive 2007/66/EC but have existed for quite a long time, they are rather briefly touched. The main questions center around a situation when the award of the contract is made in full accordance with the minimum standstill period although the information delivered did not contain remarks about the exact standstill period and its expiry (that is to say information about the earliest time possible for the award decision) or if the standstill deadline which has been announced does not correspond with the real standstill period. Analyzing the first case, § 101 b I No. 1 presupposes that an infringement of the rules anchored in § 101 a GWB (and such has obviously taken place due to the contracting body disregarding preliminary information) entails ineffectiveness. This question has been and is until now, debated controversially within German literature and jurisprudence. With view to Art. 2 d

83. Dreher, Meinrad/Hoffmann, Jens, 'Die Informations- und Wartepflicht sowie die Unwirksamkeitsfolge nach den neuen § 101 a und § 101 b GWB' NZBau 2009, p. 218.
84. Byok, Jan, 'Die Entwicklung des Vergaberechts seit 2008' NJW 2009, p. 297.

I b of the Directive,[85] some voices reiterate that ineffectiveness unconditionally calls for a sufficiently serious breach of public procurement law which is why the violation of a procedural law (establishing a duty of preliminary information) is not deemed sufficient. Other rulings however focus on the wording of § 101 a I No.1 GWB and conclude that the contract should be considered ineffective in any case. Regarding the second problem (deadline not in correspondence with the standstill period), a pathbreaking, universally accepted solution has not yet been found. Up to now, some courts consider the contract to be ineffective[86] while others preferred to keep the validity of the contract at issue.[87]

Closing, it can be said that Germany enacted a provision safeguarding the bidder`s review chances. Being kept sufficiently informed is certainly one of the most important requirements for weighing up whether the initiation of a costly and time-consuming relief procedure is worthwhile. If a contracting entity acts in violation of the standstill period (concludes the contract despite the standstill period), the contract is void (§§ 134, 138 BGB).[88]

6.3 Ineffectiveness

The particularly fundamental relief of *ineffectiveness* appeared simultaneously with the adoption of the new Remedies Directive 2007/66/EC, dictating the concern to establish fast and, more importantly, effective review mechanisms. Art. 2 d of the said Directive dictates that aggrieved bidders should be given the possibility to lodge an action against the contract award decision. According to this provision, 'Member States shall ensure that a contract is considered ineffective by a review body…or that its ineffectiveness is the result of such a body', whereas Art. 2 II Dir. 2007/66/EC prevails that consequences and conditions shall be provided for by national law. The German rules in transposition are basically governed by § 101 b GWB. It is worthwhile noticing that the main features of ineffectiveness are closely intertwined with § 101 a GWB, covering the standstill period and the duty of preliminary information at the same time.

This remedy is considered to be the most effective way to restore competition and grant new business opportunities to the aggrieved bidders who have

85. Art. 2 d I b Directive 2007/66/EC requires a breach of Directive 2004/18/EC or 2004/17/EC which has affected the bidder's chances of review.
86. OLG Düsseldorf, 23.5.2007, Verg 14/07.
87. OLG Brandenburg, 5.3.2007, Verg 4/07.
88. Weyand, Rudolf, *Praxiskommentar Vergaberecht*, 2nd. ed., Werner Verlag Köln 2007, § 114 para 2300, 2306.

been unlawfully deprived thereof earlier.[89] Ineffectiveness is particularly important regarding the prevention of direct awards whereby contracting agencies seek to establish a *fait accompli.*

6.3.1 Its scope

A successful application for ineffectiveness is tantamount to the bidder`s satisfying two main requirements cumulatively. First, the contracting authority must have acted contrary to procurement law. In order to be more concrete: an infringement of the obligations deriving from § 101 a GWB (§ 101 b I No.1 GWB) or a so- called 'de-facto'- contract award (§ 101 b I No. 2 GWB) constitute the two constitutive requirements. Beginning with § 101 b I No.1 GWB and recalling earlier remarks already made in this article (see 5.2), it is currently controversially debated in German literature and jurisdiction whether an infringement of the preliminary information rule alone is sufficient enough to promote a successful application.

Focusing on the second kind of infringement, a request for ineffectiveness is also possible if the contracting authority awarded a contract directly to a private entity without considering other competitors and without permission to do so.

Second, the alleged infringement has to be ascertained and considered ineffective by a review body and in accordance with the procedure outlined in § 101 b II GWB. This requirement can be regarded as the most decisive one in this context and finds itself in full compliance with Art. 2 d I of amending Directive 2007/66/EC, stipulating 'that a contract is considered ineffective by a review body independent of the contracting authority or that its ineffectiveness is the result of a decision of such a review body'.

Hence, the award of the contract is not ineffective per se but always implies an application and the respective decision of an independent review body.[90] In the past, German law in the field of procurement did not contain a provision for ineffectiveness. The formerly installed § 13 VgV called for (direct) voidance of the contract. Thus, an ascertainment of voidance by a judicial body was not necessarily needed. Today, the procurement tribunal's declaration of ineffectiveness is designed as a basic requirement.

Reiterating, an application for ineffectiveness requires 1) an infringement in the sense of § 101 b I No. 1 or § 101 b I No. 2 GWB and 2) the ascertainment of that infringement by the competent review body.

89. Recital 4 of Directive 2007/66/EC.
90. Dreher, Meinrad/Hoffmann, Jens, 'Die schwebende Unwirksamkeit nach § 101 b I GWB' NZBau 2010, pp. 202, 203.

As a rule, the consequences of ineffectiveness should be determined by national law (see recital 21), meaning that Germany is free to decide about either providing rules for retroactive cancellation (ineffectiveness *ex tunc*) or limit the scope of cancellation to those obligations which still have to be performed (ineffectiveness *ex nunc*).[91] Supposing that a Member State decides in favor of the latter, alternative penalties within the meaning of Art. 2 e of Directive 2007/66/EC, covering e.g. the imposition of fines or the shortening of the contract, should be made available. Generally speaking, the penalties chosen should find themselves in compliance with the requirements of legal certainty (proportionate, dissuasive and clear). To the extent that obligations following from the contract have already been fulfilled, the Member State concerned can either install provisions on the recovery of the sums which may have been paid or provide for different forms of restitution (e.g. restitution in value if restitution in kind is not possible).

6.3.2 Its main characteristics

Now that the possibilities and the scope offered by European law have been presented, it is time to dwell on the characteristics of the 'German way': with view to the truly clear wording of § 101 b GWB ('A public contract is considered ineffective *from the beginning*, if ...'), the German legislature opted for the first alternative, that is to say ineffectiveness in the sense of *ex tunc*. Notwithstanding, questions concerning the application and handling in practice, are not settled yet. On the contrary, it is highly contested if the norm should be interpreted in the sense that the contract in question is endowed with provisional effectiveness[92] or provisional ineffectiveness.[93] In any case, the relevance of this issue should not be underestimated as a relatively (see below) long time might elapse until the final ascertaining decision of the review body or the contract is immensely important due to economical reasons. Some opinions hold that the ineffectiveness is hovering over the contract unless the contract has officially been considered effective.[94] The concept of provisional ineffectiveness, is apparently more consistent with the wording of

91. See Art. 2 d II of Directive 2007/66/EC.
92. Dreher, Meinrad/Hoffmann, Jens, 'Die schwebende Unwirksamkeit nach § 101 b I GWB' NZBau 2010, p. 206; Dreher, Meinrad/Hoffmann, Jens, 'Die Informations- und Wartepflicht sowie die Unwirksamkeitsfolge nach den neuen § 101 a und § 101 b GWB' NZBau 2009, p. 218; Recommendations of the Deutscher Baugerichtstag, 7./8.5.2010, www.baugerichtstag.de.
93. Brauer, Eva, 'Das Verfahren vor der Vergabekammer' NZBau 2009, p. 297.
94. Brauer, Eva, 'Das Verfahren vor der Vergabekammer' NZBau 2009, p. 297.

§ 101 b I GWB (from the beginning).[95] On the other hand, it seems more reasonable to vote for provisional effectiveness. This is mainly for two reasons. First, a contract cannot be considered ineffective unless the procurement tribunal declares so, meaning that a contract stays valid. This directly implies that the contract has been effective from the beginning. Second, in consequence to this solution, the contractual obligations could still be fulfilled[96] and the unjust enrichment theory would not be applicable. The norms (§§ 812 I 1, 1. alternative BGB, § 818 BGB) are only relevant if the infringement under § 101 I b GWB has been declared and the exchange of services has therefore been happening devoid of a legal basis.[97] By virtue of §§ 812 I, 818 I BGB, the obtained is generally to be returned *in natura*. As this is mostly impossible, compensation for lost value has to be made (§ 818 II BGB). Since the rules on effectiveness are still very young, there are not many illustrative judgments available. Therefore, it is not fully clear and it can only be anticipated, which costs might be included.

Judging from the *telos* of the provision, a contract is endowed with provisional effectiveness as long as the review body decided upon the issue. The obligations resulting from the contract should be effective, otherwise, legal incertainty would be created needlessly.

Apart from this controversy, the Directive[98] provides for multiple derogations as the European legislature opines that ineffectiveness is not the appropriate legal consequence in any case. If exceptional circumstances require so or overriding reasons of general interest need to be respected, the effects of the contract should be maintained and the contract should not be jeopardized. Surprisingly, the relevant German provision does not explicitly allow for such derogations, which is why experts in procurement law fight for a comparable provision.[99]

Turning the focus back on further specifics concerning the admissibility of initiating a review procedure for ineffectiveness, a preclusive time limit applies. The application should be initiated on time as set up by § 101 b II

95. Brauer, Eva, 'Das Verfahren vor der Vergabekammer' NZBau 2009, p. 297; OLG Brandenburg, 22.4.2010, Verg W 5/10.
96. Dreher, Meinrad/Hoffmann, Jens, 'Die schwebende Unwirksamkeit nach § 101 b I GWB' NZBau 2010, p. 206.
97. Dreher, Meinrad/Hoffmann, Jens, 'Die schwebende Unwirksamkeit nach § 101 b I GWB' NZBau 2010, p. 206..
98. Art. 2 d III, IV and recital 22 of Directive 2007/66/EC.
99. See Recommendations of the Deutscher Baugerichtstag, 7./8.5.2010, www.baugerichtstag.de.

GWB. To be more precisely, an application for ineffectiveness must be made before the expiry of 30 calendar days taking effect from the day following the date on which the bidder becomes aware of the infringement but should in any case be made no later than the expiry of a period of at least six months after the conclusion of the contract. Alternately if the contracting authority published a contract in the Official Journal of the European Union (OJ), the time limit does not end before the expiry of 30 calendar days with effect from the day following the date on which the contracting authority published the contract award notice accordingly. The time limits chosen by the German legislator transform Art. 2 f of Directive 2007/66/EC.

Recently, the implementation of Art. 2 f I a (first indent) of the Remedies Directive 2007/66/EC in German procurement law gives cause for concern.[100] This article stipulates that the time limit for an application for ineffectiveness is only applicable if the contracting authority published a notification of the award alongside reasons for the de-facto-award. According to the national norm in transposition (§ 101 b II GWB), however, this shortened time limit already applies if the public purchaser only published a notification in the Official Journal of the European Union. It is contested, whether this transposition finds itself in compliance with European requirements. Originally, the 30-days-rule is only relevant if a correct and complete notification (covering the reasons for a de-facto award) is published in the OJ; otherwise, the desired legal certainty can only take effect after 6 months.[101] According to the ruling of a German Court,[102] the time limit set out in § 101 b II 2 GWB finds itself in accordance with European law. As long as bidders know about the award because its notification has been published in the OJ, they are able to introduce the legal remedy of ineffectiveness and inform themselves about the legal requirements for a successful remedies procedure. The information about the reasons why the contracting authority opts for a de-facto-regime has – strictly speaking – no influence on the availability of legal protection. Nevertheless, the competent body (workshop II for procurement law) of the Deutscher Baugerichtstag recommends in unision to follow the wording of the European Directive and integrate the contracting authority`s obligation to

100. Prieß, Hans-Joachim, 'Umsetzung materieller Richtlinien sowie der neuen Rechtsmittelrichtlinie in deutsches nationales Recht', Arbeitskreis II, Thesenpapier, Deutscher Baugerichtstag 2010.
101. But the applying bidder would not be affected in his right to prove the legality of the award procedure.
102. OLG Schleswig Holstein, 1.4.2010, 1 Verg 5/09.

name the reasons why a notification of the award has not been made beforehand.[103]

After the expiry of the deadline outlined above, the contract is effective once and for all.[104] Thus, legal certainty is created.

Concerning the question of *who* can bring a claim for ineffectiveness, the rules laid down in § 107 GWB apply. These have been drafted in the introductory chapter. Furthermore, § 107 III No. 2-4 GWB governing the extinction of exercising the right to apply are relevant (see introduction as well).

Ineffectiveness is predestinated to give the aggrieved bidder sufficient time to appraise correctly the success chances of an appeal. The consequences of ineffectiveness are – in any case – narrowed to a maximum time limit of six months.

7 Damages[105]

As frequently pointed out, ineffectiveness and *damages* are the only form of relief applicable once a contract has been concluded. And a damages claim can be initiated irrespective of the success in a primary legal review procedure.[106] Therefore, damages appear in a very positive light – at first sight. Allocated to the secondary legal remedies system, they do not achieve great attention when compared to primary legal protection including interim measures, ineffectiveness or the setting aside of decisions. This is due to the fact that the damages procedure in Germany (not so much on the European level)[107] has been extremely low profiled and in lack of clarity despite its many and quite elaborate regulations. Furthermore, the aggrieved bidders are

103. See Recommendation of the Deutscher Baugerichtstag, 7./8.5.2010, www.baugerichtstag.de.
104. Except if an immediate complaint is filed.
105. Regarding the following contents on damages, referral should be made to last year's conference in London, entitled 'EC procurement: Damages as an effective remedy?'. The findings and conclusions among a comprehensive article about the German perspective can be found in Fairgrieve, Duncan/Lichère, Francois (eds.), EC *procurement: Damages as an effective Remedy?*, 2010.
106. If a bidder is precluded to initiate an application for review pursuant to § 114 I GWB, for example, this does not preclude him from seeking damages. For details, see Schneider, Tobias, *Primärrechtsschutz nach Zuschlagserteilung bei einer Vergabe öffentlicher Aufträge*, Duncker & Humblot, Berlin 2007, p. 159.
107. Treumer, Steen, 'Damages for Breach of the EC Public Procurement Rules – Changes in European Regulation and Practice' 15 PPLR (2006), p. 159 ff.

first and foremost interested in obtaining the award. Not surprisingly, applications for compensation are comparatively eclipsed.

Nevertheless, the secondary remedies system is developing ever since the European Commission tried to strengthen the national remedies systems by implementing the New Remedies Directive. Art. 2 I c of Directive 2007/66/-EC encompasses that each Member State is supposed to establish both a primary and a secondary legal remedies system which is why review procedures should mandatorily include powers to 'award damages to persons harmed by an infringement'. It should be briefly noted that the damages regime is classified as an area governed by private law. Therefore, the domestic sources for breach of EU procurement law are of private law character and do not stem from a genuine public procurement basis. The only true public procurement regulations are §§ 125, 126 GWB. They will be subject to the following remarks, but in order to give a full overview, the other, and sometimes even more advantageous bases for claim should be mentioned as well. They are either of tort law (viz. §§ 823 I, II, 826 BGB) or contractual nature, such as the quasi-contractual claim arising from the rules on the *Liability due to the breach of duty prior to contract*, widely known as the principle of *culpa in contrahendo* (c.i.c.). Cartel law (viz. §§ 20, 33 GWB) and the general rules of the liability of public authorities anchored in Art. 34 Basic Law (GG), § 839 BGB serve as additional basis of claim, but they remain of minor importance in practical law life.

Again, Directive 2007/66/EC just mentions that a review system containing secondary relief should be adapted in each member state without giving further advice on *how* the transposition should be made or *which rules* should be followed. At least, the review mechanism, enabling a bidder to seek compensation should be available 'at least to any person having or having had an interest in obtaining a particular contract and who has been or risks being harmed by an alleged infringement'.[108] In addition, general European principles, especially the principles of effectiveness and equivalence apply. In accordance with the prerequisite of availability, the demand of rapidity should be met by the national legislator as well,[109] and remembering the ECJ`s ruling in different cases, the criteria and conditions set up should not be too demanding and restricted. In fact they should not render practically impossible or excessively difficult the obtainment of damages. Sadly, the Remedies Di-

108. Directive 2007/66/EC, Art. 1 III.
109. Egger, Alexander, *Europäisches Vergaberecht*, Nomos, Baden-Baden 2008, § 126 GWB para 1573.

rective is silent on the quantum[110] or the conditions of damages. Such questions can be referred to the European Court of Justice due to Art. 267 TfEU (formerly Art. 234 EC).

7.1 § 126 GWB: compensation due to the loss of a 'genuine chance'

Keeping these nebulous requirements in mind, § 126 GWB, constituting an independent basis for a damages claim, will be examined closely.

First of all, it should be noted that this paragraph is of a two-fold character: on the one hand, it tends to protect each injured bidder by granting the right to seek damages (sanctioning character). On the other hand, public authorities awarding contracts are meant to be motivated to act in accordance with public procurement law unless they do not want to pay huge sums in compensation to all claiming parties (preventive character).

A claim based on this provision is held available for each and every enterprise as long as the bidding company succeeds in laying down sufficient proof of its 'genuine chance' and the violation of procurement rules conferring a subjective right to the respective claimant. By far the most contested and complicated requirement of a damages claim pursuant to § 126 1 GWB is the condition of the so-called 'genuine chance'. Astonishingly, it is commonly accepted in German law that a claimant is not obliged to really have participated in an award procedure before seeking redress. Even in advance of participation, a candidate may be considered to be having a 'genuine chance' when seeking adequate compensation for the preparatory work done.[111] Recovery is made for the loss of a chance. As long as the claimant suffered a loss or incurred costs causal to the award, he is endowed with the right to apply for compensation. The claimant has to present sufficient proof of his chance of being awarded the public contract. As opposed to other claims, it is not important to show that the unlawfully passed-over bidder would have definitely received the award would it not have been for the violation. Pertaining to the type of chance which must be proven in order to file a damages claim successfully, the following information gives a brief over-

110. The compensation paid due to the misbehaviour of the contracting entity should be adequate.

111. Arztmann, Franz-Josef, *Schadensersatz im Vergaberecht in Deutschland und Österreich,* Peter Lang Verlag, Frankfurt a.M. 2005, pp. 95, 96; Prieß, Hans-Joachim/Niestedt, Marian, *Rechtsschutz im Vergaberecht*, Carl Heymanns Verlag, Köln 2006, p. 166.

view of the multiple interpretations in existence. Some authors[112] are convinced that § 126 1 GWB requires the bidder to belong to the short list,[113] because only then a real chance of winning the contract could be legitimately presumed. Other legal experts postulate the submission of an acceptable bid fulfilling at least all formal requirements. According to a view based on an ex-post examination, a genuine chance is only given if the bidder would have received the award with the utmost probability.[114] Highlighting one last interpretation, possibly the most severe opinion, the bidder should be part of the top flight. Despite this heavily disputed condition (of a 'genuine chance'), it is a common conception that the claimant is meant to be considered the best of all participants but giving such an interpretation, the possibilities of seeking review would be far too restricted and therefore in breach of fundamental EU law rules (principle of effectiveness). On the other hand, the tender of the complainant should not rank so low that it would surely be excluded. For example in the case of obligatory cassation, a real chance cannot be observed.[115] Furthermore, a genuine chance can only be endued if the contracting authority made correct use of its margin of discretion.[116] Despite this difficult requirement, failure by the contracting authority does not need to be proven.[117]

A successful claim on the basis of § 126 1 GWB requires the violation of a public procurement provision intended to protect the bidder, that is to say a provision falling within the scope of § 97 VII GWB. The contracting rules for the award of public service contracts, public work contracts and contracts for professional services (VOL/A; VOB/A; VOF) and the Public Procurement Regulation (VgV) grant subjective rights.[118] Nonetheless, the protective law character has to be accurately proven in the case at issue.

112. Schnorbus, York, 'Der Schadensersatzanspruch des Bieters bei der fehlerhaften Vergabe öffentlicher Aufträge' BauR 1999, pp. 77, 93.
113. In the course of the reform in Germany (1999), it was seriously discussed to require bidders seeking compensation to belong to the short list, see BT-Drs. 13/9340, p. 9.
114. OLG Thüringen, 8.12.2008, Az. 9 U 431/08.
115. Alexander, Christian, 'Vergaberechtlicher Schadensersatz gemäß § 126 GWB' WrP 2009, p. 31.
116. Dreher, in: Immenga, Ulrich/Mestmäcker, Ernst-Joachim, *Wettbewerbsrecht*, 4th edn., C.H. Beck, München 2007, § 126 GWB para 13; Willenbruch, Klaus/Bischoff, Kristina, *Kompaktkommentar Vergaberecht*, Werner Verlag, Köln 2008, § 126 GWB para 17.
117. ECJ, Case 314/09-Stadt Graz, NZBau 2010, p. 773; Prieß, Hans-Joachim/Hölzl, Franz Josef, 'Drei Worte des EuGH: Schadensersatz ohne Verschulden!' NZBau 2011, p. 21 f.
118. Willenbruch, Klaus/Bischoff, Kristina, *Kompaktkommentar Vergaberecht,* Werner Verlag, Köln 2008, § 126 GWB paras 7-12.

As far as the amount of compensation is concerned, presumptions by virtue of § 287 ZPO (Code of Civil Procedure) assist the claimant. Besides, the approximate degree of the chance has an impact on the amount of damages awarded. Beyond doubt, the range of damages awarded by the judges is predominantly dependent on the individual case and based on detailed information about the enterprise, the economic importance of the contract, the annual company accounts or its usual profits (customary in a particular trade).[119]

According to the wording of § 126 1 GWB, this norm grants recovery solely and explicitly for all expenditures relating to the preparation of the tender and participation in an award procedure. It does not allow for the compensation for the interest in the performance of the contract (*lost profit*).[120] The recoverability of lost future business chances (*anticipatory profits*) cannot be claimed on the basis of § 126 1 GWB, either. As primary legal and secondary legal review systems constitute two independent systems, substantial procedural differences do exist. The ordinary courts are competent for all kinds of damages claims (covering § 126 1 GWB and the other damages claims likewise) due to the rules written down in §§ 13 GVG (Judicature Act), 104 II 2 GWB. Since award decisions are closely linked to the commercial field, the competency of chambers for commercial matters is initiated. Actions for damages are subject to a limitation period of three years (§§ 195, 199 BGB) with effect from the end of the year in which grounds for the application first arose and in which the unlawfully passed over bidder got aware of the unlawful act.

7.2 § 125 GWB: compensation due to the abuse of legal rights

The other damages claim specifically dealt with in public procurement law is § 125 GWB. This norm lies focus on compensation for the abuse of legal rights, especially the abuse of rights to initiate review procedures.[121] Being more concrete, the applicant or claimant who has abused his right to file an application or a complaint (the application has been unjustified from the

119. OLG Naumburg, 26.10.2004, ZfBR 2005, p. 215.

120. In view of the principle of effectiveness, other opinions are present as well. An effective remedies system implies the duty to grant adequate compensation, the amount of damages should not be assessed too low, see Egger, Alexander, *Europäisches Vergaberecht,* Nomos, Baden-Baden 2008, paras 1603-1604.

121. Immenga, Ulrich/Mestmäcker, Ernst-Joachim, *Wettbewerbsrecht*, 4th edn., C.H. Beck, München 2007, § 125 GWB para 2.

start)[122] is obliged to pay sums in compensation to the procedural opponent for the damage incurred (§ 125 I GWB). The applicant or claimant does not only abuse his procedural rights, he also does prolong the award procedure. Abuse is deemed to exist in particular if the applicant gave false data either intentionally or with gross negligence (§ 125 I No. 1 GWB) and this leads to suspension or further suspension of the award procedure. Abuse is also given if he initiated an application for review solely to obstruct the award procedure or to harm one of his competitors (§ 125 II No. 2 GWB) or if he applied for review with the intention of withdrawing his application for payment of money or other benefits (§ 125 II No. 3 GWB). Generally speaking, the conditions enabling a claim pursuant to § 125 GWB are subject to a very restrictive interpretation.

If the interim measures initiated by the contracting authority pursuant to an application on the basis of § 115 III GWB and taken by the review body were unjustified *ab initio*, the applying entity shall be compensated for the loss caused due to the measures that were ordered.

The procedural opponent is being compensated for the loss he incurred. He is put in exactly the same situation he would have been in without the review procedure (§ 249 BGB natural restitution).

In contrast to § 126 GWB, § 125 GWB shows much more similarities to a typical damages claim in the field of tort law than to a damages claim in the private law sector. Therefore, the limitation period of § 852 BGB[123] applies and the competency of the ordinary courts arises from §§ 12 ff. ZPO and 32 ZPO.

In conclusion, the German damages system can be regarded as a framework of different bases of claim (provisions in the field of procurement law, tort, public and cartel law). For the time being, a more or less 'well-oiled' damages review procedure is provided for, and as such it is largely meeting the requirements set up in the European Remedies directives.

122. One opinion in German literature requires e.g. that the application shall be considered 'a dead loss', see Immenga, Ulrich/Mestmäcker, Ernst-Joachim, *Wettbewerbsrecht*, 4th edn., C.H. Beck, München 2007, § 125 GWB para 5.

123. The period does not end before the expiry of a time of 10 years after the right to claim for damages began to exist or after the expiry of 30 years since the commission of the deed or the harmful event.

7.3 Damages to the contract party losing the contract due to ineffectiveness

Art. 2 I c of the New Remedies Directive contains the prerequisite that Member States shall provide an effective damages system in order to compensate for infringements in the field of public procurement law. As a rule, Member States are thus allowed to determine the basic rules about their preferred damages system as long as the relief mechanisms are made available to any person having or having had an interest in obtaining a particular public contract and who either has been or risks being harmed by an alleged infringement. Moreover, the mechanisms installed should be effective. Therefore, the said Directive does in no way reveal or define the scope of the damages system to be established within each and every Member State of the European Union, it does not contain information or conditions as to which costs can be compensated (anticipatory or lost profits) or if negligence influences the amount of damages granted. Subsequently, one very interesting comprehensive question appears in this context: Are there any possibilities offered by national law and enabling the contract party who has lost the contract due to the newly installed relief mechanism of ineffectiveness to claim for compensation?

As evidenced in the Directive`s rules on ineffectiveness (Art. 2 d), the German legislature is mainly free to decide about consequences and conditions of an application for ineffectiveness. German public procurement law itself does not contain a claim dedicated to compensation due to the loss of a contract being ineffective, as public procurement law is traditionally applicable only from the notification of an award procedure until the conclusion of the contract. Questions and problems concerning the contract itself are dealt with by civil law norms. Furthermore, § 126 GWB is – adjudicating upon its wording – not relevant as the claiming enterprise can only be compensated for the loss of his *chance* to win the contract. The contract party concerned, having already been awarded the contract (but the contract is ineffective), loses more than just the chance if the contract is considered ineffective. Maybe one could think about interpreting § 126 GWB more broadly in the future, probably in the sense that the bidder who just won the contract loses it again due to ineffectiveness. Although the party has actually been given the contract, the 'genuine chance' needs to be proven as well, the claimant has to prove that he should have been given the contract in any case – even if the failure leading to ineffectiveness would not have happened.[124] Nevertheless §

124. BGH, 26.1.2010, X ZR 86/08, NZBau 2010, pp. 387, 388.

126 GWB would only enable the party to seek compensation for the preparation of the tender and participation in the tendering process, damage for the lost contract itself is not envisioned. Neither does § 125 GWB (requiring the misuse of procedural rights of the applicant or complainant) establish an adequate basis for a damages claim in this regard, because § 125 GWB grants compensation to the contracting authority itself and not against it (ineffectiveness presupposes that a private entity has applied beforehand).

Taking everything into consideration, the only possible bases for a damages claim in favor of the contract party (private entity) who has lost the contract due to ineffectiveness are likely to be rooted in civil law. In Germany, a contract concluded in violation of the standstill period or a directly awarded contract is considered ineffective ab initio. The contracting authority acted contrary to public procurement law and therefore infringed the trust of its contractual partner. A claim on the basis of the institute of *culpa in contrahendo* as anchored in §§ 280 I, 311 II, 241 II BGB (c.i.c.) and governing the entity`s misbehavior when concluding the contract, may arise. This provision, rendering possible the compensation for lost profit under certain circumstances, develops importance the moment the entity losing the contract already made investments because it believed in the fulfillment and in the legality of the contract. Notwithstanding, the burden of proof lies with the claimant,[125] which is why this damages claim is not easy to get access to. Furthermore, the party losing the contract may initiate a claim on the basis of § 812 I 1, 1.alt. BGB.[126] As already mentioned in the section about ineffectiveness, the exchange of services happened without a legal basis. Therefore, the rules concerning unjust enrichment are applicable.

In addition, provisions stemming from tort law are worth mentioning, too. A bidder seeking compensation on the basis of provision § 823 I BGB, probably constituting the most important and popular basis for damages in Germany, can only assert a claim in case of culpable interference in the business enterprise in exercise. As a direct award and the violation of the standstill period cannot be said to be directed against the enterprise itself, § 823 I BGB is not relevant, either. § 823 II BGB in conjunction with the protective law norms § 101 a, b GWB (standstill period and ineffectiveness) could protect the contract party, especially in view of the fact that the superior provision of § 126 GWB is not applicable (principle of subsidiarity).

125. Dreher, Meinrad/Hoffmann, Jens,., Die schwebende Unwirksamkeit nach § 101 b I GWB' NZBau 2010, p. 206.
126. Dreher, Meinrad/Hoffmann, Jens, 'Die schwebende Unwirksamkeit nach § 101 b I GWB' NZBau 2010, p. 206.

By virtue of § 826 BGB, a contract party could be entitled to obtain reparation for the lost contract as well, at least in case the grounds leading to ineffectiveness can be considered as an infringement contravening public policy. This concept is, of course, complicated to handle, as it raises the preliminary question of when such an infringement might be given. Furthermore, a claim based on § 826 BGB can hardly ever be proven (intentional infringement by the contracting entity has to be evidenced as well). Generally speaking, complaints have just been successful in case of bribery, corruption or in cases of manipulation. Recapitulatory, the relevance of § 826 BGB is a question strongly dependent on the case in question.

Closing, it can be said that at least some norms could be used as a basis for a damages claim directed at the compensation for the loss of a contract due to its ineffectiveness, and as this question will be solved with remarkable differences between European Member States, it will surely be subject to further controversies within national law as well as on the European level in the years to come. Closely related to these aspects is the question of damages for third parties suffering from the ineffectiveness of a contract. It is possible that the third party bases a claim for compensation on § 126 GWB because it has participated in an award procedure and on acccount of the direct award and the following ineffectiveness, its chances of winning the award have been infringed. With a view to the loss of trust, a damages claim pursuant to §§ 280 ff., 241 I, 311 I BGB seems possible as well. Again, it is highly interesting whether the German legislature is going to proactively solve these problems arising from the implementation of the rules on ineffectiveness.

8 Correlation between remedies

This section focuses on the interactions between damages. It is noteworthy that the German damages system does not provide for damages claims precluding one another. Therefore, a claim for compensation based on § 126 GWB does not rule out other claims on damages. As conditions and applicability of § 126 GWB differ from other damages claims, the other bases of claim are regarded as concurring claims.[127] In the case of an omission-procedure (§§ 823 I, 1004 BGB; §§ 33, 20 GWB) leading likewise to the granting of damages, the claim for compensation evolving from § 126 S.1

127. Arztmann, Franz-Josef, *Schadensersatz im Vergaberecht in Deutschland und Österreich*, Peter Lang Verlag, Frankfurt a.M. 2005, pp. 105, 126.

GWB remains unaffected and valid. In fact, the claimant can choose freely which claim he wants to bring forward. The decision is mostly dependent on the interest of the entity in what it seeks compensation for because the compensation granted can differ markedly and it should not be forgotten that each of the claims has different requirements. A claim grounded in §§ 823 I, 1004 BGB is coined by a lot of difficulties in proving its conditions, for example. From this follows, that a claim on the basis of this norm is not very attractive, the same rule applies to § 826 BGB or § 125 GWB, for example.

Besides the interactions between single damages claims, it is interesting to have a look at the relations between primary and secondary legal review mechanisms as well. Therefore the question will be (briefly) addressed, whether ineffectiveness or other review mechanisms (annulment) preclude the obtaining of damages. Although the interest of bidders in primary legal review is mostly much higher than their interest in seeking damages, there is no such rule in Germany shadowing this tendency of behavior in the sense that entities should mainly focus on applying for primary legal review. On the contrary, if an application for review on the grounds of § 114 I GWB, for example, is considered inadmissible due to § 107 GWB or other reasons, the bidder still has the chance of getting compensated. Clearly, this distinction between primary and secondary remedy and the independence given between these systems, increases the effectiveness of the remedies system in general. These rules are also applicable for the relation between ineffectiveness and a damages claim.

This is the place to state that the German system clearly is in favor of primary legal remedies and within this group, the system seems to give preference to interim measures. These two assumptions can be backed up by referring to the amount of primary legal remedies and the number of interim measures available. In contrast to this, the GWB only provides for two bases of claim for damages and the requirements and conditions enabling a bidder to seek compensation are elaborate. It is easier to apply for primary legal review than to file a successful damages claim. Another point that is relevant here is the lack of attractiveness of the secondary remedies system as it does not offer huge amounts of compensation and its exact contents are still unsure.

9 Conclusion

The importance of public procurement law on the European and national platform does not tend to cease in the years to come and the importance of efficient review systems will not, either.

Prudently speaking, the German system is tantamount to a role-model for other Member States, especially due to the effective and maybe nearly perfected interim-measures-regime it offers and, despite problems concerning its interpretation, the German damages system made available appears to be well-oiled too.

In conclusion, Germany is in fact largely meeting the requirements for an effective review system set up by the EU directives and statements observing the incompatibility of the complex German procurement law can indeed be made very rarely which is why the position of Germany as a role model regarding the establishment of an effective remedies system should be emphasized once again.

Bibliography

Alexander, Christian, 'Vergaberechtlicher Schadensersatz gemäß § 126 GWB' WrP 2009, pp. 28-36.

Arztmann, Franz-Josef, *Schadensersatz im Vergaberecht in Deutschland und Österreich* (Peter Lang Verlag, Frankfurt a.M. 2005).

Brauer, Eva, 'Das Verfahren vor der Vergabekammer' NZBau 2009, pp. 297-300.

Burgi, Martin, 'Streitbeilegung unterhalb der Schwellenwerte durch „Vergabeschlichtungsstellen“: Ein Vorschlag zur aktuellen Reformdiskussion' VergabeR 2010, pp. 403-414.

Byok, Jan, 'Die Entwicklung des Vergaberechts seit 2008' NZBau 2009, pp. 817-823. 'Die Entwicklung des Vergaberechts seit 2009' NJW 2009, pp. 644-650.

Byok, Jan/Jaeger, Wolfgang, Kommentar zum Vergaberecht, (2nd. ed., Verlag Recht und Wirtschaft, Frankfurt a.M. 2005).

Conrad, Sebastian, 'Der Rechtsschutz gegen die Aufhebung eines Vergabeverfahrens bei Fortfall des Vergabewillens' NZBau 2007, pp. 287-291.

Dreher, Meinrad, 'Rechtsschutz nach Zuschlag' NZBau 2001, pp. 244-246.

Dreher, Meinrad/Hoffmann, Jens 'Die schwebende Unwirksamkeit nach § 101 b I

GWB', NZBau 2010, pp. 201-206.

'Die Informations- und Wartepflicht sowie die Unwirksamkeitsfolge nach den neuen § 101 a und § 101 b GWB' NZBau 2009, pp. 216-219.

Egger, Alexander, *Europäisches Vergaberecht* (Nomos, Baden-Baden 2008).

Egidy, Stefanie, 'Das GWB-Vergaberecht nach der Novelle 2009; Flexibel, europarechtskonform und von Dauer?' DÖV 2009, pp. 835-844.

Franke, Horst/Kemper, Ralf/Zanner, Christian/Grünhagen, Matthias, *VOB Kommentar*, (4th ed., Werner Verlag, Köln 2010).

Gatawis, Siegbert, 'Anwalts- und Verwaltungskosten im Verfahren vor der Vergabekammer' NZBau 2004, pp. 380-381.

Grabitz, Eberhard/Hilf, Meinhard (eds.), *Das Recht der europäischen Union* (CH Beck, München 2009).

Hattig, Oliver/Maibaum, Thomas (eds.), *Praxiskommentar Kartellvergaberecht, Der 4. Teil des GWB und VgV* (Bundesanzeiger Verlag, Köln 2010).

Hertwig, Stefan, *Praxis der öffentlichen Auftragsvergabe* (4th ed., C.H. Beck, München 2010).

Hübner, Alexander, 'Das Ende der „unverzüglichen" und uneingeschränkten Rügeobliegenheit (Paragraph 107 Abs. 3 Satz 1 Nr. 1 GWB)' VergabeR 2010, pp. 414-420.

Immenga, Ulrich/Mestmäcker, Ernst-Joachim, *Wettbewerbsrecht*, (4th ed., C.H. Beck, München 2007).

Jaeger, Wolfgang., 'Neuerungen zur Rügeobliegenheit (§ 107 III GWB) durch das Vergaberechtsmodernisierungsgesetz?' NZBau 2009, pp. 558-562.

Kapellmann, Klaus/Messerschmidt, Burkhardt, VOB Teile A und B, (3rd ed., C.H. Beck, München 2010).

Kratzenberger, Rüdiger, 'Der Begriff des „Öffentlichen Auftraggeber" und der Entwurf des Gesetzes zur Modernisierung des Vergaberecht' NZBau 2010, pp. 103-106.

Krohn, Wolfram, '„Unzulässigkeit" einer unverzüglichen Rügepflicht – Uniplex' NZBau 2009, pp. 186-188.

Kühnen, Jürgen, 'Die Rügeobliegenheit' NZBau 2004, pp. 427-431, 'Das Verfahren vor dem Vergabesenat' NZBau 2009, pp. 357-360.

Kulartz, Hans-Peter/Kus, Alexander/Portz, Norbert. (eds.), *Kommentar zum GWB-Vegaberecht*, (Werner Verlag, Köln 2006).

Kulartz, Hans-Peter/Marx, Fridhelm/Portz, Norbert/Prieß, Hans-Joachim, *Kommentar zur VOB/A*, (Werner Verlag, Köln 2010).

Lausen, Irene, 'Kosten im Nachprüfungsverfahren' NZBau 2005, pp. 440-443.

Martin-Ehlers, 'Die Unterscheidung zwischen Zuschlag und Vertragsschluss im europäischen Vergaberecht' EuZW 2000, pp. 101-105.

Müller-Wrede, Malte (ed.), *Kompendium des Vergaberechts* (Bundesanzeiger Verlag, Berlin 2008).

Niebuhr, Frank/Kulartz, Hans-Peter/Kus, Alexander/Portz, Norbert, *Kommentar zum Vergaberecht* (Luchterhand, Neuwied 2000).

Niestedt, Marian/Prieß, Hans-Joachim, *Rechtsschutz im Vergaberecht* (Carl Heymanns Verlag, Köln 2006).

Prieß, Hans-Joachim, *Handbuch des europäischen Vergaberechts* (5th ed., Carl Heymanns Verlag, Köln 2007).

Prieß, Hans-Joachim, Hölzl, Franz Josef, 'Drei Worte des EuGH: Schadensersatz ohne Verschulden!' NZBau 2011, pp. 21-23.

Schneider, Tobias, Primärrechtsschutz nach Zuschlagserteilung bei einer Vergabe öffentlicher Aufträge, (Duncker & Humblot, Berlin 2007).

Schnorbus, York, 'Der Schadensersatzanspruch des Bieters bei der fehlerhaften Vergabe öffentlicher Aufträge' BauR 1999, pp. 77-106.
Trepte, Peter, *Public Procurement in the EU* (Oxford University Press, New York 2007).
Treumer, Steen, 'Damages for Breach of the EC Public Procurement Rules – Changes in European Regulation and Practice' 15 PPLR 2006, pp. 159-170.
Weyand, Rudolf, *Praxiskommentar Vergaberecht* (2nd ed., Werner Verlag, Köln 2007).
Willenbruch, Klaus/Bischoff, Kristina, *Kompaktkommentar Vergaberecht* (Werner Verlag, Köln 2008).

List of Abbreviations

BGB	German Civil Code
BHO	Federal Budgetary Regulations
Cf.	confer
e.g.	for example
EC	Treaty of the European Community/European Community
ECJ	European Court of Justice
EU	European Union
GG	Basic Law
GWB	Act against Restraints of Competition
LHO	State Budget Regulations
OJ	Official Journal of the European Union
TfEU	Treaty on the Functioning of the European Union
VgV	Public Procurement Regulation
viz.	videlicet (by name)
VOB/A	Contracting Rules for the award of public work contracts
VOF	Contracting Rules for the award of contracts for professional services
VOL/A	Contracting Rules for the award of public service contracts
ZPO	German Civil Procedure Law

5 Remedies in Public Procurement in Romania

By Dacian Dragos, Bogdana Neamtu & Raluca Veliscu

1 Introduction. Late transposition of the Remedies Directive

Currently, public procurement in Romania is regulated by Emergency Governmental Ordinance no. 34/2006[1] (with all the subsequent amendments), which transposes most, if not all, of the provisions of the EC Directives in this field: Directive 2004/18/EC, Directive 2004/17/EC, Directive 1989/665/EEC, Directive 1992/13/EEC, and Directive 2007/66/EC. In most cases, the transposition into the national legislation mimics the EU provisions; however, in the field of remedies the situation is quite different. Romania has reported the transposition of the amendments to the Remedies Directives by two Emergency Governmental Ordinances (executive decision with the legal force of a law, issued in exceptional and urgent situations – hereafter EGO). EGO no. 19/2009[2] and EGO no. 72/2009[3] were supposed to completely transpose the 2007 Remedies Directive's provisions, but the Romanian government had stopped short of doing so. In order to transpose some of the missing provisions a new regulation was issued in 2010, EGO no. 76/2010. No notice from the European Commission was issued in this sense, so it was a rather 'voluntary'completion by the Romanian Government, after realizing that the transposition was incomplete and it could attract the infringement procedure from the European Commission. Some of the missing provisions at the very core of the remedy system, *i.e.*the ineffectiveness remedy, were left out of the initial transposing legislation. In the recent years the changes brought with regard to the competent entity to solve complaints up to the

1. Published in the Official Monitor of Romania, Section I, no. 418 from 15/05/2006.
2. EGO no. 19/7.03.2009, regarding some measures in the public procurement field, published in the Official Monitor of Romania, no. 156 from 12/03/2009.
3. EGO no. 72/17.06.2009, regarding the modification of the Emergency Governmental Ordinance no. 34/2006 on public procurement contracts and concession contracts, published in the Official Monitor of Romania, no.426 from 23/06/2009.

conclusion of the contract and the effects associated with lodging such a complaint have been related to the way in which litigation in PP affected the absorption of EU structural funds in Romania. The main problem was related to the fact that litigation in PP, mainly before a court of law, meant delays up to several months (even years) and this impedes upon the absorption process, where deadlines for application/execution/reimbursement are relatively short. This problem has been raised and discussed not only in the expert community in PP but it represents a rather general public policy concern, frequently addressed by various stakeholders.[4] In light of this context, in addition to the already mentioned legislative changes, EGO no. 76/2010 was approved by the parliament at the very end of 2010, with significant changes regarding the remedies system (Law no. 278/24.12.2010).[5]

2 Review procedure and review bodies

Legal actions regarding the review of decisions to award public contracts are brought before different review bodies and following a distinct review procedure depending on the stage in the award of the public procurement contract. The changes brought to EGO no. 76/2010 by the approval law mainly regard the review bodies before which a complaint can be lodged up to the conclusion of the contract. Since these latest changes seem to go against the provisions of the Constitution and the jurisprudence of the Constitutional Court and since it is likely that these provisions will be reinstated in the future, in the following section we present both the current situation (as of 31.12.2010) and the previous one.

2.1 Legal actions up to the conclusion of the public procurement contract

Until the last changes at the end of 2010, the law allowed complainants to choose between the administrative-jurisdictional path (the National Council for Solving Legal Disputes, hereafter the Council) and the purely judicial one (court of law). The preference of complainants for one of the two review paths was associated with the implied benefits associated with each of them.

4. Recently it was the president of the state who argued in favor of speediness in court proceedings that involved litigation in PP, when contracts financed through EU structural funds are concerned.
5. Law no. 278/24.12.2010, published in the Official Monitor of Romania no. 898 from 31.12.2010.

In the early stages the preference for choosing the Council was justified by the immediate and automatic suspensive effect associated with such an action (for more details see below); more recently, after July 2010, the costs implied by an action before the Council resulted in a slight decrease in the number of actions brought before the Council. Currently, the review by the Council is mandatory.

2.1.1 Forum-shopping for a review body (prior to 31.12.2010)

Before 2011, the claimant was free to choose between the Council and the court of law (the competent court in the first instance was the tribunal). However, the law stated that it is forbidden to lodge the same complaint simultaneously with both the Council and the court of law. If this situation occurred, the procedure before the Council was automatically suspended. It was presumed that by lodging the same complaint with the court, the claimant renounced the administrative (quasi-judicial) procedure. Statistics show that during the last years the number of complaints before the Council has increased significantly;[6] incentives for going first before the Council include: speediness and flexibility of the procedure (legal obligation to solve the complaint within 20 days; possibility given to the complainant to specify the object of the complaint after lodging it), presumably lower costs (no need to hire a lawyer, no fees, at least until mid 2010); a general distrust in the judicial system and perception of major delays associated with court litigations (not necessarily in public procurement but in general), and finally but very important, the effect of automatic suspension, associated until 2010 only with the proceedings before the Council (now abrogated). This situation is already changing due to recent legislative modifications (see section 7 on establishment of a breach). In light of these data (which show the preference of tenderers for the Council as a first instance body), it seems odd that the legislator has made the action before the Council mandatory, claiming that otherwise access to EU funds will be blocked by lengthy court proceedings. This needs to be further explained – it is true that a significant number of complainants choose the Council; however, in the case of large infrastructure contracts, the economic operators preferred to go to court. The legislator, when operating the change, was mostly concerned with those tenderers who went before the court with the intention to delay the PP procedures (in many cases, though

6. National Council for Solving Legal Disputes, Statistics, [Online] at http://www.cnsc.-ro/index.php/en/reportsstatistics, accessed December 16, 2010.

they could have asked for a speedier litigation, by changing the dates allocated electronically, they opted against it).

Another benefit considered by tenderers while 'forum shopping' refers to the suspensive effect of an action before the Council (the suspensive effect evolved from automatic, immediate, and unconditioned by other actions of the contester in 2006 to an automatic suspension conditioned by the notification of the contracting authority, effective a day before the end of the standstill period in 2009 (see section 9 on interim measures). This was in place until July 2010. The award procedure was thus stopped if for example a tenderer lodged a complaint concerning the award documentation. This provision is currently abrogated – the legal action before the Council no longer stops the contracting authority from continuing the awarding procedures. The interdiction that currently operates refers to the conclusion of the contract prior to the decision of the Council. Another advantage refers to the flexibility of the administrative-jurisdictional review procedure compared to the court one. It allows the tenderers to clarify/modify some of the mandatory elements required by law, including the object of the complaint (within a five days timeframe, at the request of the Council). In practice, because tenderers have a very short time span for lodging a complaint with the Council, they tend to lodge the complaint only formally, in order to comply with the deadline, but without presenting a solid legal justification of the alleged breach, backed by the required evidence/documents. Thus, the complainant gains two additional benefits from this flexibility: the complaint is not declared inadmissible if some constitutive elements are missing and the Council indicates what is missing and how it should be remedied; second, the tardiness of the complaint as a ground for rejection by the Council is at least postponed with an additional five days.

Aside from having a mandatory review before the Council as of 31.12.2010, the advantages described above are still operating in favor of the tenderers. The only change is that the action can no longer be lodged before a court of law, as an alternative to the Council.

When the complainant decided to go directly to court, the court action was directed against the acts of the contracting authority issued within the award procedure as well as for damages caused during the award procedure (damages are discussed separately in a subsequent section of the chapter). In the absence of an action before the Council, the court of first instance was the Tribunal (established in all 41 counties), the Administrative and Fiscal Law Section. The ruling of the first instance court can be challenged with recourse within a time frame of five days from notification before the Appellate Court, Administrative and Fiscal Law Section if the legal action concerns the award procedure up to conclusion of the contract. If the legal action concerned the execution, nullity, annulment etc. of the contract (see section 2.2 below), the Commercial Law Section of the Appellate Court was the recourse instance.

2.1.2 Review procedure before the Council with the amendments brought by Law no. 278/2010

With the occasion of approval of EGO no. 76/2010 in Parliament (Law no.278/2010) a mandatory action before the Council was introduced. The Council is an independent, administrative-jurisdictional (or quasi-judicial) review body, independent from other structures with regard to its decisions. Starting with January 1st 2007, the Council gained the status of legal person and thus Romania addressed the problem regarding the independence of the Council which had been raised by the European Commission on several occasions. Through the approval Law of EGO no. 76/2010, the independence of the Council was further strengthened: if previously the law stated that the Council functioned within the institutional framework of the General Secretariat of the Government, currently all references to such dependence are eliminated from the law. The law also makes a more clear distinction between the administrative activity of the Council and its ruling as an administrative-jurisdictional body. The members of the Council are civil servants with a special status, appointed by the prime minister, based on a competitive selection process and the fulfillment of several mandatory requirements regarding previous experience/educational background. They are evaluated (with regard to the administrative and organizational activity of the Council) by a mixed Committee which comprises representatives of the National Authority for Regulating and Monitoring Public Procurement in Romania, of the Romanian Parliament, of the National Agency for Civil Servants and of the Competition Council.

The complainant can lodge a contestation before the Council in a time-frame of five or ten days, depending on the value of the contract, from the moment in which the tenderer is notified about any act/action of the contracting authority related to the public procurement procedures. When the tender documentation is published in the Electronic System for Public Procurement, the deadline starts from the day when the tender documentation is published and becomes available online.

After receiving a complaint, the Council needs to issue a decision within 10 or 20 days. Before assessing the case on its merits, the Council will review it in light of several exceptions[7] (tardiness, lack of standing, lack of object, lack of competence on the behalf of the Council etc.) which can lead to the rejection of the contestation as being inadmissible. When the decision of the Council is based on exceptions, the deadline for reaching a decision is 10 days. If the case is assessed on its merits, the deadline is 20 days (this can be extended by a maximum of ten days, once, in exceptional cases).

The deadlines within which the parties have to apply for review have to be calculated so as to give preeminence to the party, and not to the Council or the court. Thus, the date when the contestation was presented at the post office is to be considered the date of the contestation, rather than the date when the contestation reaches the Council.[8] In general, the deadlines applicable to public procurement procedures are those provided by the law, regardless of the errors made by the contracting authorities when notifying the participants about them. Thus, the courts have held that different deadlines from those stated in the law are to be disregarded by those interested, even if they were indicated by the contracting authority, because the law takes prevalence over administrative communications.[9]

There were cases when the Council delayed the solving of the contestation beyond the time frame provided by law (now 20 days with a possible extension of 10 days), reaching even to months. The penalties for the delay are only disciplinary, and they are not enforced, so practically there are no incentives to strictly follow the deadlines. The majority of the courts have held that in such cases the decision of the Council cannot be annulled only on the basis of the delay.[10] Even a delay of 3 months was considered to have no impact on

7. Exceptions are procedural means through which, under the provisions of the law, the interested party, the prosecutor or the court of law/review body, raises, without considering the case on its merits, the question of procedural irregularities regarding the composition or the competence of the court, errors concerning the right of the party to sue, with the intention to postpone the judgment, to ask to have some documents redrafted, or to reject the case altogether. In our case, the term exception refers to those irregularities discovered by the Council which prevent the case from being judged on its merits.
8. Judgment no. 970/17.09.2008, Alba Iulia Appellate Court, Division for Administrative and Fiscal Matters; Judgment no. 1861/11.09.2008, Bucharest Appellate Court, Division for Administrative and Fiscal Matters.
9. Judgment no. 118/19.01.2009, Bucharest Appellate Court, Division for Administrative and Fiscal Matters; Judgment no. 1975/01.10.2008, Craiova Appellate Court, Division for Administrative and Fiscal Matters.
10. Judgment no. 114/30.01.2008, Ploieşti Appellate Court, Division for Administrative and Fiscal Matters.

the legality of the decision issued by the Council,[11] although the 'reasonable time frame' principle from the ECHR jurisprudence was invoked. Again, not all courts have the same opinion on the issue: one of them stated that in a case when the annulment came 4 months after the opening of the offers, during which time the contracting authority had already received some products from the winning bidder, it is not admissible.[12] Currently, if the statistics of the Council are accurate, the average time span for solving a decision is approximately 19 days. There is also an evaluation procedure which can lead to disciplinary penalties for the members of the Council.

The decision of the Council may consist in the annulment, total or partial, of an act of the contracting authority; the Council can request the contracting authority to issue an act or it can adopt any other necessary measures for remedying the acts of the contracting authority which affect the award procedure. If the Council in the process of analyzing the tender documentation finds that there are other breaches apart from the ones listed in the complaint, it can only notify the National Authority for Regulating and Monitoring Public Procurement (NARMPP is the monitoring body responsible for the entire public procurement system in Romania) as well as the Unit for the Coordination and Monitoring of Public Procurements (UCMPP is a body whose competences slightly overlap with those of NARMPP, functioning within the Ministry of Public Finances). Until 2009, the Council did not have to limit its ruling to the object of the complaint at hand; it was allowed to analyze the award documentation in its entirety and to establish, *ex officio*, its legality. Based on the case law,[13] there were instances when the Council identified significant breaches of the law in the award documentation or procedure, which were not signaled by the tenderer in his complaint. Currently, the Council can only decide whether the contracting authority can continue with the award procedure or it can annul it. The Council cannot, however, decide to award the contract to a certain tenderer. The exact character of the remedies which can be offered by the Council is not always accurately perceived by the tenderers. In a significant number of complaints examined, the com-

11. Judgment no. 115/30.01.2008, Ploieşti Appellate Court, Division for Administrative and Fiscal Matters.
12. Judgment no. 2532/06.11.2008, Cluj Appellate Court, Division for Administrative and Fiscal Matters.
13. Judgment no. 2656/29.11.2008, Bucharest Appellate Court, Division for Administrative and Fiscal Matters; Judgment no. 1030/7.06/2007, Bucharest Appellate Court, Division for Administrative and Fiscal Matters; Judgment no. 1576/16.06/2008, Bucharest Appellate Court, Division for Administrative and Fiscal Matters.

plainants asked the Council to award them the contract as a result of a faulty procedure (real or perceived). Even more, the Council had in some cases ruled a complaint as inadmissible for lack of object if the tenderer, using an inappropriate legal language, complained about the result of the award procedure. The Council interpreted that the complainant requested the Council to award the contract to that specific tenderer. The Appellate Court ruled that the Council should have analyzed the complaint in light of the implicit legal breach, namely the illegality of the evaluation of the tenders and the act of the contracting authority used to award the contract. The Council was considered in breach of the flexibility requirement which allows the complainant to refine his complaint provided that the Council asks for it.[14] In this case, the court sent the case back to the Council that was required to judge it based on its merit. Currently, the law states that if a court action is brought against a decision of the Council which ruled based on exception (tardiness, lack of object etc.) and is declared admissible, the court will retain the complaint and solve it on its merits.[15]

Though the provision of the law which states that the Council cannot award the contract to a certain tenderer is very clear, the issue is more complex. Apart from some cases where the Council has decided that a certain offer is not conforming and thus ordered the resuming of the award procedure without the rejected offer,[16] the Council has refused constantly to go beyond the annulment of decisions of the contracting authority and to establish the winning offer or to award the contract.[17] The main argument used refers to the provisions of EGO no. 34/2006 (article 200) and the subsidiary legislation of implementation (Governmental Decision no. 925/2006, article 72 par.2), which state that the authority competent to award the contract by establishing the winning offer is the contracting authority. However, the question here is whether the contracting authority is the only competent authority to do that? At a closer look, both provisions invoked by the Council and by some courts refer to the *power* of the contracting authority to decide, or to the *obligation*

14. Judgment no. 214/25.02.2008, Alba Iulia Appellate Court, Division for Administrative and Fiscal Matters.
15. Article 285(2) EGO no. 34/2006 with amendments by EGO no. 76/2010.
16. See Judgment no. 2722/03.12.2008, Bucharest Appellate Court, Division for Administrative and Fiscal Matters confirming the decision of the Council, and Judgment no. 318/09.10.2008, Oradea Appellate Court, Division for Administrative and Fiscal Matters, infirming such an approach.
17. Judgment no. 2156/29.11.2007, Bucharest Appellate Court, Division for Administrative and Fiscal Matters, confirming the decision of the Council.

to decide in a certain time frame, but they do not make clear whether this power is exclusive or not, when transposed into the context of the review phase. In other words, the power to decide the winning offer and to award the contract is evidently exclusive in the administrative phase, but is it still exclusive in the review phase?

This raises the question whether the Council or the court can establish the winning offer and then award the contract, or at least establish the winning offer. The separation of powers principle, as understood in the Romanian legal system, prohibits courts to 'step into the shoes' of public authorities and decide the matter themselves. The principle of separation of powers can be invoked when talking about courts, so the answer seems to be negative in the first case, but not when the Council is involved, as the Council is a public authority belonging to the same branch as the contracting authority, and its decisions can be assessed within the administrative control paradigm.

However, some courts seem to have another take on this matter. In a noteworthy case, the court has 'put itself in the shoes' of the contracting authority, stating that the criteria for the assessment of technical specifications were lacking, therefore the assessment made by each member of the evaluation commission was subjective. Consequently, it granted the maximum score for the contested evaluation criteria to all tenderers, re-ranking the bidders according to the new scores. The court action was rejected in the end because the new ranking did not change the winner of the award procedure, but the case is interesting in itself, when comes to the extent of the review conducted by the court'.[18] In a scholarly opinion criticizing this decision, it was argued that the court had no place in re-ranking the list of bidders, because the law does not confer this power upon the courts. The solution to grant all bidders maximum score for the contested criteria is not a solution founded in law.[19] Nevertheless, the case shows the willingness of some courts to go on a path of effective dispute settlement, looking with the corner of an eye at the principle of separation of powers while at the same time interpreting in a flexible manner the provisions of the law. The case is not unique, as other courts have

18. Judgment no. 764/13.11.2008, Bacău Appellate Court, Division for Administrative and Fiscal Matters.
19. Comment on the Judgment no. 764/13.11.2008, Bacău Appellate Court, Division for Administrative and Fiscal Matters, in Şerban, D.D., *Jurisprudenţacomentatăîn-domeniulachiziţiilorpublice* [Case Law in Public Procurement], Wolters Kluwer, Bucharest, p. 99.

done the same,[20] Other courts, on the contrary, have followed a more restrictive approach, refusing to decide which offer is the winning one[21] or to comparatively evaluate the offers.[22] Following their argumentation, the court can only require the contracting authority to resume the award procedure from a certain point or start anew.

The courts have stated that the *non reformatio in pejus* principle does not apply in proceedings before the Council.[23] The conclusion is in accordance with the general opinion of the doctrine, that administrative procedures do not confer such protection.[24]

If the Council decides that measures regarding the remedying of an act are necessary, then NARMPP is notified and has the obligation to monitor the way in which the contracting authority proceeds to carry out this obligation. The decision of the Council is mandatory for the contracting authority. A public procurement contract awarded in disregard of the Council's decision is affected by nullity.

Against the decision of the Council, the tenderer can lodge a complaint with the Appellate Court in whose jurisdiction the premises of the contracting authority are located. This provision had suffered several subsequent modifications. In the initial version of EGO no. 34/2006, a complaint against the decision of the Council had to be lodged with the Council which was responsible for forwarding it to the court within 3 days after the expiration of the 10 days deadline for lodging this complaint. Following a decision by the Constitutional Court, in 2008 the law (EGO no. 143/2008) allowed the complainants to lodge the complaint with either the Council or the court. Currently, the law expressly states that the complaint needs to be lodged with the court (EGO no. 19/2009). In practice however, this last modification generates delays in the court proceedings because the Council, which could be unaware of a court action, does not send in time for the first hearing, the dossier of the case.

20. Judgment no. 1066/11.06.2007, Bucharest Appellate Court, Division for Administrative and Fiscal Matters.
21. Judgment no. 868/R/18.12.2008, Braşov Appellate Court, Division for Administrative and Fiscal Matters.
22. Judgment no. 503/15.03.2007, Bucharest Appellate Court, Division for Administrative and Fiscal Matters.
23. Judgment no. 467/16.02.2009, Bucharest Appellate Court, Division for Administrative and Fiscal Matters.
24. See, for instance, Dragoş,D.C., *Legeacontenciosuluiadministrativ. Comentariisiexplicatii* [Law on Judicial Review Commented and Explained], 2nd edition, C.H. Beck, Bucharest, 2009, p. 235.

If the Appellate Court declares the complaint admissible, it modifies the decision of the Council by ruling: the annulment, total or partial, of an act of the contracting authority; it can request the contracting authority to issue an act; it can require the contracting authority to fulfill any obligation related to the award documentation or the award procedure; or any other measures necessary to remedy breaches of the public procurement legislation. If the Council has rejected a complaint as inadmissible on the grounds of an exception (tardiness, lack of standing, lack of object etc.) the Appellate Court, in the case of admitting the complaint, will annul the decision of the Council and will solve the complaint on its merit.

2.1.3 Deadlines for lodging a complaint with the Council

As already mentioned, the deadline for lodging an action with the Council, before the conclusion of the contract, is of five or ten days, depending on the value of the contract. The five days deadline is clearly a national one, for contracts below the EU value thresholds. The existence of different national deadlines, shorter than the ones from the EU law, even if they apply to contracts below the threshold, creates confusion among the tenderers.

In an illustrative case, an economic operator lodged a complaint before the Council which was rejected on grounds of tardiness. The complainant then lodged a subsequent court action against the decision of the Council arguing that the decision does not take into consideration the deadlines from the 2004/18/CE and 2007/66/CE Directives, which have preeminence over the national legal provisions. More specifically, the Romanian PP legislation established a shorter deadline for lodging a complaint in the case of contracts under the EU value threshold (5 days starting with the next day following notification). The economic operator argued that the 10 days deadline from the Directive should apply in this case. The court ruled that the national legislation can establish different conditions for contracts/procurement under the EU value threshold.[25] This type of litigation is illustrative for a problem that has been identified in relation to PP in Romania. The Romanian legislation, in the process of transposing EU procurement law, makes relatively few distinctions with regard to contracts under and above the EU thresholds. The result is that the EU requirements apply also to low value contracts. This has led some scholars to label it as 'excessive' application of the procurement law (both to under the thresholds contracts and to economic operators other than

25. Judgment no. 1920/8.10.2009, Bucharest Appellate Court, Division for Administrative and Fiscal Matters.

contracting authorities, including NGOs). With respect to remedies, besides a shorter standstill period, there are no distinct provisions for contracts under the threshold.[26]

2.2 Legal actions brought after the conclusions of the public procurement contract

After the changes brought by Law no. 278/2010, a complainant can go to court in the first instance only after the conclusion of the contract and if the action regards the execution, ineffectiveness, termination etc. of the contract. For actions lodged after the conclusion of the contract, the competent first instance court is the tribunal, the Commercial Law Section. The procedure in front of the court has a speedy character given the nature of the public procurement field where delays can be costly for the tenderers as well as for the contracting authority.

3 Constitutionality of the administrative-jurisdictional review by the Council. The legal status of the Council. Latest developments

Since the adoption of EGO no. 34 in 2006 the constitutionality of this review was questioned. The Constitution states that administrative jurisdictions have to be elective and free of charge. The constitutionality of the review by the Council was assessed against these two main criteria.

- In the original version of EGO no. 34/2006, the tenderer who was dissatisfied with the decision of the Council, was able to lodge a court action provided that the complaint was lodged with the Council (see section 2.1.1. above) which had the responsibility to send it to the court. This meant that the tenderer was forced to lodge the complaint with the same body which ruled against him, thus having his access to justice limited. This situation resulted in a plea of unconstitutionality raised before an Appellate Court which led to a ruling by the Constitutional Court. The Constitutional Court ruled that the provision discussed above has the potential to limit the right

26. Filipon, Ş., *The Romanian Experience with Interim Measures and Automatic Suspension*, paper presented at the Public Procurement: Global Revolution V Conference, University of Copenhagen, Denmark, September 2010.

to free access to justice and to due process;[27] this is because the law required the Council to act as an intermediary between the complainant and the court, without establishing any sanction for the Council provided that it delays the process by not sending the complaint to the court. Following the decision of unconstitutionality, this provision is no longer in place.

– The law establishes that in the cases when the tenderer chooses to lodge his initial complaint with the Council, the Appellate Court is the recourse instance. Against this legal provision, several pleas of unconstitutionality were raised regarding the limitation of free access to justice and the absence of a first instance court – the Council is not a real court but an administrative-jurisdictional (quasi-judicial) body. The Constitutional Court ruled that administrative review in general is constitutional and it does not act as a limitation to the free access to justice since it is elective and free of charge. The aggrieved claimant has in addition the liberty to choose between an administrative review procedure and a court action.[28] In a subsequent decision, the Court ruled that the principle of free access to justice should be interpreted in the sense that no group or social category can be excluded from the exercise of procedural rights. It is allowed however by the Constitution to establish by law special procedural rules and specific means for the exercise of procedural rights. Therefore, free access to justice does not mean access to all judicial bodies and to all jurisdiction tiers.[29]
– EGO no. 76/2010 introduced penalties for lodging a complaint with the Council which is then rejected – the complainant will lose a portion of the deposit made with the contracting authority. This contradicts the constitutional principle of having free of charge access to administrative jurisdictions.
– Another constitutionality issue is related to the mandatory character of the review before the Council introduced as of 31.12.2010. This provision clearly violates the provision of the Constitution which states that administrative jurisdictions have to be elective. If in the case discussed above (penalties for losing the case before the Council) it is debatable if access to justice is prohibited (the penalties will be paid only after the ruling and if

27. Constitutional Court of Romania, Decision no. 569/15.05.2008, published in the Official Monitor of Romania no. 537 from 16.07.2008.
28. Constitutional Court of Romania, Decision no. 887/16.10.2007 published in the Official Monitor no. 779 from 16/11/2007.
29. Constitutional Court of Romania, Decision no. 230/4.08.2008, published in the Official Monitor no. 300 from 17/04/2008.

the tenderer losses the case); in the latter case the situation is clearer and in our opinion it represents a breach of the Constitution.

According to the law, NARMPP can also be considered an actor within the remedies system. Though the institution cannot grant remedies it has an important monitoring role concerning the implementation of the legal decisions that grant remedies to tenderers. It also has legal standing in cases concerning the ineffectiveness of the contracts.

Another debated issue refers to the legal status of the Council – although according to the law it is an administrative-jurisdictional (quasi-judicial) body, in practice it tends to behave more like a court of law. Some aspects that lead to this conclusion are analyzed below:

- In situations when it received a complaint that was not within the boundaries of its competence the Council has declined its competence in favor of the court. Such an action is considered incompatible with the legal nature of the Council, which should have rejected the complaint as inadmissible. The decline of competence is a procedure reserved for courts of law.
- The Council has no standing in court actions brought against its decisions, a feature similar to that of a court.[30] This is a unique situation in the Romanian legislation, as other administrative jurisdictions are part of the legal action brought against their decisions. This provision establishes an exceptional status for the Council. We believe that there were practical considerations justifying this measure – the Council has to be part in court proceedings all over the country since the recourse against its decisions is filed with the Court of Appeal in whose jurisdiction the contracting authority is located. Nevertheless, the legal fundament for this approach is missing.

4 Interactions between review bodies

A first situation refers to the dynamic of the interaction between the Council and the courts in the context of the review of the decisions issued by the Council. Especially in the early stages of the activity of the Council, probably because of the lack of expertise and experience of the Council, some of its decisions were stricken down by the courts on grounds of exceeding its com-

30. Pătraşcu, H., *Culegere de practică judiciară în materie de achiziţii publice*, [Case Law in Public Procurement], Wolters Kluwer, Bucaharest, 2010, p. 286.

petences. The most frequent situation identified by courts regarded the evaluation of tenders and the subsequent assessment of these tenders as non-compliant with the requirements of the award documentation.[31] Currently, the activity of the Council is publicly perceived as more trustworthy by the actors involved in the PP process (specialized forums and blogs on PP, economic operators, media etc.).The latest legislative change, which made the review before the Council mandatory, acknowledges this fact. If the decisions of the Council as a first review body will be stricken down by courts several months later, after the contract was concluded, following the standstill period, we are going to witness an increase in the number of actions for damages. The legislator seems to think that this risk is not worth considering.

In practice, interesting situations occurred concerning the decline of competences by the Council and by the courts. The nature of the Council, considered an administrative-jurisdictional (quasi-judicial) body or a special jurisdiction similar to a tribunal in the common law system, has resulted in contrary jurisprudence regarding the possibility to decline the competence to the courts and back. In early cases, the Council had refused to decline its competence to the court, while in others the courts have refused to receive such actions.[32] Other courts, on the contrary, have held that such decline is admissible.[33]

In court proceedings against decisions of the Council, the parties can invoke only evidence that was invoked before the Council, as no new evidence is admissible.[34]

In the earlier versions of the PP law, the lack of notification by the tenderer of the contracting authority generated different effects, depending on whether the action was brought before the Council or before the court. The law stated that the tenderer who goes before the Council must notify the contracting authority under the penalty of having his complaint rejected on grounds of tardiness. Thus, some courts have held that such nullity is absolute and can be invoked either before the Council or before the court,[35] while other courts make distinction between relative nullity and absolute nullity and

31. Judgment no. 2775/12.12.2008, BucharestAppellate Court, Division for Administrative and Fiscal Matters.
32. Judgment no. 229/27.02.2008 and no. 230/27.02.2008, Alba Iulia Appellate Court, Division for Administrative and Fiscal Matters.
33. Judgment no. 348/11.05.2007, Constanța Appellate Court, Division for Administrative and Fiscal Matters.
34. Judgment no. 1616/17.07.2008, Craiova Appellate Court, Division for Administrative and Fiscal Matters.
35. Judgment no. 1364/12.06.2008, Craiova Appellate Court, Division for Administrative and Fiscal Matters.

thus restrict its effects to the proceedings before the Council, considering also the abuse of the contracting authority manifested in the omission to invoke the nullity at this level in order to invoke it later, in court.[36]

Until the changes from 31.12.2010, when complainants could choose to go in the first instance either before the Council or before the court, an interesting debate concerning the administrative appeal against acts issued by contracting authorities in public procurement, in cases when the action was lodged directly with the court, was raised. The general Law on judicial review[37] provides for a mandatory reconsideration of administrative acts (administrative appeal/appeal in front of public authority) in cases when there are no other prior administrative proceedings imposed by the special legislation (this applies to the proceedings before the Council). Thus, for those who went directly in court in public procurement cases, a formal notification of the contracting authority by which the complainant asks for annulment of the decision or other measures would have been necessary. The lack of such prior appeal made the court action inadmissible (this was later changed – the lack of such a notification would no longer have prohibited the filing of a court action). Such an interpretation is in line with the provisions of the 2007/66/CE Directive which in article 1(5) states that member states may establish a mandatory review with the contracting authority provided that the use of this action leads to the immediate suspension of the conclusion of the contract. The national courts have also different views on this issue. Some courts argue that the special procedure regulated by the public procurement law is to be understood as excluding the general administrative appeal thus opening up a direct action before the court,[38] other courts, on the contrary, contend that in cases when the Council is not involved in review, the general administrative appeal to the issuer (the contracting authority) should be exercised.[39] Moreover, some courts have gone even further, arguing that a review by the Council is inadmissible after the party has exercised the administrative appeal provided by the Law on judicial review.[40] The solution is debatable, as the jurisdiction

36. Judgment no. 1284/28.05.2008, Cluj Appellate Court, Division for Administrative and Fiscal Matters.
37. Law no.554/2004.
38. Judgment no. 2954/09.12.2008, Cluj Appellate Court, Division for Administrative and Fiscal Matters.
39. Judgment no. 325/02.10.2007, Galați Appellate Court, Division for Administrative and Fiscal Matters.
40. Judgment no. 593/13.06.2008, Pitești Appellate Court, Division for Administrative and Fiscal Matters.

of the Council was optional and the administrative appeal is mandatory, so there is no contradiction between the two modes of review, even though they have the same legal nature of administrative proceedings. Following the latest changes – the review before the Council is mandatory -, this issue remains important from a doctrinary perspective. If the Constitutional Court will strike down the mandatory review, then it will regain its relevance.

For award procedures organized following the public procurement law by choice by entities that are not contracting authorities in the sense of the PP law (falling outside the scope of this law – *i.e.* NGOs), the Council has no jurisdiction to hear cases in first instance. The courts have stated that resorting voluntarily to the public procurement provisions does not expand the jurisdiction of the Council to hear such cases,[41] and that EGO no. 34/2006 regulating the jurisdiction of the Council takes prevalence against the award documentation, which may wrongfully indicate the Council as the review body.

5 Standing

By harmed person the law describes all economic operators who:

a) Currently have or had a legitimate interest concerning the award procedure;
b) Had suffered, are in the process of suffering or may potentially suffer harm following the procedure. As opposed to the past wording of the Ordinance with regard to standing, the term of harmed persons was expanded so as to include also tenderers who were excluded at some point in the award procedure, thus being potentially harmed.

Though the legal text is apparently clear and concise on the matter of standing, numerous problems occur in practice and are evident from the case law.

The courts have rightfully interpreted that the concept of interested persons or persons who have an interest in that award procedure includes also economic operators, who, due to the way in which the tender documentation

41. Judgment no. 836/R/09.12.2008, Braşov Appellate Court, Division for Administrative and Fiscal Matters; Judgment no. 1807/05.11.2007 and Judgment no. 1991/15.11.2007, Bucharest Appellate Court, Division for Administrative and Fiscal Matters.

was drafted, were excluded from participating in that tender (*i.e.* companies that use recycled materials in their production process).[42]

It is subject to considerable debate who has standing in a court action lodged against a decision of the Council. The question mainly concerns the other tenderers who were not involved in the review before the Council. It was ruled in several cases that the court proceedings intended to review the decision of the Council have to be carried out between the contracting authority and the claimant, as in the case of the proceedings before the Council.[43] Nevertheless, it can be argued that these tenderers could have standing in court against the decision of the Council, provided that this decision is aggrieving their rights or interests. The courts have held differently with regard to this matter. Some have held that there is standing regardless of the parties' participation in proceedings before the Council;[44] others have ruled that standing derives from the participation in those proceedings.[45] The critical legal provision here is the one that requires the contracting authority, notified by the claimant about the initiation of administrative or court proceedings, to inform all the other participants.[46] Based on this provision, some courts have argued that those interested should join the contestant before the Council in order to oppose the decision, and maybe prevent a decision that is contrary to their interests. Nevertheless, other courts have contended that a winning tenderer does not have any interest in participating in proceedings that are initiated by other tenderers, as long as his offer is still the winning one. The Council has no obligation either to cite the winner of the award procedure, as long as the proceedings are between the contester and the contracting author-

42. Judgment no. 1995/16.11.2007, Bucharest Appellate Court, Division for Administrative and Fiscal Matters.
43. Judgment no. 198/6.03.2008, Bacău Appellate Court, Division for Administrative and Fiscal Matters.
44. Judgment no. 380/15.05.2008, Bacău Appellate Court, Division for Administrative and Fiscal Matters; Judgment no. 1092/15.06.2007 and Judgment no. 1164/24.04.2008, Bucharest Appellate Court, Division for Administrative and Fiscal Matters; Judgment no. 252/28.08.2008, Oradea Appellate Court, Division for Administrative and Fiscal Matters.
45. Judgment no. 75/R/12.02.2008 and Judgment no. 439/R/01.07.2008, Braşov Appellate Court, Division for Administrative and Fiscal Matters; Judgment no. 1646/27.08.2008, Craiova Appellate Court, Division for Administrative and Fiscal Matters; Judgment no. 130/08.02.2008, Piteşti Appellate Court, Division for Administrative and Fiscal Matters.
46. Article 271 of EGO no. 34/2006 as amended by EGO no. 19/2009.

ity.[47] The status quo changes for the winner only when, as a consequence of the decision of the Council, the result of the award procedure is overturned. Then, the winner becomes interested in a review procedure against such a decision. We agree with this latter approach entirely, because it fits better the philosophy of the Directive.

In the context of standing cases, the courts have always made a correct application of the legal provisions as to who the defendant in public procurement cases is, making the necessary distinction among the authority *organizing* the award procedure and the *contracting* authorities. In practice, contracting authorities contracted out the actual organization of the award procedure to a different legal person *i.e.*to the Romanian Stock Exchange. It is also the case of contracting authorities other than public entities (for example NGOs which receive EU money and are required to make their procurements following PP legislation) which hire consultants for this task. Consequently, the contracting authority is considered to have standing as defendant in public procurement cases, regardless of which authority was in charge of the award procedure in the name of the contracting authority.[48] Another situation when the issue of standing was raised referred to a contracting authority which does not have the status of a legal person – *i.e.* military units which are subordinated to the Ministry of Defense, which is the legal person. In this case the court argued that the military units are contracting authorities and thus have standing in court, regardless of their legal status.[49]

Interest is a key element of standing. The courts have reiterated that the complainants have to justify an interest in the annulment of the award procedure. Thus, a winning tenderer cannot request damages by challenging the award procedure in which he was awarded the contract. Such a challenge was based on the argument that the procedure had many vices and it would surely be annulled in court at the initiative of other tenderers. Such an action was characterized as a 'preemptive action', and considered inadmissible.[50] There were no cases in which the winner seeks annulment or interim measures and

47. Judgment no. 5883/10.10.2007, Craiova Appellate Court, Division for Administrative and Fiscal Matters.
48. Judgment no. 128/22.01.2007, Bucharest Appellate Court, Division for Administrative and Fiscal Matters; Judgment no. 1092/15.06.2007, Bucharest Appellate Court, Division for Administrative and Fiscal Matters.
49. Judgment no. 1092/15.06.2007, Bucharest Appellate Court, Division for Administrative and Fiscal Matters.
50. Judgment no. 436/02.10.2008, Bacău Appellate Court, Division for Administrative and Fiscal Matters.

in the same time asks for damages, so we cannot say whether such action would be considered admissible by courts. Our opinion is that it would be admissible.

In other cases, the court had held that challenging the winning offer without also challenging the second place offer does not prove a sufficient interest of the third bidder as to obtain the annulment of the award procedure.[51] The bidder ranked on the third place has to challenge both first and second placed offers in order to have sufficient interest.[52] Also, the bidder whose offer was returned unopened was considered to have sufficient interest in challenging the decision of the contracting authority before the Council or in court.[53] On the other hand, a supplier of the tenderer does not have standing in challenging the award procedure, although indirectly it can be affected by its result.[54]

The Council has no standing in court proceedings initiated against its decisions.[55] This solution is based on the legal nature of the Council of quasi-judicial body, which cannot revoke its decisions.[56] Since 2009, the law expressly states this interdiction, with the exception of some cases when the Council fines the contracting authorities.

Also referring to standing, one court has ruled that a consortium of economic operators that had participated in the award procedure should keep its organization when challenging the award decision in court. Consequently, the designated leader of the consortium should represent it in court. The action lodged by one associate of the consortium without the consent of the others is not admissible, as the decision of the court will regard the award procedure, and will have effects on all the members of the consortium.[57]

51. Judgment no. 503/R/26.08.2008, Braşov Appellate Court, Division for Administrative and Fiscal Matters.
52. Judgment no. 2608/24.11.2008, Bucharest Appellate Court, Division for Administrative and Fiscal Matters.
53. Judgment no. 2500/13.11.2008, Bucharest Appellate Court, Division for Administrative and Fiscal Matters.
54. Judgment no. 2324/24.10.2008, Cluj Appellate Court, Division for Administrative and Fiscal Matters.
55. Judgment no. 594/14.03.2007, Cluj Appellate Court, Division for Administrative and Fiscal Matters; See also Şerban, D.D., *Calitateaprocesuala a ConsiliuluiNatioanla de Solutionare a Contestatiilor* [The Standing in Court of the NCSLD], in Dreptul [Law Review] no.9/2008.
56. Judgment no. 315/13.02.2008, Craiova Appellate Court, Division for Administrative and Fiscal Matters.
57. Judgment no. 1375/R/6.06.2008, Cluj Appellate Court, Division for Administrative and Fiscal Matters.

6 Costs

In Romania, the access to the remedies system has recently become costly as of July 2010. This happened in the context of legislative changes triggered by the abuse of the legal provisions in this field by those tenderers who were not selected in the award procedures. Thus, the remedies system has become a tool for delaying the conclusion and/or the execution of the contract. In this context, the Government publicly declared that the abuse of the legal review procedures/remedies is becoming a real threat to economic development. This statement was made especially in relation to the absorption of EU structural funds where application deadlines are short and strict. In fact, the remedies system has been used systematically by some tenderers in order to block the conclusion of the contracts, thus building a forceful position in relation to the contracting authorities. During informal discussions with practitioners we were told that in many cases the contracting authorities, in order to avoid the delays, informally agreed to award future contracts to a specific undertaking or even directly awarded other contracts to that undertaking, in exchange of tenderers renouncing the complaint. Another illegal strategy refers to informal agreements between tenderers – the tenderer with the winning bid promises the tenderer ranked in the second position to hire him as a sub-contractor provided the latter does not contest the award decision. As a proof of the magnitude of this problem, in April 2010 the Romanian Council of Competition decided to create a department that will monitor agreements among participants to public procurement.[58] Recently, on its own initiative, the Council posted on its website a list with top 100 most 'active' complainants for the last two years. We can only presume that the intention of the Council was to show that there are numerous complainants who abuse this legal remedy. However, by looking at the list, in some cases it is obvious that economic operators had no grounds for their complaint, but there are also instances when more than 50% of their complaints were accepted. So the 'list of shame' proves to be not as relevant as it was intended by the Council; on the contrary, it could be characterized as misleading.

58. Bogdan Chirițoiu, the president of the Romanian Council of Competition, cited by Săptămâna Financiară (Financial Week), on April 30, 2010; see also the report of Transparency International Romania, *Riscuri de corupție în achizițiile publice. Excelență și integritate în achizițiile publice'*, (Corruption risks in public procurement. Excellence and integrity in public procurement), 2010, [Online] at http://www.transparency.org.ro/proiecte/proiecte_incheiate/2010/proiect_3/Riscuri%20de%20coruptie%20in%20achizitii%20publice.pdf, accessed February 4, 2011.

Prior to July 2010, the action before the Council was free of charge.Table 1 below shows the costs for tenderers (lawyers' fees not included; see more below). If a tenderer lodges a complaint with the Council, the costs occur only after the ruling of the Council is made and if the legal action is rejected (on its merits or on exceptions). The fee represents a portion from the deposit of the tenderer made with the contracting authority. If the court overrules the decision of the Council, the tenderer will receive the fee back from the contracting authority within five working days. The legal action brought against the decision of the Council before a court of law is charged with a fee which is the equivalent of 50% of the sums established by law for a legal action lodged directly with the court (see Table 2 below).

***Table 1**: Costs for lodging an action with the Council*

COUNCIL	
Estimated value of the contract (RON*) (* 1 EURO=4,2 RON)	**Costs (RON* + % of the estimated value) (* 1 EURO=4,2 RON)**
63,000 - 420,000	1%
420,001 - 4,200,000 RON	4,200 + 0,1%**
4,200,001 – 42,000,000	7,980 + 0,01%
42,000,001 - 420,000,000	11,760 + 0,001%
420,000,001 - 4,200,000,000	15,540 + 0,0001%
4,200,000,001 and up	19320 + 0,00001%

** The additional percentage on top of the fixed sum applies for values that exceed the lower end of the range

Source: compiled by the authors from EGO no.34/2006 with subsequent amendments (article 278^1)

On top of the fee charged for a rejected legal action, the Council has discretion to order the party whose complaint was rejected, to pay the expenses incurred by the review procedure. The Council can decide this 'on request', presumably of the party that the review was directed against, because the law does not state who can make the request. In practice however, the Council approached this situation very carefully and has been reluctant to grant this penalty. Though there are numerous requests made by both tenderers and contracting authorities, we did not find any case in which this penalty was granted by the Council. The courts, on the other hand, have usually granted the costs incurred during the review procedure. It is however open for debate what costs can be included here – *i.e.* the Council ruled that attorney fees are not such a cost while the court overruled this decision.[59]

In another case, the complainant has requested the annulment of the award procedure and the modification of the award documentation. The Council, after rejecting the argument of the party, has annulled the award procedure *ex officio*, on the basis of most of the arguments invoked by the party. Consequently, the court held that the Council unlawfully refused to grant compensation for expenses incurred by the contestation.[60] Other courts, on the contrary, have argued that such an approach is lawful.[61]

Tenderers can go to court in the first instance in two situations – for an action in damages, which can occur both before and after the conclusion of the contract and for any actions after the conclusion of the contract (execution of the contract, ineffectiveness, termination etc). In these cases the costs for lodging a court action are presented below in Table 2.

Table 2: *Costs for lodging an action with the court*

COURT	
Estimated value of the contract (RON*) (* 1 EURO=4,2 RON)	**Costs (RON* + % of the estimated value) (* 1 EURO=4,2 RON)**
Up to 40,000	1%
40,001 - 400,000	400 + 0,1%**
400,001 - 4,000,000	760 + 0,01%
4,000,001 - 40,000,000	1120 + 0,001%
40,000,001 -400,000,000	1480 + 0,0001%
400,000,001 -4,000,000,000	1840 + 0,00001%
Over 4,000,000,000	2200

** The additional percentage on top of the fixed sum applies for values that exceed the lower end of the range

Source: compiled by the authors from EGO no. 34/2006 with subsequent amendments (article 287^17)

59. Judgment no. 519/25.04.2008, Alba Iulia Appellate Court, Division for Administrative and Fiscal Matters; Judgment no. 1436/19.06.2008, Craiova Appellate Court, Division for Administrative and Fiscal Matters.
60. Judgment no. 953/16.09.2008, Alba Iulia Appellate Court, Division for Administrative and Fiscal Matters; Judgment no. 1572/04.07.2008, Craiova Appellate Court, Division for Administrative and Fiscal Matters.
61. Judgment no. 263/10.09.2008, Oradea Appellate Court, Division for Administrative and Fiscal Matters.

The fees established need to be understood in the context discussed throughout the paper – excessive litigation on the behalf of tenderers. For example, for a value of the contract of 420,001 RON (10,000 EURO) the fee before the Council is 4,200 RON (1,000 EURO). If the tenderer is dissatisfied with the decision of the Council, and decides to challenge it in court, the fee is 380 RON (90 EURO). For an action in damages or for any type of action after the conclusion of the contract, the fee is 760 RON (180 EURO). By looking at these numbers the intention of the legislator becomes clear: a very high fee, payable in case of a rejected action, if the tender goes before the Council (mandatory). The goal was to discourage those tenderers who only wanted to block the conclusion of the contract from lodging a complaint. In case tenderers wanted to challenge in court the decision of the Council, the fees are a lot smaller, presumably with the goal of not restricting tenderers' access to justice.

As discussed in section 3, the decision of the legislator to establish a fee for an action before the Council, will most likely have to withstand the test of constitutionality. It is debatable whether or not the current provision of the EGO no. 34/2006 still ensures free of charge access to this administrative-jurisdictional procedure. Technically, the procedure is free of charge in terms of access as the law states that the tenderer needs to pay only after the conclusion of the action and only if his complaint is rejected. In our opinion, the cost implied by the review procedure before the Council does represent a limitation of the free access to justice as well as of the principle of free and elective special jurisdictions, and it is most likely that the Constitutional Court will consider the same.

With regard to the costs of litigation in PP, the issue of mandatory representation by a lawyer and also lawyers' fees should be discussed. Both in front of the Council and of the court there is no requirement concerning mandatory representation by a lawyer. In practice, in front of the Council, economic operators tend not to use a lawyer but rather a legal adviser, which is already an employee of that undertaking. From scrutinizing cases before the Council, it was rather obvious that some complaints had no legal assistance, being drafted in a rather 'informal' manner. Before a court there are few cases in which economic operators represent themselves given the complexity and technicality of court proceedings. Based on interviews with several lawyers who work in PP, we were told that fees are calculated based on the estimated value of the contract – between 1% and 2% but no less than 1.500 RON (approximately 350 EURO). This fee is received regardless of the outcome of the action; in case of successful litigation, the bonus may be up to 10% of the value of the contract.

7 Standstill provisions

The main change introduced by the new directive is the so-called 'standstill period'. This is a minimum suspensive period intended to allow for an effective review between a contracting authority's decision to award a contract and the conclusion of that contract. The new provision is intended to give unsuccessful tenderers the time to examine the decision of the contracting authority and to decide whether or not it would be appropriate to initiate a review procedure, without the risk of having the contract concluded and be left with financial damages as their means of redress. The Remedies Directive allows Member States to establish a minimum[62] of 10 days for the standstill period, with different options for the case when the communication is not done electronically or by fax – at least 15 days of standstill if other means of communication are used, or 10 days after receiving the communication regarding the award decision.[63] The standstill period operates starting with the day following the communication. In the initial transposition, the Romanian legislator did not take into account that the 10 days start with the day following the communication. Thus, the initial standstill of 10 days included the day of the communication by the contracting authority. Thus, the standstill was shorter by one day than the minimum required standstill. Currently, after two subsequent amendments,[64] the standstill is 11 days from the day of the communication (including this day) but with an extension of 5 days for cases when the communication is done by means other than fax or e-mail. The standstill period applies even in the case when a court decision regarding the award procedure was already communicated to the parties.[65]

EGO no. 76/2010 makes partial use of the provision of article 2b of the 2007/66 Directive to except from the standstill period the awards of contracts that are not subjected to the obligation of publication in the OJEU. Nevertheless, the Romanian law establishes a shorter standstill of 6 days for such contracts. We can conclude that in this case the Romanian legislation goes further then what was required by the Directive.

62. Initially, the transposing legislation EGO no. 94/2007 established exactly 10 days for the standstill. Following a different (and correct) reading of the Directive, EGO no. 76/2010 changed the standstill period to 11 days, in order to comply with the 'minimum' requirement resulting from article 2a of the Directive.
63. Article 2a par. 2 Directive 2007/66/CE.
64. EGO no. 94/2007 and EGO no. 19/2009.
65. Article 287 8 of the EGO no. 34/2006 as amended by EGO no. 76/2010.

8 Interim measures

Interim measures include the suspension of the award procedure or other measures that would cease the implementation of the decisions taken by the contracting authority. Before 31.12.2010, interim measures were granted primarily by courts. Currently, tenderers have to go first before the Council with an action requesting the suspension of the award procedure. The Council needs to make the decision within three days. Against the decision of the Council, tenderers can go before a court of law in five days from the communication of the Council's decision. The contracting authorities up to the conclusion of the contract can also decide to take the necessary measures for remedying the breaches occurred during the award procedure. These measures are triggered by a contestation by the tenderer.[66] It is debatable whether contracting authorities can suspend the award procedure as an interim measure taken until the Council issues its decision. In practice the Council seems to dislike this remedy adopted by the contracting authorities.

Directive 2007/66/CE states in art. 2(4) that, with two exceptions, review procedures need not necessarily have an automatic suspensive effect on the contract award procedures to which they are related. The first exception, referring to a review before the contracting authority, does not apply to the Romanian context, since this review is not mandatory (only in the doctrine was discussed the possibility of such a mandatory review, if the tenderer lodges an action directly with the court, when such an action was possible). The second exception, referring to a review procedure with a body of first instance, imposes the obligation for the member state to guarantee that the contracting authority cannot conclude the contract before the review body issues the decision. This is being fulfilled by the Romanian legislation through art. 253^3 of EGO no. 34/2006.

Until the legislative changes from July 2010, the automatic suspension referred to the award procedures, thus going beyond the explicit requirement of the EU Directive. The contracting authorities were prohibited to continue with the award procedure until the decision of the Council was issued. Since 2006 and up to present there have been at least four distinct types of automatic suspension: automatic, immediate and unconditional, which operated *de jure* from the moment when the complaint was lodged with the Council (06/2006-10/2007); automatic, immediate, conditioned by the notification of the contracting authority (10/2007-12/2008); automatic, semi-delayed, start-

66. Article 256^3(1).

ing one day before the deadline for submission of tenders or one day before the end of the standstill period, and conditioned by formalities (12/2008-03/2009); automatic, fully delayed, starting one day before the end of the standstill period, and conditioned by formalities (03/2009-06/2009). There was also a transition period between 06/2009 and 07/2010, when it was unclear if automatic suspension still operated.[67] Currently, there is no automatic suspension of the award procedure triggered by lodging an action with the Council.

This complicated evolution of the automatic suspension of the award procedures triggered by an action with the Council reflects the struggle of the Romanian legislator to keep a balance between proper access to the remedies system and the need to increase the efficiency and speediness of the public procurement process. The latter has been extremely important in the Romanian context. Over time mass media and think thanks[68] have repeatedly reported on individual instances when economic operators abused the remedies system for economic purposes, namely to block the awarding of the contract. The Council argued that most complaints are unjustified, based on its statistics which show that approximately more than half of the complaints is rejected. Of course, that this is not a conclusion that can be verified, as the access to the findings of the case is restricted, and it is hard to prove the actual grounds of the economic operators who lodge a complaint, but it shows a perception which has entered the public sphere, leading other state authorities (such as the Romanian President)[69] to draw attention to this practice.

The law allows the Council discretion regarding when and how the suspension of the award procedure is granted. In all cases, a test is to be performed, the public interest being measured against the private interests of the parties. The consequences of the interim measures cannot outweigh their foreseen benefits. The concept is as unclear as a legal concept can be, so the margin of discretion is very large. There is no indication whether the public

67. Filipon, Ş., *The Romanian Experience with Interim Measures and Automatic Suspension*, paper presented at the Public Procurement: Global Revolution V Conference, University of Copenhagen, Denmark, September 2010.
68. SAR (Romanian Academic Society) Policy Brief no. 43, ‚*O evaluare a eficienţei, integrităţii şi transparenţei sistemului de achiziţii publice din România. Banul public şi interesul privat*', (An assessment of efficiency, integrity, and transparency in the Romanian public procurement system. Public money and private interest), 2009, [Online] at http://www.sar.org.ro/files/409_paper-final.pdf, accessed February 4, 2011.
69. Media Fax, 6 May 2010, The President of Romania on the necessity to amend the law on public procurement.

interest should prevail or not when assessing the negative consequences against the possible benefits, and the law does not state whether public interest can be looked at as having the same weight as private interests. The only specification regards the interdiction to affect other rights of the person concerned.[70] Until the changes from 31.12.2010, a similar article existed with regard to the discretion of the courts in assessing the need for granting these interim measures. Since now the decision of the Council regarding the suspension of the award procedure can be challenged in court, it is important to see how courts have previously ruled in this matter. For example, in a case concerning the suspension of the award procedure for a road infrastructure contract, the court, taking into consideration the public interest, ruled that the infrastructure project is of national interest, being funded by EU money, and that any delay in fulfilling the project affects the financial relations between Romania and the EU, and there is also the risk of losing non-refundable financing in case of delays in completing the project. It is worth mentioning however that the court has indicated that the economic operator will not be harmed in the absence of the suspension of the award procedure.[71] It is clear that the private interests were balanced against the public ones.

An interesting debate with regard to interim measures refers to the suspension of the decisions reached by the Council. Although the public procurement legislation in place does not provide for the possibility to request the suspension of the decision of the Council,[72] based on the general Law on judicial review the decision can be suspended by the court in cases where 'there is doubt regarding its legality' and there is a 'danger of a serious imminent damage' for the interested person.[73] This legal instrument is important because the decisions of the Council are mandatory for the contracting authorities, and a court action does not automatically suspend their execution. In our opinion, this legal tool can be considered as an interim measure ordered by the court in cases when an initial brief analysis of the decision entitles the conclusion that there are grounds for annulment; the courts have not shown

70. Article 287^7 of the EGO 34/2006.
71. Judgment no. 1259/12.05.2008, Bucharest Appellate Court, Division for Administrative and Fiscal Matters.
72. The former article 284 which was allowing such suspension was abrogated by EGO no. 94/2007 without any provision to replace it.
73. Article 2 of the Law no. 554/2004. See, in this sense, Judgment from 19.06.2009, Cluj Appellate Court, Division for Administrative and Fiscal Matters, in RevistaRomână de Drept al Afacerilor [Romanian Review of Business Law], no.7/2008, p. 107.

any reluctance to use it when deemed appropriate.[74] The 'imminent damage' criterion has to be used currently with precaution, because until the implementation of the ineffectiveness remedy in 2010, the conclusion of the contract would have entitled the interested person initiating a court action only to damages, while now, the foreseen 'damage' of not being able to get annulment of the contract cannot be invoked any more.

Before the changes brought in 2010 (mandatory Council review), some courts have held that the suspension of the award procedure can be obtained not only by the means provided by the public procurement legislation, but also by invoking the Code of civil procedure. Thus, requesting an ordinance from the president of the court[75] was admissible in public procurement award procedures, to be applied for periods that are not covered by the effects of the suspension ordered on the basis of the public procurement law. This suspension can prove useful in between the decision of the Council and the action in court,[76] ever more if the interpretation of the provisions regarding the suspension of the procedure according to the public procurement legislation by court will be done restrictively, in the sense that the suspension can be granted only after a court action was lodged. In the context of the new regulation (mandatory review before the Council), it seems that such a possibility is no longer available. However, it would be interesting to see whether complainants will seek suspension by the court only to invoke the unconstitutionality of the mandatory review before the Council and thus trigger the intervention of the Constitutional Court.

Among the 'sufficient reasons' for the suspension of the award procedure, before the introduction of the ineffectiveness remedy, the most important one referred to the fact that the contract, once concluded, will only entail damages.[77] Other arguments, relating to unrealized profit or the impossibility to develop experience in such contracts were rejected by the courts.[78]

74. Judgment no. 3/R/22.05.2008, Braşov Appellate Court, Division for Administrative and Fiscal Matters.
75. Article 581 of the Code of civil procedure.
76. Judgment no. 129/17.01.2008, Bucharest Appellate Court, Division for Administrative and Fiscal Matters; for a critique of this decision, see Şerban, D.D., *Despreordonanţa preşedinţialăînmateriaachiziţiilorpublice* [Regarding the Admissibility of President's Ordinance in Public Procurement], înPandecteleRomâne [Romanian Pandectaes] no.6/2008, pp.77-86.
77. Judgment no. 140/19.01.2009, Bucharest Appellate Court, Division for Administrative and Fiscal Matters.
78. Judgment no. 174/19.01.2009, Bucharest Appellate Court, Division for Administrative and Fiscal Matters.

Until the end of 2010, when only courts were able to grant suspension, in-practice it was rather difficult to obtain it. This is based on previous case law when in several cases the court rejected the action as lacking object because by the time of the ruling the contracting authority had already awarded the contract so there was no pending award procedure to be suspended.[79] Currently, the question of speediness of proceedings in this matter is solved in light of the requirement that the Council needs to issue its decision in three days. It remains to be seen if courts will be able to address the recourse against the decision of the Council in time for it to be useful for the tenderer.

9 Establishment of a breach

The data presented below and their interpretation need to be considered in the legislative context in place until 31.12.2010 which allowed tenderers to go 'forum shopping'. Since the review by the Council is now mandatory, we will most likely witness an increase in the number of cases brought before the Council. Some practitioners estimate that the number of actions in court against the decisions of the Council will increase as well.

9.1 Before the Council

As already mentioned, tenderers can lodge an action with the Council only up to the conclusion of the contract. The Council offers statistical data on its website regarding the number of cases per year, type of solutions, decisions challenged in court etc.

First, we looked at how the number of contestations before the Council has evolved over the years. After 2006, there was a constant increase in the number of contestations, most likely triggered by the existence of the immediate suspensive effect (2006 – 673 complaints; 2007 – 4976; 2008 – 6517; 2009 – 9019). In 2010, we witnessed for the first time a decrease in the number of complaints brought before the Council (7633), estimated to be around 25% compared to 2009, according to representatives of the Council. This decrease can be explained by changes in the legislation. There are two such changes – on the one hand, the potential costs that tenderers may suffer, provided that their complaint is rejected; this explains the decrease in the number of complaints in the second semester of 2010, following a change in legisla-

79. Judgment no. 2166/03.12.2007, Bucharest Appellate Court, Division for Administrative and Fiscal Matters; Judgment no. 1400/27.09.2007, Bucharest Appellate Court, Division for Administrative and Fiscal Matters.

tion in July 2010. On the other hand, the automatic suspension that applied until 2009 no longer operates; this will explain the general reduction of complaints throughout the entire year.

A second set of data analyzed referred to the rate of success in lodging a complaint. For 2009, the rate of success declared by the Council (decisions in favor of the economic operators) was 30.99%. In 2010 (for the first six months) the rate is 31.09%. Also for 2009, the percentage of complaints declared admissible and judged on their merits was 64.4. This data is hard to verify, as the Council refuses to publish its decisions, so we couldn't look into the concrete findings of the case. Before the Council, the object of the complaint refers in 36.22% of the cases to the tender documentation and in 63.78% to the result of the award procedure (data regarding the first six months from 2010).[80] In 2010, in 73.83% of the cases judged on their merits, the Council ruled the remedying of the award procedure (ordering measures to be taken by the contracting authority, *i.e.* the contracting authority could be required to add or take out certain technical specifications or to redraft them) and in 26.17% of the cases for its annulment. From a selection of Council's rulings available online, we found the following instances as grounds for the annulment of the award procedure: tenders considered unacceptable for lack of conformity with the technical specifications; as the result of the annulment of the illegal award documentation; as the result of a breach by the contracting authority of a previous decision of the Council regarding the same award procedure; the impossibility to remedy the award documentation as to allow all interested economic operators to participate.

A third set of data refers to the rate of success in court, when a decision of the Council is challenged. In 2009, 10.65% out of the total number of decisions issued by the Council were challenged in court; only in 1.2% of the cases the court declared the complaint admissible/modified the decision of the Council. In 2010 (first 11 months) 12.65% of the decisions were challenged, and in 1.84% of the cases the decision of the Council was overturned.[81]

9.2 Before the court

In Romania the courts do not publish or post online all of their decisions. Therefore, we can only look at selections of case law made by various pub-

80. Activity report of the National Council for Solving Legal Disputes, 2009, [Online] at http://cnsc.ro/images/stories/rapoarte/2010/raport_activitate_CNSC_2009.pdf, accessed December 16, 2010.
81. Data obtained from the Council, following a request under the national FOIA.

lishers. We reviewed a number of 525 decisions. The most common breaches of the law by the contracting authorities are:

a) Restrictive qualification and selection criteria; the contracting authorities are in breach of the legal provisions by not accepting alternative certification, alternative means of proof, or certification pending.
b) Evaluation criteria that are unclear or unquantifiable; lack of transparency and equality in the application of the evaluation criteria.
c) Restrictive technical specification resulting in the limitation of competition.
d) Wrong type of award procedure for a particular contract. Illegal use of procedures that are not stated in the PP law.
e) The illegal annulment of the award procedure by the contracting authority.
f) Abnormally low tenders; lack of any measures of the contracting authority to investigate this tender.
g) Some other less common breaches: the conclusion of the contract during the standstill period; starting of the award procedures without the publication of a notice of intention or participation announcement; modification of the tender documentation during the procedure (change of technical specifications); changes in the financial proposals of the tenderers after the evaluation of the tenders, allowed by the contracting authority; the refuse to provide potential tenderers with access to tender documentation.

The sample of cases includes actions in court in first instance (limited number) and actions against the decisions of the Council. From analyzing them, it is obvious that the success rate for tenderers is low, even in cases when the decision of the Council is challenged. In many cases the action is rejected on exceptions (lack of standing, tardiness, different object than in front of the review body in first instance).

The intensity of the control exercised by courts is not very high, as they tend to keep at the surface and strike down only manifest illegal measures. Apart from some isolated cases when the courts have gone deeper and 'put themselves in the shoes' of the contracting authority,[82] the review is one of illegality.

82. Judgment no. 764/13.11.2008, Bacău Appellate Court, Division for Administrative and Fiscal Matters.

10 Annulment of the award procedure

With regard to the annulment of the award procedure (and/or decisions issued by the contracting authority during the award procedure) a distinction needs to be made between annulment by the *contracting authority* (1) and *annulment by the review bodies* (2).

10.1 Annulment by the contracting authority

In this case, annulment of the award procedure is not a remedy for those interested in annulment. An unlawful annulment of the procedure, on the other hand, can be challenged in front of the Council and this is a remedy for those interested in the continuation of the procedure.

In practice numerous situations occurred when tenderers have contested the legality of such annulments (according to a 2009 study, in 25% of the cases studied the contracting authorities annulled the award procedure, which is likely to raise suspicions).[83] This has resulted in court litigation and there are contradictory decisions as to what represents a legal ground for annulment. The law expressly states a limited number of circumstances under which the contracting authority can annul the procedure: a) The number of candidates selected in the procedure used by the authority is smaller than the one provided for by the law; b) The offers were unacceptable or not in conformity with the technical specifications; c) No offers were made or the offers made cannot be compared due to their different way of approaching the technical/financial solutions; d) Serious breaches affecting the award procedure or the impossibility to conclude the contract; e) As a result of a decision by the Council which forces contracting authorities to eliminate any technical, economical or financial specifications from the award announcement, award documentation or any other documents issued in relation to the award procedure. Aside from these circumstances, the annulment of the award procedure by the contracting authority is illegal and potentially abusive. In practice, contracting authorities have tried to annul award procedures invoking one of the legal circumstances described above (mostly the impossibility to conclude the contract).

83. SAR (Romanian Academic Society) Policy Brief no. 43, *‚O evaluare a eficienţei, integrităţii şi transparenţei sistemului de achiziţii publice din România. Banul public şi interesul privat'*, (An assessment of efficiency, integrity, and transparency in the Romanian public procurement system. Public money and private interest), 2009, [Online] at http://www.sar.org.ro/files/409_paper-final.pdf, accessed February 4, 2011.

Among the grounds invoked by the contracting authority for the annulment of the award procedure, a peculiar instance is the one when contracting authorities invoke the lack of funding for carrying out the award procedure, in the context of the ground specified at article 209 (d) of the EGO no. 34/2006 regarding the 'impossibility to conclude the contract'. When in between the initiation of the award procedure and the award of the contract the funding public entity has encountered a budget cut, in some cases the Council agreed that the award procedure can be annulled, but the winning tenderer should be compensated. Some courts, however, held that the estimated value of the contract should be relevant, not the existing funding at the date of the award. Consequently, if the winning bid is within the available budget, after the cut, the contract has to be concluded. The contracting authority has therefore unlawfully annulled the procedure, and it was forced to conclude the contract.[84] This approach was not accepted though by other courts, which held that impossibility to conclude the contract can arise also from the lack of funding for the procurement, due to changes in the funding agreements between the financing body and the contracting authority.[85]

Another situation of abusive annulment by the contracting authority, then challenged in court by an economic operator, referred to a case in which the contracting authority annulled the award procedure a long time after the opening of the offers. The court held that the contracting authority cannot invoke its own fault in conducting the procedure after such a long period of time, during which it refused to conclude the contract with the winning tenderer. The contracting authority should have either decided the annulment earlier, or concluded the contract. The court could not see any reasons for the 'impossibility to conclude the contract', as provided by the law, in order to justify such conduct.[86] Consequently, the court has ordered the resuming of the procedure from the opening of the offers. This case shows that contracting authorities need to tread very carefully when deciding whether to annul the award procedure or to take remedial measures.

84. Judgment no. 436/10.06.2008, Bacău Appellate Court, Division for Administrative and Fiscal Matters.
85. Judgment no. 819/07.05.2007, Bucharest Appellate Court, Division for Administrative and Fiscal Matters.
86. Judgment no. 2532/06.11.2008, Cluj Appellate Court, Division for Administrative and Fiscal Matters.

10.2 Annulment by the review bodies – in this case annulment is a true remedy

An interesting development is currently taking place in Romania with regard to the annulment of the award procedure by the Council. Due to the fact that the current legislation eliminated the automatic suspension of the award procedure when a complaint is lodged with the Council, there is a big increase in the number of cases when the Council rules the measure of annulment of the award procedure. In practice, this measure which was intended to speed up the conclusion of the contract has generated unwanted effects. For example, if there are minor breaches with regard to the drafting of the tender documentation, since the automatic suspension effect no longer operates, the contracting authority carries out the award procedure with the faulty documentation. If the suspension operated immediately (period 06/2006-12/2008), then such breaches could have be elimineated while now the only remedy is annulment (the same effect was associated with the delayed automatic suspension; for details see section 9 on interim measures).

An assessment needs to be made with regard to the effectiveness of the annulment of the award procedure in the context of the remedy system. From the perspective of the economic operator who challenges aspects of the award procedure, the annulment is very effective. On the other hand, from a broader perspective, the changes made to the PP legislation, mostly those regarding suspension, were meant to increase the speediness of the PP procedures and the spending of EU structural funds. From this broader standpoint, annulment results in more delays since the contracts need to be retendered. From a public policy perspective, in order to reach the goals mentioned above, in the context in which there is no longer an automatic suspension in place, there are several issues that need to be understood by the contracting authorities: in the first place, contracting authorities should take advantage of the current legal provisions which allow them to take any remedial actions, including annulment of decisions issued, following the notification about an alleged breach invoked by the complainant; second, it is possible for them to voluntarily suspend the award procedure, until the Council reaches a decision.

In order for the courts to grant the annulment of the award procedure, the grounds invoked by the complainants have to be serious and to make the annulment unavoidable in the sense that it is the only foreseeable solution for redress. The mere absence of some information from the award notification does not always justify the annulment of the whole award procedure. The information that is lacking has to be relevant and to affect the award procedure. For instance, the omission to specify the address and fax number of the contracting authority in the participation notification cannot be considered essential for the award procedure, as long as the contestant has participated after all in the procedure.[87] In another case, the lack of the signature of some members of the evaluation commission on the document describing the opening of offers was considered also irrelevant as the contestant has failed to demonstrate how he was aggrieved by that omission.[88] The court has stricken down decisions of the Council considering the opposite.[89]

As a conclusion, annulment by the contracting authority (on matters of substantive law) and annulment by review bodies (a remedy for those interested) are closely intertwined. Since annulment as a remedy is relatively hard to obtain (though recently there has been an increase in the number of annulments of the award procedure by the Council), contracting authorities seem to be the actors who, acting in good faith, might solve some breaches that could affect the award procedure in the early stages of the PP process.

11 Suspension of the execution of the contract

The Romanian law provides for an interesting remedy after the conclusion of the contract namely the *suspension of the execution* of the contract. After the changes from 31.12.2010, because of an error of the legislator (the old text was amended wherever possible just by eliminating the reference to the court as a first instance review body) there are now two separate articles (283^1 and 287^7) which address the suspension of the execution of the contract in a slightly different manner. According to article 283^1 the interested party can request the court in certain circumstances, in order to prevent the occurrence of imminent damages, to grant this suspension. The court needs to take into account all possible consequences of the suspension for a broad category of interests, including the public interest. As in the case of interim measures, the test to be performed is that the negative consequences cannot outweigh the benefits of such a decision. This remedy operates only when a tenderer whose complaint before the Council was rejected/not solved favorably then decides to challenge the decision of the Council in court. In the meanwhile the contracting authority can conclude the contract and start its execution. Article

87. Judgment no. 967/28.05.2007, Bucharest Appellate Court, Division for Administrative and Fiscal Matters.
88. Judgment no. 1092/15.06.2007, Bucharest Appellate Court, Division for Administrative and Fiscal Matters.
89. Judgment no. 1492/29.11.2008, Bucharest Appellate Court, Division for Administrative and Fiscal Matters.

283^1 makes no reference to the timeframe in which the court needs to issue its ruling regarding the suspension and also for how long the suspension would operate; article 287^7 on the other hand, states that the suspension operates until the court solves the case on its merits. Probably the error will be noticed in the future. However, the article that resulted presumably by mistake clarifies the timeframe for which the suspension operates.

12 Ineffectiveness (annulment of the contract)

The second significant amendment brought by the 2007/66/EC Directive along with the standstill period is the introduction of a specific remedy in situations where a contracting authority has awarded a public contract directly in breach of the procurement rules (*i.e.* without prior transparency and in the absence of a competitive tendering procedure). Because ineffectiveness does not operate automatically, in the case of Romania, national courts act as review bodies in this matter. The Council does not have jurisdiction with regard to ineffectiveness; it can only rule the annulment of decisions issued in the award procedure up to the conclusion of the contract.

It must be noted that the Remedies Directive, when translated into Romanian, used the concept '*without legal effects'* for ineffectiveness. EGO no. 76/2010 transposing the Remedies Directive uses the term '*nullity*'. Consequently, in the Romanian case, the concept of ineffectiveness and nullity overlap. However, in the law, besides the breaches associated with ineffectiveness in the sense of the Directive, there are other breaches that lead to nullity – *i.e.* the conclusion of the contract without taking into account the decision of the Council.[90]

The new remedy is expected to become a significant legal mechanism against the illegal direct award of public procurement contracts. Prior to the adoption of the new directive, the national legislation only allowed a person or undertaking which has suffered as a result of an illegally awarded contract to seek a review for damages, and did not permit the contract to be retendered. The deterrent effect on contracting authorities of a potential damages review was thus limited. Now, the risk (both in a financial and reputational sense) of having to retender the contract should cause contracting authorities to think twice before illegally directly awarding a contract.

90. Art. 280(3) of the EGO no. 34/2006.

The Romanian legislator, in the process of transposing the Remedies Directive, states the same instances of ineffectiveness of a contract as the Directive. Article 2d(1b) of the Remedies Directive states that several infringements of the public procurement provisions can be considered grounds for ineffectiveness (annulment) provided that two cumulative conditions are met: if the infringement had deprived the tenderer applying for review of the possibility to pursue pre-contractual remedies; where such an infringement is combined with an infringement of Directive 2004/18/EC if that infringement has affected the chances of the tenderer applying for review to obtain the contract. By comparison with the text of the Directive discussed above, the Romanian law goes a step further, and, in a separate article of the law,[91] states that ineffectiveness may be decided by the court even if the infringements do not meet the two said cumulative conditions. In these cases the court can evaluate whether to deem the contract ineffective or to rule in favor of alternative penalties.

Standing in a legal action regarding ineffectiveness has, in the first place, any economic operator or person concerned by the award procedure and/or the contract. In addition, the Romanian law states that the National Authority for Regulating and Monitoring Public Procurement can also require the court to deem a contract ineffective, based on the provisions of a general law regarding extinctive prescription. The Authority can invoke the same grounds for annulment as any economic operator (see the three situations mentioned both in the Remedies Directive and in the national legislation); however, there are three additional grounds for ineffectiveness:

a) The contract was concluded in breach of the minimum requirements set by the contracting authority in the tender documentation or, even though these requirements were met, the contract was concluded by the contracting authority with the acceptance of less favorable conditions than those comprised in the technical and/or financial winning offer.
b) When the contracting authority seeks to obtain the execution of works, services or goods which would make that contract a public procurement one, but the contracting authority concludes a different type of contract (*e.g.* land concession), in breach of the public procurement legislation.
c) The conclusion of the contract was made with a breach of the legal provisions regarding the conflict of interest – the PP legislation states that any family relations between representatives of the tenderer (his associates,

91. Article 287^11 of the EGO no. 34/2006 as amended by EGO no. 76/2010.

subcontractors, shareholders etc) and executive representatives within the contracting authority are forbidden. If such a situation had occurred, the tenderer should have been excluded from the award procedure; the lack of exclusion generates the ineffectiveness of the contract. This provision is clearly specific to the Romanian context; the legislator tries to address the issue of conflict of interest, which has been raised in numerous occasions in PP.

According to the Romanian legislation, in principle ineffectiveness operates *ex tunc*. The law also states circumstances under which ineffectiveness is replaced by alternative penalties (*ex nunc*). The reason for doing this is the existence of imperative reasons concerning public interest. The court is the body which determines what constitutes imperative reasons; the law only mentions the economic interests regarding the capacity of the contract to generate effects which can be considered as an imperative reason only if the absence of these effects would produce disproportionate consequences. In addition, the law details several economic consequences which cannot be considered imperative reasons: delay costs in the execution of the contract; costs related to the initiation of a new award procedure; costs generated by the change of the economic operator which will execute the contract; costs related to the legal obligations generated by the absence of the effects of the contract.

The alternative measures are:

a) Limitation of the effects of the contract by shortening its execution period; and/or
b) A fine for the contracting authority between 2%-15% of the value of the contract, the exact percentage being established by reference to the possibility to limit the effects of the contract (the smaller the possibility to limit them the bigger the fine). Although the directive allowed Member States to establish several criteria for the assessment of the alternative penalties, such as the seriousness of the infringement and the behavior of the contracting authority, the Romanian transposing legislation retained only one criterion, namely the possibility to limit the effects of the contract.

The court, when ruling for alternative penalties, will make sure that they are efficient, proportionate, and discouraging for the contracting authorities.

The alternative penalty of a fine for the contracting authority also applies to all cases where ineffectiveness cannot have a retroactive effect (*ex tunc*), because the termination of the contractual obligations already executed is impossible.

The ineffectiveness remedy was introduced after the implementation deadline by the Romanian Government, through EGO no. 76/2010, which entered into force on July 5th 2010, so making use of this new provision can be assessed only after this date. No court cases were finalized until now based on the new provisions.

Both the Remedies Directive and the national legislation, presuming the good faith of the contracting authorities, exclude the penalty of the ineffectiveness of the contract in cases where the contract has been introduced by the contracting authority in the category of contracts for which a participation announcement is not necessary provided that some transparency measures were taken and the standstill period was complied with voluntarily.[92]

With regard to this provision, there are two aspects open for debate. First, up to what extent can the courts assess the 'good faith' of the contracting authority? Second, are the courts competent to assess this aspect, considering the fact that the conclusion of the contract after the standstill period should have allowed tenderers enough opportunities for seeking review? Following the same reasoning, tenderers should be able to invoke this provision only within the frame of the standstill period. Nevertheless, in the absence of such specific legal provision, it seems that the Directive empowers courts to exercise discretion when assessing the decision of the contracting authorities falling within the scope of this provision. In our opinion, only in cases when it is obvious that the contracting authority has abused its power to opt for not tendering out, the court could overturn the decision. In not so clear cases, the benefit of the good faith should work in favor of the contracting authority. Otherwise, this entire procedure loses its presumed effects. Our interpretation is endorsed also by specific provisions of the national legislation. Thus article 69(2) of the Law no. 24/2000 on drafting legal norms states that any administrative interpretation of legal norms and provisions is valid until there is an interpretation from the issuer or from the court. In other words, the contracting authority, under the Romanian law, should be sheltered from accountability, outside the time limits provided by law, when the interpretation of the legal norm was done in good faith.

According to the Remedies Directive, the deadline for filing an application for ineffectiveness is at least 30 days from the publication of the contract award notice (or at least six months after the contract is concluded if no notice is published). The Romanian legislation provides for a maximum of 30

92. Article 287^12 of the EGO no. 34/2006 as amended by EGO no. 72/2009.

days or six months. It can be observed that the Romanian legislator opted to provide the minimum deadline required by the Directive.

With regard to deadlines for filing an action for ineffectiveness, the Romanian law created an opportunity for review outside the time limits of 30 days or 6 months, thus allowing for actions to be still admissible after the completion of these deadlines[93] (see the discussion above about the existence of more grounds than in the Directive for ineffectiveness and the possibility for NARMPP to have standing in legal actions concerning ineffectiveness). Inevitably, in this case the court has to take into consideration even more than in standard cases of ineffectiveness, all the relevant aspects in order to weigh the appropriate measure to be ordered. In our view the intention of the provision was to ease balancing the decision towards alternative measures.

This extension of the scope of the transposing legislation is evidently related to the jurisprudence of the ECJ in Commission v. Germany (C-503/04). In this landmark case, the ECJ has stated that provisions regarding the option to exclude annulment of a contract after conclusion only apply to an action before a review body in the Member States. The protection for signed contracts will not apply to proceedings brought by the Commission before ECJ requiring the Member State to comply with its procurement law obligations. Accordingly, in that case, the ECJ declared that Germany was required to ensure that contracts concluded in breach of the procurement rules were terminated, despite the fact that they had been signed 10 years ago for a 30 years period.

It is thus probable that, following the case law of the European Court of Justice, the Romanian legislator had created 'a way out' of the situation when infringement of public procurement law is held against the Romanian state and the time limits set for seeking review for ineffectiveness would have been expired. It is evident that the intention of the Romanian government was to make sure that no cases that would lead to the accountability of the Romanian state in front of the ECJ, because of the lack of means to redress the breach, are left out of the scope of review.

93. Article 287^14 combined with article287^11 of EGO no. 34/2006 as amended by EGO no. 76/2010.

13 Damages

Damages arising from the award procedure can be granted only in court, following a separate action in damages. The action in damages is conditioned by the prior annulment of the act of the contracting authority.[94] It can be decided also after the contracting authority revokes the act or takes other measures of redress. Before the changes from 31.12.2010, if the tenderer decided to go to court in first instance, it was possible to file for damages alongside with the annulment of the procedure or alternative measures. The concerned person who requests damages for preparing the offer and participating in the award procedure has to prove the causal relation that exists between the infringement of the public procurement law and the real chance of winning the contract.

The courts have held that the damages in public procurement cases can be only material, and not moral,[95] although this conclusion does not follow from the EGO no. 34/2006, which simply refers to 'damages'. The compensations have to be related to the loss, which needs to be proved; the compensation action cannot be based just on the fact that the award procedure was annulled.[96] Consequently, the award of compensations cannot be related to the value of the contract which was not obtained, but to the real expenses incurred by the tenderer in the award procedure. From the available case law, it surfaces that lost profit is not considered when granting damages, most courts have decided that only 'real' costs, that already were incurred, could be compensated. However, in a case when there was a single offer which was assessed by the contracting authority in breach of the PP legislation (because there were not enough tenders, the contracting authority should have annulled the award procedure, and not proceeded with the evaluation of the existing offer), leading in the end to the annulment of the procedure, we consider that compensation could have been granted, as the fault was entirely on the part of the contracting authority. The court has ruled otherwise, rejecting the complaint based on the fact that the offer was neither rejected nor accepted, so the complainant has suffered no damages as a result of the annulment of the proce-

94. Article 287 of the EGO no. 34/2006 as amended by EGO no. 19/2009.
95. Judgment no. 211/28.01.2008, Bucharest Appellate Court, Division for Administrative and Fiscal Matters.
96. Judgment no. 227/23.04.2008, Constanța Appellate Court, Division for Administrative and Fiscal Matters.

dure.[97] In our opinion, for the reasons discussed above, the solution of the court is debatable.

Damages following ineffectiveness. Damages can be granted to the contracting party after the court has ruled the contract ineffective. In this case, the action in damages can complement the action in ineffectiveness or be filed separately, at a later moment (but not after 3 years from the ineffectiveness).

The damages can be granted to the party that was awarded the ineffective contract (1), or to the party that filed the action in ineffectiveness (2), regardless of the fact that the court decides annulment of the contract or maintains the contract ordering instead alternative sanctions. As no cases were registered yet for ineffectiveness, we cannot assess the case law on this matter. In the first case, the court should also assess the good faith of the party that was awarded the contract.

In the case of an ineffective contract, damages may cover losses arising from the preparation of the offer and participation in the procedure, and the plaintiff shall only demonstrate the breach and that he had a real chance of obtaining the contract, which was compromised as a result of the breach.

14 Correlation of remedies

The initial version of EGO no. 34/2006 represents an instance of over-compliance with the EU Directives with regard to the automatic suspension of the award procedure following an action before the Council. This initial provision obviously operated in favor of the tenderers; the logic of the provision was to make sure that tenderers are not affected by breaches of the PP law by the contracting authorities. Over time this resulted in negative effects, namely major delays in awarding/concluding contracts due to abusive litigation. The termination of the automatic suspension, the introduction of fees for an action before the Council, and finally the mandatory review in first instance by the Council were all designed to limit excessive litigation. It is still unclear if the latest measures limit the access of tenderers to the remedies system.

From the perspective of the remedies system, we must analyze the interplay between the actors who can grant remedies; a distinction needs to be made between the PP process before the conclusion and after the conclusion

97. Judgment no. 420/12.05.2008, Constanța Appellate Court, Division for Administrative and Fiscal Matters.

of the contract, after noting that remedies available in the pre-contractual phase are not precluding the use of remedies in the contractual phase.

Up to the conclusion of the contract, the remedies available are the suspension of the award procedure, the annulment of the award procedure or of acts of the contracting authority, as well as other remedial measures, and damages (where the contracting authority stops the award process because of the illegality of it and therefore there is room for damages of the bid cost). With the exception of damages, both the Council and the courts can grant these remedies, with the mention that tenderers need to go first before the Council, which acts as a mandatory first instance review body. Because the automatic suspension is no longer operating, the remedy most often granted by the Council is the annulment of the award procedure.

After the conclusion of the contract, the courts are the only review bodies which can grant remedies and they have many remedies at hand: suspension of the execution of the contract, ineffectiveness, alternative sanctions, and damages. With the exception of damages, all the other remedies that can be granted are new (introduced in 2010). As already discussed, it is difficult to comment on their impact or how they interact for now.

There are no special rules concerning the interplay between remedies similar to those in the French law (parallel remedy theory), at least not specifically for public procurement. In the doctrine there is the theory of 'parallel recourse' that precludes the use of the procedure laid down in the *general* Law on judicial review when there are other review proceedings regulated in *specific* laws, but it is not the case for public procurement, as the review procedure here is regulated entirely by a special law. The article from the PP law stating that its provisions are supplemented with those from the general Law on judicial review is currently abrogated.

A feasible option for tenderers will be to seek annulment (ineffectiveness) alongside with damages. This brings the judge in the position of granting damages even in the case when the contract is not declared ineffective for reasons of public interest and alternative sanctions are applied to the contracting authority.

As a concluding remark, the Council seems to be the key actor of the remedies system up to the conclusion of the contract – courts can grant these remedies only following an action before the Council.

15 Alternative Dispute Resolution (ADR) in public procurement

The law creates the framework for the establishment of ADR tools in public procurement. The Government can regulate, by means of decision, the situations and the way in which tenderers and contracting authorities have the right to participate in a conciliation procedure (it applies only during the execution of the contract). Currently there is no such decision in place. Nevertheless, the general Law on judicial review[98] sends the parties of the public contracts to conciliation regulated by the Code of civil procedure[99] for commercial contracts. It is a prior requirement for lodging a court action, so it is mandatory. Moreover, among the ADR tools available there is also the procedure of mediation, regulated in a general manner in Law no. 192/2006 which can be in principle applied to public procurement procedures and contracts as well. Nevertheless, there is reluctance from the contracting authorities regarding the use of such tools in practice, as they are fearful of the controls conducted by the Court of Auditors, which does not encourage such practices. This happens in light of potential abuses by the contracting authorities.

16 Final considerations

As mentioned from the very beginning of the paper, the Remedies Directive (at least some of its provisions) has been transposed late and with errors, which triggered subsequent amendments to EGO no. 34/2006. This incremental change has resulted in a rather difficult to read legal text (the numbering of the articles is odd; sometimes it is hard to follow the logic of a certain remedy procedure). The late transposition also makes it difficult for us to assess at the beginning of 2011 the efficiency of specific remedies and how they interact with each other.

The legislative changes were triggered by two separate reasons – on the one hand, the existence of the Remedies Directive; on the other hand, the national legislator had to balance the need for effective remedies available to economic operators with the need to ensure that contracting authorities can carry out their policy objectives in a reasonable time frame. These challenges seem however specific for the Romanian context.

98. Law no.554/2004, article 7 par.2.
99. Article7201 of the Code of civil procedure.

The latest developments with regard to remedies in PP in Romania include: the mandatory review by the Council as the first instance review body; the termination of the automatic suspension of the award procedure following a complaint lodged with the Council (a remedy not required by the Directive; overcompliance); the standstill period (the correct duration introduced only in 2010), the suspension of the execution of the contract; and ineffectiveness which is new and seems to overlap with absolute nullity. At a first assessment, ineffectiveness may determine courts to grant other remedies, mostly suspension of the award procedure and/or damages, more sparingly.

Bibliography

Dragoş, D.C., *Legea contenciosului administrativ. Comentarii şi explicaţii* [Law on Judicial Review Commented and Explained], 2nd edition, C.H. Beck, Bucharest, 2009.

Filipon, Ş., *The Romanian Experience with Interim Measures and Automatic Suspension*, paper presented at the Public Procurement: Global Revolution V Conference, University of Copenhagen, Denmark, September 2010.

National Council for Solving Legal Disputes, [Online] at www.cnsc.ro.

Pătraşcu, H., *Culegere de practică judiciară în materie de achiziţii publice*, [Case Law in the Field of Public Procurement], Wolters Kluwer, Bucharest, 2010.

SAR (Romanian Academic Society) Policy Brief no. 43, O evaluare a eficienţei, integrităţii şi transparenţei sistemului de achiziţii publice din România. Banul public şi interesul privat, (An assessment of efficiency, integrity, and transparency in the Romanian public procurement system. Public money and private interest), 2009, [Online] at http://www.sar.org.ro/files/409_paper-final.pdf.

Şerban, D.D. *Jurisprudenţa comentată în domeniul achiziţiilorpublice* [Case Law in Public Procurement], Wolters Kluwer, Bucharest, 2009

Şerban, D.D., *Despre ordonanţa preşedinţială în materia achiziţiilorpublic*e [Regarding the Admissibility of the President's Ordinance in Public Procurement], in Pandectele Romane [Romanian Pandectae] no.6/2008, pp.77-86.

Şerban, D.D., *Calitatea procesuală a Consiliului Naţional de Soluţionare a Contestaţiilor* [The Standing in Court of the NCSLD], in Dreptul [Law Review] no.9/2008.

Transparency International Romania, Riscuri de corupţie în achiziţiile publice. Excelenţă şi integritate în achiziţiile publice, (Corruption risks in public procurement. Excellence and integrity in public procurement), 2010, [Online] at http://www.transparency.org.-ro/proiecte/proiecte_incheiate/2010/proiect_3/Riscuri%20de%20coruptie%20in%20-achizitii%20publice.pdf.

6 An Overview of the United Kingdom Public Procurement Review and Remedies System with an Emphasis on England and Wales

By Martin Trybus

1 Introduction

The jurisdictions of the United Kingdom: England and Wales, Scotland, and Northern Ireland, have seen a noticeable increase in public procurement review and remedies litigation recently. After decades of only a handful of cases every year, if that, the High Court (England, Wales, and Northern Ireland) and the Sheriff Court (Scotland) have become busier with the review of public procurement procedures. There are now about 20 cases each year. Many of these concern legal action against the failure of contracting entities to properly inform bidders about the award criteria, their weighting, the evaluation methodology, the failure to apply these criteria properly, more generally the unequal treatment of tenderers, lack of transparency, and the termination of the procurement procedure before the contract is awarded.

The United Kingdom Public Contracts Regulations SI 2006/6 implemented Directive 2004/18/EC and the Utilities Contracts Regulations SI 2006/5 implemented Directive 2004/17/EC. Both entered into force on 31 January 2006.[1] The United Kingdom Public Contracts (Amendment) Regula-

* The author wishes to thank Steen Treumer (Copenhagen) and François Lichère (Aix-en-Provence) for their very useful substantive and editorial comments on an earlier draft of this chapter. He also wishes to thank all the participants of the 3rd European Procurement Law Network meeting in Copenhagen in September 2010 for their comments in response to the paper delivered during that meeting. Moreover, he wishes to thank his colleague Keith Uff (Birmingham) for comments especially on the English law aspects of this chapter. Finally, he is grateful to Christopher Bovis (Hull) for discussing a few issues of this chapter with him. All mistakes, however, remain those of the author.

tions 2009 SI 2009/2992[2] and the Utilities Contracts (Amendment) Regulations 2009 SI 2009/3100[3] represent the transposition of Directive 2007/66/EC amending the Procurement Remedies Directives 89/665/EEC and 92/13/EC. These Amendment Regulations entered into force on 20 December 2009. All these Regulations apply in England, Wales, and Northern Ireland. Scotland has implemented separately and the new Scottish Regulations also entered into force on 31 January 2006 and 20 December 2009 respectively.[4] With the further progress of devolution, separate instruments for the devolved assemblies in Wales and Northern Ireland are possible. The separation of the United Kingdom into several jurisdictions is particularly important in the context of a chapter on public procurement review and remedies, since Scotland always had its separate judicial system. Both the United Kingdom and Scotland Regulations apply only to public and utilities contracts within the field of application of the EU Directives, most importantly to contracts above the value thresholds of these instruments.

This chapter will first discuss the public procurement review bodies in the jurisdictions of the United Kingdom (excluding Scotland), the limitation of the review and remedies system to contracts within the field of application of the EU Directives and the United Kingdom Regulations, and the rules on standing (1.). Second, the available remedies before and after the conclusion of the contract will be discussed, including interim measures (2.), standstill provisions (3.), the establishment of a breach (4.), the annulment and set-aside of award decisions (5.), the ineffectiveness of the contract (6.), alternative penalties (7.), damages (8.), parallel remedies (9.) and alternative dispute settlement (10.). The analysis will show that, following the traditional limited

1. See: www.opsi.gov.uk/si/si200600.htm (accessed in late July 2010). The Office of Government Commerce (OGC) web site (www.ogc.gov.uk) also contains associated guidance, including guidance on central purchasing bodies see in more detail (2006) 15 *Public Procurement Law Review* NA82-90. For a detailed commentary on the transposition of the 2004 EU Directives for England, Wales, and Northern Ireland see S. Arrowsmith, 'Implementation of the New EC Procurement Directives and the Alcatel Ruling in England and Wales and Northern Ireland: a Review of the New Legislation and Guidance' (2006) 15 *Public Procurement Law Review* 86.
2. http://www.opsi.gov.uk/si/si2009/uksi_20092992_en_1 (accessed in late July 2010).
3. http://www.opsi.gov.uk/si/si2009/uksi_20093100_en_1 (accessed in late July 2010). On both instruments see: Henty, 'Remedies Directive Implemented into UK Law' (2010) 19 *Public Procurement Law Review* NA115-124.
4. Public Contracts and Utilities Contracts (Scotland) Amendment Regulations SSI 2009/428: http://www.opsi.gov.uk/legislation/scotland/ssi2009/ssi_20090428_en_1 (accessed in late July 2010).

approach to the transposition of Directives followed in the United Kingdom, the transposition of the public procurement remedies Directives does not go beyond the requirements of these instruments. It will also be shown that while the United Kingdom systems of public procurement review and remedies is largely compliant with the requirements of EU law, there are a few important exceptions which will be specifically highlighted. The discussion will focus on the law of England and Wales unless otherwise stated, although it is mostly equally applicable to Northern Ireland as well.

1.1 Review bodies

In England and Wales (and Northern Ireland) legal actions regarding judicial review of public procurement decisions are brought in the High Court,[5] more specifically in the Administrative Court which forms part of the Queen's Bench Division of the High Court. This applies to legal action before and after the conclusion or making[6] of the contract.[7] Where the proceedings are for the enforcement of such a contract the proceedings will also be in the Queen's Bench Division of the High Court, or, if the contract so provides, before an arbitrator. Some cases are decided by the Technology and Construction Court (also part of the Queen's Bench Division)[8] or sometimes the Chancery Division.[9] The case will be heard by a single judge and processed

5. Regulation 47C Public Contracts (Amendment) Regulations 2009 reads:
(1) A breach of the duty owed in accordance with regulation 47A or 47B is actionable by any economic operator which, in consequence, suffers, or risks suffering, loss or damage.
(2) Proceedings for that purpose must be started in the High Court, and regulations 47D to 47P apply to such proceedings.
See also Regulation 45C United Kingdom Utilities Contracts (Amendment) Regulations 2006 which has almost the same wording.
6. The EU law term 'conclusion' might be confused with the English law term 'discharge' and therefore the term 'making' of the contract would be more appropriate. However, since in the context of EU law the term 'conclusion' of the public contract defines the most crucial moment for the purposes of public procurement law, the latter will be used as well as the term 'making' of the contract.
7. In the separate court and legal system of Scotland legal action is brought in the Court of Session of the Sheriff Court. See Regulation 47 (6) Public Contracts (Scotland) Regulations 2006.
8. See for example the seminal case of *Harmon CFEM Facades (UK) Ltd* v *The Corporate Officer of the House of Commons*, [2002] 2 LGLR 372.
9. If the contract is one involving building or civil engineering or matters involving technology, it is probable that the proceedings will be allocated to the Technology

in accordance with the procedural rules for the civil courts, set out in the Civil Procedure Rules 1998. The central location of the High Court is in the Royal Courts of Justice in London but there are regional court offices (District Registries) in more than 20 'provincial' cities. These regional representations of the High Court are fully competent to review public procurement cases and can award all the available remedies discussed in this chapter. If an action in the High Court is unsuccessful and the applicant believes the decision to be legally flawed, he or she may, with the permission of the High Court or the Court of Appeal, appeal to the Civil Division of the Court of Appeal where the argument will be heard by three judges. Since the coming into force of the relevant provisions of the Constitutional Reform Act 2005 on 1st October 2009, public contract cases are heard in the last instance by the Supreme Court of the United Kingdom. Before that the House of Lords was the last instance review body for such cases. Hence the High Court, the Court of Appeal and the new Supreme Court (formerly the House of Lords) will hear public procurement cases.

With regards to legal action up to the conclusion or making of a public contract, the High Court is the review body of first instance in public procurement cases under the United Kingdom Public Contracts Regulations SI 2006/05 and the Utilities Contracts Regulations SI 2006/06.

With regards to legal action brought after the conclusion or making of the public contract, in other words regarding the contract implementation or contract management phase, the common law of obligations applies.[10] Therefore legal action regarding this phase is handled by the regular courts also dealing with disputes between private parties to a contract. These are the same courts hearing cases up to the conclusion of the contract: High Court, Court of Appeal and Supreme Court (formerly the House of Lords). This is normally a dispute between the contracting authority and the private party the contract was made or concluded with. There are only relatively few cases with a public law element decided by the English (and Welsh and Northern Irish) courts. Until the 2009 Public and Utilities (Amendment) Regulations for the United Kingdom and Scotland respectively, third parties outside a contracting relationship had no possibility to seek judicial review regarding a contract between a contracting entity and a private party. Even actions regarding an

and Construction Court, which forms part of the Queen's Bench Division. See for example: *J.D. Ladbitter & Co LtD* v *Devon CC*, [2009] EWHC 930.

10. With the exception of certain rules on ineffectiveness and damages which although brought after the conclusion or making of the contract, are largely regulated by the procurement Regulations.

unlawful award could only lead to damages once the contract had been made. The 2009 amendments changed that profoundly through the introduction of the remedy of ineffectiveness discussed in more detail under 6. below.

1.2 Limitation to contracts within the field of application of the Directives

The Crown Proceedings Act 1947 normally excludes most remedies against the Crown. However, this important limitation does not apply to contracts within the field of application of the Procurement Regulations. Most importantly, according to United Kingdom Public Contracts (Amendment) Regulation 47P[11] and United Kingdom Utilities Contracts (Amendment) Regulation 45P[12] the High Court has the power to grant remedies against the Crown in proceedings under the Regulations notwithstanding sections 21[13] and 42[14] of the Crown Proceedings Act 1947.

11. Regulation 47P United Kingdom Public Contracts (Amendment) Regulations 2009 reads:
    'In proceedings against the Crown, the Court has power to grant an injunction despite section 21 of the Crown Proceedings Act 1947.'
12. Regulation 45P United Kingdom Utilities Contracts (Amendment) Regulations 2009 reads:
    'In proceedings against the Crown, the Court has power to grant an injunction despite section 21 of the Crown Proceedings Act 1947.'
13. Section 21 of the Crown Proceedings Act 1947 entitled 'Nature of relief' reads:
    '(1) In any civil proceedings by or against the Crown the court shall, subject to the provisions of this Act, have power to make all such orders as it has power to make in proceedings between subjects, and otherwise to give such appropriate relief as the case may require:
    Provided that: –
    (a) where in any proceedings against the Crown any such relief is sought as might in proceedings between subjects be granted by way of injunction or specific performance, the court shall not grant an injunction or make an order for specific performance, but may in lieu thereof make an order declaratory of the rights of the parties; and
    (b) in any proceedings against the Crown for the recovery of land or other property the court shall not make an order for the recovery of the land or the delivery of the property, but may in lieu thereof make an order declaring that the plaintiff is entitled as against the Crown to the land or property or to the possession thereof.
    (2) The court shall not in any civil proceedings grant any injunction or make any order against an officer of the Crown if the effect of granting the injunction or making the order would be to give any relief against the Crown which could not have been obtained in proceedings against the Crown.'

For contracts outside the field of application of the Regulations remedies are not available against the Crown as such. Certain remedies, however, can be obtained against a minister who acts under legislative powers conferred upon the minister himself.[15] However, it is doubtful that this limitation of the public procurement review and remedies system to contracts covered by the Regulations and Directives does comply with the requirements of the Treaty on the Functioning of the European Union (TFEU) regarding contracts outside the field of application of the EU procurement Directives as established by the Court of Justice of the European Union[16] and clarified by the European Commission in a 2006 Interpretative Communication.[17] According to this

14. Section 42 of the Crown Proceedings Act 1947 entitled 'Exclusion of certain provisions' reads:
'Section one, Part II (except section thirteen so far as relating to proceedings mentioned in the First Schedule and section twenty-one), Part III (except section twenty-six) and section twenty-eight of this Act shall not apply to Scotland.'
In other words, Section 21 *does* apply to Scotland.
15. Arrowsmith, *The Law of Public and Utilities Procurement*, (Sweet & Maxwell: London, 2nd ed. 2005) 1364 citing *M.* v *Home Office* [1994] 1 AC 377 and Craig, *Administrative Law* (Sweet & Maxwell, London, 6th ed., 2008) 949-955.
16. Case C-76/81, *Transporoute et Travaux SA* v *Ministère des travaux publics* [1982] ECR 417; Case C-263/85, *Commission* v. *Italy* [1991] ECR I-2457; Case C-45/87, *Commission* v. *Ireland* ('Dundalk') [1988] ECR 4929; Case C-3/88, *Commission* v. *Italy* ('Re Data Processing') [1989] ECR 4035; [1991] CMLR 115; Case C-21/88, *Du Pont de Nemours Italiana* v. *Unita Sanitara Locale di Carara* [1990] ECR 889; Case C-113/89, *Rush Portuguesa* v. *Office national d'immigration* [1990] ECR I-1417; Case C-243/89, *Commission* v. *Denmark* ('Storebaelt' or 'Danish Bridge'), [1993] ECR I-3353; C-360/89, *Commission* v *Italy* [1992] ECR I-3401; Case C-272/91, *Commission* v *Italy* ('Lottomatica') [1992] ECR I-3929; Case C-87/94, *Commission* v *Belgium* ('Walloon Buses') [1996] ECR I-2043; Case C-359/93, *Commission* v *The Netherlands* ('UNIX') [1995] ECR I-157; Case C-275/98, *Unitron Scandinavia* [1999] ECR I-8291; Case C-324/98, *Telaustria Verlag GmbH and Telephonadress GmbH* v *Telekom Austria AG, joined party Herold Business Data AG* ('Teleaustria') [2000] ECR I-10745; Case C-470/99, *Universale Bau AG* [2002] ECR I-11617; Case C-59/00, *Bent Mousten Vestergaard* v *Spøttrup Boligselskab* [2001] ECR I-9505; Case C-358/00, *Buchhändler Vereinigung* [2002] ECR I-4685; Case C-231/03, Consorzio Aziende Metano *(Coname)* v *Padania Acque SpA (Coname)* [2005] ECR I-7287; Case C-234/03, *Contse and others* v. *Instituto Nacional de Géstion Sanitaria (Ingesa)* [2005] ECR I-9315; Case C-264/03, *Commission* v *France*, [2005] ECR I-8831; Case C-458/03, *Parking Brixen GmbH* v *Gemeinde Brixen, Stadtwerke Brixen AG* [2004] ECR I-12055; Case C-535/03, *Commission* v *Italy*, [2006] ECR I-2689.
17. *Commission Interpretative Communication on the Community law applicable to contracts not or not fully subject to the provisions of the Public Procurement Directives*, 1 August 2006, OJ [2006] C-179/02.

case law as explained in the 2006 Interpretative Communication, a number of requirements regarding public and utilities review and remedies derive directly from the TFEU.

As far as contracts below the thresholds of the Directives are concerned, the Communication stresses the fact that on the basis of the jurisprudence of the Court of Justice, individuals are entitled to effective judicial protection of the rights that derive from EU law. As the Public (and Utilities) Procurement Remedies Directives do not apply to these contracts it is the task of the national laws of the Member States to provide the necessary rules and procedures for judicial protection. Hence the case law is interpreted as containing a requirement to provide a mechanism for the judicial review of public procurement decisions for contracts below the thresholds of the Directives:

'In order to comply with this requirement of effective judicial protection, at least decisions adversely affecting a person having or having had an interest in obtaining the contract, such as any decision to eliminate an applicant or tenderer, should be subject to review for possible violations of the basic standards derived from primary Community law.'[18]

This clause is based on the case law of the Court of Justice[19] and can generally be applied to contracts outside the field of application of the Directives that have internal market relevance. The clause is very similar to the general rule for procurement review proceedings contained in the Directives, most importantly Article 1 (3) of the *Public Sector Remedies (Amendment) Directive 2007/66/EC.*[20]

Moreover, with respect to the remedies that can be awarded by the judges in judicial review proceedings the 2006 Interpretative Communication provides:

'In accordance with the case-law on judicial protection, the available remedies must not be less efficient than those applying to similar claims based on domestic law (principle of

18. 2006 Interpretative Communication, ibid., at 6.
19. Case C-222/86, *Heylens* [1987] ECR 4097, at paragraph 14 and Case C-50/00P, *Unión de Pequeños Agricultores* v *Council* [2002] ECR I-6677, at paragraph 39.
20. Article 1 (3) of Directive 2007/66/EC of the European Parliament and the Council of 11 December 2007 amending Council Directives 89/665/EEC and 92/13/EC with regard to improving the effectiveness of review procedures concerning the award of public contracts OJ [2007] L-335/31 reads:
'Member States shall ensure that the review proceedings are available, under detailed rules which the Member States may establish, at least to any person having or having had an interest in obtaining a particular contract and who has been or risk being harmed by an alleged infringement.'

equivalence) and must not be such as in practice to make it impossible or excessively difficult to obtain judicial protection (principle of effectiveness).'[21]

The principles of equivalence and effectiveness of national judicial review involving EU law are well established in the case law of the Court of Justice.[22] Since they apply to all national proceedings involving EU law, the exclusion of public procurement cases outside the field of application of the Directives would be surprising. However, as a crucial limitation, tenderers can only bring proceedings when the contract has relevance for the internal market.

Finally, regarding the effective exercise of the right to public procurement review, the 2006 Interpretative Communication provides:

'To allow for an effective exercise of the right to such a review, contracting entities should state the grounds for decisions which are open to review either in the decision itself or upon request after communication of the decision.'[23]

Similar requirements apply within the field of application of the Directives.[24] The clause facilitates effective review and remedies, which facilitate non-discriminatory and transparent procurement procedures, which facilitate the internal market.

Overall, the case law of the European Court of Justice and the European Commission's 2006 Interpretative Communications regarding contracts falling outside the field of application of the EU procurement Directives, merely clarify the application of principles derived from the TFEU and previously the EC Treaty, such as non-discrimination, equal treatment, transparency, mutual recognition, proportionality, equivalence and effectiveness. These principles apply to all Member State activities related to the internal market, without any explicit *de minimis* rule. The fact that the EU legislator has subjected public procurement contracts above certain value thresholds to detailed substantive Directives and procurement review Directives does not exclude the internal market relevance and therefore the application of EU law to these contracts.

21. 2006 Interpretative Communication, *supra* note 17, at 6.
22. Case C-46/93, *Brasserie du Pêcheur* [1996] ECR I-1029, at paragraph 83 and Case C-327/00, *Santex* [2003] ECR I-1877, at paragraph 55.
23. 2006 Interpretative Communication, *supra* note 17, at 6. Case C-222/86, *Heylens*, *supra* note 19, at paragraph 14.
24. See Article 2a (2) subparagraph 4 amended Public Sector Remedies Directive 89/665/EEC and 41 (2) Public Sector Procurement Directive 2004/18/EC.

United Kingdom Public Contracts (Amendment) Regulation 47C and United Kingdom Utilities Contracts (Amendment) Regulation 45C empowering the High Court to grant remedies against the Crown in proceedings under the Regulations, apply only to contracts above the thresholds of the EU Directives and United Kingdom Regulations. Thus sections 21 and 42 of the Crown Proceedings Act 1947 excluding most remedies against the Crown apply to contracts below these thresholds. The very limited remedies which can be obtained against a Minister who acts under legislative powers conferred upon the minister himself[25] do not meet the requirements of the TFEU as clarified in the 2006 Interpretative Communication outlined above. If these remedies met the requirements of the TFEU the express granting of powers 'notwithstanding sections 21 and 42 of the Crown Proceedings Act 1947' would not have been necessary to comply with the Directives within the field of application of the Regulations. The limitations of the Crown Proceedings Act 1947 for the public and utilities procurement review and remedies system for contracts below the thresholds are not in compliance with EU law.

1.3 Standing

Third parties can only launch judicial actions against the award of a public contract if they have standing to bring review proceedings.[26] The rules on standing are similar but different with regards to contracts to which the United Kingdom Public Contracts and Utilities Contracts Regulations apply on the one hand and those outside their field of application on the other. Within the field of application of the Regulations, any person who sought or seeks, or would have wished to be the person to whom a contract is awarded and is a national of, and established in, a relevant State, can bring an action if he or she suffers or risks suffering loss or damage due to the contracting authority's breach of duty. This is provided in Regulation 47C of the United Kingdom Public Contracts (Amendment) Regulation 2009 and Regulation 45C of the United Kingdom Utilities Contracts (Amendment) Regulations 2009. Standing might extend beyond those that actually participated in the tendering procedure if they believe that they were prevented from participating as a result of a breach of the Regulations.

Outside the field of application of the Regulations, a party with 'sufficient interest in the matter' has standing for judicial review according to Section 31

25. See: Arrowsmith, *The Law of Public and Utilities Procurement*, *supra* note 15, 1364 citing *M.* v *Home Office* [1994] 1 AC 377 and Craig, *supra* note 15, at 949-955.
26. Craig, ibid., Chap 24.

(3) of the Senior Courts Act 1980, a very flexible and liberal test.[27] Within the context of public procurement any competitor with a prospect of obtaining the contract is likely to have standing.[28] Moreover, representative trade organisations may be granted standing, provided they have a special expertise and a genuine concern in the matter.[29] Council tax[30] payers no longer have standing when local standing orders on procurement have been violated, save perhaps in very serious cases.[31]

1.4 Time limits

Time limits for initiating proceedings protect the smooth flow of the procurement process and promote legal certainty.[32] According to the Court of Justice Member States may impose 'reasonable' time limits for the initiation of review proceedings against breaches of procurement law.[33] The time limits for challenging violations of procurement law start to run 'from the time they become known to those concerned.'[34] This importance of knowing about the breaches, which might well happen a long time after they occurred, is crucial for the effectiveness and fairness of the remedies system since only those knowing about breaches can reasonably be required to 'get their act together' and initiate proceedings.

According to Regulation 47D (2) United Kingdom Public Contracts (Amendment) Regulations 2009 and Regulation 45D (2) the Utilities Contracts (Amendment) Regulations 2009 procurement decisions must be challenged promptly and in any event within three months from when the grounds for review first arose.[35] Hence the time limit starts to run from the

27. Arrowsmith, *The Law of Public and Utilities Procurement*, *supra* note 15, at 1367.
28. Ibid. citing *Regina.* v *Avon CC Ex. p. Terry Adams* [1994] Env LR 442, CA; *Birmingham City Council* v *Mass Energy* [1993] Env LR 298, CA and *Regina.* v *National Lottery Commission Ex p. Camelot Group plc* [2000] All ER (D) 1205.
29. Craig, *supra* note 15, 805-807.
30. A local tax payable directly to the local authority of your area of residence.
31. *Regina.* v *Her Majesty's Treasury Ex p. Smedley* [1985] QB 657.
32. Arrowsmith, *The Law of Public and Utilities Procurement*, *supra* note 15, at 1400.
33. Case C-470/99, *Universale Bau*, *supra* note 16; Case C-327/00, *Santex*, *supra* note 22.
34. C-470/99, ibid., at paragraph 78.
35. Regulation 47D United Kingdom Public Contracts (Amendment) Regulations 2009 entitled 'General time limits for starting proceedings' reads:
    '(1) This regulation limits the time within which proceedings may be started where the proceedings do not seek a declaration of ineffectiveness.

time the grounds for review first arose and not 'from the time they became known to those concerned.' This arrangement is not in compliance with the requirements of EU law, an assessment already clear from *Universale Bau*[36] and recently confirmed by the Court of Justice in the *Uniplex* case[37] which directly concerned the relevant United Kingdom time limits. According to EU law limitation periods have to run from the time when the applicant 'knew or ought to have known' that an infringement of public procurement rules occurred.[38] This will make it necessary to amend Regulations 47D (2)

(2) Subject to paragraphs (3) and (4), such proceedings must be started promptly and in any event within 3 months beginning with the date when grounds for starting the proceedings first arose.
(3) Paragraph (2) does not require proceedings to be started before the end of any of the following periods –
(a) where the proceedings relate to a decision which is sent to the economic operator by facsimile or electronic means, 10 days beginning with –
(i) the day after the date on which the decision is sent, if the decision is accompanied by a summary of the reasons for the decision;
(ii) if the decision is not so accompanied, the day after the date on which the economic operator is informed of a summary of those reasons;
(b) where the proceedings relate to a decision which is sent to the economic operator by other means, whichever of the following periods ends first –
(i) 15 days beginning with –
(aa) the day after the date on which the decision is sent, if the decision is accompanied by a summary of the reasons for the decision; or
(bb) if the decision is not so accompanied, the day after the date on which the economic operator is informed of a summary of those reasons;
(ii)10 days beginning with –
(aa) the day after the date on which the decision is received, if the decision is accompanied by a summary of the reasons for the decision; or
(bb) if the decision is not so accompanied, the day after the date on which the economic operator is informed of a summary of those reasons;
(c) where sub-paragraphs (a) and (b) do not apply but the decision is published, 10 days beginning with the day on which the decision is published.
(4) The Court may extend the time limits imposed by this regulation (but not the limits imposed by regulation 47E) where the Court considers that there is a good reason for doing so.
(5) For the purposes of this regulation, proceedings are to be regarded as started only when the claim form is served in compliance with regulation 47F(1).'
See also Regulations 45D United Kingdom Utilities Contracts (Amendment) Regulations 2009 with almost the same wording.

36. Case C-470/99, *supra* note 16.
37. Case C-406/08, *Uniplex*, nyr.
38. McGovern, 'Two important decisions of the European Court of Justice on time-limits in proceedings for review procedures in public procurement: the Uniplex case (C-

and 45D (2), for public contracts and utilities contracts respectively, as an implementation of the *Uniplex* case is required to comply with EU law.[39]

With a time limit that is triggered by the knowledge of the prospective applicant, proceedings might be initiated much later than three months after the breach of procurement law occurred. On the one hand this compromises the objectives of the time limits, to protect the smooth flow of the procurement process and promote legal certainty. On the other hand it is largely within the control of the contracting entity to avoid this effect through transparency. They can avoid this effect by communicating their decisions to the bidders.[40]

1.5 Available remedies

The English term 'remedy' describes the desired result of judicial review. The court will for example set aside a procurement decision or award damages to 'remedy' a wrongful act that has harmed the applicant. This is not so different from the medical context where the doctor will apply a 'remedy', for example medication or therapy, to heal the patient's ailments. Public procurement review and remedies in England and Wales are differentiated into remedies regarding contracts to which the Regulations apply and contracts outside their field of application. Moreover, remedies before and up to the conclusion or making of the contract on the one hand and remedies after the conclusion or making of the contract have to be viewed separately. A standstill period between the communication of the award decision and the important conclusion or making of the contract prevents the latter from pre-empting the 'pre-conclusion' or 'pre-making' remedies. A 'race to the conclusion or making of the contract' to make it immune from most remedies is thus prohibited.

Remedies are currently regulated in Part 9 of the United Kingdom Public Contracts Regulations and Utilities Contracts Regulations as amended in

406/08) and Commission v Ireland (C-456/08)' (2010) 19 *Public Procurement Law Review* 101.

39. Henty, 'Remedies Directive Implemented into UK Law', *supra* note 3, at NA122, whereas Taylor, 'Bridging the remedies gap' (2010) 21 *Practical Law Company* 29, at 31 suggests interpreting Regulation 47D (4) in the light of the *Uniplex* judgment.
40. In the recent case of *Sita UK Ltd v Greater Manchester Waste Disposal Authority* (Rev 1) [2010] EWHC 680 the High Court decided against a bidder who had initiated proceedings after the contract award when the time limit had elapsed. The bidder had known about the breach in question well before the limitation period had elapsed. According to Skilbeck, 'Developments in Public Procurement Law' (2010) 20 *Computers & the Law* 16, at 18 this will make breaches of procurement law which occur earlier in the procedure more often the subject of review proceedings.

2009. Should the High Court find in favour of the applicant, it may grant an order to set aside or to amend a relevant decision by the contracting authority, suspend the implementation of its decisions and of the procedure itself, or to amend a document (for example regarding the specifications).[41] Before the 2009 amendments damages were the only available remedy after the conclusion or making of the contract,[42] with the exception of rare cases of fraud or bad faith. The SI 2009/2992 United Kingdom Public Contracts (Amendment) Regulations 2009 and the SI 2009/3100 United Kingdom Utilities Contracts (Amendment) Regulations 2009 introduced the new remedy of ineffectiveness discussed under 6. below.[43]

41. Regulation 47I Public Contracts (Amendment) Regulations 2009 entitled 'Remedies where the contract has not been entered into' reads:
'(1) Paragraph (2) applies where –
(a) the Court is satisfied that a decision or action taken by a contracting authority was in breach of the duty owed in accordance with regulation 47A or 47B; and
(b) the contract has not yet been entered into.
(2) In those circumstances, the Court may do one or more of the following –
(a) order the setting aside of the decision or action concerned;
(b)order the contracting authority to amend any document;
(c) award damages to an economic operator which has suffered loss or damage as a consequence of the breach.
(3) This regulation does not prejudice any other powers of the Court.'
See Regulation 45I Utilities Contracts (Amendment) Regulations 2009 with almost the same wording.
42. Even SI 2006/05 United Kingdom Public Contracts Regulation 47 (9) reads:
'In proceedings under this regulation the Court does not have power to order any remedy other than an award of damages in respect of a breach of the duty owed in accordance with paragraph (1) or (2) if the contract in relation to which the breach occurred has been entered into.'
43. The 2009 United Kingdom Public Contracts (Amendment) Regulation 47J entitled 'Remedies where the contract has been entered into' reads:
'(1) Paragraph (2) applies if –
(a) the Court is satisfied that a decision or action taken by a contracting authority was in breach of the duty owed in accordance with regulation 47A or 47B; and
(b) the contract has already been entered into.
(2) In those circumstances, the Court –
(a) must, if it is satisfied that any of the grounds for ineffectiveness applies, make a declaration of ineffectiveness in respect of the contract unless regulation 47L requires the Court not to do so;
(b) must, where required by regulation 47N, impose penalties in accordance with that regulation;

2 Interim measures

Before the Public Contracts (Amendment) Regulations 2009 and the Utilities Contracts (Amendment) Regulations 2009, the lodging of an application for review had normally no automatic suspensive effect on the ongoing tendering procedure.[44] However, at any stage of the proceedings before the conclusion or making of the contract the court could grant interim relief upon an urgent request by the applicant and issue an injunction which had a suspensive effect on the relevant actions of the contracting authority. When determining whether interim relief was appropriate, the court would have regard to the need, on the one hand to provide an effective review and remedies system, to uphold EU procurement rules and to protect the applicant and, on the other hand, the interests of the public in the progress of public projects.[45] Therefore to obtain an injunction suspending the tendering procedure or implementation of a decision taken in respect of the tendering procedure, the applicant would have had to show 'a prima facie legitimate case with serious chances of success in its substantive stage.'[46] Moreover the applicant had to prove that the balance of interests was leaning towards his case and would have to show that damages would not be an adequate remedy.[47] The EU law compatibility

(c) may award damages to an economic operator which has suffered loss or damage as a consequence of the breach, regardless of whether the Court also acts as described in sub-paragraphs (a) and (b);
(d) must not order any other remedies.
(3) Paragraph (2)(d) is subject to regulation 47O(3) and (9) (additional relief in respect of specific contracts where a framework agreement is ineffective) and does not prejudice any power of the Court under regulation 47M(3) or 47N(10) (orders which supplement a declaration of ineffectiveness or a contract-shortening order).'
See Regulation 45J Utilities Contracts (Amendment) Regulations 2009 with almost the same wording.

44. Henty, 'Remedies Directive Implemented into UK Law', *supra* note 3, at 117.
45. See Bovis, *EC Public Procurement: Case Law and Litigation* (Oxford University Press: New York, 2006) at 526, paragraph 11.169.
46. Iibd.
47. Bovis, *supra* note 45, at 526, paragraph 11.169. At paragraph 11.168 he also summarised the court procedure as follwows:
'Applications for interim measures orders such as injunctions or suspension orders commence by a summons application to the court in conjunction with a supporting affidavit or a sworn statement. The application may be dealt with by the court before the summons and affidavit are served on the other party (ex parte) or after the summons and affidavit have been served on the other party (inter partes). A claim for an interim injunction will not normally involve oral evidence but will, instead, involve leag susbmissions to the judge on the basis of the affidavit evidence. The summons

of this approach that if damages are available interim relief would be precluded or even affected was rather doubtful. Moreover, obtaining this injunction often proved difficult in practice. There was very little time to take decisions, gather the necessary evidence, mandate lawyers, etc. Finally, the requirements for the granting of an injunction[48] were very difficult to meet and the balance of convenience regularly favoured the contracting entity.[49]

The new Regulation 47G of the United Kingdom Public Contracts (Amendment) Regulations 2009 SI2009/2992 contains a provision entitled: 'Contract making suspended by challenge to award decision'.[50] Where proceedings are started with respect to a contracting authority's decision to award the contract, and the contract has not been entered into, the starting of the proceedings requires the contracting authority to refrain from entering into the contract. The requirement continues until the court brings the requirement to an end by interim order under Regulation 47H (1) (a) or 45 (1) (a), for public or utilities contracts respectively, or the proceedings at first instance are determined, discontinued or otherwise disposed of and no order has been made continuing the requirement, for example in connection with an

for interim measures may be issued prior to, simultaneously with, or after the issue of a writ. The applicant will usually have to give an undertaking that he will compensate the contracting authority for any loss suffered if, at the final hearing of the proceedings, the application for the injunction is rejected. Similar procedures apply in relation to interim injunctions in the context of judicial review proceedings.'

48. *American Cyanamid C* v *Ethicom Ltd* [1975] AC 396.
49. Taylor, *supra* note 39, at 31.
50. Regulation 47G United Kingdom Public Contracts (Amendment) Regulations 2009 reads:
'(1) Where –
(a) proceedings are started in respect of a contracting authority's decision to award the contract; and
(b) the contract has not been entered into, the starting of the proceedings requires the contracting authority to refrain from entering into the contract.
(2) The requirement continues until any of the following occurs –
(a) the Court brings the requirement to an end by interim order under regulation 47H(1)(a);
(b) the proceedings at first instance are determined, discontinued or otherwise disposed of and no order has been made continuing the requirement (for example in connection with an appeal or the possibility of an appeal).
(3) For the purposes of paragraph (1), proceedings are to be regarded as started only when the claim form is served in compliance with regulation 47F(1).
(4) This regulation does not affect the obligations imposed by regulation 32A.
See also Regulation 45G United Kingdom Utilities Contracts (Amendment) Regulations 2009 with the same wording.

appeal or the possibility of an appeal. Hence the recently amended Regulations introduced an automatic suspensive effect on the making of the contract until the court decided on the case. The procedure described above in the first paragraph of this section, an application for an injunction suspending the tendering procedure, is no longer necessary. An automatic suspensive effect ensures that the *status quo* is maintained until a review body decides on the lawfulness of the challenged act.[51] Commentators have been very positive about this change which addresses many of the shortcomings outlined in the first paragraph of this section above, representing an 'extremely powerful new tool'[52] for aggrieved bidders and striking the right balance between the effectiveness of the review system on the one hand and avoiding abuse and excessive obstruction of procurement proceedings on the other hand.[53]

Moreover, the possibility of 'reverse suspensive effect' by interim order was introduced in Regulation 47H and 45H in 2009 for public and utilities contracts respectively. This will allow the High Court to remove the now automatic suspensive effect, normally on the application of the respective contracting entity. In deciding on such an application the Court will apply the same test formerly – under the 2006 Regulations – used for deciding on the granting of interim relief in the form of a suspension of the procurement procedure outlined above. However, this turns the tables: the contracting entity rather than the aggrieved bidder has to invest time and effort, and has the difficult burden to establish the requirements of the test.[54] Moreover, the new rules give the aggrieved bidder more time.[55]

3 Standstill provisions

With regards to contracts covered by the Regulations, the United Kingdom has introduced a ten-day standstill period between the notification of the results of the tendering procedure to the bidders and the formal conclusion or making of the contract in United Kingdom Public Contracts Regulation 32 (3) and United Kingdom Utilities Contracts Regulation 33 (3). Aggrieved

51. Arrowsmith, Linarelli, and Wallace; *Regulating Public Procurement: National and International Perspectives* (Kluwer Law International: London, 2000), at 773.
52. Skilbeck, *supra* note 40, at 16.
53. Henty, 'Is the standstill period a step forward? The proposed revision of the EC Remedies Directive' (2006) 15 *Public Procurement Law Review* 253, at 259.
54. Henty, 'Remedies Directive Implemented into UK Law', *supra* note 3, at 117.
55. Taylor, *supra* note 39, at 31.

bidders thus have the opportunity to mount a challenge to an award decision they believe to be legally flawed.

This standstill period was introduced in 2006 following the *Alcatel* judgment of the European Court of Justice[56] and was recently amended to a 10 or 15 day period by SI 2009/2992 implementing Directive 2009/66/EC. The Amendment Regulations of 2009 have altered the structure of the standstill period.[57] Under the old 2006 Regulations the standstill period was a two-stage process. First, in a standstill letter to the unsuccessful bidders the contracting entity would provide only the basic information about their bids. Second, the recipient of this letter, in other words the unsuccessful bidder, would then have the opportunity to request a debriefing with additional information including the strengths of the successful tender. As there was only a standstill period of ten days, it was very difficult in practice for an aggrieved bidder to collect the necessary information, gather the evidence, instruct lawyers, and apply for an injunction before the conclusion or making of the contract.[58] In contrast, under the 2009 Amendment Regulations 32A and 33A, for public contracts and utilities contracts respectively, unsuccessful bidders have to be informed about the reasons for the award decisions in the standstill letter already. Moreover, the standstill period will only begin once that information has been provided.[59] This gives bidders enough time to collect the relevant information, gather the evidence, mandate the lawyers, and to initiate proceedings as envisaged in Recital 6 of Directive 2007/66/EC.

Respect for the standstill period is also enforced by the new remedy of ineffectiveness outlined under 6. below, since the conclusion or making of a contract before the standstill period has expired is one of the only three violations for which ineffectiveness can be granted.

56. Case C-81/98, *Alcatel Austria AG* v *Bundesministerium für Wirtschaft und Verkehr* [1999] ECR I-7671.
57. Henty, 'Remedies Directive Implemented into UK Law', *supra* note 3, at 116.
58. Taylor, *supra* note 39, at 30.
59. Regulation 32A of the Public Contracts (Amendment) Regulations 2009 entitled 'Standstill period' reads:
    'Where regulation 32(1) applies, the contracting authority must not enter into the contract or conclude the framework agreement before the end of the standstill period. [...]'
    See Regulation 33A of the United Kingdom Utilities Contracts (Amendment) Regulations 2009 with almost the same wording.

4 Establishment of a breach

In English law a 'declaration' is understood as a distinctive remedy in which the Court establishes that a violation of the procurement regulations and EU law or a breach of the duties owed by contracting authorities or entities has occurred or that a future conduct would constitute such a breach.[60] The declaration is not stipulated in the Regulations but has its origin in common law. It is available inside and outside the field of application of the Regulations and Directives. However, using the medical metaphor explained above again, it could be asked whether this can really be classed as a remedy or only as a 'diagnosis'. However, since the 'patient' can gain some satisfaction from such an establishment by the Court the better view is that this is a remedy.[61] Using the medical metaphor yet again there might at times also be a 'placebo effect', where a placebo treatment is prescribed, which although scientifically not effective as a cure makes the patient feel better. Moreover, since it can also be used for future conduct it may be enough to achieve the desired change of behaviour of a contracting authority or entity. It may also have an impact on a later action for damages. From an English law point of view there is no doubt that declaration counts as a remedy.[62]

5 Annulment or set-aside of award decisions

Outside the field of application of the United Kingdom procurement Regulations, an injunction or a declaration might be granted by the court to restrain a breach of the law or to command compliance. Injunction and declaration are among the common law remedies for breach of public law or private law duties. Moreover, specific public law remedies, the 'prerogative orders' might be granted. A 'quashing order' eliminates a decision, a 'mandatory order' compels the authority to render a lawful decision, and a 'prohibiting order' prevents unlawful action.[63] While it is disputed whether procurement cases are matters of public law, a question mainly affecting the competence of the administrative court, the better view is that they are for the purposes of the

60. Arrowsmith, *The Law of Public and Utilities Procurement*, *supra* note 15, at 1364.
61. Arrowsmith, ibid. covers the declaration in the context of her remedies and enforcement chapter which suggests that it is a remedy.
62. Thanks to my colleague Keith Uff (Birmingham) for pointing this out to me.
63. Arrowsmith, *The Law of Public and Utilities Procurement*, *supra* note 15, at 1364; Bovis, *supra* note 45, at 571 paragraph 11.317.

prerogative orders since their rationale is the public law nature of the contracting authority or the influence of public authorities over other contracting entities.[64] With regards to the breach of legislative rules on procurement applicable only to public bodies, for example Section 19 Local Government Act 1988, there is clearly the possibility to enforce those by prerogative orders.

Inside the field of application of the Regulations the court may, according to Regulation 47I[65] (8) (b) United Kingdom Public Contracts (Amendment) Regulations 2009, and if satisfied that a decision or action taken by a contracting authority was in breach of a duty to comply with the provisions of the Regulations or any enforceable EU law:

'(a) order the setting aside of that decision or action concerned;
(b) order the contracting authority to amend any document; [...]'

According to Regulation 47I (2) (c) this can even be done in addition to damages and according to Regulation 47I (3) does not prejudice any other powers of the court. It is submitted that these rules comply with the requirements of the EU public procurement remedies Directives.[66]

A set aside decision will eliminate the legal basis the contract. If there is a race to the making or conclusion of the contract, prior to the 2009 Amendment Regulations and the introduction of the remedy of ineffectiveness disucssed under 6. below, damages were the only available remedy as a result of the set aside. Moreover, the set aside was often a standing requirement for an action for damages.[67] It appears that there has so far not been an interven-

64. Arrowsmith, ibid., at 1365.
65. Regulation 47I.of the Public Contracts (Amendment) Regulations 2009 reads:
'(1) Paragraph (2) applies where –
(a) the Court is satisfied that a decision or action taken by a contracting authority was in breach of the duty owed in accordance with regulation 47A or 47B; and
(b) the contract has not yet been entered into.
(2) In those circumstances, the Court may do one or more of the following –
(a) order the setting aside of the decision or action concerned;
(b) order the contracting authority to amend any document;
(c) award damages to an economic operator which has suffered loss or damage as a consequence of the breach.
(3) This regulation does not prejudice any other powers of the Court.
See Regulation 45I of the Utilities Contracts (Amendment) Regulations 2009 with almost the same wording.
66. See Bovis, *supra* note 45, at 570-572, paragraphs 11.312 to 11.317 on the details of the court procedure in the High Court.
67. Thanks to my colleague Chris Bovis (Hull) for pointing this out to me.

tion of the Hight Court in the contract after the set aside of a decision.[68] There are no reports on whether this changed with the introduction of ineffectiv-ness.

6 Ineffectiveness of the contract

Following the requirements of the new Remedies Directive 2007/66/EC,[69] 'ineffectiveness' was introduced in the United Kingdom procurement Regulations in December 2009. According to Regulation 47K of the United Kingdom Public Contracts (Amendment) Regulations 2009 and Regulation 45K of the United Kingdom Utilities Contracts (Amendment) Regulations 2009 the respective courts may declare a public or utility contract ineffective if there are extreme violations of the Public or Utilities Contracts Regulations. These are the three grounds also provided in the Directive: direct illegal awards, violation of the standstill obligation and of the suspension of the tender procedure, and call-offs above the threshold values of the Directives in the context of framework agreements or dynamic purchasing systems.[70] This

68. Ibid.
69. Directive 2007/66/EC with regard to improving the effectiveness of review procedures concerning the award of public contracts [2007] OJ L-134/114.
70. Regulation 47K of the Public Contracts (Amendment) Regulations 2009 reads:
'(1) There are three grounds for ineffectiveness.
The first ground
(2) Subject to paragraph (3), the first ground applies where the contract has been awarded without prior publication of a contract notice in any case in which these Regulations required the prior publication of a contract notice.
(3) The first ground does not apply if all the following apply [...]
The second ground
(5) The second ground applies where all the following apply –
(a) the contract has been entered into in breach of any requirement imposed by –
(i) regulation 32A (the standstill period);
(ii) regulation 47G (contract-making suspended by challenge to award); or
(iii) regulation 47H(1)(b) (interim order restoring or modifying a suspension originally imposed by regulation 47G);
(b) there has also been a breach of the duty owed to the economic operator in accordance with regulation 47A or 47B in respect of obligations other than those imposed by regulation 32A (the standstill period) and this Part;
(c) the breach mentioned in sub-paragraph (a) has deprived the economic operator of the possibility of starting proceedings in respect of the breach mentioned in sub-paragraph (b), or pursuing them to a proper conclusion, before the contract was entered into; and

will enable legal action by third parties against concluded or made contracts possibly leading to the court nullifying at least parts of the obligations of a concluded or made contract.

According to Regulation 47E of the Public Contracts (Amendment) Regulations 2009 and Regulation 45E Utilities Contracts (Amendment) Regulations 2009 an action for ineffectiveness has to be brought within a time limit of six months after the conclusion or making of the contract. The exception to this rule is when a contract award notice was published or where the contracting authority has informed the economic operator of the conclusion of the contract and provided a summary of the relevant reasons. In these two cases the time limit is 30 days from the date of the publication of the notice.[71]

(d) the breach mentioned in sub-paragraph (b) has affected the chances of the economic operator obtaining the contract.
The third ground
(6) Subject to paragraph (7), the third ground applies where all the following apply –
(a) the contract is based on a framework agreement or was awarded under a dynamic purchasing system;
(b) the contract was awarded in breach of any requirement imposed by –
(i) regulation 19(7)(b), (8) and (9) (award of particular contracts under framework agreements through re-opening of competition); or
(ii) regulation 20(11) to (14) (award of contracts under dynamic purchasing systems); and
(c) the estimated value of the contract exceeds the relevant threshold for the purposes of regulation 8.
(7) The third ground does not apply if all the following apply [...]'
See Regulation 45K United Kingdom Utilities Contracts (Amendment) Regulations 2009 with almost the same wording.

71. Regulation 47E Public Contracts (Amendment) Regulations 2009 reads:
'(1) This regulation limits the time within which proceedings may be started where the proceedings seek a declaration of ineffectiveness.
(2) Such proceedings must be started –
(a) where paragraph (3) or (5) applies, within 30 days beginning with the relevant date mentioned in that paragraph;
(b) in any other case, within 6 months beginning with the day after the date on which the contract was entered into.
(3) This paragraph applies where a relevant contract award notice has been published in the Official Journal, in which case the relevant date is the day after the date on which the notice was published.
(4) For that purpose, a contract award notice is relevant if, and only if –
(a) the contract was awarded without prior publication of a contract notice; and
(b) the contract award notice includes justification of the decision of the contracting authority to award the contract without prior publication of a contract notice.

There is no time limit for the court to issue a decision on an action for in-effectiveness. There are generally no limits for English courts to issue decisions. The time for a court to reach a decision will depend on 'the complexity of the issue under consideration and will vary widely.'[72]

The approach of 'prospective ineffectiveness'[73] in Regulation 47M (5) will limit the contractual obligations that can be nullified to those which have yet to be performed at the time of the legal action. This means that '[o]bligations that have been performed by any contractor will not therefore have to be undone.'[74] According to the Office of Government Commerce's *Explanatory Memorandum to the Public Contracts (Amendment) Regulations 2009 No. 2992*, 'UK stakeholders strongly favoured the prospective method, even though that would need to be coupled with an additional method, [...]'.[75] The Directive left the choice between prospective and retrospective ineffectiveness to the Member States. Moreover, consultation of the stakeholders is good legislative practice. However, this citation from the OGC document could be interpreted as suggesting that the choice was mainly made by the stakeholders or at least that their opinion was a decisive factor. Ineffectiveness and public procurement law in general aims to regulate the behaviour of contracting authorities and bidders. Ineffectiveness aims to deal with the most extreme violations. While, again, consultation is good legislative practice, it is doubtful whether the details of an instrument devised to punish

(5) This paragraph applies where the contracting authority has informed the economic operator of –
(a) the conclusion of the contract; and
(b) a summary of the relevant reasons, in which case the relevant date is the day after the date on which the economic operator was informed of the conclusion or, if later, was informed of a summary of the relevant reasons. [...]'
See Regulations 45E Utilities Contracts (Amendment) Regulations 2009 with almost the same wording.

72. Trybus, Blomberg, and Gorecki, *Public Procurement Review and Remedies Systems in the European Union* (SIGMA Paper 41, Paris, 2007), http://www.oecd-ilibrary.org/governance/public-procurement-review-and-remedies-systems-in-the-european-union_5kml60q9vklt-en (accessed in February 2011), at 109.
73. Henty, 'OGC Consultation on Implementation of the New Remedies Directive' 2009) 18 *Public Procurement Law Review* NA48, at NA50 citing (United Kingdom) Office of Government Commerce, Consultation on the Approach to Implementation, at paragraphs 28-32
74. *Explanatory Memorandum to the Public Contracts (Amendment) Regulations 2009 No. 2992*, (Office of Government Commerce, 2009) http://www.ogc.gov.uk/-documents/Remedies_EXPL_MEMO.pdf (accessed in December 2010), at 7.3.1.
75. Ibid.

extreme violations of the law should be decided by stakeholders the new instrument is directed against, if they violate the law in such an extreme way. Prospective ineffectiveness is 'ineffectiveness light' and potentially less effective as it is less of a deterrent against the extreme violations it is directed against. Moreover, the distinction between the two forms of ineffectiveness can be difficult to establish.[76]

Regulation 47L of the Public Contracts (Amendment) Regulations 2009 and Regulation 45L of the Utilities Contracts (Amendment) Regulations 2009 contains an exception to ineffectiveness when overriding reasons relating to the general interest can justify that the contract is continued.[77] While this exception provides the judges with a certain degree of flexibility which allows them to take individual circumstances into account, it might also lead to legal uncertainty. Skilbeck suggests that the general interest should be an 'external general interest',[78] which would include risks to public health and safety, threats to the environment, or national security. This would exclude economic interests, including third party interests, which are directly linked to the contract. Nevertheless, the interpretation of Regulation 47L Public Contracts (Amendment) Regulations 2009 remains difficult especially due to the fact that many public contracts are by definition in the general interest.[79] If as a

76. Skilbeck, *supra* note 40, at 17.
77. Regulation 47L Public Contracts (Amendment) Regulations 2009 reads:
    '(1) Where the Court is satisfied that any of the grounds for ineffectiveness applies, the Court must not make a declaration of ineffectiveness if –
    (a) the contracting authority or another party to the proceedings raises an issue under this regulation; and
    (b) the Court is satisfied that overriding reasons relating to a general interest require that the effects of the contract should be maintained.
    (2) For that purpose, economic interests in the effectiveness of the contract may be considered as overriding reasons only if in exceptional circumstances ineffectiveness would lead to disproportionate consequences.
    (3) However, economic interests directly linked to the contract cannot constitute overriding reasons relating to a general interest.
    (4) For that purpose, economic interests directly linked to the contract include –
    (a) the costs resulting from the delay in the execution of the contract;
    (b) the costs resulting from the commencement of a new procurement procedure;
    (c) the costs resulting from change of the economic operator performing the contract; and
    (d) the costs of legal obligations resulting from the ineffectiveness. [...]'.
78. Skilbeck, *supra* note 40, at 17.
79. This is perhaps lees the case for utilities contracts and Regulation 45L Utilities Contracts Regulations 2009.

consequence to this lack of clarity the courts rely too heavily on the exception and thus do not apply ineffectiveness in practice, Regulations 47L and 45L might well prove too large a loophole undermining the effectiveness of ineffectiveness and thus of the entire public procurement review and remedies system.[80] However, such a practice would not be in compliance with Article 2 (d) of Directive 2007/66/EC which clearly requires ineffectiveness to be the regular consequence of the three most severe procurement law violations, especially in cases of direct illegal awards.[81] Another connected problem arises out of the lack of clarity of Regulations 47L and 45L. The effectiveness of a remedies system depends to a certain extent on their 'user-friendliness'. Rules need to be understandable to the bidders who are supposed to be the backbone of the review system, especially with regards to ineffectiveness. The unpredictability of review proceedings has already been a considerable disincentive for United Kingdom bidders to initiate proceedings in the past.[82] Hence not only the judges but also the bidders might 'refuse' to 'use' ineffectiveness in practice. However, it is too early to assess this question on the basis of empirical evidence: ineffectiveness has not yet been used in practice. It is therefore not clear whether the Hight Court will avoid annulling contracts for reasons of public interest, alter contract conditions, actually annul contracts, or just impose fines. If contracts are annulled this may lead to claims for damages by the pviate party to an ineffective contract.[83] Again, it is too early to discuss the conditions under which this would operate in practice.

Despite all the criticism expressed above, the introduction of ineffectiveness significantly changes the traditional approach to concluded public contracts in England and Wales (and Northern Ireland and Scotland). At least in theory, which is no small feat, the principle of *pacta sunt servanda* is overcome by the amended Regulations. Again, it is not clear yet how ineffectiveness will operate in practice. However, even with the current lack of clarity it is assumed that it is a major deterrent due to the possible costs, delay to the project, the hassle of re-commencing the procurement procedure, the impact

80. Henty, 'Is the standstill period a step forward? The proposed revision of the EC Remedies Directive', *supra* note 53, at 265, thinks that it is 'unlikely that this ultimate sanction [of ineffectiveness] will routinely be applied.'
81. For example: Recital 13 Directive 2007/66/EC: '[...] a contract resulting from an illegal direct award should in principle be considered ineffective.'
82. Pachnou, 'Bidders' use of mechanisms to enforce EC procurement law' (2005) 14 *Public Procurement Law Review* 256, at 258 et seq.
83. Thanks to by collerague Chris Bovis (Hull) for pointing this out to me.

on the budget if fines are imposed,[84] as well as the risk of bad publicity and political pressure.[85]

7 Alternative penalties

Traditionally, there were no provisions in relation to periodic penalty payments and no financial or other alternative penalties available in the United Kingdom. However, this changed with the implementation of Directive 2007/66/EC in the United Kingdom (and Scotland).[86] According to Regulations 47N and 45N for public contracts and utilities contracts respectively 'civil financial penalties' may and in some cases have to be imposed by the court.[87] Moreover, the same provisions allow 'contract shortening' as a pos-

84. Clifton, 'Ineffectiveness – the new deterrent: will the new Remedies Directive ensure greater compliance with the substantive procurement rules in the classical sectors?' (2009) 19 *Public Procurement Law Review* 165
85. Henty, 'Remedies Directive Implemented into UK Law', *supra* note 3, at 116.
86. As foreseen by Henty, 'OGC Consultation on Implementation of the New Remedies Directive', *supra* note 73, at NA51-52.
87. Regulation 47N of the Public Contracts (Amendment) Regulations 2009 entitled 'Penalties in addition to, or instead of, ineffectiveness' reads:
'(1) Where the Court makes a declaration of ineffectiveness, it must also order that the contracting authority pay a civil financial penalty of the amount specified in the order.
(2) Paragraph (3) applies where –
(a) in proceedings for a declaration of ineffectiveness, the Court is satisfied that any of the grounds for ineffectiveness applies but does not make a declaration of ineffectiveness because regulation 47L requires it not to do so; or
(b) in any proceedings, the Court is satisfied that the contract has been entered into in breach of any requirement imposed by regulation 32A, 47G or 47H(1)(b), and does not make a declaration of ineffectiveness (whether because none was sought or because the Court is not satisfied that any of the grounds for ineffectiveness applies).
(3) In those circumstances, the Court must order at least one, and may order both, of the following penalties –
(a) that the duration of the contract be shortened to the extent specified in the order;
(b) that the contracting authority pay a civil financial penalty of the amount specified in the order.
(4) When the Court is considering what order to make under paragraph (1) or (3), the overriding consideration is that the penalties must be effective, proportionate and dissuasive.
(5) In determining the appropriate order, the Court must take account of all the relevant factors, including –

sible remedy in certain circumstances.[88] Both of these 'alternative penalties' can be imposed in addition to or instead of an order of ineffectiveness. In the context of the latter case, they can be imposed if the court is satisfied that any of the grounds for ineffectiveness apply but does not make such a declaration because of overriding reasons in the public interest (see above). Finally, they can be imposed where the standstill period, the automatic suspension of the procurement procedure, or an interim order has not been respected and the court does not make an order of ineffectiveness, 'because none was sought or because the court is not satisfied that any of the grounds for ineffectiveness applies.' When the court is considering what 'alternative penalty' to impose, 'the overriding consideration is that the penalties must be effective, proportionate and dissuasive.' In that context the court will take account of all the relevant factors, including the seriousness of the relevant breach of the duty, the behavior of the contracting authority, and in certain contexts the extent to which the contract remains in force.

(a) the seriousness of the relevant breach of the duty owed in accordance with regulation 47A or 47B;
(b) the behaviour of the contracting authority;
(c) where the order is to be made under paragraph (3), the extent to which the contract remains in force. [...]'
See Regulation 45N of the Utilities Contracts (Amendment) Regulations 2009 with almost the same wording.

88. The relevant part of Regulation 47N of the Public Contracts (Amendment) Regulations 2009 entitled 'Contract shortening' reads:
(10) When making an order under paragraph (3)(a), or at any time after doing so, the Court may make any order that it thinks appropriate for addressing the consequences of the shortening of the duration of the contract.
(11) Such an order may, for example, address issues of restitution and compensation as between those parties to the contract who are parties to the proceedings so as to achieve an outcome which the Court considers to be just in all the circumstances.
(12) Paragraph (13) applies where the parties to the contract have, at any time before the order under paragraph 3(a) is made, agreed by contract any provisions for the purpose of regulating their mutual rights and obligations in the event of such an order being made. [...]'
See Regulation 45N of the Utilities Contracts (Amendment) Regulations 2009 with almost the same wording.

8 Damages

According to Regulation 47I of the United Kingdom Public Contracts (Amendment) Regulations 2009, if the Court is satisfied that a decision or action taken by a contracting authority was in breach of a relevant duty owed in accordance with the Regulations and the contract has not yet been entered into it may inter alia 'award damages to an economic operator which has suffered loss or damage as a consequence of the breach.'[89] According to Regulation 47J of the United Kingdom Public Contracts (Amendment) Regulations 2009 this option is also available to the court after the contract has been entered into.[90] The common law of obligations applies to these damages. Therefore legal action regarding the phase after the conclusion or making of the contract is handled by the courts also dealing with disputes between private parties to a contract. These are the same courts hearing cases up to the conclusion of the contract: High Court, Court of Appeal, and Supreme Court. With regards to contracts of a lower value, below the thresholds of the Regulations and Directives, a county court may decide on claims for damages.[91]

8.1 Actions in tort

Damages may be recovered in actions in tort, such as the tort of breach of statutory duty and the tort of misfeasance in public office. The tort of breach of statutory duty is relevant with respect to contracts within the field of application of the Directives and Regulations.[92] The tort of misfeasance in public office is relevant for contracts inside and outside their field of application. Moreover, as explained above, there is an implied contract governing the conduct of the contract award procedure and in some cases a breach of these rules might coincide with the private law obligations in this contract and thus damages might be available for breach of contract.

As damages are generally subject to long-established common law rules,[93] they feature only briefly in the 2006 and 2009 Regulations. Regulation 47J of

89. See Regulation 45I United Kingdom Utilities Contracts (Amendment) Regulations 2009 with the same wording.
90. See Regulation 45J United Kingdom Utilities Contracts (Amendment) Regulations 2009 with the same wording.
91. Arrowsmith, *The Law of Public and Procurement*, *supra* note 15, at 1384.
92. Arrowsmith, *The Law of Public and Utilities Procurement*, ibid., at 1422: 'Since the claim [for damages under the Regulations] can be categorised as one in tort for breach of statutory duty.'
93. See Bovis, *supra* note 45, at 594, paragraph 11.391.

the United Kingdom Public Contracts (Amendment) Regulations 2009 stipulates that if 'the Court is satisfied that a decision or action taken by a contracting authority was in breach' of the regulations and 'the contract has already been entered into' the Court 'may award damages to an economic operator which has suffered loss or damage as a consequence of the breach.'[94] This rule which applies to contracts within the field of application of the Regulations and Directives appears to apply irrespective of whether the contracting authority was fully aware of the fact that it was breaching the procurement rules or disregarded a risk of doing so.

Under the general rules of tort law a 'balance of probabilities rule' will be applied by the court: the applicant is required to prove that had the rules been followed he or she would have been awarded the contract 'on the balance of probabilities.' In the context of public procurement cases, however, the courts have applied a 'loss of chance' rule.[95] The court will assess the chance the tenderer in question had of being awarded the contract that was denied due to the contracting authority's failure to observe the procurement rules and award damages based on the estimated profit the tenderer would have gained from the contract.[96] The requirements of the 'loss of chance' rule are easier to meet than those of the 'balance of probabilities' rule. However, the earlier requires a 'real' or 'substantial' chance of being awarded the contract, which may lead to problems when a tender was submitted[97] as will be discussed further under 9. below.

8.2 Loss or damage

With regards to claims for damages regarding both contracts inside and outside the field of application of the EU Directives and United Kingdom Regulations, Arrowsmith has summarised the position as follows:

94. See Regulation 45J United Kingdom Utilities Contracts (Amendment) Regulations 2009 with the same wording.
95. *Allied Maples Group* v *Simmons and Simmons* [1995] 1 W.L.R. 1602 and *Chaplin* v *Hicks* [1911] 2 K.B. 786 as cited by Arrowsmith, *The Law of Public and Procurement*, *supra* note 14, at 1382.
96. Applied with regards to determining damages under the procurement Regulations in *Harmon CFEM Facades (UK) Ltd* v *The Corporate Officer of the House of Commons*, [2002] 2 L.G.L.R. 372 and *G Luck Arboricultural & Horticultural* v *Tower Hamlets LBC*, [2003] 2 CMLR 12, CA, affirming High Court Decision [2002] EWHC 717, QBD as cited by Arrowsmith, *The Law of Public and Utilities Procurement*, ibid.
97. See Arrowsmith, *The Law of Public and Procurement*, *supra* note 15, at 1382.

'The general principle of damages in tort requires the claimant to be put in a position as if the tort had not occurred. In the present context, this requires the aggrieved provider to be put in the position in which it would have been had the purchaser complied with its obligations. Thus it is necessary to ask: what would the firm's position have been if the proper rules had been observed?'[98]

This means that the tender costs cannot be recovered since they would have been spent even without any violation of procurement rules. What can be recovered is what could broadly be termed the profit which was lost because the bidder was not awarded the contract:

'This will be the difference between the amount that would have been paid to [the tenderer] under the contract, and the costs that would have been incurred as a result of the contract.'[99]

Again, this would exclude the tender costs, unless the bidder can show that he or she would not have participated in the procurement procedure at all had the rules been followed.[100] The bidder has to prove the precise amount of the likely amount and that can be difficult.[101]

9 Parallel remedies?

Another issue is whether a 'parallel remedies theory' as described in the chapter on France applies in the United Kingdom public procurement remedies system. This concerns the question whether more than one remedy can be awarded, declared, or imposed at the same time and in the same case or if certain remedies are mutually exclusive.

With regards to contracts that have not been entered into, Regulation 47I (2) United Kingdom Public Contract (Amendment) Regulations 2009 stipulates that the court may award 'one or more' of the remedies of set aside, amendment, or damages.[102] This suggests that the award of remedies is not mutually exclusive and that more than one remedy may be awarded. More-

98. Ibid., at 1381.
99. Arrowsmith, *The Law of Public and Procurement, supra* note 15, at 1381.
100. *Harmon CFEM Facades (UK) Ltd* v *The Corporate Officer of the House of Commons, supra* note 8.
101. See Arrowsmith, *The Law of Public and Procurement, supra* note 15, at 1383-4.
102. See Regulation 45J United Kingdom Utilities Contracts (Amendment) Regulations 2009 with the same wording.

over, according to Regulation 47I (3): '[t]his regulation does not prejudice any other powers of the Court.' However, if the court orders a procurement decision to be set aside the bidder will normally have a second chance for the contract and thus no longer be able to claim damages 'for loss of a chance'. Hence is will be difficult to satisfy the tort requirements outlined under 8. above when a procurement decision violating the procurement rules has been set aside making set aside and damages mutually exclusive.

With regards to contracts that have already been entered into, the Regulations are more limited since according to Regulation 47J (d) the court 'must not order any other remedies' than the three remedies prescribed in the Regulation. According to Regulation 47J the Court '(a) must, if it is satisfied that any of the grounds for ineffectiveness applies, make a declaration of ineffectiveness in respect of the contract unless regulation 47L requires the Court not to do so;' and '(b) must, where required by Regulation 47N, impose penalties in accordance with that regulation[.]' This means that if the requirements are met the court has to declare or impose the remedies. There is no passage in the text of the Regulations that would suggest that these two remedies are mutually exclusive. It is submitted that the court could make a declaration of ineffectiveness and impose penalties at the same time.

Moreover, the Court '(c) may award damages to an economic operator which has suffered loss or damage as a consequence of the breach [.]' The award of damages is possible '[...] regardless of whether the Court also acts as described in sub-paragraphs (a) and (b) [.]' This suggests that the court could (1) impose penalties and award damages, (2) impose penalties and make a declaration of ineffectiveness (see above), or (3) make a declaration of ineffectiveness and award damages. Based on a literal interpretation of Regulation 47J and especially the second part of Regulation 47J (3), the court could, as a third possibility, award all three remedies. However, if the court makes a declaration of ineffectiveness, the bidder will normally have a chance to be awarded the contract and thus no longer be able to claim damages 'for loss of a chance', although this will depend on which of the three reasons of ineffectiveness applies and more generally on the individual circumstances of the case. Nevertheless in many cases ineffectiveness and damages will be mutually exclusive. Moreover, the requirement for the bidder to have had a 'real' or 'substantial' chance of being awarded the contract as part of the loss of chance principle applied to claims for damages outlined under 8. above, is difficult if not impossible to meet in the case of direct illegal awards as the litigant did not participate in a procurement procedure and can therefore not demonstrate such a chance. This left bidders without a remedy before the introduction of ineffectiveness in 2009 which now appears to be the only remedy for such a case.

Again, the traditional approach before the 2009 public and utilities contracts amendment Regulations was that once the contract is concluded or made, the possibilities of litigation by third parties were very limited. As explained above, damages were normally the only available remedy and a violation of procurement rules did not normally invalidate the contract.[103] The old strict approach was designed to protect the successful tenderer as well as the public interest in the realisation of the project in question. Moreover, save in very rare cases of fraud or bad faith, the court did not have the power to overturn a contract award once the contract had been concluded. This changed after the introduction of ineffectiveness in the implementation process of Directive 2007/66/EC, as explained under 9. above. In the context of the common law of contracts, which governs most other aspects of public contracts during the performance stage after their conclusion, third parties may not bring judicial actions against such contracts.

10 Alternative dispute settlement

There are various United Kingdom organisations providing alternative dispute settlement services, especially at the performance stage. Public bodies and their contractors may use these services on occasion, but they are not obliged by law or policy to do so.

Apart from the alternative dispute settlement mechanisms described above, the Utilities Contracts Regulations had implemented the conciliation mechanism established by Directive 92/13/EC in Regulations 44 and 46 respectively. The option for such a mechanism was taken out of the EU regime in Directive 2007/66/EC and therefore also removed from the Utilities Contracts Regulations in the course of the implementation process in the United Kingdom through the Utilities Contracts (Amendment) Regulations 2009.

103. Section 135 Local Government Act 1972 requiring local authorities to adopt standing orders providing for competitive tendering also provides that a breach of such standing orders does not invalidate the contract. By contrast, Section 51 Environmental Protection Act 1990 expressly provides that a breach of its tendering rules will render the contract void.

11 Conclusions

The attitude of judges towards the interests involved in public procurement cases is considered to be completely independent and unbiased.[104] However, compared to the case loads discussed in the chapters on Germany and France, there are relatively few public procurement cases each year. While this is partly due to the effort and costs[105] involved in having to bring proceedings in the High Court and possibly beyond and the unavailability of cheaper lower level procurement review bodies, the small number of public contracts cases in England and Wales (and Scotland and Northern Ireland) is also a result of the general attitude of tenderers towards review proceedings. The Wood Review found that British tenderers are reluctant to challenge mainly due to the negative consequences of their business relationships and the difficulties of proving a wrongdoing.[106] This changed recently. For the last few years there have been about 20+ public procurement cases each year, amounting to an overall body of case law since the beginnings of public procurement litigation of about 200 cases with about 60 in Northern Ireland alone.[107] While there has been no research into the reasons for this change of attitude regarding litigation, it appears that the findings of the Wood Review are now at least to an extent outdated. An increased awareness of the available public procurement remedies amongst tenderers is likely to be one factor leading to their increased readiness to seek them. Moreover, there is anecdotal evidence that the introduction of the standstill period following the *Alcatel* judgment in the 2006 regulations made a considerable difference.

The small number of cases, high litigation costs, and the absence of lower level procurement review bodies below the High Court (and Sheriff Court) led to criticism questioning whether the United Kingdom and Scotland public procurement review and remedies systems were sufficiently effective. The

104. Trybus, Blomberg, Gorecki, *Public Procurement Review and Remedies Systems in the European Union*, *supra* note 72, at 110.

105. The costs indentified as a detrerent to litigation already by Pachnou, 'Bidder remedies to enforce the EC procurement rules in England and Wales' (2003) 12 *Public Procurement Law Reveiw* 35.

106. Wood Review: *Investigating UK business experiences of competing for public contracts* in other EU countries (November 2004) www.ogc.gov.uk/documents/-woodreview.pdf (accessed in January 2011).

107. This estimate figure emerges from the increased number of United Kingdom and Scotland judgments published in the law reports and discussed in the *Public Procurement Law Review*, other law journals, and the websites of law firms and barristers' chambers.

number of cases is increasing and might increase even further in the future. While this is partly due to innovations in the review and remedies systems initiated by the implementation of EU law, there also appears to be a shift from the attitude of many tenderers 'not to bite the hand that feeds'. This shift might become more dramatic in the future since the new Coalition Government is not feeding as much as its predecessor did.

Bibliography

Arrowsmith, S, *The Law of Public and Utilities Procurement* (Sweet & Maxwell, 2nd ed., 2005)

Arrowsmith, S, 'Implementation of the New EC Procurement Directives and the Alcatel Ruling in England and Wales and Northern Ireland: a Review of the New Legislation and Guidance' (2006) 15 *Public Procurement Law Review* 86

Arrowsmith, S, Linarelli, J, Wallace D; *Regulating Public Procurement: National and International Perspectives* (Kluwer Law International: London, 2000)

Bovis, C, *EC Public Procurement: Case Law and Regulation* (Oxford University Press: New York, 2006)

Clifton, M-J, 'Ineffectiveness – the new deterrent: will the new Remedies Directive ensure greater compliance with the substantive procurement rules in the classical sectors?' (2009) 19 *Public Procurement Law Review* 165

Craig, PP, *Administrative Law* (Sweet & Maxwell, 6th ed., 2008)

De Koninck, C and Flamey, P (eds.), *European Public Procurement Law, Part III – Remedies* Kluwer Law International: London, 2009)

Golding, J and Henty, P, 'The new Remedies Directive of the EC: standstill and ineffectiveness' (2008) 17 *Public Procurement Law Review* 146

Henty, P, 'Remedies Directive Implemented into UK Law' (2010) 19 *Public Procurement Law Review* NA115-124.

Henty, P, 'United Kingdom: Public Procurement Remedies Directive – an update on the implementation process' (2010) 19 *Public Procurement Law Review* 1

Henty, P, 'OGC Consultation on Implementation of the New Remedies Directive' (2009) 18 *Public Procurement Law Review* NA48

Henty, P, 'Is the standstill period a step forward? The proposed revision of the EC Remedies Directive' (2006) 15 *Public Procurement Law Review* 253

McGovern, P, 'Two important decisions of the European Court of Justice on time-limits in proceedings for review procedures in public procurement: the Uniplex case (C-406/08) and Commission v. Ireland (C-456/08)' (2010) 19 *Public Procurement Law Review* 101

Pachnou, D, 'Bidders' use of mechanisms to enforce EC procurement law' (2005) 14 *Public Procurement Law Review* 256

Pachnou, D. 'Bidder remedies to enforce the EC procurement rules in England and Wales' (2003) 12 Public Procurement Law Reveiw 35

Pachnou, D, 'Enforcement of the EC procurement rules: the standards required of national review systems under EC law in the context of the principle of effectiveness' (2000) 9 *Public Procurement Law Review* 55

Skilbeck, J, 'Developments in Public Procurement Law' (2010) 20 *Computers & the Law* 16

Taylor, S, 'Bridging the remedies gap' (2010) 21 *PLC* 29

Trepte, P-A, *Public Procurement in the EU: A Practitioner's Guide* (Oxford University Press: Oxford, 2nd ed. 2007)

Tridimas, T, *General Principles of EU Law* (Oxford University Press, Oxford, 2nd ed. 2006)

Trybus, M, Blomberg, P, Gorecki, PN, *Public Procurement Review and Remedies Systems in the European Union* (SIGMA Paper 41, Paris, 2007)

National Audit Office -- http://www.nao.org.uk/

Office of Government Commerce -- http://www.ogc.gov.uk/

Treasury and Procurement http://www.hm treasury.gov.uk./media/E/6/government-_procurement_pu147.pdf

Wood Review: Investigating UK business experiences of competing for public contracts in other EU countries (November 2004) www.ogc.gov.uk/documents/woodreview.pdf.

7 Enforcement of EU Procurement Rules. The Italian System of Remedies

By Mario Comba

1 Introduction: the Italian system of remedies against the Public Administration and, in particular, in the field of public procurements

The Italian system of remedies for public procurements has not been differentiated from the general system of remedies against the Public Administration until recently. It is well known, in comparative administrative studies,[1] that the Italian system is based on the distinction between 'interesse legittimo' and 'diritto soggettivo' where the latter is a full right, while the first is 'something less' than a full right and is given legal protection in front of special courts, called 'administrative tribunals', while the 'diritto soggettivo' is protected by ordinary Courts.[2] According to the classification proposed by the Sigma Re-

1. See A. Piras – *M. Stipo, Administrative Justice in Italy*, in M. Motzo – A. Piras (eds.) *Administrative Law, the Problem of Justice*, Milano Giuffré, 1997, vol. III, p. 237-327; in particular, p. 267-327 for the distinction between 'diritto soggettivo' and 'interesse legittimo'; D. Sorace, *Administrative Law*, in J. S. Lena – U. Mattei (eds), *Introduction to Italian Law*, Kluwer, 2002, pag. 125-158, spec. pag. 138-158 for the Italian system of administrative justice; F. G. Scoca, *Administrative Justice in Italy: Origins and Evolution, in Italian Journal of Public law*, n. 2/2009, p. 118-161 (www.ijpl.eu). For the specific case of judicial review in the competition field, see R. Caranta – B. Marchetti, *Judicial Review of Regulatory Decisions in Italy; Changing the Formula and Keeping the Substance?* In O. Essens – A. Gerbrandy – S. Lavrijssen (eds), *National Courts and the Standard of Review in Competition Law and Economic Regulation*, Groningen, Europa Law Publishing, 2009, p. 145. In French, see M. Fromont, *Droit administratif des Etats européens*, Paris, PUF, 2006, p. 149-152; more recently, see R. Caranta, *Le contentieux des contrats publics en Italie, in Revue française de droit administratif*, 2010 (forthcoming)
2. This 'double jurisdiction' system was created with the Law n. 5992 of 1889 which gave to the Consiglio di Sato, based in Rome, the power to judge litigation against Public administrations. Law 1034 of 1971 created a Tribunale Amministrativo Regionale for each Region, as a first instance judge against whose decision an appeal

port n. 41 on Public Procurement Review and Remedies Systems in the European Union[3] (which does not include an Italian national report) the Italian model could be qualified as a 'Dual system of remedies', along with the French, the Belgian and the Swedish, but with the difference that in Italy the criterion of distinction between the administrative and the ordinary Court is not based on the legal form of the contract (public procurement/concession) nor on the object of the same (services, works, supplies/utilities) nor on the legal nature of the buyer (public entity/mixed company) but on the legal nature of the relationship between the (public) buyer and the (private) seller: exercise of a public power by the buyer/equal rights between buyer and seller. This distinction often overlaps with the distinction between remedies given before and after the conclusion of the contract,[4] but it has some relevant differences which will be explained further below .

This is not the place to analyse the difference between 'interese legittimo' and 'diritto soggettivo', nor the evolution of the Italian system of administrative justice, but in a rough synthesis, the position of 'interesse legittimo' arises when the individual's full right is limited by a contrasting public interest which is pursued by the Administration by exercising a public power: for example, my right of property is a full right against another private who wants to limit it by passing through my estate with his car; but if the State decides to build a new highway and to place it on my estate, my right of property is downgraded to an 'interesse legittimo' and the State is entitled to expropriate my estate for public interest through an act of expropriation. The only limitation to the expropriation is given by the due process of law and thus I can ask the Administrative judge to annul the expropriation if I can give evidence that it was issued in contrast with the due process established by the general law about expropriation.

The position of 'interesse legittimo' can be negative or positive ('oppositivo' or 'pretensivo'), in the sense that I can expect the Public administration not to do something (like, for example, in the case of expropriation, not to expropriate my estate) or, on the contrary, positively to do something (like, for example, when I am asking for a public grant or a contribution, or for the licence to exploit a mine). In this general framework, the position of the private in the public procurement field is that of a positive 'interesse legittimo':

was possible to the Consiglio di Stato. D. Lgs (Legislative Decree) n. 104 of 2010, effective from 15 September 2010, has now incorporated all those provisions into the new Italian Code for the administrative process.

3. GOV/SIGMA (2007)5, point. 2.2, which can be found on the website of OECD.
4. See the Sigma report cited above, point. 2.3

if I am an economic operator in the field I have an 'interesse legittimo' to have the public procurement awarded to me and thus I can ask the Administrative judge to annul any decision of the contracting authority taken in violation of public procurement rules.[5]

From 1889[6] to 2000, the Italian administrative process was not differentiated: it was the same for cases relating for example expropriation, the award of grants or contributions, zoning, building licences and public procurements. The process provided for the possibility of injunctive relief and, since 1999, of damages[7] and no particular problems arose under the perspective of the implementation of the European directive 89/665/CE on remedies.

Law n. 205 of 2000 introduced for the first time a different procedure for some specific cases, among which public procurements (introducing article 23bis in the general law about administrative process – Law 1034 of 1971). It was not exactly a different procedure, but mainly the acceleration of the ordinary procedure: in fact all the deadlines of the process were cut by half (but leaving the regular 60 day time for the notification of the recourse); a fast track was introduced for cases where the recourse was patently well grounded and finally an injunctive power was given to the President of the Tribunal, in cases where it was not possible to wait until the first regular hearing for the discussion about the interim measure required.

With the approval of D. Lgs (Legislative Decree) n. 163 of 2006, implementing Directives 2004/17/CE and 2004/18/CE, the Italian public procurement code was enacted (hereinafter, the p.p. code), containing all provisions related to public procurements, including special sectors and procurements under the threshold. Even if the public procurement code does not tackle directly remedies in the process it regulates, however, the procedure for the conclusion of the contract and thus, in article 11 cl. 10 introduces the stand-

5. To be precise, the 'interesse legittimo' in the positive sense is not 'something less' than a full right: in the case of public procurement, for example, there is not a full right to have a contract awarded in the private sector; on the contrary, an economic operator who makes an offer to a private company is much less protected than an economic operator making an offer to a contracting authority because 'il diritto dei privati sostanzialmente si disinteressa dei modi impiegati per individuare un partner contrattuale' (private law is substantially uninterested in the way by which the contractual partner is chosen) R. Caranta, I contratti pubblici, Torino, Giappichelli, 2004, p. 6.
6. See footnote 2.
7. It was only with the decision of the Corte di Cassazione, sezioni unite, n. 500 of 22 july 1999 that Italian case law recognized the possibility for the petitioner to get damages for violation of an 'interesse legittimo'.

still clause forbidding the conclusion of the contract before 30 days from the communication to the other participants to the procedure of the award of the contract. In order to make this provision effective, article 79 of the p.p. code imposes some obligations of communication to the contracting authority: a message has to be sent to all participants in five days time from the award communicating that the contract was awarded and a message has to be sent to all participant excluded from the procedure, with the motivation of the exclusion.

The p.p. code featured a few articles directly dealing with remedies: article 244, stating that all litigation dealing with the award procedure falls under the jurisdiction of the administrative judge (but without mentioning the contract); article 245 'strumenti di tutela' (tools for enforcement) and article 246 about enforcement for procurements of public works of particular relevance. Article 245 is nothing more than a repetition of what was already stated by Law 205 of 2000, while article 246 reduces the tools of enforcement for public works procurements of particular relevance, excluding the possibility to declare ineffectiveness of the contract and leaving only the possibility of damages.

Given the text of article 244 p.p.code which did non mention contracts among the jurisdiction of the administrative judge, the case law of the Italian Corte di Cassazione[8] decided that the power to annul the contract was up to the ordinary judge and not the administrative judge, with the consequence that an economic operator who wanted to challenge the award of a public procurement to a competitor had to lodge a complaint first before the administrative judge, in order to have the award annulled, and then in front of the ordinary judge, in order to have the contract annulled. The question was the cause of a deep conflict (between the Consiglio di Stato (acting as the higher administrative jurisdiction) and the Corte di Cassazione (the higher ordinary jurisdiction, having the power to decide questions over conflict of juridiction).[9] Only one month before the enactment of the Italian law implementing Directive 2007/66/EC (and when the deadline for the implementation was al-

8. Corte di Cassazione, Sezioni Unite, sentenza 28 dicembre 2007, n. 27169.
9. With a decision of 2003 (Cons. St., sez. VI, 5 may 2003 n. 2332), the Consiglio di Stato declared that he annullment of the award had the consequence of provoking the ineffectiveness of the contract, but in 2007 the Corte di Cassazione (Sezioni Unite, sentenza 28 dicembre 2007, n. 27169) decided that only the ordinary judge and not the administrative judge could declare the ineffectiveness of the contract and the Consiglio di Stato, with a decision of 2008 (Cons. St., ad. plen., 30 luglio 2008 n. 9) went along with the decision of the Corte di Cassazione. It has to be reminded that, according to Italian law, the Corte di Cassazione has the power to decide over the conflict of jurisdiction between ordinary and administrative judges.

ready expired) did the Corte di Cassazione change its mind, stating that the annulment of the contract belongs to the jurisdiction of the administrative judge.[10]

Directive 2007/66/EC was implemented in Italy with D. Lgs. (Legislative Decree) 20 march 2010, n. 53, effective on 27 april 2010. D. Lgs. 53/10 modifies the p.p. code in two main areas: as for substantive rules (mainly the standstill clause and related obligations of communication) it modifies articles 11 and 79 of the p.p. code; as for remedies in the process, it modifies article 244 of p.p. code, giving to the administrative judge also the power to annul the contract and modifying deeply article 245 through the introduction of articles 245bis, 245ter, 245quater and 245quinquies. Substantially, the new articles 244 to 245quinquies contain the rules of a special process for public procurement litigation, rooted into the administrative process but with relevant differences.

A few months after the enactment of D. Lgs. 53/10, the Code of the Administrative Process (D. Lgs. n. 104 of 2010) was approved, (the third Italian code of procedure, after the code for civil and that for criminal process), effective from 15 september 2010. The regulation of remedies in public procurements was thus concentrated in the CAP (Code for Administrative Process) through the amendment of articles 244 to 245quinquies of the p.p. code which now only refer to the CAP for remedies. Article 133, cl. 1.e.1 CAP confirms that the annulment of the contract falls under the jurisdiction of the administrative judge.

After this short history of remedies for public procurements in Italian law, it can now be said conclusively that, presently, Directive 2007/66/EC is enacted in Italy by two different pieces of legislation: articles 11 and 79 of the p.p. code tackle the standstill clause and the related obligations of communications, while articles 119 to 125 CAP deal with the process for public procurements, considered as a special process rooted into the principles of the administrative process.

It follows that presently, in Italy, only Administrative Courts (TAR as first instance judge and Consiglio di Stato as judge of appeal) are involved in the enforcement of public procurement provisions, until the conclusion of the contract. Since the rule is that all litigation involving the exercise of a public power goes to the Administrative Court, while if the Administration is acting

10. Corte di Cassazione, Sezioni Unite, sentenza 10 febbraio 2010, n. 2906. Directive 2007/66/EC does not say that the power to annull the award and the contract should be given to the same judge, but the Corte di Cassazione recognizes that doubling the judges could be too burdensome for an effective system of remedies.

on a private law basis (iure privatorum) the litigation goes to the ordinary judge (Tribunale civile, as first instance judge, Corte d'Appello as appeal judge and Corte di Cassazione as third level judge), then it is generally understood that all litigation arising after the conclusion of the contract falls into the jurisdiction of the ordinary judge because it is considered as being a litigation between two private parties, as the contracting authority does not exercise a public power in the mere execution of the contract.[11]

The Italian system does not provide for an independent authority to hear litigations in public procurement. It has to be noted that until the enactement of D. Lgs. 53/10, it was always possible to choose an alternative remedy for challenging every decision of the Public administration, that is requesting the annulment from the President of the Republic, through an administrative – and not a judicial – procedure regulated by Law n. 1199 of 1971. But this possibility was eliminated, for public procurements only, by D. Lgs. 53/10 and the prohibition is now confirmed by article 120 cl. 1 CAP according to which the only legal way to challenge decisions of the contracting authority in the process of awarding the contract is lodging a complaint before the administrative judge. The Italian Authority on Public contracts (AVCP) is not a substitute for the administrative judge in litigation for public procurements; it can only issue non binding advice when asked by the contracting authority or by one of the participants to the awarding procedure (article 6, cl. 7.n p.p. code).

As for the *locus standi*, there is not a specific provision for public procurement. Case law is pretty precise on the matter, stating that as a general rule in order to lodge a complaint against the award of a public procurement one must have participated to the procedure having presented an offer or a manifestation of interest. There are some exceptions, the first and most important being the case in which no publicity was done with regard to the procedure: in this case the *locus standi* is given to all economic operators who could have participated to the procedure, had the contracting authority made a regular publication Another case is admitted when the economic operator wants to challenge the bid, pretending it does not allow him to participate (for example because technical contitions are too difficult for him to fulfil): he is

11. Of course there are some exceptions to this rule, and perhaps more than one can expect, because it can happen that in certain cases the contracting authority exercises public powers also in the execution of the contract. For example it can revoke the award of the contract if it is found out that the contractor did not fulfil some specific subjective conditions (article 135 p.p. code) and in this case the question falls into the jurisdiction of the administrative judge.

allowed to challenge the bid even if he has not presented an offer, because his offer surely would have been rejected and was thus useless. Another discussed case about *locus standi* is that related to groups of economic operators: Italian case law was divided between the position that excluded the possibility for a single operator to lodge a complaint, if not together with all the other economic operators of the group, and the position that admitted the recourse even if lodged by a single economic operator of the group. Recently the Consiglio di Stato has chosen the latter interpretation, stating that the group of economic operators is not an autonomous legal entity.[12]

As for costs, a fixed tax of two thousands euros is required for starting a public procurement litigation in front of an administrative judge, irrespective of the economic value of the question (art. 13, d.P.R. n. 115 of 2002) and the same tax has to be paid in case of appeal before the Consiglio di Stato. That is the higher judicial tax required in the administrative process (only recourses against independent administrative authorities have the same cost). A lower tax of one thousand Euros is required for all recourses subject to the fast track procedure provided by CAP and listed by article 119 (among them, for example, privatization and expropriation procedures, appointments made by the Government, emergency orders), while the tax for all other administrative litigations is five hundred Euros (except for recourses for citizenship or for getting documents from the Public administration, in which cases it is reduced to 250 Euros). In addition one has to assess the cost of the lawyer, whose tariffs are settled by a Decree of the Minister of Justice (D.M. 8 aprile 2004). The tariffs are not binding but can be a useful reference; they vary depending on the value of the litigation and on the activity to be done. According to article 26 CAP, the judge must condemn the party who lost the judgment to pay all costs, so that the winning party can recover them. But the normal practice up to now was that the administrative judge did not do so, deciding for 'compensation' of expenses, or in some cases condemned the losing party to pay a limited sum (very rarely higher than 10.000 euros, more commonly around 3-5.000 euros).[13]

The following points of this paper will analyze the main issues tackled by Directive 2007/66/EC in order to verify how they are implemented in Italian law, whether the Directive have just been complied with or the enforcement system is more efficient than required by the European legislator.

12. Consiglio di Stato, Adunanza Plenaria, decision n. 1 of 15 april 2010.
13. See Consiglio di Stato, sez. V – sentenza 26 agosto 2010 n. 5961, stating the administrative judge has a vey high discretion in deciding the condemnation to the payment of legal expenses and taxes and is not bound by tariffs settled in D.M. 8 aprile 2004.

2 Stand-still provisions

A standstill provision was already included in article 11, cl. 10 of the p.p. code of 2006 and thus even before the enactment of Directive 2007/66/EC the contracting authority could not conclude a contract before thirty days from the communication to the other participants of the award of the contract. This rule was however not accurate some respects: (i) the 30 days deadline was not coordinated with the deadline for notifying the recourse, which was 60 days from the communication, so that if the recourse was notified after 30 days (and before 60 days) the contracting authority could sign the contract and thus nullify the effect of the standstill provision; (ii) the standstill provision was subject to a general exception 'per motivate ragioni di particolare urgenza' ('for justified reasons of particular urgency') and (iii) no consequences were provided in case of violation of the standstill provision.

D. Lgs. 53/10 has tried to solve these problems by modifying article 11 cl. 10 of the p.p. code in the sense that the deadline for the recourse is reduced to 30 days (from the previous 60) and the standstill provision is extended to 35 days (from the previous 30), so that when the recourse is lodged, the contract cannot already be concluded. According to the directive it was not an obligation to have a longer deadline for the standstill than for the recourse, but the Italian law provided for it, thus giving a more efficient protection to the petitioner. As for the derogations from the standstill period, the new article 11 cl. 10bis of the p.p. code does not say anything in relation to article 2.b of the directive (prior publication not required by directive), while it mentions the case of article 2.c of the directive (if the only tenderer concerned is the one who is awarded the contract and no candidates are concerned) and article 2.d (contract based on a framework agreement or on a dynamic purchasing agreement). As for sanctions in case of violation of the standstill period, article 123, cl. 3 CAP stipulates that the pecuniary sanction between 0,5% and 5% of the value of the contract can be applied to the contracting authority which violated the standstill provision.

The automatic suspension of the effectiveness of the contract for the notification of a complaint against the award of the contract provided by the directive (article 2.3 of the Directive) is introduced in article 10ter of the p.p. code. For this purpose the first day of the ten days period is the day when the recourse is notified to the contracting authority, that is when it receives the notification, and not when the petitioner delivers the recourse to the public officer for the notification, as it is as a general rule (see note 11) . Since the petitioner has 30 days for the notification and the standstill period is 35 days, the law presumes that the notification procedure does not last more than five days so that even if the petitioner delivers the recourse for notification on the 30th day, the contracting authority is not permitted to conclude the contract until the 35th day, and by then the notification should arrived and thus the new period of suspension starts. If it is not,[14] it can happen that the contracting authority concludes the contract in good faith even if a recourse has been notified but the notification is still pending on the 35th day; in this case the contracting authority cannot be fined with sanctions for violation of the standstill period. The last day of the ten days period chosen by Italian law is somewhere in the middle between the two possibilities provided by the directive: it is the day in which the interim measure is taken (more precisely, the day in which the interim decision is communicated to the parties), unless the Tribunal decided to follow the fast track procedure (described in article 60 CAP), issuing the final decision after the hearing for the interim measure, in which case it is the day of the final decision.

Italian law contains a specific provision[15] allowing the contracting authority, in cases of urgency, to begin the execution of the contract before the conclusion of the contract itself. This may be considered as an infringement of the directive rules because it consists in the anticipation of the effects of the contract notwithstanding the standstill provision.[16] On the other hand, this anticipated execution is only a *de facto* situation, with the consequence that, if the conclusion of the contract does not follow because, for example, the award is nullified by the administrative tribunal, the economic operator who has already executed part of the contract is not entitled to get a full payment

14. In Italy, the notification is considered to be completed when the petitioner delivers the recourse to the public officer in charge of the notification (Corte costituzionale, decision of 23 January 2004, n. 28) and not when the recourse is delivered by the public officer to the adressee. Then the public officer can bring it personally to the adressee, if it resides in the same town, or give it to the National postal service, if the addressee resides in another town. Thus the recourse can take more than five days to reach the adressee, due to the time necessary for the National postal service to deliver it, even if the notification is legally completed on the day when it was given to the public officer.
15. Articles 337 and 338 of Law n. 2248 of 1865, annex. F; article 129 of D.P.R. (Decree of the President of the Republic) n. 554 of 1999 and now article 11.9 of the p.p. code.
16. R. De Nictolis, Il recepimento della direttiva ricorsi, in www.giustizia-amministrativa.it, point 5.4.f. However, one could argue that the standstill provision (art. 2.a.3 of the Directive) only prohibits the 'conclusion' of the contract and not the execution of the same. The point thus is if the contract can be executed without being previously concluded and the answer can be positive considering that public contracts must be concluded in writing (article 2.a Directive 2004/18) and therefore they cannot be concluded by the mere activity of the parties.

but can only ask for a restoration of his expenses, and only in proportion to the utility obtained by the contracting authority, (according to article 2041 Italian civil code: 'arricchimento senza causa').[17] For example, if he has already built one building, he will get back his expenses, but if he has only prepared the building site he will not recover his costs because this is useless for the contracting authority. This situation is similar to that where the judge declares the *retroactive* ineffectiveness of the contract (see point 5).

3 Interim measures

Article 61 CAP provides the possibility for the petitioner to ask for an interim measure, when there is such an urgency as to make it impossible the preparation and the notification of a recourse and with the obligation for the petitioner to notify the recourse in 5 days time after the decision on the interim measure. However, it seems that this measure is useless in case of public procurement, since the standstill provision forbids the conclusion of the contract for 35 days from the communication of the award to the interested participants to the procedure and thus the realization of such an urgency seems very difficult.

Given the automatic suspension of the effectiveness of the contract after the notification of a complaint against the award of the contract, it is crucial to speed up the procedure for the decision on the interim measure, since the contracting authority has a great interest in a quick decision on interim measures in order to know if it can conclude the contract. When a complaint against the award of a contract is notified, the President of the Tribunal must assign it to the first available hearing after five days from the notification, which means that the recourse can be discussed in the hearing also six or seven days after the notification, depending on the calendar of the hearings. There is, however, a mismatch with the deadline for the lodging of the recourse before the Tribunal, which is ten days: the law seemed to admit the (absurd) possibility that the hearing be assigned (five days from notification) before the recourse is lodged (ten days from notification). Of course it was impossible to do so and the problem is now solved by CAP (effective from 16 september 2010) according to which the decision on the interim measure is assigned by the President of the Tribunal to the first hearing after ten days

17. Cass. civ., sez. I, 27 marzo 2007, n. 7481

from the notification, that is to the first hearing after the expiration of the deadline for lodging the complaint.

In order to guarantee the highest speed possible to the interim measure process and to the administrative process in general, article 3 CAP says that judges and lawyers must draw up their writings in a clear and synthetic way. There is not a specific sanction for drawing up too long or unclear writings, but it seems that the judge can take into account this element when deciding about the recovery of expenses so that he can decide that a party whose writings were extremely and unnecessarily long have caused an unjust damage to the other party and must therefore be condemned to pay, at least partially, the other part legal expenses.

The administrative tribunal must grant the interim measure if the petitioner provides evidence of the presence of both the conditions of *fumus boni iuris* and *periculum in mora*. The first element means that the recourse has to seem formed, at least at a first exam: no interim measure can be given for a patently unfounded recourse. Of course, the judgment on the solidity of the recourse can be reversed in the final decision, after disclosure of evidence. The *periculum in mora* requires that the petitioner gives evidence of damage caused by the execution of the contract: damage must be relevant and irrecoverable, that is they cannot be restored with the payment of money (for example the demolition of a building, supposedly built without building permission, cannot be recovered merely by giving money to the owner because he could not get back the same building; or the case where health or environment are involved). In the case of public procurement, the *periculum in mora* can be difficult to prove because it is a question of contracts and payments and thus, in theory, the petitioner should prove that without that contract he is likely to go bankrupt, which is an irrecoverable situation. But case law of administrative tribunals is usually less strict in assessing the presence of an irrecoverable damage, saying that it is not only a question of economic damage, but also of 'danno curricolare' that is a damage to the curriculum of the petitioner who is deprived of the possibility to add the public procurement to his curriculum and thus increase the technical experience he can use as an advantage in future bids. In this case, of course, the main locus standi consists in the expectation to win the bid and the 'loss of curriculum' is only a criterion for the quantification of damages.

The interim measure of the temporary suspension of the award is not rare in Italian administrative tribunals and this is probably because, on the other hand, administrative judges are less likely to award damages.[18]

4 Establishment of a breach

The reasons why a breach can be established are not, of course, determined by the Directive. Italian case law and doctrine elaborated the three classical faults after French influence: violation of law, incompetence and 'eccesso di potere' (too difficult to be translated, but originally similar to the French '*détournement de pouvoir*')[19] and subsequently law n. 241 of 7 august 1990, as amended in 2005, codiefied the case law declaring in art. 21, § 8 that an administrative decision can be annulled for violation of law, 'eccesso di potere' or incompetence.

There are not official statistics about the main breaches in the field of public contracts. It is, however, not difficult to say that a great number of annulments are based on the direct awarding of public procurements contracts without any public procedure, often due to a misapplication of the doctrine of in house providing. Another frequent reason for annulment is due to procedural and formal mistakes made by the contracting authority during the procedure of award, which the administrative tribunals are happy to chase for.[20]

It is more difficult to assess the position of Italian case law when the recourse deals with discretionary choices of the contracting authority. As a general rule, the administrative tribunals (TAR and Consiglio di Stato) tend to exercise a kind of self restraint when such a question is involved, because they are not likely to substitute the contracting authority in its judgment. Thus, the judicial annulment of a discretionary decision of the contracting authority is admitted only when that decision is clearly and patently incoherent and unreasonable.[21] A wide discretion is recognized to the contracting author-

18. See R. Caranta, *Le contentieux des contrats publics en Italie*, cit.
19. See R. Caranta, *Le contentieux des contrats publics en Italie*, cit.
20. Consiglio di Stato, sez. V – sentenza 21 settembre 2005, n. 494 warns administrative judges not to follow the 'spirito della caccia all'errore' ('spirit of the hunt to mistakes'). The case was about a participant to a public procedure who was excluded because he had not closed the envelope containing the offer with sealing wax – as required by the bid – but only with a scotch tape. The TAR annulled the award, but the Consiglio di Stato upheld the TAR decision for excess of formalism.
21. Consiglio di Stato, Sez. V – decision n. 837 of 16 february 2009.

ity in deciding whether to go for a public procurement procedure or to provide the service within its own internal organization[22] as well as in determining the score to be awarded by the contract notice to the different elements to be taken into consideration,[23] while case law seems to be slightly stricter when it requires proportionality in the determination of admission criteria, which cannot be too strict in order to avoid illegal restrictions to the participating in the tending procedure.[24] A motivation is required to the contracting authority for the application of the score to the offers received in order to determine the more advantageous economic tender and thus award the contract (obviously it is not necessary when the criterion for awarding the contract is the lowest price only). But a purely numeric motivation is considered sufficient if the criteria set in the contract notice are precisely and accurately specified, while, if they are not, a motivation is required.[25]

5 Annulment/set aside

The annulment of the decision taken by the contracting authority to award the contract to an economic operator presupposes that the award is something different from the conclusion of the contract: the award is a decision of the contracting authority exercising its public power and its discretion, while the conclusion of the contract is the first act of a long series of 'private law' acts enacted by the contracting authority. But in Italian law this distinction was not so clear until the p.p. code was approved in 2006 stating, in article 11.7,

22. Consiglio di Stato, Sez. V, decision n. 5808 of 28 september 2009.
23. It is a well established case law; see recently Consiglio di Stato, Sez. V – decision n. 5952 of 26 august 2010.
24. For example, TAR Lombardia – Brescia Sez. II – decision n. 326 of 27 agosto 2010, annull a call for offer for a one-year meal providing service requiring a five years experience in the sector of kitchen cleaning.
25. Consiglio di Stato, Sez. V – decision n. 3481 of 11 luglio 2008. Obviously the problem is to know when the awarding criteria are sufficiently precise and accurate: the case law does not give a general rule, but it is possible to reconstruct for the cases decided that awarding criteria are considered precise and accurate when they give not more than 5-7 point for any single sub-criterion: see Consiglio di Stato, Sez. V – decision n. 2355 of 11 maggio 2007 and other decisions therein cited. In particular, Consiglio di Stato, Sez. V – decision n. 237 of 27 aprile 2006 which considers the case in which 50 points were given for the technical offer, divided in 7 criteria, each of which having thus in average a weight of about 7 points.

that the final award[26] is not equivalent to the approval of the offer and, in article 11.9, that the contracts has to be signed by the contracting authority and the contractor within 60 days after the award (and not before 30 – now 35 – days). Before the p.p. code there was some confusion about the distinction between the final award and the contract and in some cases, according to the law, the final award was considered replacing the contract. In other cases, the contract was considered to be only a formal confirmation of the decision taken with the final award, without autonomous legal effects.

Presently, given the sharp distinction between final award and contract, the annulment of the award has different effects depending on whether the contract is already concluded or not. In the first case, the annulment of the final award itself is substantially useless since the focus is on the contract, while in the latter case the annulment of the final award causes the impossibility for the contracting authority to conclude the contract.

With the final award annulled before the conclusion of the contract,[27] the contracting authority has often no other chance than to start a new procedure for the award of the contract, beginning from the point at which the administrative tribunal has annulled. If, for example, the award is annulled for procedural reasons, the procedure has to be repeated and thus the petitioner has only reached the goal to be readmitted to a new procedure, with a new chance to win it. In the meantime, usually in cases of public services (f. eg. transportation, natural gas distribution, cleaning in hospitals and schools etc.), the contracting authority awards a temporary contract without public procedure on an urgency basis for providing the services during the time necessary for the new public procedure to be completed.

It happens less frequently that the annulment of the award prior to the conclusion of the contract ranked to the immediate award of the contract to

26. The procedure of award sees first a provisional award, which is proclaimed by the technical commission immediately after the assessment of the technical and the economic offer. After the provisional award, the contracting authtority checks if the candidate fulfils the general and specific conditions he has declared to possess; after this control, the contracting authority proclaims the final, or definitive award.
27. A final decision of the Consiglio di Stato (and not only an interim measure) may take place before the contract is completely executed, if the execution time of the contract is two years or more. In fact, according to the Annual Report on the administrative justice written by the President of the Consiglio di Stato on february 2010, point 3, (P. Salvatore, *Relazione sull'attività della Giustizia amministrativa del presidente del Consiglio di Stato*, Roma, 11 febbraio 2010, in www.giustizia-amministrativa.it), the average length of the administrative process for public procurement cases does not exceed 18 month for both levels of judgment (TAR and Consiglio di Stato).

the petitioner: it is the case when, for example, the petitioner was leads at the second place and the administrative tribunal ruled that the economic operator ranked at the first place did not fulfil the necessary conditions and thus had to be excluded, or if the economic operator ranking first was excluded and the administrative tribunal annulled the exclusion.

6 Ineffectiveness

In Italy, the possibility for the administrative judge to declare the ineffectiveness of the contract and not only to annul the final award was the great innovation brought by the 2007/66 directive, and consequently by D. Lgs. 53/2010, even if anticipated by one month from the Corte di Cassazione after a long conflict between the Consiglio di Stato and the Corte di Cassazione (see point 1 of this paper). In reality, one can say that given the standstill provision and the automatic suspension of the conclusion of the contract in case of notification of a complaint, the necessity for the judge to declare the ineffectiveness of the contract concluded after an illegal award is now very limited, because the whole system is intended to eliminate the possibility that the contract be concluded before a first judgment, at least for an interim measure, on the legality of the award.

It is, however, still possible that the award be declared illegal and then nullified when the contract is already concluded: it is the case when exceptions to the standstill clause are admitted, or when the standstill clause is violated, or else when the interim measure is refused by the judge and thus the contract is concluded, but then, in the final judgment, it is decided that the award was in fact illegal and it is thus annulled. In addition, a more common case is when the contract is directly awarded without a prior publication of a contract notice without it being permissible under Directive 2004/18/EC.

In these cases if the award is annulled, the contract is automatically declared ineffective by the judge, even if the petitioner has not asked for it, but in certain cases the judge can decide to 'save' the contract after a careful assessment of the interplay between public and private interests. According to what is stated by the directive (article 2.d of directive; article 121 CAP), the contract must be declared ineffective in cases where the violation is particularly serious unless overriding reasons relating to a general interest (thus not only public interest of the contracting authority)[28] require that the effects of the contract should be maintained, applying alternative penalties. If ineffectiveness is declared, the judge will decide if it has retroactive effects or not and, in the latter case, he will apply alternative penalties.

If the award is annulled for violations which are not those listed in article 2.d of the directive the judge can decide whether to declare or not the ineffectiveness of the contract (article 122 CAP), taking into account: (i) the interests of parties (ii) the real chance of the petitioner to get the contract in relation to the established violations (iii) the technical possibility for the petitioner to continue the execution of the contract instead of the first contractor,[29] unless the violation leads to the necessity to reopen the public procedure and only if the petitioner has asked for continuing the execution. In this case the judge will not apply alternative penalties, but will award the petitioner with damages. It has to be noted that in case of public procurements for strategic infrastructures, if the violation is not listed in art. 2.d of the directive article 125 CAP imposes to the judge not to declare the ineffectiveness of the contract but only to award damages, and that can probably be considered not compliant with the directive.

Since the declaration of ineffectiveness of the contract follows the annulment of the award and since the award can be annulled only after a recourse notified not later than 30 days after the communication of the award itself, the deadline for the action aimed at the declaration of ineffectiveness of the contract is 30 days. It does not seem possible to act only for the declaration of ineffectiveness of the contract without asking the judge also to annul the award since the action for the ineffectiveness of the contract has to be considered as indissolubly bound to the action for the ineffectiveness of the contract.

If the judge declares the retroactive ineffectiveness of the contract, the part of the contract already executed from the first contractor who (illegally) got the award turns out to be executed sine titulo, because there is no more a contract that can justify the activity done by the contractor, nor the money paid

28. The difference between the 'simple' public interest and the 'wider' general interest is stressed by De Nictolis, cit., where it is explained that the public interest is proper to the contracting authority, while the general interest is wider and more qualified. In any case, the simple economic interest of the contracting authority can not be considered overriding and thus cannot justify the maintenance of the contract.

29. It can happen, for example, that the public work is already executed almost entirely, which means that it is not technically possible (or not convenient) for the petitioner to substitute the original contractor in performing the contract. Of course this is a judgment not about an absolute impossibility, but about a reasonable assessment of excessive costs in the change of the contractor.

by the contracting authority. In this situation the contracting authority could ask his money back from the first contractor, who can raise an exception of 'arricchimento senza causa', that is an action given by article 2042 of the Italian civil code by which the one who has received *sine titulo* an economic advantage from another person must pay a restoration of the expenses borne by the latter, but only in proportion to the benefit obtained. According to Italian case law the 'arricchimento senza causa' with a Public administration is different from that with regard to a private party, because with regard to a Public administration it is necessary that the public administration explicitly recognizes the utility of the advantage received, while with a private party the utility is presumed.[30] But in the case of the retroactive declaration of ineffectiveness of a contract, the utility of the contract itself for the contracting authority derives from the fact that the contracting authority issued a bid for purchasing the public procurement.[31]

7 Alternative penalties

Alternative penalties are provoded for in article 123 which follows the directive. The judge can sentence the contracting authority to an alternative penalty if (i) there is a serious violation and the judge decides to continue the contract for overriding reasons or (ii) there is a serious violation and the judge declares the contract ineffective only ex nunc or (iii) if there is a violation on the standstill provision and this has not caused a diminution of remedies for the petitioner.

Alternative penalties can be a pecuniary sanction, between 0,5% and 5% of the value of the contract, or the reduction of the length of the contract. The judge decides the amount of the sanction in order to guarantee its effectiveness, proportionality with the value of the contract and with the seriousness of

30. Cassazione civile, Sez. I, decision. n. 3322 of 12 february 2010.
31. See Corte di Cassazione, sezioni unite, decision n. 23385 of 11 september 2008. A public works contract, stipulated between the Municipality of Acireale and CRC company, was annulled by the Consiglio di Giustizia amministrativa per la Regione siciliana (acting as Supreme Administrative Court in the Sicily Region) when the works were almost completed. The CRC asked for the complete payment of the contract price, included the loss of profit, but the Corte di Cassazione decided that the loss of profit was not due. See also Corte dei Conti, sezione controllo di legittimità sugli atti del governo e delle Amministrazioni dello Stato, delibera n. 1/2007/P of 1 february 2007.

the violation and taking into account what the contracting authority has done in order to reduce the consequences of the violation.

8 Damages

Until 1999 the Italian case law did not recognize the possibility for the petitioner to get damages from the public administration in case of violation of an 'Interesse legittimo' since, according to the Italian civil code (art. 2043), only the holder of a full right is entitled to damages. The Corte di Cassazione changed its mind on July 1999 admitting damages for violation of an 'interesse legittimo'[32] and a year later Law n. 205 of 21 july 2000 consolidated this position.

A lot of problems have arisen since 2000 in relation to the application of the damages rule. First of all, the question if the previous annulment of the award was necessary for the condemnation to damages, or if the action for damages is an autonomous action, not bound to the action for annulment.[33] The question is now resolved by articles 7.4 and 30.1 of CAP which admit the action for damages independently from the action for annulment, even if introducing a time limitation for the action of damages of 120 days, while for the same action the civil code gives five years to the petitioner

Article 124 CAP introduces a rule by which damages are awarded only if the petitioner asks for continuing the contract and the judge, having annulled the award, decides not to declare the ineffectiveness of the contract. On the contrary, if the petitioner has not formally asked in his recourse to continue the execution of the contract or, if asked to do so, refuses, the judge will evaluate his behaviour in deciding about damages, which means that he will be not so likely to grant damages or at least he will reduce them. The rule is intended to limit the phenomenon of companies who file recourses against public procurement awards with the only scope of get damages but without the real intention to get the contract and execute it. On the other hand, the rule reduces even more the probability to get damages, which is already not so likely in Italian administrative courts.[34]

32. Corte di Cassazione, sezioni unite, decision n. 500 of 22 july 1999
33. For the first position, Consiglio di Stato, adunanza plenaria, decision n. 12 of 22 october 2007; for the latter, Corte di Cassazione, sezioni unite, decision n. 13659 of 13 june 2006 and n. 9040 of 8 april 2008. See R. Caranta, *Le contentieux des contrats publics en Italie*, cit.
34. See R. Caranta, *Le contentieux des contrats publics en Italie*, cit.

As a general rule of thumb, it can be said that, when compensation is awarded, the amount is given by the sum of (i) expenses paid by the petitioner and (ii) the loss of profit. For both elements the burden of proof falls on to the petitioner, but for the latter (loss of profit) there is a 'light' presumption of about 10% of the value of the contract, which means that the petitioner has to prove that he would have be in a position for winning the contract, had the contracting authority acted correctly. The compensation is then divided in relation to the chances the petitioner had to get the contract, which is generally proportional to the number of participants to the procedure. If, for example, the judge annuls the award because the winner didn't fulfil the necessary conditions, but the contract has already been fully executed and thus only damages are possible, if the petitioner was the only other participant in addition to the winner he will be awarded a full 10% of damages; if there was another participant, in addition to the petitioner and the winner, the petitioner will be awarded only a 5% damages because his chances to win the contract, had the winner been excluded in time, are shared by 50% with the other participant.[35]

It is not easy to say what will be the effect of the new CAP on the decisions of administrative judges in awarding compensatory damages. Notwithstanding some pessimistic positions,[36] it not unreasonable to say that perhaps the tendency to 'save' existing contracts could lead to an increase in damages, which are however the only admitted solution in cases of strategic infrasctructures, where if the violation is not particularly serious (according to the definition of the directive) article 125 CAP compels to the judge not to declare the ineffectiveness of the contract but only to award damages (see par. 6).

Italian case law required also the demonstration of culpability of the contracting authority as a condition for the condemnation to damages,[37] but it

35. For a recent and accurate synthesis of the criteria used by Italian case law for the assessment of damages, see TAR Piemonte, sez. II, decision n. 3939 of 29 october 2010
36. R. Caranta, *Le contentieux des contrats publics en Italie*, cit.
37. This was a well established case law, from the first decision admitting the possibility to condemn the Public administration for damages (Corte di Cassazione, Sezioni unite, decision n. 500 of 22 july 1999, till very recent decisions like Corte di Cassazione, sez. III, decision n. 22021 of 28 october 2010 (but discussed on 10 june 2010 and thus before the publication of the *Strabag* decision of the ECJ). It is however to be noted that a presumption of culpability was recognized by the case law against the contracting authority.

seems that now it is likely to go along with the decision of the ECJ on the *Strabag* case,[38] not requiring any more the establisment of culpability.[39]

Bibliography

For a general description of the Italian system of administrative litigation in English, see:

F. G. Scoca, *Administrative Justice in Italy: Origins and Evolution,* in *Italian Journal of Public law*, n. 2/2009, p. 118-161 (www.ijpl.eu).

The new Italian system of administrative litigation introduced by the new Code of Administrative Process (D. Lgs. n. 104 of 2000) is described mainly in Italian:

R. Caranta (ed.), *Il Nuovo processo amministrativo*, Zanichelli, Bologna, 2010

R. Garofoli – G. Ferrari (eds), *Codice del processo amministrativo*, ed. Neldiritto, 3 voll., 2010;

F. Caringella – M. Protto (eds) *Codice del nuovo processo amministrativo*, Dike Giuridica Editrice, 2010;

R. Chieppa (ed.), *Il codice del processo amministrativo*, Giuffré, 2010;

Specifically about litigation in the public procurement field, with reference to the new Code of Administrative Process:

R. Caranta, *Le contentieux des contrats publics en Italie*, in *Revue française de droit administratif*, 2010 (forthcoming);

R. De Nictolis, *Il recepimento della direttiva ricorsi*, in www.giustizia-amministrativa.it, 2010;

G. Ferrari, *Il contenzioso degli appalti nel nuovo codice del processo amministrativo*, Neldiritto, 2010.

The law journal *Rivista di diritto processuale amministrativo*, published by Giuffré, is specialized in administrative litigation.

All decisions of TAR (regional administrative tribunals) and Consiglio di Stato since the year 2000 can be found on the website www.giustizia-amministrativa.it.

38. Judgment of 30 September 2010, *Strabag* and others (C-314/09). With the Judgment of) December 2010, Spijker (C-568/08) the Court of Justice seems to have partially reversed the Strabag decision, stating that it is up to national Courts to state the conditions for the application of damages (point 84-92). I am not aware of any decision by Italian Administrative Courts citing the Spijker decision.
39. See TAR Lombardia – Brescia Sez. II – decision n. 4552 of 4 November 2010.

8 Enforcement of The EU Public Procurement Rules: Danish Regulation and Practise

By Steen Treumer

1 Introduction to the Danish enforcement system

Denmark has prioritized the regulation of and compliance with the EU public procurement rules for about two decades. This approach appears at least initially to be a follow-up on the ruling from 1993 of the Court of Justice in the case C-243/89, *Commission v Denmark*. In this judgment the principle of equal treatment of tenderers was established together with various fundamental breaches of the rules. The Danish interpretation of substantial public procurement rules in the Public Procurement Directives is relatively restrictive[1] and the enforcement system appears to be one of the most efficient in the EU.

It is actually so efficient that by many practitioners and politicians it is considered to be *too efficient* which allegedly makes many contracting entities hesitate to tender out. It is expected that the Danish enforcement system will be changed fundamentally in order to secure that the Complaints Board for Public Procurement (herafter the Complaints Board) focuses on the most fundamental breaches and that the number of cases is reduced. Whether the analysis behind these anticipated changes is correct and whether this is the best way to address such a problem is questionable. However, this issue shall not be considered in further detail here as the primary aim is to present the

1. The approach to the EU public procurement rules differs from Member State to Member State, not only due to variations caused by the implementation of the Public Procurement Directives, but also due to a difference in the balancing of the relevant interests of the parties involved in public procurement. It appears that the approach in the United Kingdom for example is clearly more flexible than in Denmark as there is more emphasis in the United Kingdom on a pragmatic approach and value for money. There appears to be more emphasis on the principles of equal treatment and transparency in the Nordic countries.

state of the law and not to engage in a very complex and time-consuming policy discussion.

Nevertheless, the Danish system is clearly more efficient than required by the EU on a number of important points. As will be further elaborated below the range of potential complainants has been widened, the economic risk of submitting a complaint has been substantially reduced, a fast working Complaints Board with extensive competences has been established and numerous complainants have been successful.

Denmark has established a tradition for speedy implementation or at least implementation on time of the Public Procurement Directives and as some will know Denmark was the first Member State to implement the Public Sector Directive on January 1, 2005. This tradition was not followed with regard to the implementation of Remedies Directive 2007/66. The relevant legislation was delayed and entered into force on July 1, 2010.[2] The new legislation is based on a second draft version with elaborate preparatory works to the draft.[3] The reader with a common law background must be aware that the preparatory works according to Danish legal tradition are of utmost importance and often decisive for a given interpretation.

The new Act on Enforcement of the Public Procurement Rules from 2010 fundamentally changed the division of work between the bodies involved in enforcement of the public procurement rules. Until the above-mentioned Act entered into force aggrieved tenderers and a number of other entities had a free choice between the Complaints Board for Public Procurement and the ordinary courts when they wanted a formal dispute settlement. Ever since the establishment of the Complaints Board in the early 1990s it has been a pure exception that a case has been brought before the ordinary courts instead of the Complaints Board. The consequence of this was that the ordinary courts in reality only received public procurement disputes on appeal from the Complaints Board. It now follows from §5 of the Act on the Enforcement of the Public Procurement Rules that complaints cannot be submitted to the ordinary courts during the standstill-period. The Complaints Board for Public

2. Act no. 492 of 12 May 2010 on the Enforcement of the Procurement Rules. The Act was subsequently amended by Act no. 1556 of 21 December 2010 §13 which adjusted §7 and the start of the preclusive time-limits.
3. Proposal for an Act on Enforcement of the Procurement Rules of 27 January 2010 (Forslag til lov om håndhævelse af udbudsreglerne m.v.). This is an adjusted version of the original proposal of 10 November 2009 with the same title. Unless something else is indicated the reference to the preparatory works to the Act in this chapter refers to the latest proposal and the accompanying remarks.

Procurement has become the obligatory first instance in procurement disputes in most cases.[4] However, the ordinary courts still remain competent in the first instance if the complaint is submitted after the standstill period which presumably will be the case at least in some of the cases on ineffectiveness.

The Complaints Board has the power to grant interim measures, the power to establish that the rules have been violated and the power to issue set aside orders to contracting authorities. It can also declare a contract ineffective and award damages. The latter competence is remarkable and atypical both in a Danish and European context. The award of damages is normally exclusively a matter for the ordinary courts and the Complaints Board is an administrative body. The Complaints Board did not have the competence to award damages when it was established in the early 1990s but the legislation was changed in 2000 so the Board was also vested with the power to award damages for infringements of the EU public procurement rules.[5] Many of the parties that were consulted during the legislative process opposed the suggestion that the Complaints Board should be competent to award damages. The Association of Judges was against the change because it strengthened the judicial characteristics of the Complaints Board. Other organisations argued that an administrative body such as the Board should not be competent to award damages. This point of view is firmly rooted in Danish legal tradition whereby the award of damages in all fields of law has been considered a task for the ordinary courts.

The background for the extension of the competences of Complaints Board back in 2000 was that the Danish system had been criticised in public debate for lack of efficiency on the basis of a number of concrete cases brought before the Complaints Board, even though the legal literature in general had refrained from criticism. The preparatory works to the law from 2000 referred to the public debate and underlined various weaknesses in the system at that time.[6] The importance of easy and effective enforcement of the

4. With the exceptions mentioned in §5(2) and §5(3) of Act.
5. See the article of S. Treumer, 'Increased Effectiveness of Public Procurement Remedies in Denmark', Public Procurement Law Review 2000, NA 120 for an analysis of the change of the legislation and its background.
6. One the most important being that the Complaints Board's main function, in practice, was to rule on the legality of completed tender procedures. Another weakness was the lack of consequences when the Board had established that the public procurement rules had been infringed, which happened in about two out of three of the cases brought before the Board. At that time there did not seem to be a single case where the contracting authority had cancelled the contract after the Board had ruled that the

procurement regime was also stressed in the preparatory works to the new Act on the Enforcement of the Public Procurement Rules from 2010. The above-mentioned anticipated change in the approach based on an assessment of the enforcement system is therefore the first of its type. All prior changes of the enforcement system have aimed at making the system more effective in order to remedy apparent weaknesses in the enforcement regime. There has been a clear increase in the claim for damages in the field of public procurement after the Complaints Board was vested with the power to grant damages. The Board has awarded damages for violation of the public procurement rules on many occasions including compensation for the loss of profit.

The Complaints Board for Public Procurement is an administrative body and not a part of the judiciary. However, the Complaints Board is chaired by judges and it can make references for preliminary rulings to the Court of Justice. The other members of the Board are experts in fields of relevance to functioning of the Board i.e. public procurement, law and utilities, cf. §9 of the Act. A complaint can be filed by anybody with an individual interest in the tender procedures.[7] In addition, the Competition and Consumer Authority and a broad range of organizations and authorities have been granted locus standi by a Decree.[8] This remarkable widening of the access to file a complaint was created in order to remedy the fear of blacklisting. The admissibility of complaints from many of the professional organisations have been important as there have been several cases in Denmark where a professional organization has complained on behalf of anonymous firms engaged in the tender procedures.

The legislation of several Member States of the European Union has for many years set relatively short time-limits for applications relevant to review in the field of public procurement, with the consequence that an application for review that does not comply with the relevant time-limit is refused. These preclusive time-limits have been a very important feature of their enforcement systems and obviously limit the number of disputes considerably. The state of law in Denmark has been fundamentally different in this respect as

public procurement rules had been violated, cf. also the preparatory works to the Act on the Complaints Board.

7. In Danish 'retlig interesse' which essentially covers the circumstances described in Art.1(3) of the Remedies Directives and at least covers any person having or having had an interest in obtaining a particular contract and who has been or risks being harmed by an infringement. However, the concept has a broader coverage.
8. Decree no. 602 of 26 June 2000. About 40 professional organizations and authorities have been granted locus standi by the Decree.

preclusive time-limits have not been a part of the Danish enforcement system in the area of public procurement. However, various preclusive time-limits were introduced in the new Act on the Enforcement of the Public Procurement Rules which implemented Remedies Directive 2007/66. The latter does not require that preclusive time-limits are established but allow them and establishes that the complainants at least should have various minimum periods of time to react. The Danish legislator has established some of the preclusive time-limits considered in the Remedies Directive but not all. The periods for bringing complaints are also very favourable to the complainants in the sense that the time-limits exceed the minimum periods established by the Remedies Directives. As an example the Remedies Directives generally allow preclusive time-limits of 10-15 days[9] whereas the Act on the Enforcement establish 1) a time-limit of 30 days for challenge of a rejection for selection (prequalification) and 2) a main rule according to which the complainant has to initiate the case before 6 months from the notice in the Official Journal on the conclusion of the contract. However, as specified in the preparatory works this preclusive time limit does *not* apply to cases where the contract illegally has been concluded without a tender notice in the Official Journal. The new rules on preclusive time-limits are therefore presumably clearly more favourable to the complainants than in the majority of Member States.

The rules on costs are also atypical in a European context both in a public procurement context and in other fields of law as well. The present legislation favours the complainants to an unusual degree in relation to the costs. If the complainant wins the case, the Board can order the contracting authority to cover the costs of the complainant in whole or in part. The Board will settle the costs according to its discretion but in practice the complainant typically does not receive an amount that fully covers the costs to the law firm representing it. However, the contracting entities do not enjoy the same rights, as the Complaints Board cannot grant costs to a contracting entity. The implies that a complainant risks only covering his own legal costs and losing the symbolic fee paid in connection with the initiation of the complaints procedures. The complaints fee is as modest as about 500 € (4000 DKK).

Many contracting authorities have understandably been very dissatisfied with this state of law and various parties have suggested changing the provisions on costs in order to allow the Board to grant costs to the contracting entities. The rules on costs were adopted in 1995 and it was stressed in the pre-

9. Depending on the means of communication (by ordinary mail or electronic communication).

paratory works to the legislation that the purpose of the provisions on costs is to avoid the situation where costs alone make a small business refrain from complaining. However, the current government wishes to change the rules on costs so that also complainants can be ordered to cover the costs.[10] It can be added that the allocation of costs in public procurement cases before the ordinary courts follow the traditional approach in court procedures so that they are divided on the basis of the outcome of the case. In extreme situations this can make a complainant that actually won a complaints case before the Complaints Board accept to settle the case in order to avoid the risk of loosing the case with the consequence that the costs of the contracting authority and its own costs should be covered.[11]

It is an exception that the rulings of the Complaints Board are appealed before the ordinary courts which happens in about 10 % of the cases. The number of complaints has increased during the years and considerably in most recent years. The Complaints Board received only about 15 complaints around 2000 but 84 complaints in 2008,[12] 115 in 2009 and 182 in 2010. The background for the increase in the number of disputes is uncertain. However, it is likely that it is partly caused by the financial crisis making the outcome of at least some of the public procurement procedures of utmost importance for the tenderers in question. Another feature could be the increased willingness to complain and dispute decisions that can be detected in many areas of law spurred by the Complaints Boards competence to award damages for infringements of public procurement disputes.

2 Interim measures and automatic suspensive effect of complaints

Access to interim measures is crucial in order to ensure efficient enforcement of the public procurement rules especially since it is difficult successfully to challenge a concluded public contract. Remedies Directive 2007/66 introduced new rules on automatic suspension for review in the standstill period. These rules supplement the original regulation of interim measures in Art.2(1)(a) of the Remedies Directives according to which the Member States

10. See 'Vækst og fornyelse gennem øget konkurrence', p. 18 on envisaged changes of the public procurement regime, report on a meeting in Vækstforum, 25 and 26 November 2010.
11. The author is familiar with a concrete example of the latter.
12. Cf. the preparatory works to the Act on the Enforcement of the Public Procurement Rules.

shall ensure that interim measures can be granted in the review procedures. The new rules on automatic suspension will be addressed first as they are a novelty and of utmost importance in practice.

2.1 Automatic suspensive effect

The background for the introduction of these new rules is spelled out in recital 12 to Remedies Directive 2007/66: 'Seeking review shortly before the end of the minimum standstill period should not have the effect of depriving the body responsible for review procedures of the minimum time needed to act, in particular to extend the standstill period for the conclusion of the contract. It is thus necessary to provide for an independent minimum standstill period that should not end before the review body has taken a decision on the application ...'. It follows from §3(1) of the Act on the Enforcement of the Public Procurement Rules that a contracting authority must observe a standstill period of 10 or 15 calendar days when it awards the contract. The period is 10 days if the notification of the reasons behind the decision has been forwarded by electronic means of communication and 15 calendar days from the dispatch by mail. The former Danish rules on standstill only applied to contracts covered by the Public Sector Directive whereas the new rules also apply to contracts covered by the Utilities Directive. It is explicitly stated in the preparatory works to the Act on the Enforcement of the Public Procurement Rules that it is not obligatory to observe the above-mentioned rules on standstill if the contract in question is excluded from the Public Sector Directive or the Utilities Directive. It is questionable whether this is in accordance with EU public procurement law as it can be argued that a standstill period also is mandatory outside of the scope of the Public Procurement Directives.[13]

A complaint to the Complaints Board for Public Procurement[14] has automatic suspensive effect if it is filed during the standstill period, cf. §12(1) of the Act on Enforcement of the Procurement Rules. The suspensive effect ends when the Complaints Board has decided whether interim measures

13. See Carina Risvig Hansen, 'Pligt til annoncering af offentlige kontrakter – uden effektiv håndhævelse af reglerne?', Ugeskrift for Retsvæsen, 2011 B101. French lower courts have also ruled that a standstill period must be observed for contracts outside the scope of the Public Procurement Directives, cf. the chapter of F. Lichère and Nicholas Gabayet on France in the present publication. The case law from the lower French courts has recently been overruled by the French Supreme Court.
14. The Complaints Board has exclusive competence during the standstill period, cf. §5(1) of the Act on Enforcement of the Procurement Rules. It is therefore in principle only after the expiry of this period that the ordinary courts can consider complaints in the field of public procurement.

should be granted until the final decision in the case is rendered. When the complaint is filed during the standstill-period the Complaints Board[15] shall decide on interim measures within 30 calendar days from the receipt of the complaint,[16] cf. §12(3) of the Act on Enforcement of the Procurement Rules. It is noteworthy that the Danish implementation on this point goes further than required by the new rules which is explicitly pointed out in the preparatory works to §12 of the Act on Enforcement of the Public Procurement Rules. The Remedies Directives only require that complaints on contract award decisions[17] imply automatic suspensive effect whereas a complaint as such entails automatic suspensive effect in the Danish system.

It follows from the preparatory works to the Act on Enforcement of the Procurement Rules that the contracting entity is not allowed to sign the contract before the expiry of the standstill period even if the Complaints Board has decided not to grant interim measures to a complainant. The background for this is that others could complain and ask for interim measures in the same case.

2.2 Interim measures

It has been and still is very common to apply for interim measures in cases before the Complaints Board for Public Procurement. About 2/3 of the complainants applied for interim measures when the new Act on the Enforcement of the Public Procurement Rules was drafted.[18] However, it has been a clear exception that the complainants have been granted interim measures as will be further commented upon below.

The Complaints Board for Public Procurement and the ordinary courts have the competence to grant interim measures in the field of public procurement.[19] Member States may provide that the body responsible for review procedures may take into account the probable consequences of interim

15. The ordinary courts are not competent when the complaint is filed during the standstill period. There is not specified a time limit for the decision of the Complaints Board or the ordinary courts on interim measures in cases where the complaint is submitted after the expiry of the standstill period.
16. The time limit was extended from 10 to 30 days with the new provision in §12 and the former time limit started when the Complaints Board had sent a notification to the contracting entity on the complaint.
17. Cf. Art.2(3) of Remedies Directive 2007/66.
18. See the point 3 of the ordinary remarks to the Act on the Enforcement of the Public Procurement Rules.
19. However, it is an absolute exception that public procurement cases in Denmark are brought before the ordinary courts as first instance.

measures for all interests to be harmed, as well as the public interest, and may decide not to grant such measures when their negative consequences could exceed their benefits, cf. Art.2(5) of the Remedies Directives. Art.2(5) does not establish the criteria for the assessment of whether interim measures should be granted or not. As a consequence the national legislator has a wide frame to regulate within and the criteria and procedures established in national legislation on interim measures vary to a considerable degree.

It follows from §12(1) of the Act on Enforcement of the Procurement Rules that the Complaints Board or one or several of its members presiding in the concrete case can grant interim measures when 'special reasons' speaks in favour of such a decision. This wording does not cast much light on the conditions for the grant of interim measures even though it clearly follows from the rule that the grant of interim measures should be an exception. The publicized rulings of the Complaints Board do also normally not cast light on the applied criteria. The Board typically just specifies that the complainant has asked for interim measures and that the application was rejected.

However, the Board has to a considerable extent remedied the abovementioned lack of transparency as regards the conditions for the grant of interim measures. The Complaints Board made an exception in the ruling of 16 October 2007, *Kuwait Petrolium A/S v Sønderborg Kommune*, as it made an elaborate reasoning for the grant of interim measures part of the published ruling. It is submitted that the purpose of this publication was to clarify the conditions for the grant of interim measures to those working in the field of public procurement. The Complaints Board outlined three cumulative conditions 1) the complainant must establish that it has a prima facie case (fumus boni juris)[20] 2) there must be urgency in the sense that the complainant has to show that it will suffer serious and irreparable harm if interim measures are not granted 3) the complainant must pass a balance of interest test considering the interest of the complainant/the tenderers and the public interest in completion of the tender procedure. It can be added that the reasoning in the rulings on interim measures has been made much more detailed from 2006 onwards[21] and that the President of the Complaints Board recently co-

20. Not all breaches of the public procurement rules will be considered to fulfil this condition. The Complaints Board will consider whether the breach is so qualified that the decision for rejection of a tenderer in the qualification phase or the award decision is likely to become annulled, cf. M.F. Hansen and K. Thorup, Standstill og opsættende virkning i udbudsretten, Ugeskrift for Retsvæsen 2010 B 303.
21. Prior to this the Complaints Board instead typically limited itself to stating that the special reasons could not justify the grant of interim measures.

authored an article on standstill and interim measures in the leading Danish law journal.[22] The three conditions are cumulative which implies that the Complaints Board will not necessarily consider all of the conditions. If it obvious that one of the conditions is not fulfilled it is customary only to refer to this fact in the reasoning for the rejection.[23]

Many will be familiar with the above-mentioned conditions as they correspond to the conditions applied by the Court of Justice in cases concerning the grant of interim measures, cf. Art.279 of TFEU (formerly Art.243 of the EC Treaty). The Rules of Procedure of the Court of Justice spell out the conditions for the grant of interim relief and that the application for interim measures must be made by a party to the case before the Court. It is noteworthy that a national review body has adopted exactly the same conditions as the Court of Justice in a situation where the national legislation gave this body discretion to adopt its own approach to interim measures, cf. the words 'special reasons' in §12 of the Act on Enforcement of the Procurement Rules.

It is presumably the second condition 'urgency' that rules out the grant of interim measures in most cases. If this condition is interpreted strictly it will be extremely difficult to obtain interim measures. In the case law of the Court of Justice this condition usually[24] implies that the applicant has to show that it will suffer serious and irreparable harm if interim measures are not granted. It appears that the condition of urgency is satisfied whenever there is a threat of a breach of EU law and this constitutes a serious breach. The breach must also be 'irreparable' which in the procurement case law appears to have been applied in the sense of 'irreversible'.[25] The Court of Justice has in the few procurement cases on interim measures emphasized the need to prevent a breach and to avoid presenting the Court with a fait accompli and has even granted interim measures where a contract has been concluded.[26] The outcome of the many Danish applications for interim measures and the very limited number of grants of interim measures point towards a very strict ap-

22. See M.F. Hansen and K. Thorup, 'Standstill og opsættende virkning i udbudsretten', Ugeskrift for Retsvæsen 2010 B 303.
23. See M.F. Hansen and K. Thorup, fn.22 above.
24. This is the usual approach even though the Court of Justice does not always explicitly or consistently assess the condition this way, cf. P. Trepte, *Public Procurement in the EU (A Practitioner's Guide),* chapter 9, 2nd ed., 2007, p. 586.
25. Cf. P. Trepte, fn. 21 above, p. 587.
26. Cf. C-194/88 R, *Commission v Italy (Lottomatica).*

proach even though this appears not to be the declared intention of the legislator.[27]

It is typically difficult to obtain interim relief at national level[28] and Denmark is clearly no exception in this respect. It has been and still is so difficult to obtain interim measures in Danish practice that it is questioned whether the requirements following from the principle of effectiveness has been met with regard to interim measures.[29] It was recently pointed out in an article co-authored by the President of the Complaints Board that it is to be presumed that the grant of interim measures also in the future will be an exception.[30]

The Complaints Board has received numerous applications for grant of interim measures but it is an exception that they are granted and for several years the Complaints Board abstained from granting interim measures.[31] The Board did not grant interim measures from late 2000 until the very start of 2007. In some of the cases from 2000 until 2007 where applications for interim measures where rejected the Complaints Board subsequently established several breaches of the public procurement rules and even annulled the decisions to award the contract.

There could be several explanations for the widespread rejection of applications for interim measures in the Danish case law. An obvious explanation

27. It follows from the preparatory works to the former Act on the Complaints Board from 2000 that instead of granting damages the possibilities of correcting breaches by temporary suspension of the tender procedures must be used as far as possible having regard to the involved resources of the society.
28. A. Brown, 'Effectiveness of Remedies at National Level in the Field of Public Procurement', Public Procurement Law Review 1998 p. 89. See also section 3 in the article of S. Treumer, 'National håndhævelse af EU's udbudsregler – er håndhævelsessystemet effektivt på EU-udbudsområdet?', p. 99 in J. Fejø and S. Treumer (eds.), *EU's Udbudsregler – implementering og håndhævelse i Norden* (The EC Public Procurement Rules-Implementation and Enforcement in the Nordic Countries), 2006.
29. See S.T. Poulsen, P.S. Jakobsen and S.E. Kalsmose-Hjelmborg, *EU Udbudsretten*, 2nd ed. 2011, p. 543. See also the article of S. Treumer, 'National håndhævelse af EU's udbudsregler – er håndhævelsessystemet effektivt på EU-udbudsområdet?' p. 99 in J. Fejø and S. Treumer (eds.), *EU's Udbudsregler – implementering og håndhævelse i Norden* (The EC Public Procurement Rules-Implementation and Enforcement in the Nordic Countries), 2006 with references.
30. See M.F. Hansen and K. Thorup, 'Standstill og opsættende virkning i udbudsretten', Ugeskrift for Retsvæsen 2010 B 303.
31. A listing of the cases where the Complaints Board has granted interim measures can be found on p. 540 in S.T. Poulsen, P.S. Jakobsen and S.E. Kalsmose-Hjelmborg, S.T. Poulsen, op.cit in fn. 21.

could be that the conditions for the grant of interim measures were not met in the cases in question. However, it is likely that there are or have been other circumstances behind the remarkable trend in the case law. It is also possible that the phenomenon could be linked to the Court of Appeal's criticism of the grant of interim measures in a concrete case.[32] It also appears that the restrictive approach has been linked to the characteristics and functioning of the Complaints Board. As stressed by a now former member of the Presidency of the Complaints Board, H.P. Rosenmeier,[33] urgent cases are better dealt with by a review body whose members are permanent staff working on full time as this would entail that they could address the case with short notice. However, the Complaints Board is not composed of such staff. The requests for interim measures are normally dealt with by the Members of the Complaints Board that are judges in the ordinary courts whose primary responsibility lies elsewhere – in the ordinary courts. Rosenmeier submitted in November 2005[34] that the result was that it in practice was very difficult for the Board to address these cases on short notice and that this in reality led to the lack of grant of interim measures. However, this appears no longer to be the background for the limited grant of interim measures, cf. the now elaborate reasoning in the cases on interim measures and the clarification of the criteria for the grant of interim measures in the ruling of 16 October 2007, *Kuwait Petrolium A/S v Sønderborg Kommune* mentioned above.

The effect of a grant of interim measures is not spelled out in the Act on Enforcement of the Procurement Rules. Instead this has been addressed in the preparatory works to the Act according to which interim measures imply that the contracting entity cannot conclude the contract before the Complaints Board final decision in the case.[35] This is most likely too simplistic and interim measures presumably have additional consequences. It is to be presumed that the contracting entity normally must abstain from making other decisions relating to the tender procedure in question.[36] However, the Com-

32. The Court of Appeal (Østre Landsret) criticized the grant of interim measures in judgment of 16 August 2000 in case B-1654-97 and others, *Handelshøjskolen i København og Forskningsministeriet v Højgaard & Schultz A/S.*
33. See H.P. Rosenmeier, 'Det danske klagesystem', p. 135 in J. Fejø and S. Treumer (eds.), *EU's Udbudsregler – implementering og håndhævelse i Norden* (The EC Public Procurement Rules-Implementation and Enforcement in the Nordic Countries), 2006.
34. See H.P. Rosenmeier, fn. 29 above.
35. Cf. the remarks on §12 to the draft Act of 27 January 2010.
36. For the same point of view see S.T. Poulsen, P.S. Jakobsen and S.E. Kalsmose-Hjelmborg, *EU Udbudsretten*, 2nd ed. 2011, fn. 29 above on p. 544 and J. Fabricius,

plaints Board has at least in one case decided to grant interim measures with a more limited effect. The Board decided in the course of the procedure leading to the ruling of 9 March 1999, *Technicom A/S v DSB*, that the interim measures only implied that the contracting entity was excluded from concluding the contract but not from continuation of the tender procedure as such.

Another issue relates to the effect of interim measures once the contract has been concluded. The typical case where interim measures are granted relates to a situation where the contract has not yet been concluded. However, it is not excluded to grant interim measures after the conclusion of the contract in the Danish enforcement system[37] and the Complaints Board has done so as an exception *prior* to the Act on the Enforcement of the Public Procurement Rules.[38] The effect of interim measures in such a situation is debatable. It is submitted that the consequence is that the contracting entity should stop the execution of the contract in cases where the ineffectiveness of the contract is an issue.[39] If the contracting authority in such a situation just continues to execute the contract it decreases the impact of a possible application of the remedy ineffectiveness. Granting interim measures after the conclusion of the contract is atypical and it would appear relevant that the Complaints Board in future case law of this type specifies its understanding of the implication of the interim measures in question just as it did in the ruling of 9 March 1999, *Technicom A/S v DSB.*

Offentlige indkøb i praksis, 2010 p. 536. However, the latter text relates to the Act on the Complaints Board from 2006 which has now been replaced by the Act on the Enforcement of the Public Procurement rules.

37. See also M.F. Hansen and K. Thorup, 'Standstill og opsættende virkning i udbudsretten', Ugeskrift for Retsvæsen 2010 B 303 according to which the Complaints Board can grant interim measures even though the contract has been concluded.
38. An example is the ruling of 27 June 2000, *Deponering af Problem-affald ApS v I/S Vestforbrænding.* However, this appears not to have been in accordance with the competence of the Complaints Board at the time, cf. See M.F. Hansen and K. Thorup, 'Standstill og opsættende virkning i udbudsretten', Ugeskrift for Retsvæsen 2010 B 303 in section 3. The authors refer also to the ruling of the Complaints Board of 16 June 2010, *KMD A/S v Middelfart Kommune.* The grant of interim measures was rejected in the latter ruling exactly because the contract was concluded. The ruling relates to the state of law prior to the entry into force of the Act on the Enforcement of the Public Procurement Rules.
39. Contrary to the point of view expressed by S.T. Poulsen, P.S. Jakobsen and S.E. Kalsmose-Hjelmborg, op.cit. in fn. 29 on p. 544. According to these authors a grant of interim measures lacks purpose when the contract is awarded as there is nothing to 'suspend'.

As mentioned in section 2.1 the Complaints Board shall decide on interim measures within 30 calendar days from the receipt of the complaint in cases where the complaint has been submitted during the standstill period, cf. §12(3) of the Act on the Enforcement of the Public Procurement rules. There is not specified a time limit for the decision on interim measures in cases where the complaint is submitted after the expiry of the standstill period. However, in such cases the Complaints Board must consider the application for interim measures as quickly as possible, cf. also the remarks in the preparatory works.[40]

3 Establishment of a breach

A ruling of illegality is the typical form of sanctioning applied by the Complaints Board for Public Procurement. In numerous cases brought before the Complaints Board the complainant has limited the case to a claim for a ruling on the illegality of the decisions of a contracting authority. In several of these cases the purpose of the complaint has been to get an overruling of a specific procedural approach applied by the contracting authority or occasionally to the get an overruling of common Danish procurement practice. The motivation for such a claim can also be that the complainant wishes to pave the way for a subsequent claim for damages or wishes to facilitate a settlement of the dispute outside of court.

A considerable number of cases before the Complaints Board have dealt with technical dialogue prior to submission of bids and the principle of equal treatment of tenderers, the ban on negotiation, the termination of tender procedures and the award criteria. In recent years there have also been several cases concerning the legality of the applied evaluation models.[41]

The Complaints Board has in numerous cases established that the ban on negotiations has been violated. It is frequently the acceptance of bids that deviate from the substantive tender conditions that has led to complaints. Non-compliance with formalities has also been considered in several cases. The competitors will in some cases become aware that the contracting authority has accepted a breach of the formal tender conditions but the Complaints Board has also addressed the issue ex officio several times.

40. Cf. the remarks on §12 of the draft Act of 27 January 2010.
41. For an earlier overview of the typical complaints case see S. Treumer, 'Enforcement of the EC Public Procurement Rules in Denmark', Public Procurement Law Review 2005, NA 186.

Illegal award criteria are frequently seen in Danish public procurement practice. Such a violation often has a major impact as the award criteria is decisive or at least ought to be decisive for the choice of contractor. Despite this the Complaints Board has typically refrained from annulment of illegal decisions of the contracting authorities with direct reference to the illegality of the award criteria. However, it surely has been a part of the assessments leading to annulment in several cases.

Termination of tender procedures occur rather frequently in Danish practice also after the opening of the bids. This phenomenon is rather striking as this increases the costs of the contracting authorities and inevitably delays the completion of the tender procedures, which clearly is contrary to the interest of the contracting authority in concluding the contract as quickly as possible. The termination of the tender procedures can be abused to discriminate the tenderers and has often been perceived as discrimination by tenderers in Denmark. The Complaints Board has held that the contracting authority had an objective reasoning for the termination of the tender procedures in the majority of the cases where the legality of the termination of the tender procedures has been challenged. However, the Board has occasionally stated that the contracting authority did not have an objective reason for the termination of the tender procedures but this has normally[42] not led to the annulment of the illegal termination decision in the concrete cases.

There have also been numerous cases where the complainant has argued that a participant should have been excluded as a consequence of technical dialogue prior to submission of tenders on the basis of the principle of equal treatment. This important consequence of the principle of equal treatment was not considered in the case law of the Court of Justice of the European Union until spring 2005 in the Fabricom-case. However, this theme has been considered in many Danish cases prior to this ruling and also in some cases after the judgment from the Court. A restrictive interpretation of the principle of equal treatment in this context would imply that the starting point normally would be exclusion of firms that have been involved in technical dialogue with the contracting authority concerning the contract in question. The Complaints Board did for many years not choose this approach and typically accepted the participation of the firms previously involved in technical dialogue in the subsequent tender procedures. The approach of the Complaints Board has been more restrictive in later years[43] even though the recent ruling of 31

42. An exception is the ruling of 12 August 2002, *Milana A/S v Vestsjællands Amt*.

43. The first ruling indicating a changed approach was the important ruling of 13 January 2004, *Pihl & Søn v Hadsund Kommune*, where the Board clearly took a more restric-

May 2010, *Danske Arkitektvirksomheder v Udenrigsministeriet* could be interpreted as allowing the contracting authorities a considerable discretion as to whether or not to exclude due to technical dialogue prior to submission of tenders.

The Board scrutinizes the decisions of the contracting authorities with intensity and has also frequently used it competence to consider issues of law ex officio which definitely has not been welcomed by all lawyers specialized in the field. Nevertheless, the Board would normally show considerable appreciation of the wide margin of discretion of the contracting entities in accordance with the legal tradition in the Danish ordinary courts.[44]

4 Annulment/set aside of award decisions

It follows from the Remedies Directives that Member States shall ensure that annulment of illegal decisions is a part of the available remedies at national level, cf. the Remedies Directives Art. 2(1)(b). It follows from §12 in the Act on the Enforcement of the Public Procurement Rules that the Complaints Board can annul the illegal decisions of a contracting authority or the tender procedure as such. There is no doubt that the ordinary courts in Denmark have the same competence even though this does not follow explicitly from the wording of the Act or the preparatory works. There are many examples of annulments of the decisions of contracting authorities in Danish practice whereas the annulment of the tender procedures has been an exception.[45]

Traditionally most Member States have limited the powers of their review bodies to the award of damages after the conclusion of the contract, cf. Art. 2(7) of the Remedies Directives (Art.2(6) in the original version of the Remedies Directives). The approach in Denmark deviates from this approach as it is possible to annul the decision *to conclude* the contract and has been so from the first implementation of the Remedies Directives. As follows from

tive approach and also for the first time stressed that the advantage in time following from the technical dialogue is an element to be considered in the assessment of whether the principle of equal treatment has been violated or not.

44. The same approach is well-known in other Member States and is also taken by the Court of Justice of the European Union. For an analysis of the latter see S. Treumer, 'The Discretionary Powers of Contracting Entities – Towards a Flexible Approach in the Recent Case Law of the Court of Justice?', Public Procurement Law Review 2006, p. 71.
45. An example of the latter is ruling of 10 July 2009, *NCC Construction Danmark A/S v Billund Kommune*.

below it is complex to establish the legal implications of this unusual approach to the remedy annulment.

Danish complainants have in numerous cases asked for annulment of the illegal decisions and in particular of the annulment of the award decision or the decision to conclude the contract. There have also been a number of cases where the complainants have asked for the annulment of a decision of termination of the tender procedures without an award. The interest has clearly been focused on annulment of award decisions or the decision to conclude the contract as the complainants primary motivation typically have been a reopening of the competition for the contract. However, this has normally not been the outcome of these cases for various reasons. Once the contracts were concluded they have remained effective also in Denmark regardless of the annulment of decisions to conclude the contracts.

The legal implications of an annulment of the award decision and/or the decision to conclude the contract has been debated in Denmark and still remains unclear. The annulment of an *award decision* could be expected to be rather obvious: the contracting authority cannot base its decisions on the annulled decision. This is obvious where the tender procedures are suspended until the annulment but must also apply where the tender procedures are not suspended.[46] The contracting authority would therefore presumably have to make a new award decision or recommence the tender procedures depending on the circumstances behind the annulment. In some situations the tender procedures are so flawed that the contracting authorities have to terminate the tender procedures and retender. This could for instance be the case in a situation where the award criteria are illegal.

The legal implications of an annulment of the decision *to conclude* the contract are much more complicated to determine. The understanding of the Danish legislator has been that the annulment only has an impact on the administrative decision and not on the contract as such.[47] In other words the validity of the concluded contract remained unaffected of the annulment of the decision to conclude the contract. However, this does not necessarily imply that the contracting authority in question is entitled to execute the contract as

46. The grant of interim measures has been a pure exception in Danish public procurement practice until recently. The new Act on the Enforcement of the Public Procurement Rules changes this fundamentally as it introduces automatic suspension, cf. section 2.1. of this chapter.
47. See the preparatory works to L243 of 26 May 2000 (Official Journal of the Danish Parliament 1999-2000, A 6861). See also the remarks in the preparatory works of 27 January 2010 to §13 in the Act on the Enforcement of the Public Procurement Rules.

if nothing had happened. It has been debated in Danish legal literature since the middle of the 1990s whether such an annulment had any legal consequences. One point of view has been that the contracting authority as a starting point has a duty to terminate the concluded contract when the decision to conclude the contract has been annulled.[48] Another has been that the contracting authority at least should consider whether it was relevant to terminate the contract taking into consideration the interest of the contracting party and the interest of the complainant in renewed competition for the contract.[49] Others would rely on the point of view expressed in the preparatory works by the legislator. It suffices to state that the majority of authors have argued in support of some sort of duty to act following from the annulment. However, this did *not* influence the behaviour of practitioners throughout the years. The contracting authorities have almost without exception executed the contracts according to their wording and have thereby refrained from terminating or shortening the contracts in question. This practice has implicitly been accepted by the bodies involved in the enforcement of the public procurement rules. The terminology 'annulment' appears misleading in light of the extremely limited consequences this remedy has had in Danish procurement practice. In reality the sanction annulment has just indicated that the Complaints Board considered the infringements to be serious with implications for the competition for the contract. The Complaints Board has usually only applied the sanction when the complainant has reacted very qiuckly after having become aware of the infringements in the case. As previously mentioned preclusive time-limits for review have only recently been introduced in the Danish remedies system with the implementation of Remedies Directive 2007/66.

The new remedy of ineffectiveness that is analysed in section 5 below is therefore very important as it ensures termination or shortening of the contract in cases which previously would only have been sanctioned with 'annulment' as outlined above. It is also worth to notice that the Court of Appeal in 2009 accepted that a tenderer can get a ruling from the court establishing whether a contracting authority has a duty to set aside the contract or not. This is a landmark ruling based on an interpretation of C-503/04, *Commission v Germany*.[50] The Court of Appeal also recently ruled[51] that such a duty

48. See S. Treumer, *Ligebehandlingsprincippet i EU's udbudsregler*, 2000 pp. 56-57 with references.
49. See J. Fabricius and R. Offersen, *EU's udbudsregler i praksis*, 1st. ed. 2002, p. 294.
50. See S. Treumer, 'Towards an Obligation to Terminate Contracts Concluded in Breach of the EC Public Procurement Rules: the End of the Status of Concluded Public Contracts as Sacred Cows', Public Procurement Law Review 2007 p. 371.

could come into existence with regard to very serious violations of the public procurement rules and thereby clarifying that the duty not only comes into existence with regard to direct illegal procurement.[52] This development in the case law will be further commented upon in the subsequent section on the closely related remedy 'ineffectiveness'.

5 Ineffectiveness of the contract

The following analysis will not focus strictly on the implementation of the new remedy 'ineffectiveness' in the latest version of the Remedies Directives as recent developments in the Danish case law is at least equally as interesting – be it from a European or a Danish perspective.

The Danish development in this area appears to deviate from the situation in the majority of the Member States as the Danish courts and Complaints Board for Public Procurement in recent years have considered several cases in which a plaintiff or complainant have argued that a contract concluded in breach of the EU public procurement rules should be terminated/declared ineffective *prior* to the implementation of the remedy 'ineffectiveness' of Remedies Directive 2007/66. A couple of concluded contracts have also been terminated with effect for the future and with some delay after the procurement disputes. In other words there has been a very insistent pressure in Danish case law for a development of a remedy of ineffectiveness independent of the implementation of Remedies Directive 2007/66. Some of these cases have even been initiated before the Court of Justice considered the issue in C-503/04, *Commission v Germany*,[53] and not surprisingly efforts were intensified after this landmark ruling from the Court of Justice. It should also be emphasized that the above-mentioned cases are not based on Remedies Directives 2007/66 but on other sources of law namely C-503/04, *Commission v Germany*, and apparently also on the EU law principles of loyalty and effectiveness.

51. Judgment of 30 March 2009 in the case *Region Syddanmark v Sectra A/S*, (No. B-2541-07 from Østre Landsret).
52. C-503/04, *Commission v Germany*, concerned direct illegal procurement which is considered as the most serious violation of the public procurement rules by the Court, cf. Case C-26/03, *Stadt Halle* at paragraph 37.
53. See S. Treumer, 'Towards an Obligation to Terminate Contracts Concluded in Breach of the EC Public Procurement Rules: the End of the Status of Concluded Public Contracts as Sacred Cows', Public Procurement Law Review 2007 pp. 371-386.

Section 5.1 concerns recent case law on ineffectiveness before the deadline for implementation of Remedies Directive 2007/66 and also a case on ineffectiveness after the deadline for implementation of this Directive. Section 5.2 provides an analysis of the implementation of the new remedy ineffectiveness in Denmark.

5.1 Recent Danish case law on effectiveness before the implementation of Remedies Directive 2007/66

The case law in this section concerns disputes in which it has been argued that a contract concluded in breach of the EU public procurement rules should be terminated/declared ineffective *prior* to the implementation of the remedy 'ineffectiveness'. The Complaints Board and the ordinary courts have not yet rendered decisions on ineffectiveness based on the Act on the Enforcement of the Public Procurement rules implementing Remedies Directive 2007/66.

One of the first cases that led to the partial termination of the contract was not a direct consequence of ruling to this effect from a court or a complaints board. Nevertheless, the case is illustrative of the uncertainty linked to termination/ineffectiveness of concluded public contracts in Denmark. Readers should be aware that the partial termination of the contract took place shortly after the presentation of the opinion of the Advocate General in C-503/04, *Commission v Germany*. The Complaints Board for Public Procurement established in ruling of 28 March 2007, *Fujitsu Siemens Computers A/S v Finansministeriet & Statens og Kommunernes Indkøbsservice A/S*, that a framework contract had been wrongfully concluded with one out of several firms as the bid from this firm did not comply with the tender conditions. The Board therefore annulled the decision to conclude the contract with this firm. The contracting authority, The Ministry of Finance, clearly expressed a lack of will to terminate the contract in whole or in part after the above-mentioned ruling from the Board. However, this approach was questioned by the media and the undersigned and shortly after gave rise to a critical question addressed to the Ministry of Finance in the Danish Parliament. The Ministry initially maintained its position and was supported by a memorandum on the issue from the Legal Adviser to the Danish Government[54] ('Kammeradvokaten'). According to the memorandum the Ministry of Finance could not terminate the concluded contract.[55] The Ministry then altered its position. It

54. The sole legal adviser of the Danish State.
55. Memorandum of 30 March 2007 on the ruling of 28 March 2007 from the Danish Complaints Board for Public Procurement.

upheld the contract for one year and terminated the subsequent options for a prolongation of the contract. It should be mentioned that the contract value was considerable and the hesitation of the Ministry understandable considering the unclear state of EU law and the values concerned.

Another case which is highly interesting concerned the possible duty to terminate a contract after a fundamental breach of the public procurement rules had been established by the Complaints Board for Public Procurement. This case is *Centralforeningen af Taxiforretninger i Danmark representing Taxi Stig/Stig Marcussen v Region Sjælland (formerly Vestsjællands Amt)*, that was brought before the Court of Appeal (Østre Landsret).[56]

This case is of particular interest for at least three reasons. Firstly, like C-503/04, *Commission v Germany*, the case concerned a contract where the contract had been illegally concluded without a tender and this had been established by the Danish Complaints Board for Public Procurement. In addition the Danish Competition and Consumer Authority urged the contracting authority to terminate the contract and to make a tender in order to take the necessary measures in order to comply with the ruling of the Complaints Board.[57] Secondly, the Danish Complaints Board subsequently ruled[58] that there was no obligation to terminate the contract in question according to the Remedies Directive and according to additional EU law.[59] This conclusion was questionable and even more so after the subsequent ruling from the Court of Justice in C-503/04, *Commission v Germany*. Thirdly, the case is of particular interest because the plaintiff requested the national court to make a reference for a preliminary ruling the Court of Justice. One of the two[60] preliminary questions suggested to the Court of Appeal addressed the question of whether there was an obligation to terminate the contract in a situation such as the concrete case. However, the Court of Appeal rejected the request

56. U.2009.1331Ø.
57. Letter of 22 December 2004 from the Danish Competition Authority to the contracting authority.
58. Ruling of 3 May 2005, *Taxi Stig and others v Vestsjælland Amt,* from the Danish Complaints Board.
59. Ruth Nielsen, 'Standstill og ugyldighed/uvirksomhed af offentlige kontrakter' (standstill and invalidity/ineffectiveness of public contracts), Ugeskrift for Retsvæsen 2007 B 120 remarks that it had been obvious to consider relevant case law from the Court of Justice which presumably did not support the point of view of the Complaints Board.
60. The other suggested question concerns the issue of damages for violation of the EU public procurement cases.

for the preliminary ruling.[61] The rejection was challenged but was curiously enough upheld after the ruling in C-503/04, *Commission v Germany*, even though this ruling made the state of law very unclear as regards enforcement of ineffectiveness at national level. It can be added that a German national court made a preliminary ruling regarding termination and ineffectiveness at national level shortly after.[62] The reasoning for the rejection of the Court of Appeal was clearly founded on the traditional and common perception that there is no duty to terminate a contract regardless of a fundamental breach of the rules.[63]

The Court of Appeal eventually ruled that there is not a general duty to terminate a contract concluded in breach of the EU public procurement rules and held with reference to various circumstances that a tender initiated in 2007 and 2008 was sufficient follow-up to the ruling from the Complaints Board in April 2003 which established the violation of the procurement rules. It can be added that the contract was concluded 20 December 2001 and that the dispute took so long that the contract expired before the ruling from the Court of Appeal.[64] It follows implicitly from the ruling of the Court of Appeal that it recognized that a national court could establish a duty to terminate a contract concluded in breach of the public procurement rules even though the defendant had argued that such a competence was limited to the Court of Justice.[65]

The case *Region Syddanmark v Sectra A/S,*[66] is a subsequent and very important judgment from the Court of Appeal (Østre Landsret) which followed shortly after the above-mentioned Taxi Stig case. The Sectra-case did not relate to direct illegal award but was a follow-up to a ruling[67] from the Complaints Board for Public Procurement in which the Board had ruled that the

61. Order of 30 May 2007 in case B-1989-05.
62. C-91/08, *Wall.*
63. The Court of Appeal quoted Art.2(1), (6) and (7) in Remedies Directives 89/665 and paragraphs 25 and 26 in C-126/03, *Commission v Germany*, corresponding to paragraphs 10 and 11 in C-414/03, *Commission v Germany*, and concluded on this basis that according to EU law there is not a general duty for a contracting authority to terminate a contract concluded in breach of the EU public procurement rules.
64. The contract expired 20 December 2007 and the Court ruled on 28 December 2008.
65. See section 5 'Is there a duty to terminate contracts following actions before national courts and review boards' in S. Treumer, fn. 48 above.
66. Judgment of 30 March 2009 from the Court of Appeal (Østre Landsret) in case B-2541-07.
67. Ruling of 29 August 2007, *Sectra A/S v Region Syddanmark*, from the Complaints Board for Public Procurement.

contracting authority had violated the public procurement rules in the evaluation of the bids. The contracting authority brought the ruling before the Court of Appeal and the tenderer asked the Court to rule that the contract should be terminated and claimed damages. The tenderer was awarded damages for the costs of preparing the bid but the Court did not rule that the contract should be terminated. The Court of Appeal again ruled that there is not a general duty to terminate a contract concluded in breach of the EU public procurement rules. However, the Court came with a very important addition. It added that such a duty follows from the case law of the European Court of Justice[68] in cases of very gross and serious violations of EU public procurement rules such as direct illegal procurement. Nevertheless, the Court of Appeal did not consider the mistakes in the concrete case to be sufficiently serious. According to the interpretation of the Court of Appeal the duty to terminate based on other legal sources than the Remedies Directives is not only limited to situations of direct illegal procurement, cf. also what has been submitted in the literature.[69]

The Court of Appeal also had to consider a fundamental question addressed in legal literature[70] which is whether the duty to terminate contracts was limited to a follow-up to rulings on a breach of the EU public procurement rules from the Court of Justice or whether it could also be a relevant consequence of rulings from national courts or review bodies on the basis of other legal sources than the Remedies Directives.[71] The contracting authority argued that the claim for the termination of the contract should be dismissed based on the underlying rationale that a national court did not have such a competence/such a claim was reserved for the European Commission in cases before the Court of Justice, cf. the former Art.228 of the EC Treaty (now Art. 260 of the TFEU). This argument was essentially supported by the former wording of Art.2(6) of the Remedies Directives that allowed Member States to provide in their legislation that, after the conclusion of the contract following the award of a public contract, the bringing of an action can give rise only to an award of damages.[72] The Court of Appeal explicitly overruled this ar-

68. Cf. C-503/04, *Commission v Germany*, invoked by the aggrieved tenderer Sectra A/S in the proceedings.
69. See the article mentioned in footnote 48.
70. See section 5 'Is there a duty to terminate contracts following actions before national courts and review boards?' in S. Treumer, fn. 48 above.
71. The other legal sources being C-503/04, *Commission v Germany*, and the principles of loyalty and effectiveness.
72. Compare now with Art.2(7) of the Remedies Directive.

gument and established that the tenderer had locus standi. This point of the ruling is noteworthy because the court established that it had the competence to terminate a public contract independently of the Remedies Directive and based this on an interpretation of other sources of EU-law. This approach could be an opening for a sharpening of the ineffectiveness remedy and for a widening of its scope compared to the remedy outlined and delimited by the Remedies Directive. Further comments on this aspect can be found in the very end of section 5.2.

A recent judgment from the Court in Herning in the case *Holstebro Kommune and others v AV Form A/S*,[73] ought also to be mentioned. The judgment was a follow-up to a ruling from the Complaints Board of 27 March 2008 between the parties. The Complaints Board had established that a number of municipalities had violated the public procurement rules and annulled a decision concerning a conclusion of the contract. It is undisputed in Danish legal practice that such an annulment does not automatically make the contract void. However, the complainant subsequently asked the court to establish that the contracting authority should recognise that the contract should be terminated. The Court ruled that the municipalities should recognize to be obliged to seek the contract with the third party terminated. The Court specified that the contract party of the contracting authority was not a party to the court case and that the judgment therefore was not binding for this party. The contract was subsequently terminated some months after the ruling.

Finally, it should be mentioned that the Complaints Board for Public Procurement recently had to address the issue of ineffectiveness in the ruling of 25 March 2010, *Visma Services Odense A/S v Hillerød Kommune*. This case also concerned a case of direct illegal procurement supplemented by dubious behaviour[74] by some key players involved in the process leading to the conclusion of the contract. However, the conclusion of the contract had taken place in 2009 before the deadline for implementation of the Remedies Directive 2007/66. This is worth to notice as this is likely to have 'saved' the Complaints Board from considering whether the remedy of ineffectiveness had direct effect as the Danish implementation was delayed. The Complaints

73. Judgment of 5 November 2009 in case BS 1-542/2008.

74. It appears that a manager in the municipality/the contracting authority in question had received tickets to a rock concert and had been invited to a gourmet dinner by the contractor shortly before the conclusion of the contract. The manager was later suspended. The contractor appears to have given golf travels, tickets for rock concerts and football matches etc. to a variety of civil servants in Danish municipalities involved in the conclusion of public IT contracts.

Board established that it did not have the competence to establish whether a contracting authority according to EU-law is obliged to terminate a concluded contract. The complainant had also asked the Board to order the complainant to terminate the contract but this claim was also dismissed.

5.2 The implementation of the new remedy ineffectiveness

As mentioned in the introduction the Danish implementation of Remedies Directive 2007/66 was delayed and it appears that disagreement as regards the new sanctions ineffectiveness and alternative penalties caused the delay.

It follows from Art.2(d)(2) of Remedies Directive 2007/66 that the consequences of a contract being considered ineffective shall be provided for by national law. The relevant provision in the Act on Enforcement of the Procurement Rules is §18 which establishes that the starting point is to limit the ineffectiveness to those obligations which still have to be performed (ex nunc). However, the remedy can have retroactive effect (ex tunc) when the circumstances are particular. It follows from the preparatory works to the Act that retroactive effect first and foremost is expected to be relevant when the contract relates to goods and not to services or public works. Alternative measures in the form of economic sanctions and fines are provided for in §§19 and 20. It is explicitly specified in the preparatory works on §18 that ineffectiveness does not exclude that the original contract party is awarded damages according to the common rules on damages in Danish law. Claims for damages when a contract becomes ineffective are considered in further detail in section 8.1.

It follows from Art.2(d)(1) of the Remedies Directives that the Member States shall ensure that a contract is considered ineffective by a review body independent of the contracting authority or that its ineffectiveness is the result of a decision of such a review body in circumstances outlined in that provision. It follows from §17(1)(1) of the Act on Enforcement of the Procurement Rules that the Complaints Board for Public Procurement or the ordinary courts shall declare a contract ineffective in the case of illegal direct award even though there are exceptions to this rule as will be outlined below.[75] The same principle is established in §17(1)(2) with regard to violation of the standstill provisions or the rules on interim measures provided that infringement has affected the chances of the tenderer applying for a review to obtain the contract.

75. There is an explicit reference to the exception in §4(2) in §17(1)(1).

The above-mentioned Art.2(d)(1) establishes in principle a duty to consider the contract ineffective. Art.2(e)(1) of the Remedies Directives requires less as it establishes that the review bodies should have competence to provide for ineffectiveness or to impose alternative sanctions in certain situations. §16 of Act on the Enforcement of the Procurement Rules implements Art.2(e)(1) where it is established that ineffectiveness is an option where the standstill-provisions or interim measures have been violated. The violation can relate only to the latter provisions and there is not a requirement for an additional violation of the public procurement regime.

The Remedies Directives stipulates in Art.2(d)(4) that Member States shall provide that ineffectiveness in the case of direct illegal award, cf. Art.2(d)(1) does not apply where the contracting authority considers that the award of the contract without prior notice in the Official Journal of the European Union is permissible and has published a notice as described in Art.3a of the Remedies Directives expressing its intention to conclude the contract. It is an additional condition that the contract has not been concluded before the expiry of at least 10 calendar days with effect from the day following the date of the publication of the notice for voluntary ex ante transparency. These provisions of the Remedies Directive are implemented by §4 of the Act on the Enforcement of the Procurement Rules. §4(2) of the Act specifies the requirements to the notice, cf. Art.3a of the Remedies Directives.[76]

However, the remarks in the preparatory works regarding §4 are very interesting as they create doubts as to the range of the protection against ineffectiveness for those that comply with the procedure outlined in §4. It is stipulated in the preparatory works that the Complaints Board for Public Procurement (and thereby surely also the ordinary courts) can declare the contract ineffective even though the conditions outlined in §4 of the Act corresponding to Art.2(d)(4) of the Remedies Directives are fulfilled. The remarks relate to the situation that the Complaints Board later rules that a contract could not legally be concluded without a notice in the Official Journal of the European Union and finds that the contracting authority has made an apparently incorrect assessment of whether a notice was needed or not. It is specified in the preparatory works that the assessment of the Complaints Board shall be based on an objective consideration of the character of the violation of the EU public procurement rules where the clarity of the rules should be taken into consideration. This limitation of the range of the exception in §4 of

76. However, the reference in Art 3(a)(e) regarding 'any other information deemed useful by the contracting authority' is 'implemented' with a remark in the preparatory works to §2(2).

the Act is remarkable as it does not seem to follow clearly from or to be supported by the wording of Art.2(d)(4) of the Remedies Directives.[77]

The Danish interpretation appears to be sound and appropriate even though the Danish legislator seems to adopt a stricter approach than required by the EU public procurement rules. This approach is not excluded as specified by consideration 20 of the Preamble to Remedies Directive 2007/66. It follows from this consideration that 'this Directive should not exclude the application of stricter sanctions in accordance with national law.' However, it cannot be excluded that a contracting authority would challenge the narrow interpretation suggested in the Danish preparatory works as it could be argued that this is a limitation of a right granted by the Remedies Directive to contracting authorities as such.

An approach similar to the Danish one was suggested by a law firm in connection with the Swedish implementation of Remedies Directive 2007/66. However, the Swedish legislator did not adjust the law on this point as it did not limit the scope of the immunity granted to those that follow the procedure of voluntary ex ante transparency.[78] The UK Government appears to share the idea that abuse of the procedure outlined in Art.3a of the Remedies Directives does not protect against ineffectiveness.[79] It is very important that contracting authorities are aware of this interpretation and of the risk that they are not granted immunity from ineffectiveness even though they formally complied with the procedure of voluntary ex ante transparency.

Art.2(d)(3) of the Remedies Directives allows for another important exception to ineffectiveness as a main rule in situations covered by Art.2(d)(1). It follows from this provision that Member States may allow review bodies not to consider a contract ineffective where overriding reasons relating to the general interest require that the effects of the contract should be maintained. The Danish legislator has used this option in §17(3) of the Act. It follows from Art.2(d)(3) that economic interests directly linked to the contract con-

77. The use of the word 'considers' in Art.2d(5) clearly gives the impression that the contracting authorities are allowed a wide discretion just like the use of the word in Art.29 on competitive dialogue. It is not the case with regard to competitive dialogue but presumably in the current context.
78. Prop. 2009/10:180, p. 142.
79. See Implementation of the Remedies Directive: OGC Guidance on the 2009 amending regulations (Part 3: The new remedies rules), p 36. It is stated that 'An overly brief or vague explanation may not therefore be sufficient, and failure to include the right information could have the same effect as having published no VEAT [Voluntary Ex-Ante Transparency Notice] notice if a court was to find that the information published was insufficient.

cerned shall not constitute overriding reasons relating to the general interest. It is problematic that this is not specified in the substantive provisions of the Act on the Enforcement of the Public Procurement Rules but only follows from the preparatory works. Danish judges would be inclined to consider exactly the economic interests when they would access whether to make a declaration of ineffectiveness or not. It is mentioned in the preparatory works that such overriding reasons in the general interest could be present when ineffectiveness makes it impossible for the contracting authority to comply with its duty to deliver services or goods to the citizens or endangers the life or health of human beings or animals.

Preclusive time limits can also be introduced by the Member States according to Remedies Directive 2007/66. The most interesting provision with regard to ineffectiveness is Art.2(f)(1)(a) that allows the stipulation of a time limit of 30 calendar days relating to review of ineffectiveness in accordance with Art.2(d)(1) either from the contract award notice or from the date on which the contracting authority informed the tenderers and candidates concerned of the conclusion of the contract. However, such a general preclusive time limit concerning ineffectiveness is *not* a part of the new enforcement regime in Denmark[80] which probably is a deviation from the common approach in the Member States. Nevertheless, it follows from §7 of the Act that a complaint[81] against a contracting authority which has followed the procedure outlined in §4 (notice according to Art.3a in the Remedies Directives) must be submitted within 30 calendar days from the day after the announcement of a notice on the conclusion of the contract.[82] Remedies Directive 2007/66 also ensures that the Member States can stipulate that a complaint concerning ineffectiveness based on Art.2(d)(1) in any case must be made before the expiry of a period of 6 months with effect from the day following the date of the conclusion of the contract. This opportunity has partially been used by the Danish legislator. It follows from §7(2)1) of the Act that a complaint – with some exceptions – must be submitted within 6 months after the award notice.

80. The Act on Enforcement introduced a new fundamental and general limitation on complaints concerning qualification as they must be submitted within 30 calendar days from the notice to the applicants on the outcome of the qualification process, cf. §7(1) of the Act on the Enforcement of the Procurement Rules.
81. Or a law suit before the ordinary courts, cf. §7(4) of the Act that clarifies that the provisions on preclusive time limits also apply to cases before the ordinary courts.
82. This presupposes that the notice contains the reasoning for the decision without prior publication of a tender in the Official Journal. The provision in §7 was amended on this point, cf. footnote 2.

However, as specified in the preparatory works this preclusive time limit does *not* apply to cases where the contract illegally has been concluded without a tender notice in the Official Journal. The Danish approach is also likely to deviate from the common pattern on this point as most Member States probably have ensured or will ensure that complaints or law suits are cut off after 6 months.

The Act on the Enforcement of the Procurement Rules fundamentally changed the division of competences in Danish enforcement regime as mentioned in section 1 of this chapter. Complaints cannot be submitted to the ordinary courts during the standstill-period and the Complaints Board will typically be an obligatory first instance in procurement disputes. Nevertheless, the ordinary courts can consider the case in the first instance if the complaint is submitted after the standstill-period which presumably will be the case at least in some of the cases on ineffectiveness.

It could be worthwhile to consider using the ordinary courts as an alternative to the Complaints Board in cases concerning ineffectiveness. The background for this is that the ordinary courts as elaborated in section 5.1 have shown some willingness to push the concept of ineffectiveness forward without relying on the Remedies Directives as the legal basis. It is therefore possible that the conditions for the application of the sanction ineffectiveness could differ from what is outlined in the Remedies Directives and in the Danish legislation implementing the Directive. The Act on the Enforcement of the Procurement Rules refers mainly to the competence of the Complaints Board and outlines to a limited extent the competence of the ordinary courts.[83]

The Danish legislator has been aware of this progressive interpretation of the rules which follows from the *original* draft from November 2009 and its preparatory works.[84] It followed from §16(2) of the original draft that a contract covered by the EU public procurement rules could be declared ineffective if this was considered necessary to comply with Community law. It was specified in the preparatory works that this was *not* a reflection of a provision in the Remedies Directives and that the provision was proposed in order to ensure that the Complaints Board for Public Procurement had the competences needed in order to comply with Community law. It was further stated that in particular the case law from the Court of Justice should be considered

83. However, it should be noted that the legislator has specified that the preclusive time limits in §7 of the Act also apply to procurement disputes before the ordinary courts, cf. §7(4).

84. The original proposal of 10 November 2009. See footnote 2.

with explicit reference to C-503/04, *Commission v Germany*. The preparatory works also emphasized that the Court of Appeal (Østre Landsret) recently recognized that Danish courts can have a duty to terminate a concluded contract and that the Court of Appeal in one of those cases clarified that this duty could be present in cases of very gross and serious violations of EU public procurement rules including direct illegal procurement. Such an approach clearly makes the conditions for the use of the sanction 'ineffectiveness' different and probably also less demanding than outlined in the Remedies Directives and contains no reference to a violation of standstill-provisions or interim measures.

The provision in §16(2) of the original draft and the above-mentioned remarks in the preparatory works were subsequently removed. Many would probably argue that the remarks and the provision were superfluous as this would already follow from EU law. This is admittedly the case from a formalistic point of view. However, such a provision supplemented with the remarks in the preparatory works would have sent a clear signal from the legislator: Please do not hesitate to live up to your obligations according to EU public procurement law even though they 'only' follow from recent case law from the Court of Justice and/or from principles of EU-law such as the principles of loyalty or effectiveness. The change of the wording of the Act on this point was therefore a move that took some steam out of the new remedy of ineffectiveness in Denmark.

Finally, it can be added that the number of claims for ineffectiveness after the entry into force of the Act on Enforcement of the Public Procurement Rules is easy to overview. It appears that there is only one pending case before the Complaints Board at present and that another case was settled by the parties. The contract was shortened in the latter case.

The issue of claims for damages from the contracting party when a contract becomes ineffective is considered in further detail in section 7.1. below.

6 Alternative penalties

The 'alternative penalty' is an alternative to ineffectiveness of the contract (ineffectiveness ex tunc of the full contract) and will therefore become relevant in several and fundamentally different situations. These situations are outlined in §18(3) of the Act on the Enforcement of the Public Procurement Rules. Firstly, an alternative penalty has to be measured out when the Complaints Board does not declare a contract ineffective in spite of contracting during the standstill period or in breach of suspension of the tender procedures due to a complaint.[85] Secondly, it becomes relevant when the Complaints Board has decided not to declare the contract ineffective on the basis of overriding reasons relating to the general interest, cf. §17(3) of the Act on the Enforcement of the Public Procurement Rules. Thirdly, alternative penalties will be imposed when only a part of the contract is declared ineffective including the situations where the ineffectiveness has been limited to those obligations which still have to be performed.

As the standard solution according to the Danish legislation is ineffectiveness ex nunc it will typically be relevant to impose alternative penalties in the form of 'fines', cf. Art.2(e)(1) of Remedies Directive 2007/66. If the contracting authority is a part of the public administration the Complaints Board can impose an economic sanction, cf. §19 of the Act. However, if the contracting authority is not a part of the public administration it can be fined by the ordinary courts, cf. §20 of the Act. In the latter situation the case is initiated by the Prosecution.[86] The economic sanction can be imposed even if the breach of the public procurement rules is not intentional or negligent, cf. §19(3) and §20(2).

The level of and criteria for the measurement of the economic sanctions are not specified in the Act on the Enforcement of the Public Procurement Rules but are instead specified in detail in the preparatory works. Nevertheless, it follows from the preparatory works to §19 of the Act that the economic sanctions[87] as a main rule should be minimum 25000 DKK (about 3000 €) and maximum 10 mio. DKK (about 1,33 mio €). The preparatory works contains a model for the calculation of the economic sanctions and several illustrative examples. The idea behind the model is to base the calculation on two variables: the gravity of the breach of the public procurement rules and the percentage of the contract that remains unaffected by the ineffectiveness.

The legislator appears to have established a priority between the application of ineffectiveness and alternative penalties. It is stated in the preparatory works to §18 that ineffectiveness is a far-reaching consequence with implications for tenderers, the contracting authority and the society. It is added that the contracting authorities will often prefer the application of alternative pen-

85. The Complaints Board has in this situation assessed that it would not be proportionate to declare the contract ineffective.
86. Presumably Statsadvokaten for Særlig Økonomisk Kriminalitet, cf. the preparatory works on §20.
87. It is specified in the preparatory works to §20 that the model and indicated minimum and maximum amount is also expected to apply with regard to fines.

alties instead of ineffectiveness. This statement lacks in clarity. One interpretation could be that the Complaints Board should give priority to the application of ineffectiveness as this would have the strongest deterrent effect. However, this interpretation does not appear to be correct in light of the remarks on the far-reaching implications of ineffectiveness inserted before the statement on the preference of the contracting authorities. The preparatory works must therefore be interpreted as giving preference to alternative penalties. The legislator has communicated that the use of ineffectiveness should be limited and softened up with the use of alternative penalties. This prioritization is probably the most balanced taking into consideration the entirety of involved interests. However, it seems inappropriate that the legislators' reasoning on this point is linked to the preferred choice of remedies of the contracting authorities. Obviously this should not be decisive for an important choice between remedies.

It is highly interesting that there are also indications of a similar approach and confusion in the United Kingdom where the 'UK stakeholders' strongly favoured ineffectiveness to be limited to future obligations instead of ineffectiveness ex tunc. The approach was subsequently to limit ineffectiveness to those which have yet to be performed at the time of the legal action and it appears that the choice was mainly made by the stakeholders or at least that their opinion was a decisive factor. This is criticized in the chapter on United Kingdom in the present publication.[88] As pointed out in the chapter on United Kingdom it is doubtful whether the details of an instrument devised to punish extreme violations of the law should be decided by the stakeholders that the new instrument is directed against. Prospective ineffectiveness (ineffectiveness ex nunc) is 'ineffectiveness light' and is less of a deterrent.[89]

7 Damages

As mentioned in the introduction to this chapter not only the ordinary courts but also the Complaints Board has the power grant damages which are remarkable and atypical both in a Danish and a European context. The Complaints Board did not have this competence when it was established in the early 1990s but the legislation was changed in 2000. The background for the

88. See the chapter of M. Trybus, 'An Overview of the United Kingdom Public Procurement Review and Remedies System with an Emphasis on England and Wales', section 6 on ineffectiveness.
89. See M. Trybus, fn. 86 above.

extension of the competences of Complaints Board back in 2000 was that the Danish system had been criticised in public debate for lack of efficiency on the basis of a number of concrete cases. There has been a clear increase in the claim for damages in the field of public procurement in Denmark after the above-mentioned change of the division of competences. The Board has awarded damages for violation of the public procurement rules on many occasions including compensation for the loss of profit.

It was explicitly stated in the preparatory works to the Law on the Complaints Board from 2000 that the Complaints Board must apply the ordinary Danish rules on damages in business relations. As previously mentioned according to Danish legal tradition, the preparatory works are of utmost importance and often decisive for a given interpretation. The Complaints Board has clearly been aware of this limitation of its powers, but one could question whether the Board actually applied the traditional approach in a couple of highly interesting cases in its first case law.[90] These cases will be further commented upon below but it should be stressed that the Complaints Board in its current practice applies the traditional approach.

The first case from the initial case law to be commented upon in further detail is the Magnus case[91] where the Board submitted various general statements on the application of its power to grant damages, bearing in mind that the rulings on damages also contribute to the motivation of the contracting authorities to comply with the EU public procurement rules. It then went on to stress that as a consequence it will not set restrictive requirements on proof concerning the causal link or the quantum of the loss. A traditional approach would instead have been to focus on compensation of loss and not on the prevention of infringements of the law. The claimant also received damages for external costs and internal costs. The damages for the internal costs were noteworthy, as the traditional legal approach would be not to award compensation for such an expense, based on the consideration that there is no loss since the salary of the employees had to be paid in any circumstances. However, the Complaints Board also awarded damages for this expense, even though it reduced the damages a little. The Complaints Board introduced its ruling on the internal costs by stating explicitly that damages for external costs shall be influenced by the deterrent effect of the rules on damages. However, as mentioned above the Complaints Board now follows the traditional approach to claims for damages in its case law.

90. For a detailed analysis of this see S. Treumer, European Business Organzation Law Review, 2004 p. 564 (in particular pp. 573-575).
91. Ruling of 22 November 2001, *Forlaget Magnus A/S v Told-og Skattestyrelsen.*

Another very interesting case concerned the conditions for granting compensation for loss of profit that are of utmost importance in practice. The starting point according to Danish law is that the successful action of this type presupposes that the tenderer can establish that it would have won the contract had there been no infringement. It is extremely difficult to document this because contracting authorities tend to award contracts on the basis of the 'most advantageous offer'. In the ruling of 3 July 2002 *Judex A/S v Århus Amt* from the Complaints Board a tenderer had fundamentally violated the public procurement rules. The Complaints Board considered that it was not feasible to assess the likelihood that the complainant would have won the contract if the contracting authority had not violated the EU public procurement rules. It then emphasized that this was the result of the illegal actions of the contracting authority and that this should not be to the disadvantage of the contracting authority, thereby effectively reversing the burden of proof. As a consequence, the tenderer was granted compensation for the loss of profit. The ruling was instantly appealed and the Court of Appeal overruled the Complaints Board. The Court of Appeal held that the requirements concerning the proof in support of the claim of the tenderer should be reduced but did not consider it proven that the tenderer would have been likely to win the contract.

A low percentage of the rulings of the Complaints Board have been appealed to the ordinary courts. The tendency has been that the judgments in these cases are firmly rooted in the traditional approach to the law.

7.1 Claims for damages when a contract becomes ineffective

Until recently it was very difficult to come up with examples of cases be it in Denmark or in other Member States where a contracting authority had terminated a contract covered by the EU public procurement rules due to a breach of the procurement rules.[92] However, this situation is likely to materialize in several cases in future practice. This is a consequence of the new rules on ineffectiveness combined with the recent case law from Court of Justice of the European Union addressing the duty to terminate tender procedures in case of breaches of the public procurement rules.[93]

92. Some examples are mentioned in section 5 of this chapter and in section 1 of the article of S. Treumer,'Towards an Obligation to Terminate Contracts Concluded in Breach of the EC Public Procurement Rules: the End of the Status of Concluded Public Contracts as Sacred Cows', Public Procurement Law Review 2007 pp. 371-386.
93. C-503/04, *Commission v Germany*, and C-91/08, Wall.

It follows from Art.2(d)(2) of the Remedies Directive that the consequences of a contract being considered ineffective shall be provided for by national law. The grant of damages to the contracting party when a contract becomes ineffective is not addressed in the provisions of the Act on the Enforcement of the Public Procurement Rules. However, the question is considered in the preparatory works[94] to the Act where it is stated the damages are not excluded provided that the ordinary conditions for damages are fulfilled. The assumption is therefore that the contracting party can claim damages. The preparatory works does not address the question of whether the contracting party can obtain compensation for the loss of profit. This question is difficult to answer with certainty and the interpretations on this issue are likely to be divided until the issue is settled in the case law.

One approach would be to draw an analogy from the approach in cases where a contract is invalid. In such a case it would in Danish law be excluded to obtain compensation for loss of profit as this is reserved to valid contracts where you seek to maintain the economic consequences of the contract to the benefit of the contracting party. At first sight this would appear to be a relevant approach as this would be in accordance with the aim of the introduction of the new remedy 'ineffectiveness'.[95] The latter is considered in consideration 21 of the Preamble to Remedies Directive 2007/66 where it is stated that 'The objective to be achieved ... is that the rights and obligations of the parties under the contract should cease to be enforced and performed.

Another approach could be to emphasize that the new remedy is invalidity sui generis – a close relative of invalidity but with characteristics and legal implications that on some points deviate from the well-known features of invalidity. The public procurement context is special and it is the duty of the contracting authority to comply with the EU public procurement rules. Ineffectiveness is ultimately a consequence of a fundamental failure of the contracting authority and one could question whether it is reasonable that a tenderer in good faith should be excluded from claiming damages for the loss of profit. It would appear appropriate to let the contracting authority carry the financial risk of a contract's possible ineffectiveness as if is the addressee of the public procurement rules and a tenderer should be able to rely on their observance of the public procurement rules. This approach could also have a positive effect on the observance of the public procurement regime as it would be a clear incentive for compliance. The contracting authority could at

94. See the remarks regarding §18 of 27 January 2010.
95. This was the preferred approach in the Norwegian preparatory works on enforcement in the field of public procurement, NOU 2010:2, p. 175.

least theoretically face a double claim for damages for loss of profit: A claim from one or more of the tenderers that did not win the competition for the contract and a claim from the contracting party loosing the contract because it becomes ineffective.[96] For obvious reasons the contracting authority would in practice never be obliged to cover the loss of profit twice as only one tenderer in principle can document that it would have won the competition for the contract if the public procurement rules had been observed.

It can be added that the Swedish legislator also considered the issue of damages in case of ineffectiveness. It follows explicitly from the preparatory works to the implementation of Remedies Directive 2007/66[97] that the contracting party can claim damages. There is a reference to case law[98] concerning damages for loss of profit in the preparatory works and it would therefore appear implicitly to follow from these that the contracting party can make a claim for loss of profit in Sweden. The Government stressed in the preparatory works that damages to the contracting party was considered to be reasonable and that the preventive effect supports this solution.[99]

The above-mentioned approach with a theoretical acceptance of a claim for damages for loss of profit from the contract party will without doubt be questioned by many. However, the reader should bear in mind that it would be highly unlikely that a contracting authority has to pay damages for loss of profit to a contracting party. There are several reasons for this and it suffices to stress three of them. Firstly, the tenderer has to be in good faith which will frequently not be the case. In most cases the contracting authority can undermine the claim by challenging the good faith of the tenderer as the tenderer has been or ought to have been aware that the contract should have been tendered out or of the other violations that leads to ineffectiveness. Secondly, the contracting party has to fulfil the ordinary conditions for damages and therefore has to establish a casual link. The contracting party therefore has to establish that it would have won the contract had the public procurement rules

96. If the contracting party wins the competition for the contract again in a subsequent tender procedure the consequence is presumably that a claim for damages for loss of profit is without legal basis as this would lead to an unjustified enrichment of the contracting party. The law suit for damages would normally be considered after the conclusion of the contract in the second tender procedure.
97. The changes of the Swedish public procurement laws LOU (classic sectors) and LUF (utilities) entered into force 15 July 2010. The issue of damages in cases of ineffectiveness is considered in K. Pedersen, *Upphandlingens grunder – en introduktion til offentlig upphandling och upphandling i försörjningssektorerna*, 201, p.167.
98. NJA 2000 p. 712 and NJA 2007 p. 349.
99. Prop. 2009/10:180, pp. 225-226.

been complied with. This will be almost impossible in cases where there has been no tender but also very difficult when the ineffectiveness is caused by other breaches. Thirdly, it is highly likely that the Complaints Board or ordinary courts will hesitate to grant damages for loss of profit to the contracting party and that they therefore will be inclined to interpret the facts of each individual case to the disadvantage of the contracting party claiming damages for loss of profit. It is still a clear exception that tenderers receive compensation for loss of profit in the traditional scenario where a loosing competitor claim damages of this sort.[100] If the above-mentioned approach is accepted it will probably be even rarer that the contracting party makes a successful claim for loss of profit.

Finally, it should be noted that many contracting authorities have started to insert contract clauses in their public contracts limiting or cutting of the responsibility of the contracting authority in case the contract is declared ineffective or terminated due to breach of the public procurement rules. These clauses could subsequently be challenged on the basis of contract law principles and possible also on the basis of EU public procurement rules as it could be argued that they undermine the effect of the remedy ineffectiveness.

8 Correlation between remedies

A very interesting question is whether more than one remedy can be applied in the same case or whether certain remedies are mutually exclusive. The latter is the case in the French system according to the 'parallel remedy theory' described in the chapter on France in the present publication. Another equally as interesting question is whether the national enforcement system gives preference to certain remedies above others and the background for this. These issues are not directly addressed in the Act on the Enforcement of the Public Procurement Rules or earlier legislation implementing the Remedies Directives. However, they are to a certain extent clarified in the preparatory works to this legislation and in the case law of namely the Complaints Board for Public Procurement.

100. See S. Treumer, 'Damages for Breach of the EC Public Procurement Rules-Changes in European Regulation and Practice', Public Procurement Law Review, 2006 p. 159 for an overview of trends in European practice. A striking feature of the case law in the field was the almost total absence of successful actions for damages. However, this feature has rapidly changed, as there are now several examples of successful actions in various Member States.

The first question as regards mutual exclusivity is not clearly addressed in legal theory. It also essentially remains unanswered when the case law is considered. The answer is therefore as a starting point that the remedies are not mutually exclusive. It has been questioned in a recent case[101] whether the application of the remedy ineffectiveness or the related establishment of a duty to terminate the contract excludes the claim of damages for loss of profit. As the complainant lost the case the issue was not considered by the Complaints Board. For obvious reasons a complainant should not be excluded from claiming both the ineffectiveness of the contract and damages for breach of the public procurement rules including loss of profit. The ineffectiveness only implies that the complainant gets a second chance to win the contract provided that it is tendered out again after the termination of the original contract. The complaining tenderer has typically only a small chance of winning the contract in the subsequent tender procedures as the outcome is very uncertain for various reasons. One of them being that the outcome is uncertain by its very nature as it is a competition for the contract.[102] It is far from certain that the complainant will deliver the lowest bid or the economically most advantageous tender and the quality of the complaint does not necessarily reflect the competitiveness of the complainant. The contracting authority will also most likely be a little hesitant to award the contract to the complainant that forced it to retender the contract and in some instances it will presumably blacklist the complainant thereby excluding all chances of winning the contract. To sum up it will be rare that the successful complainant will be awarded the contract in a subsequent tender procedure and a pure exception that the complainant can also meet the strict requirements for the grant of damages for loss of profit. Should this be the case the extraordinarily successful complainant could probably be met with a law suit for unjustified enrichment as it has both been awarded the contract and been compensated for the loss of profit.

101. Ruling of 25 March 2010, *Visma Services Odense A/S v Hillerød Kommune*, from the Complaints Board.

102. It is also by no means certain that the content of the contract is identical in the subsequent tender procedure. The contracting authority may have developed new preferences; the market has been innovative and has come up with new products etc. It should also not be forgotten that the contracting authority has a much clearer picture of the competitive situation after running the first tender procedure. It can therefore relatively easily adjust the contract to the advantage of some of the tenderers – and the disadvantage of others including perhaps the complainant.

The likelihood of a successful claim for damages has surely excluded the grant of interim measures in many cases. This does not follow explicitly from the formulation of the conditions for grant of interim measures in the Danish legislation but is a likely consequence of the conditions adopted in the case law of the Complaints Board for Public Procurement. One of these conditions is urgency and the prospects of damages can lead to a finding that this condition is not fulfilled. As previously pointed out in section 2 on interim measures the grant of interim measures has been a clear exception in Danish Complaints Board practice. However, the reasoning for the rejections in the case law is normally not accessible[103] because they are not inserted as a part of the published rulings of the Board. On this point the state of law in Denmark appears to correspond to United Kingdom.[104]

The Complaints Board for Public Procurement was indirectly instructed to be hesitant with the grant of damages in the preparatory works to the Act on the Complaints Board which entered into force in 2000. It was stated in these preparatory works that the use of interim measures, annulment of illegal decisions, orders on legalization of the tender procedures should be applied to the widest extent possible instead of grant of damages. This was based on consideration to the involved resources of the society the idea being to limit the consequences of the breach through correction as fast as possible and avoiding that the conclusion of the contract without due consideration to the public procurement rules.

It was stated in the preparatory works to §13 of the Act on the Enforcement of the Public Procurement Rules that it is expected that the Complaints Board to the widest extent possible issues orders when violations of the public procurement rules has been established. The background for this expectation was explicitly stated as being that the primary aim of the Act is to make the enforcement of the public procurement rules more effective. It remains to be seen whether the Complaints Board will apply its competence to issue orders in many of the complaints cases. The Board has in its previous practice rarely used the competence to order the legalization of the tender procedure.

The new competence to order the termination of a contract after a declaration of ineffectiveness is very unlikely to be applied in many cases for various reasons. Firstly, complainants will most likely think twice before asking for a declaration of ineffectiveness and the Complaints Board will also presumably

103. That is unless you explicitly request access to the file in the individual case.
104. See the chapter in the present publication written by M. Trybus, fn. 86 above, section 2. M. Trybus questions the EU law compatibility of the approach that if damages are available interim measures would be affected or even precluded?

hesitate to apply this remedy. As previously mentioned in the section on alternative penalties the Danish legislator appears to have established a priority between the application of ineffectiveness and alternative penalties. Statements in the preparatory works to the Act on the Enforcement of the Public Procurement Rules must be interpreted as giving preference to alternative penalties, cf. the analysis in section 6. The idea being that the use of ineffectiveness should be limited and preferably softened up by the use of alternative penalties in cases where the contract nevertheless is declared ineffective with effect for future obligations.

9 Alternative dispute settlement

Alternative dispute settlement currently lacks importance in the Danish public procurement system. It used to be different as the Competition and Consumer Authority played a very special role in the enforcement of the public procurement rules and very successfully exercised an effective alternative dispute resolution mechanism for public contracts. However, this has recently changed as will be explained below.

The Authority can deal with complaints concerning alleged infringements but *cannot* issue a binding order in the field of public procurement. However, it can instead bring a case before the Complaints Board if a contracting authority does not comply with the recommendations of the Competition Authority. This allowed the Competition and Consumer Authority to function as an easy and also rather informal alternative to the Complaints Board for Public Procurement. Furthermore, it ensured that disputes could be solved at a relatively low dispute level in many instances. The potential complaint of the Contracting Authority to the Complaints Board helped in reality to convince many contracting authorities and it was not necessary to enter into the more formal, costly and time-consuming dispute before the Complaints Board for Public Procurement or the ordinary courts. However, the resources of the Competition and Consumer Authority are now primarily used on other tasks. The contracting authorities have also recently been more unwilling to suspend the tender procedures until the Authority have had a chance to look into the substance of the complaint. As mentioned above the Authority cannot issue a binding order and also not grant interim measures. The alternative dispute settlement is therefore to a large extent dependant on the willingness of the contracting authorities to suspend the procedures. If this willingness is not present the complainants will then normally have to bring the case to the Complaints Board for Public Procurement if it wants to have its complaint considered. It can be added that the Competition and Consumer Authority only on rare occasions have used its standing to refer a complainant to the Complaints Board and with a very low success rate.

10 Conclusion

Denmark has prioritized the regulation of and compliance with the EU public procurement rules for about two decades. The Danish interpretation of substantial public procurement rules in the public procurement directives is relatively restrictive and the enforcement system appears to be one of the most efficient in the EU.[105] It is actually so efficient that by many practitioners and politicians it is considered to be *too efficient* which allegedly makes many contracting entities hesitate when they should decide whether to tender out or not. It is expected that the Danish enforcement system will be changed fundamentally in order to secure that the Complaints Board for Public Procurement focuses on the most fundamental breaches and that the number of cases is reduced.

Denmark has established a tradition for quick implementation or at least implementation on time of the public procurement directives. This tradition was not followed with regard to the implementation of Remedies Directive 2007/66. The relevant legislation was delayed and entered into force on July 1, 2010.

The new Act on Enforcement of the Public Procurement rules from 2010 fundamentally changed the division of work between the bodies involved in enforcement of the public procurement rules. Until the above-mentioned Act entered into force aggrieved tenderers and a number of other entities had a free choice between the Complaints Board for Public Procurement and the ordinary courts when they wanted a formal dispute settlement. Ever since the establishment of the Complaints Board in the early 1990s it has been a pure exception that a case has been brought before the ordinary courts instead of the Complaints Board. The Danish legislator has taken the consequences of this as the Complaints Board for Public Procurement now has become the obligatory first instance in procurement disputes in most cases.

105. The range of potential complainants has been widened, the economic risk of submitting a complaint has been substantially reduced, a fast working Complaints Board with extensive competences has been established and many complainants have been successful. The Complaints Board has also been vested with the competence to award damages even though it is an administrative body that is not a part of the judiciary.

The Complaints Board has the power to grant interim measures, the power to establish that the rules have been violated and the power to issue set aside orders to contracting authorities. It can also declare a contract ineffective and award damages. The latter competence is remarkable and atypical both in a Danish and European context. The award of damages is normally exclusively a matter for the ordinary courts and the Complaints Board is an administrative body. The Complaints Board did not have the competence to award damages when it was established in the early 1990s. The legislation was changed in 2000 and vested the Board with the power to award damages for infringements of the EU public procurement rules. This change was made in order to increase the effectiveness of the Danish complaints system. There has subsequently been a clear increase in the claim for damages in the field of public procurement after the Complaints Board was vested with the power to grant damages. The Board has awarded damages for violation of the public procurement rules on many occasions including compensation for the loss of profit.

It is an exception that the rulings of the Complaints Board is appealed before the ordinary courts which happens in about 10 % of the cases. The number of complaints has steadily increased during the years. The Complaints Board received 84 complaints in 2008, about 115 in 2009 and about 182 in 2010. The complainants have been successful[106] in numerous cases brought before the Complaints Board.

Even though the Danish enforcement system appears to be one of the most efficient in the EU it still has a few shortcomings. One of them has been the uncertain legal effects of an annulment of the award decision or of decisions to conclude the contract. The new remedy of ineffectiveness is therefore of utmost importance for insuring of a well-functioning remedies system also in Denmark.

Another weakness is linked to interim measures. It was extremely difficult to obtain interim measures for several years and the approach is still restrictive in the case law of the Complaints Board. When a request for interim measures is rejected the consequences of a possible breach will often be very limited. The concluded contract will typically remain in force and damages for loss of profit are a clear exception. The new rules on automatic suspension of the tender procedures in complaints cases would appear to repair this

106. Successful in the sense that the Complaints Board established a breach of the public procurement rules in these cases. This need not be considered a success from the perspective of the complainants. The complainant's primary aim with the dispute will often be the retendering of the contract or damages for the loss of profit.

at least to some extent. However, it is unlikely that the Complaints Board will be more willing to grant interim measures after it has used its thirty days to consider whether the automatic suspension should be prolonged. It should be noted that the criteria for the grant of interim measures have not changed with the Act on the Enforcement of the Public Procurement Rules. It is therefore to be assumed that the typical Complaints Board ruling still will consider the legality in a case where the contract has been concluded implying that a breach of the public procurement rules typically has limited consequences. A general widening of the scope for the application of the remedy ineffectiveness could remedy this weakness if ineffectiveness could be declared in all cases where infringement has affected the chances of the tenderer.

It will be highly interesting to follow the future developments in the field and to evaluate if the latest revision of the Remedies Directives led to a substantial improvement of effective enforcement of the EU public procurement rules also in Denmark.

Bibliography (selected publications)

M.F. Hansen and K. Thorup, 'Standstill og opsættende virkning i udbudsrettten', Ugeskrift for Retsvæsen 2010 B 303.

C. Risvig Hansen, 'Pligt til annoncering af offentlige kontrakter – uden effektiv håndhævelse af reglerne?', Ugeskrift for Retsvæsen, 2011 B 101.

L. Hummelshøj and H. Bang Schmidt, 'EU-udbud: Retsvirkningen af at undlade udbud', Ugeskrift for Retsvæsen 2006 B 80.

T. Høg, *Udbudsretlige erstatningsspørgsmål*, 2005.

J. Fabricius, *Offentlige indkøb i praksis*, 2010.

J. Fejø and S. Treumer (eds.), *EU's Udbudsregler – implementering og håndhævelse i Norden* (The EC Public Procurement Rules-Implementation and Enforcement in the Nordic Countries), 2006.

Ruth Nielsen, 'Standstill og ugyldighed/uvirksomhed af offentlige kontrakter', Ugeskrift for Retsvæsen 2007 B 120.

R. Offersen and M. Frank, 'Ugyldighed og annullation af kontrakter indgået i strid med udbudsreglerne', Ugeskrift for Retsvæsen 2008 B 372.

R. Offersen, 'Lovliggørelse af fejlbehæftede udbud', Ugeskrift for Retsvæsen 2010 B 55.

S.T. Poulsen, P.S. Jakobsen and S.E. Kalsmose-Hjelmborg, *EU Udbudsretten*, 2nd ed. 2011.

H.P. Rosenmeier, 'Det danske klagesystem', p. 135 in J. Fejø and S. Treumer (eds.), *EU's Udbudsregler – implementering og håndhævelse i Norden* (The EC Public Procurement Rules-Implementation and Enforcement in the Nordic Countries), 2006.

S. Treumer, 'Increased Effectiveness of Public Procurement Remedies in Denmark', Public Procurement Law Review 2000, NA 120.

S. Treumer, 'Damages for Breach of the EC Public Procurement Rules from a Danish Perspective', European Business Organization Law Review, 2004 p. 563.

S. Treumer, 'Enforcement of the EC Public Procurement Rules in Denmark', Public Procurement Law Review 2005, NA 186.

S. Treumer, 'National håndhævelse af EU's udbudsregler – er håndhævelsessystemet effektivt på EU-udbudsområdet?', p. 99 in J. Fejø and S. Treumer (eds.), *EU's Udbudsregler – implementering og håndhævelse i Norden* (The EC Public Procurement Rules-Implementation and Enforcement in the Nordic Countries), 2006.

S. Treumer, 'Damages for Breach of the EC Public Procurement Rules-Changes in European Regulation and Practice', Public Procurement Law Review, 2006 p. 159.

S. Treumer, 'Towards an Obligation to Terminate Contracts Concluded in Breach of the EC Public Procurement Rules: the End of the Status of Concluded Public Contracts as Sacred Cows', Public Procurement Law Review 2007 p. 371.

9 Enforcement of the EU Public Procurement Rules in France

By François Lichère and Nicolas Gabayet

1 Introduction of the institutions of the French system

The French legal system is divided between, on the one hand, administrative law, applied by administrative courts ('juridictions administratives') and on the other, private law, applied by civil and criminal courts ('juridictions judiciaires'). As far as a public procurement contract is concerned, most of the time, litigation falls under the competence of administrative courts, no matter if it deals with the making of the contract (including the application of EU award procedures) or the performance of the contract. As a consequence, any plaintiff who wants to obtain a remedy for a breach of EU procurement rules has usually to bring his claim before the administrative judge. There are exceptions to this competence when the public procurement contract is considered as being private, which is not generally the case if the contract is signed by a public authority representative, but which is generally the case if the contract is signed between two private parties in the French meaning. However, this article only deals with the enforcement of EU public procurement rules before administrative courts which is the general situations in practice, bearing in mind that in any case the remedies introduced by transposing the EU directives are the same before the civil courts. Within the administrative courts system, the litigants first go before one of the 42 administrative courts of first instance ('tribunaux administratifs'), then before one of the administrative courts of appeals ('cours administrative d'appel') and then before the Council of State ('Conseil d'Etat'). By exception, for the 'référés' (see below), the appeals of the judgments of first instance go directly before the Conseil d'Etat.

Even though, i.e. even if the system is only scrutinized through the administrative courts procedure, the French system can be characterized firstly as complex. This is due to the fact that the remedies introduced by transposing the EU directives on public contracts review have been added to the remedies already existing in a purely national or domestic context. The the government decided to clean up the latter remedies when introducing the new remedies, which therefore involves a superposition of remedies. The system is also complex as the distinction between interim relief and annulment does not always correspond to a distinction between different remedies. In other words, there is one remedy which can lead to either a suspension of the award procedure or the annulment of an award decision (see below 'référé précontractuel'). Interestingly, this référé précontractuel has been introduced by the French legislator when transposing the first public contract review directive of 1989 and such a system was a real novelty at the time, although the directive did not impose to give such various power to a judge ceased by a sole action.

On the other hand, the French system can be deemed as relatively efficient in terms of the number of ways of actions and the power given to the courts. It often goes beyond the requirements of the two review directives by, for example, extending the review mechanisms for contracts below the European thresholds, an illustration of the famous 'spill over effect' of the EU law.

Regarding the legal costs, there are not very high. Most of the time, the losing party is condemned to pay the trial expenses called '*dépens*', which includes, *inter alia*, the cost of assessments, if any, and the costs of particular pleadings if any, but no taxes are to be paid in principle. Usually, under the article L 761-1 of the *Code de justice administrative*, the litigant condemned to pay the '*dépens*' is also condemned to pay the so-called '*frais non-compris dans les dépens*', which are basically the fees paid by the parties to their lawyers. However, when due to an abusive behaviour from the winning party, the expanses increased during the trial, the judge can condemn him to pay at least a part of the '*frais non compris dans les dépens*' when it is equitable not to let them to the expanses of the other party.[1] It is nevertheless worth mentioning that when the trial was only meant to obtain an interim relief, the temporarily losing party cannot be condemned to pay the '*frais non compris dans les dépens*'.[2] However, it can be condemned to pay these fees when it comes to 'référé précontractuel' and 'référé contractuel' (see below) as in this case, the judge can adopt definitive decisions.

The claimant has to have recourse to a lawyer for claims on public contracts when the performance of the contract is at stake, but no lawyer is re-

1. CE, 2 June 1989, *SA Finelec*, *AJDA* 1989. 722. All the case law referred to in this article and posterior to 1979 can be found in free access on www.legifrance.gouv.fr. (jurisprudence administrative)
2. CAA Paris, 2 November 1994, *Groupe des sociétés Eiffage*, *Lebon* p. 712, *AJDA* 1995. 147.

quired for judicial review and interim measures in the field of public contracts, with the exception of a cassation before the Council of State. The hiring of a lawyer is pretty cheap in France in the field of public procurement, ranging for example from 3 000 to 10 000 euros in average for a 'référé précontractuel'.

The Council Directive 2007/66/CE has been implemented by an ordinance of 7 May 7, 2009 (N°2009-515), completed by decree of 27 November 2009, creating the relief of *'référé contractuel'* and improving the *'référé précontractuel'*. The Directive has been implemented on time, since the deadline to proceed to the implementation was the 11th of December 2009.

2 Interim Mesures

Under French law, a so-called 'référé' is an interlocutory procedure meant to be led quickly by a single judge in order to settle, in principle temporarily, a contentious or pre-contentious situation, thanks to interim measures. This kind of procedure has long existed in French administrative law. However, two *référés* especially dedicated to public contracts do not originate from domestic law, but from EU law. The 'référé précontractuel' allows the judge to adopt either interim measures or definitive measures (i.e. measures that he cannot change). This concept is unknown to me before the signing of the contract. The 'référé contractuel' allows the adoption of definitive measures after the signing of the contract. The latter will then be analysed in the section dealing with ineffectiveness.

Regarding the 'référés', it is worth distinguishing between, on the one hand, the interlocutory procedure coming from EU directives specifically dedicated to cope with breaches in the tendering procedure of public procurement contracts,[3] and on the other hand, several non-specialized and 'domestic' interim reliefs that can apply to settle litigations arising during the tendering procedure.

3. Which are not the only public contracts at stake since concessions contracts, which are subject to specific French rules for their award (Act of 29 january 1993), are also subject to this référé.

2.1 Interim Measures dedicated to public procurement contracts originating from eu law: the 'refere precontractuel'

2.1.1 Locus standi common to 'référé précontractuel' and 'référé contractuel'

There are quite a lot of similarities between *locus standi* applying to both 'référés' procedures in the field of public contracts (*'référé pré-contractuel* and *'référé-contractuel' – see section on ineffectiveness for the latter*). Indeed, under articles L 551-10 (dealing with standings to apply for a *'référé pré-contractuel*') and L 551-14 (dealing with the standings for a *'référé contractuel*') of the *Code de justice administrative*, both procedures may apply, as far as the claimant have had an interest to sign the contract or if his interests have been likely to be harmed by the alleged breach in the tendering procedure. The case law interpreted strictly originally this condition for the non candidates by requiring that they have been prevented from tendering. The case law is less demanding now as the judge will simply check that the speciality of the firm which did not tender is sufficient with regard to the subject matter of the contract.[4] But on the other hand, the requirements are quite high regarding the illegalities that can be invoked since the *SMIRGEOMES* case.[5] Since then, it is the duty of the judge to ckeck if the claimant has actually been harmed or is likely to be harmed by the breach in publicy and competition rules of the tendering procedure, even indirectly, in favoring a challenging company whereas before any breaches could be alleged, which had first made this remedy to be considered as an 'objective' remedy. This case was only dealing with the *'référé pré-contractuel*' procedure but most of the authors consider that the standings to allow a *'référé contractuel*' should be interpreted following *SMIRGEOMES*.[6] Even more, and quite surprisingly, the awarded firm can use a 'référé précontractuel' as it always has an interest in signing a contract flowing a lawful award procedure.[7]

Besides, in both procedures (*'référé précontractuel'* and *'contractuel'*), under the articles L 551-10 and L 551-14 of the *Code de justice administra-*

4. CE, 8 August 2008, Région de Bourgogne, n°304163
5. CE, Sect., 3 octobre 2008, *Syndicat Mixte Intercommunal de Réalisation et de Gestion pour l'élimination des Ordure Ménagères du Secteur Est de la Sarthe*, n° 305420, *Lebon* 242, *RFDA* 2008. 1128, concl. B. Da Cosa, note P. Delvolvé).
6. e.g. S. Braconnier, « L'autonomie contrastée du contentieux des contrats publics d'affaires», *RDP* 2010, n° 2. 327, at 339; J.-F. Lafaix, «Systématisation inachevée du contentieux de la commande publique. Commentaire de l'ordonnance n° 2009-515 du 17 mai 2009», *Jurisclasseur Contrats et marchés publics*, Fasc.2, 8 mai 2009, § 25.
7. CE 19 septembre 2007, Communauté d'agglomération de Saint Etienne, n°296192.

tive, the Prefect always has standings to refer a breach of tendering procedure to the judge as long as the awarding authority is a local authority. Finally, the government can also act when asked by the European Commission.

However, as we shall see, there are some more requirements applying to '*référé contractuel*'.

2.1.2 Definition / Purpose of the 'référé précontractuel'

The '*référé précontractuel*' originates from the Council Directive 89/665 on Review Procedures, which has been implemented in France by the Law of 4 January 1992. The rules applicable to this *référé* have been complemented and modified by the Law of 7 May 2009 (N°2009-515) implementing Council Directive 2007/66/CE.[8] This interlocutory procedure applies in case of a breach of EC or French public procurement rules related to the requirements of publicity and competition during the tendering period. Under *référé précontractuel*, a claimant can go before a single judge in the administrative court, holding that the awarding authority has infringed the requirements of the tendering procedure.

About the suspension of the procedure for the award of a public contract entailed by the review the awarding procedure,[9] French law has gone further than EU law provisions in 2009. Before this date, the legal action had no automatic suspensive effect. Nonetheless, the judge seiced in 'référé précontractuel' could immediately suspend for a maximum of 20 days the award procedure and decide on the merits in the meantime. From Dec. 1, 2009 onwards, whereas Article 2(4) of the Council Directive 2007/66/CE provides that the suspension is mandatory in two cases (when there is a review with the awarding authority – which is not possible in France – and in case of a claim against the awarding decision), the Law of 7 May 7, 2009 (N°2009-515) provides that suspension is mandatory in all cases, when the procedure is a '*référé précontractuel*', as soon as the case is referred to the judge. The contract cannot be signed until the decision of the judge has been notified to the awarding authority.[10] The suspension is therefore automatic within the '*référé précontractuel*', whatever the contested part of the awarding procedure. However, the suspension concerns only the signature of the contract. Therefore, the award procedure can still be implemented until the signature stage.

8. Ordonnance n° 2009-515 du 7 mai 2009 relative aux procédures de recours applicables aux contrats de la commande publique.
9. Council Directive 2007/66/CE, Article 2(3).
10. *Code de justice administrative,* art. L 551-9.

2.1.3 Scope of the judge's powers

Contracting authorities and utility operators

The powers of the '*référé précontractuel*' judge vary in accordance with the nature of the awarding authority.

When the awarding authority is a 'contracting authority',[11] according to article 1 (9) of Council Directive 2004/18,[12] the judge may request the authority in breach to comply with the tendering procedure requirements, he may request the suspension of any decision related to the awarding procedure. However, since the implementation of the Council Directive 2007/66/EC,[13] the tendering procedure is automatically suspended as soon as a '*référé précontractuel*' is referred to the court. The judge may also set aside any decision related to the awarding procedure, and cancel, within the contract, those of the clauses which would be, according to him, opposite to the requirements of the tendering procedure.[14] These two last possibilities were already in place in 1992 which was, at the time, a clearly highly new and important power given to a single judge and moreover almost counter nature since a 'juge des référés' is supposed to adopt provisional measures.

When the awarding authority is a 'utility operator',[15] according to the Council Directive 2004/17/EC, the '*référé pré-contractuel*' claim applies,[16] but as opposed to the case where the awarding body is a 'contracting authority', the powers of the judge are limited. Indeed, he cannot annul any decision, nor can he cancel any clauses of the contract. In such a case, the judge may only request the suspension of any decision related to the awarding procedure or request the authority in breach to comply with the tendering procedure requirements, with daily penalties, if necessary.[17]

Measures spontaneously decided by the judge

One of the contributions of the Law of 7 May 7, 2009, in the field of the powers of the '*référé précontractuel*' judge is to enable him to take measures

11. '*pouvoir adjudicateur*'.
12. 'The State, regional or local authorities, bodies governed by public law, associations formed by one or several of such authorities or one or several of such bodies governed by public law'.
13. Ordonnance n° 2009-515 du 7 mai 2009 relative aux procédures de recours applicables aux contrats de la commande publique.
14. *Code de justice administrative*, art. L 551-2.
15. '*entité adjudicatrice*' or '*opérateur de réseau*'.
16. *Code de justice administrative*, art. L 551-5.
17. *Code de justice administrative*, art. L 551-6.

'*d'office*', meaning without being asked to by the claimant.[18] This possibility does not derive from the Directive 2004/17/EC. It is a consequence of a previous case law, stating that the '*référé précontractuel*' judge could rule on the case either *infra petita* or *ultra petita*.[19] In such a case however, the ordinance of 7 May 2009 imposes to the judge to respect the 'principe du contradictoire' and therefore must ask for the opinion of the parties before deciding to grant a remedy that was not asked for.

2.2 Interim Measures dedicated to Public Procurement Contracts Originating from French Law

2.2.1 'Référé suspension'

The so called '*référé-suspension*' is an interlocutory procedure enabling a claimant, having applied for a 'recours pour excès de pouvoir' (which aims to obtain the annulment of an *ultra vires* administrative decision – see below) or having applied to a 'recours Tropic' (see below) to seek the stay of the administrative decision until the judge has settled the main litigation, that is to say the question of whether the decision is *ultra vires* and consequently, the question of its annulment. There are two requirements related to the nature of the decision and of the illegality committed by to be met to allow the claim. First, there must be a situation of emergency; second, there must be 'a serious doubt about the legality of the decision'. The requirement of emergency has been defined by the case law as the situation in which '*the administrative act harms seriously and irretrievably a public interest or the situation of the claimant or of any interest he is protecting*'.[20] This requirement of emergency '*must be assessed concretely by the judge*',[21] using legal and factual elements.[22] Most of the time though, the illegality only harms the claimant's interests and neither the public interest nor other interests the claimant would defend. For that reason, the courts had been quite reluctant to recognize such an emergency situation when the '*référé-suspension*' was made against an

18. *Code de justice administrative*, art. L 551-12.
19. CE, 20 October 2006, *Commune d'Andeville*, n° 289234, *Lebon* 434; *AJDA* 2006. 2340, concl. D. Casas.
20. CE, Sect., 19 January 2001, *Confédération nationale des radios libres*, n° 228815, *Lebon* 29; *AJDA* 2001. 152, chron. M. Guyomar & P. Collin.
21. CE, Sect., 28 February 2001, *Préfet des Alpes-Maritimes*, n° 229562, Lebon 109; *AJDA* 2001, 464, chron. M. Guyomar & P. Collin.
22. CE, Sect., 25 avril 2001, Association des habitants du littoral du Morbihan c/ commune de Baden, *Lebon* 220; *RDP* 2002, 765, obs. C. Guettier.

award decision.[23] The only situation in which the judges always recognize the emergency is when the illegality comes from the fact that the awarding authority has signed the contract in violation of the *'référé pré-contractuel'* judge's decision to suspend the awarding procedure. In such a case, the emergency is presumed.[24] Also, there can be cases where the signing of the contract with a firm A might compromise the viability of the firm B – depending on its economic situation – and in this case the emergency exists.[25]

The interlocutory procedure of *'référé suspension'* cannot be used on its own. According to article 521-1 of the *Code de justice administrative*, it has to be the secondary claim of a main one. Traditionally the main claim could only be a *'recours pour excès de pouvoir'*. It is worth specifying that the *'recours pour excès de pouvoir'* is normally not possible against a public procurement contract.[26] Indeed, this claim is by nature a claim aiming to seek annulment of an administrative unilateral act. However, it has been stated that this interim relief is available in case of a so-called *'Tropic travaux'* claim, which is a claim against a contract.[27]

Since the only available remedy here is then the stay of the decision, one can consider that this relief is not as advantageous for the claimant as the *référé-précontractuel*. Indeed, in this procedure, there are much more remedies available: suspension or annulment of any decision related to the awarding procedure, cancellation of some clauses (when the awarding authority is a contracting authority). However, the *'référé suspension'* might be applied for together with a *'Tropic travaux'* claim when at the first place a *'référé pré-contractuel'* has been unsuccessful or when the awarding authority has signed the contract in violation of one of the standstill periods. Moreover, it does not limit the number of legal arguments against the award decisions as does the 'référé précontractuel' (limited to legal arguments dealing with public pro-

23. TA Besançon, 12 février 2008, *Société CBS*, n° 800115, *JCPA* 2008, 2075, note F. Linditch.
24. CE, 6 mars 2009, *Société Biomérieux*, n° 324064, *JCPA* 2009, 2107, note F. Linditch. Unless the signature of the contract was particulary urgent for the needs of the awarding authority: TA Nice, 15 mars 2010, n° 100070, *Société Ricoh France*, *JCPA* 2010, 2325, note F. Linditch. The authority of this judgement is debatable though, since it does not have the authority of a binding precedent.
25. CE, 3 Mars 2006, n° 287960.
26. CE, 13 May 1899, *Levieux*, *Lebon* 701. It may be applied against a so-called 'acte détachable du contrat', see infra or if it is asked by the State representative against a local contract.
27. See infra.

curement rules and among them, only if the alleged breach has harmed or is likely to have harmed the claimant).

It must be added that exists a specific interim relied in the hand of the State representative against local public contract which does not require an emergency. Moreover, when applied within a period of 10 days following the reception of the contract, such a claim has an automatic suspension effect.[28]

2.2.2 'Référé provision'

Article R 541-1 of the *Code de justice administrative*, provides that a claimant can go before a single judge directly, asking him to recognize that the pecuniary loss he has suffered because of the loss of a chance to be awarded the contract is 'not seriously debatable' and to grant him an interim payment.[29] This interim payment cannot exceed the limits of the 'not seriously debatable part' of the loss. There is no need for a main damages claim before a court to make a '*référé-provision*'.

3 Stand-Still Provisions

Under article 80 of the *Code des Marchés publics*, the standstill period is only one day longer than required by the article 2.4 of the 2007/66 directive, either when the contract award decision is sent to the tenderers concerned by electronic means or, when other means of communication are used. Under article 80, in the former case, the standstill period is 11 days (instead of ten) and in the latter, the period is 16 days (instead of 15). This difference is only apparent since the starting date is the day of the sending ('envoi de la notification') and not the day 'following the date on which the contract award decision is sent to the tenderers and candidates concerned' as put by the directive in its article 2.

Interestingly, there is no 'spillover effect' since this standstill period applies only to public procurement contracts within the scope of the EU directive on public contracts. However, several lower courts have decided that there must be a reasonable period of time between the award decision and the signing of those contracts outside the scope of the EU directive (below the

28. CE 3 march 2006, Société François-Charles Obterhur Fiduciaire, n° 287960.
29. Art. R. 541-1 CJA: «*le juge des référés peut, même en l'absence d'une demande au fond, accorder une provision au créancier qui l'a saisi lorsque l'existence de l'obligation n'est pas sérieusement contestable.*»

threshold or public contracts for services of Annex II.B of the 2004/18 directive) but the Council of States has now ruled out the cases.[30]

This standstill period was already in place prior to the ordinance of 2009 since 2004 but with a shorter period (10 days).[31] In 2006, the new public procurement contract code added that this period could be reduced in case of emergency. This reference to emergency has disappeared with the implementation of directive 2007/66 and been replaced by the exceptions provided by this directive (article 2): '(a) if Directive 2004/18/EC does not require prior publication of a contract notice in the Official Journal of the European Union; (b) if the only tenderer concerned within the meaning of Article 2a(2) of this Directive is the one who is awarded the contract and there are no candidates concerned; (c) in the case of a contract based on a framework agreement as provided for in Article 32 of Directive 2004/18/EC and in the case of a specific contract based on a dynamic purchasing system as provided for in Article 33 of that Directive.'

The question of what information shall be given is a sensitive one. The directive simply requires 'a summary of the relevant reasons as set out in Article 41(2) of Directive 2004/18/EC, subject to the provisions of Article 41(3) of that Directive, and a precise statement of the exact standstill period applicable pursuant to the provisions of national law transposing this paragraph'. Although the second requirement has been transposed into French law with no difficulties, the French public procurement code sets a limitation to the first one: 'The person in charge of the contract cannot provide information if its disclosure: a) Would be contrary to the law, b) Would be contrary to the public interest; c) Could prejudice fair competition between companies.'

Prior to the implementation of directive 2007/66 there existed a fourth exception when such disclosure 'would prejudice companies' legitimate commercial interests'. It is presumed that such a limitation might be deemed as contrary to EU requirements.

30. 29 Bis CE, 19 Janvier 2011, n° 343435.
31. Article 76 public procurement contract code 2004, available in English on www.legifrance.gouv.fr: 'Once it has made its choice concerning the applications or bids, the public entity informs all the other bidders of the rejection of their applications or bids. At least ten days must elapse between the date on which the bidders whose bids were selected are informed of the decision and the date on which the contract is signed.'

4 Establishment of a Breach

In this section, we will mainly deal with breaches leading to interim measures under the '*référé précontractuel*' procedure. It must be noted that the number of action is pretty high in France. According to a study made by the OECD in 2007, around 4000 cases a year deals with the making of public contracts – most of them through a 'référé précontractuel' with a success rate of 53 %.[32] There are no more recent statistics but this rate is very likely to have decreased since the SMIRGEOMES case which impose the claimant to prove they have been harmed by the alleged breach.

4.1 Illegality within the Invitation to Tender

4.1.1 Illegality in the choice of the tendering procedure

The awarding authority is required to use the appropriate procedure provided by the *Code des marchés publics*. If the awarding authority does not, e.g. because they have considered the contract was not among those concerned by the requirement of publicity and competition[33] or because having been regarded as a contract subject to publicity and competition requirements, the requirements have still been infringed, invitation to tender will be regarded as illegal.[34]

4.1.2 Illegality of the splitting of the contracts

When the awarding authority is willing to split an 'operation' into different public contracts, this will be enough to render the invitations to tender illegal.[35]

This must not be confused with the new requirements of the article 10 of the *Code des Marchés publics*, prescribing that there a duty to split the public contracts in lots, as in such case the amount to be compared to the threshold is the amount of the total of the lots. This requirement is also controlled by the judge in a 'référé précontractuel' as it is deemed to favour the competition between firms, although this duty is not imposed by the EU directives.

32. http://www.oecd-ilibrary.org/fr/governance/public-procurement-review-and-remedies-systems-in-the-european-union_5kml60q9vklten;jsessionid=iwp3l72wk6ea.delta
33. CE, Ass., 10 June 1994, *Commune de Cabourg*, n° 141633, *Lebon* 300.
34. CE, 8 July 2005, *Communauté d'agglomération de Moulins*, n° 268610.
35. CE, 8 february 1999, Syndicat des eaux de la Gatine, n°156333.

4.1.3 Illegality in the technical specifications

When the technical specifications go beyond the needs of the awarding authority, they may be regarded as being intentionally mentioned in order to prevent companies from bidding, the invitation to tender is illegal.[36]

4.1.4 Illegality in the publicity document

When the specifications included in the publicity document are not sufficient to properly inform the bidders, the invitation to tender will also be held illegal.[37]

4.1.5 Illegality in indication of the relevant criteria used for the choice of a bid

Article 53 of the *Code des Marchés publics* provides that the awarding authority has to choose the 'most economically advantageous' tender. The article also provides a list or criteria to be a applied to determine which of the tenders is the 'most economically advantageous', among which: '*the operating costs, the bid's technical merit, its innovative nature, its environmental friendliness, its performance in terms of occupational integration of populations in difficulty, the time for completion, its esthetic and functional features, after-sales service and technical support, the delivery time and date, and the price of the provisions*'. When it appears that an award criterion has not a sufficient link with the subject matter of the contract, such as a 'social' criterie, the invitation to tender is illegal.[38] The case law is also very demanding regarding the transparency of the award criteria: a subjective award criterion must be complemented by 'subcriteria'; i.e. by sufficient information regarding the way contracting authorities will apply this criterion, such as the esthetical and functional criterion.[39] Moreover, any use of subcriteria must be rendered public to the candidates.

4.2 Illegalities Related to the Treatment of Candidates

4.2.1 Illegality in the admittance of bids

Any illegality in the way the awarding authority has not admitted some tenderers to bid for the awarding of the contract will vitiate the awarding procedure, which is the case if a firm is automatically excluded as having taken

36. CE, Sect., 3 November 1995, *District de l'agglomération nancéienne*, n° 152484, *Lebon* 391.
37. CE, 10 February 1997, *OPAC du Puy-de-Dôme et du Massif central*, n° 167569.
38. CE, 25 July 2001, *Commune de Gravelines*, n° 229666, *Lebon* 391.
39. CE, 28 April 2006, Ville de Toulouse, n° 280197

part in the definition of the public contract.[40] The judge always checks if the motives of the authority in refusing to allow a tenderer to bid are relevant regarding the general rules of public procurement law.[41]

4.2.2 Breach of the principle of equal treatment between candidates
The most common example is the fact that changing the documents included in the invitation to tender in a way which does not enable the bidders to have the same time to prepare their tenders is a breach of the principle of equal treatment.[42]

4.2.3 Illegality in the rejection of a bid
Under article 80 of the *Code des marchés publics*, for all the rejected bids, the awarding authority has to inform the bidders their offer has been rejected and give them the reasons of the rejection. Then, during the standstill period starting with the information of the rejection of offers, the bidders may apply for '*référé précontractuel*'. Therefore, any infringement of the information of unsuccessful tenderers will be vitiating the awarding procedure.[43]

5 Annulment/Set Aside of Award Decisions

As it has been earlier stated, it is possible to seek annulment of the award decision with the 'référé précontractuel' which is also an interlocutory procedure. However, this section will only deal with annulment sought with claims on the merits of the cases.

Opposite to interlocutory procedures dedicated to public contracts, originating from EU law, the two claims on the merit of the case aiming to annul an award decision originate in French national law. None of them comes from EU law. One of them have been created by the *Conseil d'Etat* (in the

40. CE, 29 July 1998, *Ministre de la Justice, garde des Sceaux c/ Société Genicorp*, n° 177952.
41. CE, 6 November 1998, *Assistance publique des hôpitaux de Marseille*, n° 194960.
42. CE, 9 February 2004, *Communauté urbaine de Nantes*, n° 259369: the awarding authority has changed the documents 11 days prior to the deadline to tender.
43. CE, 21 January 2004, *Société Aquitaine Démolition*, n° 253509: the motives for rejecting the offer have not been specified within the communication of the decision to reject the bid.

Martin case),[44] whereas the second one has been created by statute law: the '*déféré préfectoral*', reserved for the Prefect, has been created by an Act of Parliament in 1982.[45] These two remedies must not be confused with a special remedy created in 2007 by the Conseil d'Etat in the '*Tropic travaux*' case,[46] creating the 'claim on the validity of the contract' (see below the section on ineffectiveness).

5.1 The Recours pour Exces de Pouvoir Against a Detachable Act

The '*recours pour excès de pouvoir*' against an '*acte détachable du contrat*'[47] is a long known possibility[48] for any claimant who meets the classical *locus standi* applicable to the *recours pour excès de pouvoir*[49] which is widely interpreted as giving standing for action to taxp payers or environmental societies for example. The substance of the so-called '*acte détachable du contrat*' theory is to consider that any administrative decision enacted in the contract making process may be regarded as separable from the contract, and consequently, as any administrative unilateral act, it is challengeable through the *recours pour excès de pouvoir*. Once the judge has annulled a decision separable from the contract, he may, if he considers the annulled decision was mandatory for the legality of the contract, pronounce an injunction towards the parties, asking them to go before the 'judge of the contract' (who might not be the same than the first judge) to ask him to pronounce the voidance of the contract (see below the section on ineffectiveness).

Here, a distinction has to be made between unsuccessful bidders and all the other potential claimants. Since, the *Tropic travaux* case, the former can only apply for *recours pour excès de pouvoir* before the contract has been signed, whilst the later may use this procedure during the tendering procedure as well as once the contract has been signed. Indeed, French administrative law applies the rule of '*exception de recours parallèle*', stating that when there is an available procedure to make a claim on a matter which is normally

44. CE, 4 août 1905, *Martin*, *Lebon* 749, G.Braibant, P. Delvolvé, B.Genevois, M. Long, P.Weil, *Les Grands arrêts de la jurisprudence administrative*, Dalloz, 2007, n° 16, 94.
45. *Loi n° 82-213 du 2 mars 1982 relative aux droits et libertés des communes, des départements et des régions.*
46. CE, Ass., 16 July2007, *Tropic travaux signalisation Guadeloupe*, RFDA 2007. 696, concl. D. Casas; RFDA 2007. 923, note D. Pouyaud.
47. This phrase could be translated by 'a decision separable from the contract'.
48. CE, 4 août 1905, *Martin, op. cit.*
49. The decision must harm the interest of the claimant as far as he is in a particular situation regarding the decision.

excluded from '*recours pour excès de pouvoir*', the claimant has to use this particular procedure and not a '*recours pour excès de pouvoir* against an *acte détachable*'.[50] Thank to the creation of the '*recours en contestation de validité du contrat*' in the *Tropic travaux* case (see below), unsuccessful bidders have now on a special claim to seek *inter alia* annulment of the contract once it has been signed. Therefore, under the '*exception de recours parallèle*' doctrine, they cannot use the '*recours pour excès de pouvoir*' against detachable act anymore. All the other potential claimants who are excluded from the '*recours en contestation de validité du contrat*' may still use the '*recours pour excès de pouvoir*' against an '*acte détachable*' because this is the only main claim they have against the contract once it has been signed.

Referred to the judge by an unsuccessful tendered or any other claimant, the '*recours pour excès de pouvoir*' against an '*acte détachable*' must always be made within two months after the contested decision has been taken.

The contested unilateral act may be, for instance, the final awarding decision or the decision to make a contract itself, voted by the assembly of a local authority and materialized by the signing of the contract.

5.2 The Defere Prefectoral

To counterbalance the fact that the *loi n° 82-213 du 2 mars 1982 relative aux droits et libertés des communes, des départements et des régions* gives more rights and freedoms to local authorities, who are not under the admnistrative supervision of the Prefect[51] anymore, the Act provides that local authorities must send most of their acts – either unilateral of contractual – to the Prefect, to enable him to check le legalty of the acts.[52] If the Prefect estimates that a detachable act or a public procurement contract[53] is *ultra vires*, he may, under the *loi n° 82-213 du 2 mars 1982*, use a particular claim for which he is the only one to meet the standings: the so called '*déféré préfectoral*'.[54] This claim looks like the '*recours pour excès de pouvoir*'[55] in that it aims to annul

50. On this question Cf. R. Chapus, *Droit du contentieux administratif,* 13th Edition, Monchrestien, 2008, 702-703.
51. The Prefect represents the State in each *départments.*
52. *Code Général des Collectivités Territoriales (CGCT),* Article L 2131-1.
53. Under Article L 2131-2, 4°of the *CGCT,* only the public procurement contract must be send to the Prefect but in the *Département de la Sarthe* case, the *Conseil d'Etat* held that all the contracts made by local authorities must be sent to the Prefect (CE, 4 november 1994, *Département de la Sarthe, Lebon* 801).
54. *CGCT,* Article L 2131-6.
55. CE, Sect., 26 July 1991, *Commune de Sainte-Marie, AJDA* 1991, 693, chron. C. Maugüe & R. Scwartz.

an *ultra vires* administrative decision, but notwithstanding *locus standi*, the main difference between the two claims is that the '*déféré préfectoral*' may be directed not only against a detachable act but also against a contract, whereas the '*recours pour excès de pouvoir*' may not be directed again a contract.[56]

6 Ineffectiveness of the Contract and Alternative Penalties

Ineffectiveness was already in place before the implementation of the 2007/66 directive thanks to two remedies that differs from each other because of the third party involved. Then the implementation of the 2007/66 directive led to the introduction of a third way to ineffectiveness. We must recall in addition the possibility for the Prefect to ask for the annulment of a local public contract directly but this will not be dealt with in this section as it is pretty rarely used.

6.1 The Domestic Remedies Leading to Ineffectiveness

– The consequences of the annulment of the detachable act upon the contract

Once the detachable act is declared void, it does not follow that the contract will be declared void. In fact, for decades, the annulment of the detachable act had no real effect on the contract, a situation called in the beginning of the XXth century the 'platonic effect of the annulment of the detachable act' by Romieu. The only consequence would have been if one party of the contract was willing to get rid of the contract (for instance, if it appears as economically disadvantageous), he could then ask the 'judge of the contract' to declare contract void as a consequence of the annulment of the detachable act. But there was not remedy opened to third parties against the contract. The situation has changed with two statute laws of 1980 and 1995 which have as their object the implementation of judgments of administrative courts. Since then, a third party who has obtained the annulment of a detachable act can ask the judge the detachable act (at the same time it asks for the annulment or latter on) to give an order to the contracting authority to cease the 'judge of the contract'. The judge in charge of the annulment of the detachable act will only give such an injunction if the request meets three conditions. In short, the success of the action depends on the importance of the detachable act, the

56. See above the '*acte détachable*' doctrine.

gravity of the breach and the general interest in maintaining the contract.[57] In a recent case, the Conseil d'Etat has held that the judge of the voidance of the contract must comply with the decision of the judge of detachable act.[58] This remedy still applies for third parties who are not considered as 'rejected competitors' in the meaning of the Tropic case law (see below).

Annulments of the contract always have an *ex tunc* effect. Therefore, once annulment has been pronounced, the contract is not binding anymore and is reputed not having ever been binding. Thus, parties cannot take advantage of the contractual provisions,[59] nor can they seek performance of the contract before the judge,[60] no more than seeking compensation in triggering the other party's contractual liability.[61] This situation might therefore be particularly harsh for the parties, especially for the private contractor having had expenses in starting to perform the contract. However, they can gain compensation of the useful expenses by application of the 'enrichissement sans cause' theory but not for the lost profits, unless they prove the illegality is a fault by the public authority and that they could not be aware of the illegality (see below the section on damages).[62]

– The 'claim on the validity of the contract' or 'Tropic travaux' claim

The 'claim on the validity of the contract' originates from case law.[63] The *Conseil d'Etat* has created this claim in 2007 in the *Tropic travaux signalisation Guadeloupe* case.[64] This claim is only open to unsuccessful bidders of an awarding procedure requiring publicity and competition. It has to be brought before the judge within two months after the publicity of the signature of the contract.

To settle a litigation which has given rise to a '*Tropic travaux*' claim, the court has the power to annul partially or totally the contract, or to terminate it with no retroactive effect, or to delete illegal clauses or to grant damages to the claimant. The possibility to the benefit of a third party to seek direct an-

57. CE 10 December 2003, Institut recherches pour le développement, n° 248950, CE 21 Feb. 2011, n° 337349.
58. CE, 9 April 2010, *Commune de Levallois-Perret*, n° 309480.
59. CE, Sect., 13 July1961, *Société d'Entrprises générales des travaux publics pour la France et les colonies*, *Lebon* 473.
60. CE, 13 October 1972, *SA Banque Le Crédit du Nord et OPHLM du Calvados*, *Lebon* 630.
61. CE, 29 January1982, *Martin*, *Lebon* 44; CE, Sect., 2000, *Citécâble Est*, n° 196553.
62. CE 10 April 2008, Société Jean-Claude Decaux, n° 244950.
63. '*Recours en validité du contrat*'.
64. CE, Ass., 16 July2007, *Tropic travaux signalisation Guadeloupe*, *op. cit.*

nulment of a public procurement contract was absolutely new at the time when *Tropic travaux* was settled. Until then, only the parties had possibility to make an direct action for voidance of the public procurement contract, with the exception of the Prefect.]

The kinds of breaches likely to give rise to a 'claim on the validity of the contract' are pretty numerous. Not only can the claimant apply for a Tropic travaux claim for a breach of the tendering rules, but he also can apply for this claim for the incompetency of the authority having allowed the signature of the contract or having signed the contract, for the illegality of the subject-matter of the contract or of some of its clauses, and so forth. In the Tropic travaux case, the alleged breach of law was an abuse of power of the awarding authority. According to the claimant, the reason why the authority decided to make a contract was not to satisfy its needs but to increase the activity of a particular company.

6.2 The 'European' Remedy Leading to Ineffectiveness: The 'Référé' Contractuel

Once the contract has been signed, unsuccessful bidders cannot apply for a '*référé-précontractuel*' anymore. There is still an actionable interlocutory procedure though: the so-called '*référé contractuel*'. This procedure originates from the Law of 7 May 7, 2009 (N°2009-515), implementing the Council Directive 2007/66/CE. As the '*référé-précontractuel*', it aims to sanction infringements of the duties of publicity and competition during the tendering procedure. Moreover, in line with the requirements of the Council Directive 2007/66/CE, which imposes a 10 days or 15 days standstill period, the '*référé-contractuel*' enables the unsuccessful tenderers to have a claim when the awarding authority has signed the contract in breach of the standstill period.

However, the '*référé-contractuel*' shall not be regarded as a procedural alternative to '*référé-précontractuel*'. Indeed, the prior use of a 'référé précontractuel' is in principle a cause of rejection of a 'référé contractuel' and furthermore the case law now shows that in the absence of a 'référé précontractuel', the 'référé contractuel' can only be used when specific circumstances happened.[65] The purpose of this particular interlocutory procedure is actually to enable the claimant to have a claim when infringements of the awarding authority would preclude him from efficiently using the '*référé-précontractuel*' procedure. Therefore there are only limited hypotheses in which

65. CE 19 january 2011, Grand Port autonome du Havre, n° 343435.

it is possible for a claimant to have a claim under '*référé contractuel*' procedure: (a) when no publicity was made illegally or when the publicity at the OJEU has been illegally omitted; (b) when the public contract following a framework agreement has breached the initial competitive rules of the framework agreement; (c)when the awarding authority has signed the contract in breach of the 11 (or 16) days stand still period; (d) when the awarding authority has not complied with the automatic suspension of the procedure applying when a '*référé-précontractuel*' is referred to the judge or when they have not complied with the injunctions made by the judge of the 'référé précontractuel'. As a consequence, in all the cases in which the claimant has been precluded by the awarding authority's behaviour to efficiently use the '*référé précontractuel*', the '*référé contractuel*' procedure will not open. In other words, the French law has not extend the référé contractuel above the cases set by the EU directive. The only 'spill over' effect lies in the fact that this référé can be used for public procurement contract below the thresholds, as shown in the first case ruled by the Conseil d'Etat.[66]

E.g., if a bidder applies for a '*référé précontractuel*' ignoring that his bid has actually been unsuccessful because the awarding authority has not informed him of the dismissal of the bid and has signed the contract, his application for a forthcoming 'référé-contractuel' will nonetheless be allowed.[67] This case law shows a flexible approach of the Conseil d'Etat as it follows from it that under certain circumstances, a 'référé précontractuel' can be transformed into a 'référé contractuel' without bringing a new action.

In practise, although there have been cases before judges of the administrative courts of first instance ('tribunaux administratifs'), the restrictive approach of the 'référé contractuel', which is reserved to main violation following the EU directive conception, will certainly lead to a limited number of cases.

Scope of the judge's powers

Suspension of the performance of the contract

Under Article L. 551-17 of the *Code de justice administrative*, the '*référé-contractuel*' judge can pronounce a stay of the performance of the contract, for the duration of the proceedings, unless the harmful consequences of such a stay would be excessive considering the interests likely to be harmed (especially the public interest).

66. Ibid.
67. CE, 10 November 2010, *France AGRIMER*, n° 340944.

Annulment or cancellation of the contract (Implementation of article 2(5) of the Council Directive 2007/66/CE)

Under Articles L. 551-18 of the *Code de justice administrative*, the judge must annul the contract when no publicity required by the tendering procedure has been made or when there has been no publicity in the Official Journal of the European Union, whereas the publicity was mandatory. Likewise, the judge must annul the contract the awarding authority has infringed the competition requirements for the making of contracts originating from framework agreement or dynamic purchasing system. Articles L. 551-18 also provide that the judge must annul the contract when it has been signed before the end of the stand-still period or in violation of the automatic suspension effect of a 'référé précontractuel',[68] if two other requirements are met: the violation of must have deprived the claimant to use a '*référé-précontractuel*' and the publicity and competition duties within the awarding procedure has been breached in a manner that jeopardizes the chances of the claimant to be awarded the contract. It is not yet sure whether the latter condition will be identical to the 'loss of a chance' theory used when damages and compensation for the loss of expected profits is concerned (see below the section on damages). Interestingly, the Conseil d'Etat rules that the référé contractuel can be used in the case of public contract that are outside the scope of the EU directives, although there cannot be a violation of the standstill period as there aren't any.[69]

In those cases, the annulment is in principle compulsory, i.e. there is no margin of discretion for the judge,. unless there is a 'compelling motive of public interest'[70] at stake which allows an alternative penalty (see below). This can be explained by the fact that the consequences of annulment are sometimes more harmful for the public interests at stake than alternative measures such as termination. Indeed, the former has an *ex tunc* effect, whereas the latter only has an *ex nunc* effect.

68. *Code de justice administrative*, art. L 551-9.
69. CE 19 january 2011, Grand Port autonome du Havre, n° 343435.
70. '*Raison impérieuse d'intérêt général*'. Article L 551-19 specifies that an economic interest can be taken into account in the scope of the public interest if one out of the two requirements is met: the annulment of the contract entails disproportionate consequences and the economic interest at stake is not directly related to the contract, or the contract is a contract giving the economic operator the performance of a public service (e.g. a concession contract).

Alternative penalties

When the annulment of the contract because of a violation of the stand-still period or of the automatic suspension of the 'référé précontractuel' would come up against a 'compelling motive of public interest', or when one of the two last conditions set in article L 551-18 is not met, articles L. 551-19 and L. 551-20 provide that the judge can either annul or terminate (for the future) the contract, reduce its length or pronounce pecuniary penalties against the awarding authority. The two latter remedies are brand new in French administrative law and the latter can lead to consideration when the public authority at stake is the State. It is likely that in this case, as the penalties will be paid to the Treasury, this will not be a good incentive for the Ministers to strictly follow the public procurement rules.

Measures spontaneously decided by the judge

The above-mentioned measures may be pronounced spontaneously by the judge, meaning even if the claimant has not asked for,[71] providing that the claimant has at least asked for one of the remedies available. In such a case however, the persons concerned must be asked to make any observation before the judge's decision, as it is also the case for the 'référé précontractuel'.

Restrictions: No 'référé contractuel' against a contract which is excluded from the publicity and competition duties

According to the article L 551-15 of the Code de justice administrative, 'the claim [of référé contractual] cannot be used towards the contracts whose tendering procedure is not subject to publicity and competition duties, provided that the awarding authority has, before the signature of the contract, communicated to the public his intention to sign the contract, and observed an 11 days stand-still period starting from the communication'.

7 Damages

In order to trigger the awarding authority's extra-contractual liability, as well as to trigger any public body's extra-contractual liability, the claim is called 'recours indemnitaire'. This kind of claim is included in a broader kind of procedure called 'the recours de plein contentieux'. This kind of procedure is typical from the French sharing of administrave law contentious procedures

71. *Code de justice administrative*, art. L 521-21.

in two parts. One part aims to review decisions of public bodies and to annul ultra-vires unilateral administrative acts: 'recours pour excès de pouvoir'. The other part aims to enable citizens or corporates to have claims in order to defend rights attached to their person and harmed by the activity of a public body: 'the recours de plein contentieux'. As it has been earlier stated, in a 'recours indemnitaire', any claimant may try to trigger the awarding authority's extra-contractual liability by proving a loss, a fault committed by the awarding authority, and a causal link between them. No particular other conditions have to be met.

7.1 A Traditional Action in Tort

French law has not waited for the review directive of 1989 to allow for damages in case of breach of public procurement rules. Indeed, the possibilities are quite wide opened when one compares to other jurisdictions.[72] Moreover, the possibility suggested by article 2(6) of the Directive 2007/66 EC that the Member States may provide that when 'damages are claimed on the grounds that a decision was taken unlawfully, the contested decision must be first set aside by a body having the necessary powers'[73] has not been implemented in French law. In administrative law, damages are never subject to any set aside of a decision by an administrative court.

In case of infringements in the procedure for the award of a public procurement contract, the rules governing the award of damages are the same as those applicable generally for the liability of public authorities before an administrative court. Here the liability is an extra-contractual one, since the contractual liability only applies to the contracting parties. Thus, the damages claim sought by the claimant is a remedy in tort, not in contract. Indeed, the rules governing the liability of public authorities apply each time a public body commits a fault harming someone, including in infringing tendering procedure requirements, and any illegality is a fault. The harmed citizen or corporate may trigger the liability of the public authority, in proving that the public body has committed a fault consisting in a breach of the awarding procedure, and that there is a causal link between the fault and the loss,[74] the loss being the loss of a chance of being awarded the contract. The extent of the

72. See in particular PPLR 2006 n°4 and the forthcoming book of D. Fairgrieve and F. Lichere (eds), 'Damages as an effective remedy', Hart, to be published in 2011.
73. Council Directive 2007/66 EC, article 2(6).
74. N. Gabayet, 'Damages as an Effective Remedy: A French Perspective', in D. Fairgrieve and F. Lichére (eds), 'Damages as an effective remedy', Hart, to be published in 2011.

compensation depends on the probability of a successful outcome in the tender. According to case law, there are three degrees of probability:[75] the bidder had no chance to win the contract; the bidder 'would not have been devoid of a chance to win the contract'; the bidder had a serious chance to win the contract. If he can prove that had the procedure been lawful, and he would have had a serious chance of winning the contract, the claimant will be awarded compensation recovering the loss of potential profit.[76] If he can only prove that 'he would not have been devoid of a chance to win the contract', he will be compensated only for the loss of bid costs. Obviously, if he is unable to prove, at the very least, that had the procedure been lawful, he 'would not have been devoid of a chance of winning the contract', no compensation will be granted.[77] This claim aiming to trigger awarding authorities' extra-contractual liability must be referred to a judge within four years starting on 1 January following the date on which they have become aware of the loss.

Although no statistics exist in this regard, there have been several cases dealing with this issue. It is remarkable that the courts grant damages quite often for the bid costs and not rarely for loss of profits.

7.2 The Claim of 'Objection on the Validity of the Contract

This claim, belonging to the category of 'the recours de plein contentieux', originates from the *Tropic travaux'* case. Opposite to the traditional and single 'recours indemnitaire', this claim is not only dedicated to compensation. The claimant may seek annulment too as we have seen already. But it then must act within 2 months following the publicity of the contract regarding the annulment and 4 years regarding demages.

75. CE, 18 June 2003, *Groupement d'entreprises solidaires ETPO Guadeloupe, Sté. Biwater, Sté. Aqua TP*, *AJDA* 2003, 1676; CE, 11 September 2006, *Commune de Saran*, req. n° 257545; CE, 29 December 2006, *Sté. Bertele SNC*, req. n° 273783: '*When a tendering company claims compensation for the loss resulting from its unlawful eviction from the tendering procedure, it is up to the judge to check whether the company was devoid of any chance to win the contract or not; if the company was devoid of any chance, then it will not have any right to compensation; if the company was not devoid of any chance to win the contract, it should have a right to compensation for the bid costs; then the judge has to check if the company had a serious chance to be awarded the contract. Should it be so, the company has a right to compensation for the loss of profit, necessarily including the bid costs, which would then not to be compensated separately, unless it is otherwise provided by the contract*'.
76. CE, 13 May 1970, *Monti*, req. n° 74601, *Lebon* 322; CE, 21 November 2001, *SA Quillery*, req. n° 21822; CE, 27 January 2006, *Ville d'Amiens*, *CP-ACCP* mars 2006, 62, concl. N. Boulouis.
77. CE, 30 June 1999, *Sarfati*, n° 193925.

7.3 Unjust Enrichment

Once a contract has been declared void, the contractor is allowed to try to trigger the extra-contractual liability of the contracting public body, to seek damages for unjust enrichment.

This public law claim is although slightly different from the classical *de in rem verso* claim existing in French private law and inspired by Roman law. Before the administrative judge, the claim is available even when a contract has existed, although in private law, it is only available when there have never been any contract between the person whose patrimony has been impoverished and the person whose patrimony has been enriched. This may then be named a special 'administrative law unjust enrichment doctrine'.[78] This may be explain by the 'lack of cause' doctrine[79] (the Roman law concept of 'causa' being somehow quite close to the Common law 'consideration' doctrine). Indeed, one party has started to perform the contract whereas the other has not and therefore, the performance by the former has no counterpart.

One main requirement has to be satisfied to apply the administrative law *de in rem verso* claim: the debtor's (the contracting public body) enrichment by the delivery from the creditor must benefit the public interest.[80]

8 Articulation of Claims

Claimants can seek annulment of awarding decisions and compensation through several claims. Not only those claims may be used together, but they can even go with interim reliefs (which may themselves be used together), making the whole scope of claims on public contracts in French law a tremendously complicated topic.

8.1 Claim on the Merits of the Case: Annulment with Compensation

8.1.1 Annulment with annulment

Combination of both claims on the merits of the case seeking annulment ('*Tropic travaux*' with a '*recours pour excès de pouvoir*') is not possible in the same time by the same claimants. Indeed, on the one hand, before the

78. D. Pouyaud, *La nullité des contrats administratifs*, LGDJ, 1991, 492.
79. Théorie de l'absence de cause. On this topic, see more generally F. Lombard, *La cause dans le contrat administratif*, Dalloz, Nouvelle bibliothèque des thèses, 2008.
80. CE, 19 April 1860, *Commune de Gonnord*, Lebon 338; CE, Sect., 2000, *Citécâble Est*, n°196553.

contract has been signed, all the claimants, including the tenderers, can seek annulment of a detachable act through a '*recours pour excès de pouvoir*'. On the other hand, once the contract has been signed, due to the 'Parallel remedy theory' ('exception de recours parallèle'), unsuccessful bidders do not have access to the '*recours pour excès de pouvoir*' anymore. The only claim on the merits of the case to seek annulment they have access to is a '*recours en contestation de validité du contrat*' (Tropic travaux claim), whereas the other claimants proving a sufficient interest have access to '*recours pour excès de pouvoir*' but not to the *Tropic travaux* claim. As a consequence, a bidder can make a '*recours pour excès de pouvoir*' against an '*acte détachable*' before the contract has been signed, and a *Tropic Travaux* claim after it has been signed but then the 'recours pour excès de pouvoir' is automatically rejected.

8.1.2 Annulment with Compensation

8.1.2.1 Annulment with compensation through Tropic travaux claim

In the case of the '*recours en contestation de validité du contrat*', it is not really an articulation of claims in that there would be two distinct procedures. With a single procedure dealing with the merits of the case, the unsuccessful bidder can both seek annulment of the contract and compensation for his loss due to the unlawful awarding procedure but the judge would choose either one or the other.

8.1.3 Annulment with compensation through a recours pour excès de pouvoir with a claim on extra-contractual liability

Before the contract has been signed, all the claimants including the bidders can make both a '*recours pour excès de pouvoir*' against a decision separable from the contract and a claim on extra contractual liability against the awarding authority. If the judge, within the '*excès de pouvoir*' procedure, settle the case in stating that the public authority has taken an *ultra vires* decision in the contractual making process, the fact that the awarding authority has taken the unlawful decision will be regarded by the judge ruling the claim on liability as a fault. And if the award decision is annulled, it does not preclude from a claim on damages.[81]

Once the contract has been signed, only the claimants who did not bid for the award of the contract will be allowed to make a '*recours pour excès de*

81. CAA Nancy, 1er février 2007, n° 04NC01114. In this case, the court however refused to grant damages because the claimant had not a serious chance to win the contract.

pouvoir' with, possibly, a claim on extra contractual liability against the awarding authority.

8.2 Articulation of Interlocutory Procedures (Référés)

Since '*référé-provision*' can go with any other procedure, it is not worth mentioning it for the articulation of each kind of claim.

8.2.1 'Référé précontractuel' with 'référé contractuel'

As already mentioned, when the claimant has already made an application for '*référé-précontractuel*' before the contract has been signed and has been unsuccessful with his claim, he will not be allowed to apply for '*référé-contractuel*'. There are only two possibilities for the claimant to be allowed to apply for '*référé-contractuel*' after he has used '*référé-précontractuel*': when they have signed the contract before the judgment, i.e. by violating the automatic suspension effect or when, the awarding authority has not complied with the requirements of the judges (or contested) decision.

8.2.2 'Référé précontractuel' with 'référé suspension'

Illegalities that may be brought before the judge are not the same under '*référé précontractuel*' and under '*référé suspension*'. Under the former, the claimant may only bring illegalities of the publicity and competition requirements of the tendering procedure and moreover only illegalities likely to have harmed the claimant as we have seen with the SMIRGEOMES case, whereas under the latter, any illegality may be brought. To have good chances to have the contract suspended, the claimant should then use both, which however requires the evidence of an emergency.

There are three hypotheses in which claimants may use both '*référé précontractuel*' and '*référé suspension*'. Two out of the three hypotheses apply after the contract has been signed, whereas one applies before.

As it has been earlier specified, '*référé suspension*' is only actionable when in the same time, a claim on annulment on the merits of the case (seeking '*recours pour excès de pouvoir*' against a separable decision or a claim on the validity of the contract) has been referred to the court, whereas '*référé précontractuel*' procedure may be used on its own, prior to the signature of the contract. Before the contract has been signed, any claimant who has an interest in signing the contract can apply for '*référé précontractuel*' and in the same time, for a '*recours pour excès de pouvoir*' against a decision separable from the contract, together with the '*référé suspension*' of the contentious decision.

Another possibility is that a bidder had applied for '*référé précontractuel*' before the contract has been signed and because the claim has been rejected or because the awarding authority has refused to comply with '*référé précontractuel*' judge's orders or because they have signed the contract during the suspension period entailed by the '*référé précontractuel*', or simply because he realized there were grieves he had not noticed prior to the signature, the unsuccessful bidder can apply for a '*Tropic travaux*' claim, together with a '*référé suspension*'. This way, both '*interlocurory procedures*' do not apply in the same time: one is made before the signature of the contract ('*référé précontractuel*') and the other one after ('*référé suspension*').

The last hypothesis is when a claimant who had an interest to sign the contract (but did not or could not make it) applies for '*référé précontractuel*' and once the contract has been signed, he applies for '*recours pour excès de pouvoir*' against a decision separable from the contract, together with the '*référé suspension*' of the contentious decision. One again, the '*référé précontractuel*' has been applied for prior to the signature and '*référé suspension*' has been applied after the signature.

8.2.3 'Référé suspension' with 'référé contractuel'

Once again, due the nature of these two claims, the hypothesis in which the contract has been signed must be distinguished from the hypothesis in which it has not.

On the one hand, it is impossible to make both claims in the same time before the contract has been signed, because the '*référé contractuel*' is only available after the signature. However, there may well be a '*recours pour excès de pouvoir*' together with a '*référé suspension*' prior to the signature of the contract and a '*référé contractuel*' afterwards.

On the other hand, once the contract has been signed, the claimant can make both a '*référé contractuel*' and a '*Tropic travaux*' claim with a '*référé suspension*'.

8.3 Claim on the Merits of the Case with Interlocutory Procedure

It is sometimes mandatory to make a particular claim on the merits of the case to be allowed to apply for an interlocutory procedure but in most of the cases, interlocutory procedures are absolutely independent from claims on the merits of the case and there is therefore a scary number of possibilities of combination of a claim on the merits of the case with an interlocutory procedure.

8.3.1 When the claim on the merits of the case is a 'claim in contesting the validity of the contract' (Tropic travaux)

8.3.1.1 Tropic travaux with référé précontractuel

The matter of articulation between *Tropic travaux* and *référé précontractuel* may be relevant as far as the claimant is an unsuccessful bidder, since other claimants can never make a '*claim in contesting the validity of the contract*'.

The difference here, as it has already been stated above, between both claims is that the interlocutory procedure of *référé précontractuel* is only available before the contract as been signed, whereas the claim on the merits of the case of '*Tropic travaux*' is only available once the contract has been signed. Both claims can therefore never be used in the same time.

8.3.1.2 Tropic travaux with référé contractuel

Both claims have a lot of similarities. They have similarities on the claimants who are allowed to make a claim, about the time when it can be made, regarding the signature of the contract and on the purposes of the claim. This has led academics to consider the two claims as having a '*fratricidal struggle*'.[82] Indeed, both of them are open once the contract has been signed. Plus, the *locus standi* to make a *Tropic travaux* claim or a '*référé contractuel*' are very similar. On the one hand, *Tropic Travaux* is open to unsuccessful bidders and on the other, a *référé contractuel* is open to claimants having an interest in signing the contract and likely to be harmed by any infringement of the publicity and competition duties. These two categories of claimants are slightly the same, whereas le latter one seems broader than the category of unsuccessful bidders, since it can gather on the mean time unsuccessful bidders plus other economic operators who has not bid.

It is also worth comparing the powers of the *Tropic travaux* judge *with* those of the *référé contractuel* judge and kinds of illegalities which can be held before the judge. In '*référé contractuel*', only illegalities dealing with publicity and competition requirements can be held, whereas under '*Tropic Travaux*', the claimant may broadly hold any illegality likely to render unlawful the contract. The main similarity between the powers of the judge in both claims is that he may annul the contract *ex nunc* or *ex tunc*. The other powers of the judge or remedies are different. On the one hand, under *Tropic travaux*, the judge may decide that the contract should be implemented, de-

82. S. BRACONNIER, «L'autonomie contrastée du contentieux des contrats publics d'affaires», *RDP* 2010, n° 2, 327, at 342.

spite of an illegality and he award damages. On the other, the '*référé contractuel*' judge may suspend the contract and pronounce pecuniary penalties.

The choice between one out of the two claims will certainly depend, on the one hand, if the claimant seeks damages or if he only seeks annulment. It will also depend how quick he needs the proceedings to be. Proceedings under '*référé contractuel*' are supposed to be a quicker than proceedings under '*Tropic travaux*' (even if, the claimant may use '*référé suspension*' with '*Tropic travaux*'). However, the claimant does not have to choose one out of the two claims. Nothing precludes him to use both.

8.3.1.3 Tropic travaux with référé suspension

In the '*Tropic travaux*' case, the *Conseil d'Etat* explicitly provided that the 'claim on the validity of the contract' could go with a'*référé suspension*'. This way, the '*référé suspension*' judge can pronounce a suspension of the performance of the contract, until the court has settled the main litigation on the validity of the contract in case of emergency, when there is a serious doubt on the legality of the contract. As it has been mentioned above, the '*mariage*'[83] of, on the one hand, the '*référé suspension*', dealing by nature with administrative decisions and a claim on the validity of a contract does not seem pretty natural to a French lawyer. Some would even say it is a '*failure*'.[84] Indeed, cases in which the judge agreed to suspend the performance of a contract when the claimant applied for a '*référé suspension*' with a '*Tropic travaux*' claim are particularly rare.[85]

8.4 When the claim on the merits of the case is a '*recours pour excès de pouvoir*'

8.4.1 Recours pour excès de pouvoir against an 'acte détachable' with référé suspension

This is the *par excellence* hypothesis of articulation between a claim on the merits of the case and an interlocutory procedure. Indeed, under the Act of 30 June 2000 on the emergency procedures, the articulation with '*recours pour excès de pouvoir*' claims is mandatory to be allowed to apply for '*référé suspension*'.[86] The latter is always subordinate to the former. Therefore, any

83. G.BERTHON, '*La suspension juridictionnelle du contrat administratif entre 'référé suspension' et 'référé contractuel' '*, *RFDA* 2009. 1215, at1218.
84. G.BERTHON, *op. cit.* 1217.
85. See however CE 16 Novembre 2009, Cimade, n° 328826, where the emergency results in the need to respect a statute law.
86. *Code de justice administrative*, article L 521-1.

claimant allowed to apply for '*recours pour excès de pouvoir*'[87] against a decision separable from the contract will be allowed to apply for the interim suspension of the contentious unilateral act, provided that the conditions of emergency and of serious doubt on the legality of the act are satisfied.[88]

8.4.2 Recours pour excès de pouvoir against an 'acte détachable' with référé précontractuel

Prior to the signature of the contract, any claimant with a sufficient interest may apply for a '*recours pour excès de pouvoir*' against a decision separable from the contract, whereas only the claimants having an interest in signing the contract may apply for '*référé précontractuel*'. After the contract has been signed, the unsuccessful bidders cannot apply for '*recours pour excès de pouvoir*' against a decision separable from the contract anymore, due to the '*exception de recours parallèle*' doctrine.[89] Therefore, the only hypothesis of genuine combination of '*référé précontractuel*' and '*recours pour excès de pouvoir*' against a decision separable from the contract is the case in which the claimant has had an interest in signing the contract.

It also possible for a claimant who did not bid for the award of the contracts but who had an interest in signing the contract to apply for '*référé précontractuel*' prior to the signature of the contract and for '*recours pour excès de pouvoir*' against a decision separable from the contract once the contract has been signed.

8.4.3 Recours pour excès de pouvoir with référé contractuel

The question of the right of standings is the same here as it has been for the articulation between '*recours pour excès de pouvoir*' against an *'acte détachable'* with '*référé précontractuel*'. However, since the '*référé contractuel*' is only possible once the contract has been signed, the only possibility of simultaneous combination is the hypothesis in which the claimant had an interest in signing the contract and did not take part in the tendering procedure (he would otherwise not be allowed to apply for '*recours pour excès de pouvoir*' against an *'acte détachable'* since he has a reserved claim in contesting the validity of the contract).[90] This way, the claimant having an interest in signing the contract, who can only bring infringements of publicity and competition requirements within the '*référé contractuel*' procedure, may also bring

87. See above.
88. See above.
89. See above.
90. See above.

any other illegality within the '*recours pour excès de pouvoir*' against an '*acte détachable*' procedure. Plus, as it has already been emphasized, the recours pour excès de pouvoir may always go with '*référé suspension*'. Then if the tests to allow '*référé suspension*' are satisfied, the claimant will be able to obtain the suspension of a decision separable from the contract quicker than he would obtain the suspension of the contract through '*référé contractuel*'.

To conclude, these articulations and combinations of remedies are in theory numerous and, as we have seen, complex. In practice, it appears that a claimant usually uses one or the other but rarely several remedies. Indeed, the candidates and potential candidates tend to privilege the 'référé précontractuel', and to use the Tropic travaux claim and the référé suspension quite rarely as there are less efficient for the first one (because of alternative powers of the court) or more demanding for the second one (condition of emergency). The damages action is also less successful as there is a strong uncertainty as to whether the claimant will be reimbursed of the loss of his potential profits. Although there has already been case law regarding the new 'référé contractuel', it is unlikely that it will be very often used since it is only build to fight grave illegalities. The other third parties have fewer remedies available and tend to use the recours pour excès de pouvoir against a detachable act with no 'référé suspension'.

With so many remedies, not surprisingly, no alternative dispute resolution can be found regarding the award of public contract. There are reserved indeed to litigations related to the performance of a public contract.

The previous development clearly shows that the state of law could be simplified by limiting the remedies available to rejected bidders to the European ones and by easing the detachable act remedy for the other third parties. France has not take the opportunity to delete domestic remedies when transposing the EU review directives and this leads to a complex system and to a lack of harmonization with other European countries. Indeed EU law has not had a complete effect of harmonization when it comes to remedies, despite the two EU review directives of 1989 and 2007, and this can be explain both by the relative brevity of the directive and also by the reluctance to regulate deeply because of the procedural autonomy principle.

Bibliography

- BERTHON G., «La suspension juridictionnelle du contrat administratif entre «référé suspension» et «référé contractuel», *RFDA* 2009, p. 1215

- BOULOUIS N., «Vers une simplification du contentieux des contrats publics', *CP-ACCP* 2010, n° 100, p. 80.
- BRACONNIER S., «L'autonomie contrastée du contentieux des contrats publics d'affaires», *RDP* 2010, n° 2, p. 327
- CLAMOUR G., «Décret du 27 novembre 2009 relatif aux procédures de recours applicables aux contrats de la commande publique: dispositions applicables aux marchés publics», Contr. et MP 2010, n° 1, comm. 2
- CLAMOUR G., «Décret du 27 novembre 2009 relatif aux procédures de recours applicables aux contrats de la commande publique', Contr. et MP 2010, n° 1, comm. 8
- CLAMOUR G., «Ordonnance du 7 mai 2009 relative aux recours applicables aux contrats de la commande publique», Contr. et MP 2009, n° 6, comm. 177
- DREYFUS J.-D., «L'émergence d'un droit commun de la commande publique en matière de procédures de recours', *AJDA* 2010, p. 148.
- ERSTEIN L., «Référé administratif», *Jurisclasseur Contrats et marchés publics*, Fasc.30, 30 novembre 2009.
- GOURDOU J., TERNEYRE P., «Les référés précontractuels et contractuels après l'ordonnance du 7 mai 2009», *BJCP* 2009, n° 66, p 358.
- GUEZOU O., «Référé contractuel: mise en perspective», *Le Moniteur Contrats publics*, III. 670.
- HAIM V. «De l'usage du référé dans le cas d'irrégularités lors de la passation d'un marché public», *AJDA* 2010, p. 871
- LAFAIX J.-F., «Systématisation inachevée du contentieux de la commande publique. Commentaire de l'ordonnance n° 2009-515 du 17 mai 2009', *Jurisclasseur Contrats et marchés publics*, Fasc.2, 8 mai 2009.
- TERNEYRE P., «Les principaux recours contentieux en matière de contrats administratifs», *BJCP* 2010, n° 69, p.74
- TERNEYRE P., «Les conséquences de la nullité des marchés publics et des délégations de service public', *CJEG* 2002, n° 592, p. 571
- VANDERMEEREN R., «Référé précontractuel', *Le Moniteur Droit des marchés publics et Contrats publics spéciaux*, III. 650.

About the Authors

Roberto Caranta (1963) is full professor of administrative law with the Law Faculty of the University of Turin (Italy). He is Director of the Master on Public Procurement for Sustainable Development jointly managed by his University and ITC-ILO Turin. He is member of the Procurement Review Board of the European Space Agency. He is directing (with Steen Treumer) the *European Procurement Law Series*, DJØF, Copenhagen. He is member of both the research networks *Public Contracts in Legal Globalization/Contrats Publics dans la Globalisation Juridique* and *PLAN – Procurement Law Academic Network*. Among his recent works on public procurements: (editor with Martin Trybus) *The Law of Green and Social Procurements in Europe*, Copenhagen, DJØF, 2010; *The In-House Providing: The Law as It Stands in the EU*, in M. Comba and S. Treumer (edds.), *The In-House Providing in European Law*, Copenhagen, DJØF, 2010.

Steen Treumer is a Professor of Public Procurement Law and Privatization Law at the Faculty of Law, University of Copenhagen. He published his prize awarded Ph.D.-dissertation in 2000 on the principle of equal treatment of tenderers in the EU public procurement rules. His numerous international publications on public procurement law include many in the recognized international journal *Public Procurement Law Review* which he has co-edited as from 2006. Steen Treumer is also editing the *European Procurement Law Series* together with Roberto Caranta. He has arranged more than 30 international conferences and seminars including two global public procurement conferences in 2010 in collaboration with Professor Sue Arrowsmith, University of Nottingham. Steen Treumer is also Chairman of the Danish Association for Public Procurement Law and has been a consultant in numerous public procurement cases.

Prof. *Gabriella Racca* is Full Professor of administrative law and Deputy Dean at the Faculty of Economics of the University of Turin (Italy). She is Member of the Teaching Staff of Ph.D in Public Law at the University of Turin, Member of the Scientific Board of the Master of Science in public procurement management for sustainable development organized by the ITC-

ILO in partnership with the University of Turin. She's on the editorial staff of the 'Foro amministrativo – Consiglio di Stato' review, she is member of the Scientific Board of the Diritto Amministrativo Review and writes also for Public Procurment Law Review. She has several publications on public contracts and has presented papers at several international conferences (Paris 2010; New York University 2010; George Washington University 2010; IPPC 2010, Seoul; Arizona University 2011). Her research interests include public service, accountability of public administration, public contracts, collaborative procurement and central purchasing bodies as well as the use of framework agreements.

Professor Dr. *Martin Burgi* is Professor of German and European Public Law (since 1999) and Director of the only research institute in Germany for the Modernisation of Administrative Law and Government Procurement Law at the Ruhr-University Bochum (since 2004). He is a member of the board of directors of the Institute for Mining and Energy Law at the Ruhr-University Bochum and a Research Fellow at the George-Washington-University Law School in Washington D.C.

Professor Martin Burgi areas of expertise are modernisation and privatisation of the state, administration and local governments and privatisation in the international context; privatisation in Europe; government procurement law; protection of fundamental rights of enterprises; legal protection at international courts; the roles of regions and municipalities in the global change. He is an official expert for parliamentary institutions and legal consultant for stock exchange enterprises, states and local municipalities. Furthermore, he is the scientific supervisor of the 'Düsseldorfer Vergaberechtstag', which is one of the leading annual conferences on government procurement paw in Germany. He has written numerous books and articles (more than 10 books and over 100 essays) on all his research areas, e.g.: 'The German public supply industry within the European legal framework – with special view to articles 16 and 86 II ECT', in Burgi, M. & Pielow, J.-C. (eds.), Public Utilities in Germany and Italy: An Overview, 25 Bochumer Forschungsberichte zum Berg- und Energierecht, 45-55 (2003); 'Small and medium-sized enterprises and procurement law – European legal framework and German experiences' in PPLR, 284-294 (2007); Kommunalrecht, Verlag C.H. Beck, 2 ed. (2008); 'Die Bedeutung der allgemeinen Vergabegrundsätze Wettbewerb, Transparenz und Gleichbehandlung' in NZBau, 29-34 (2008); 'Tagungsband zum 10. Düsseldorfer Vergaberechtstag', 2009; 'The Policy on Regulating Electronic, Communications in Germany', in: Arrowsmith (Hrsg.), Reform of the Uncitral Model Law on Procurement: Procurement Regulation for the 21st

Century, 305-327 (2009); 'Die Modernisierung des Vergaberechts als Daueraufgabe' in DÖV, 829-835 (2009); 'Federal Republic of Germany', in: Steytler (Hrsg.), Local Government and Metropolitan Regions in Federal Systems, 136-165 (2009); 'Damages as an effective remedy? – German Perspective', Oxford University Press (2010). You can contact Professor Dr. Martin Burgi at: ls.burgi@jura.ruhr-uni-bochum.de.

Dacian C. DRAGOS is Jean Monnet Associate Professor of Administrative and European Law at Babes Bolyai University, Cluj Napoca, Romania, and Vice Dean of the Faculty of Political, Administrative and Communication Sciences (since 2008). He has been awarded the Romanian Writers Association National Prize for legal research (2003). He was Scientific Coordinator of the Commission for drafting the Administrative Procedure Code of Romania (2006-2008), member of the Presidential Commission for Analyzing the Constitutional System of Romania (2008-2009) and currently Expert Member in the Commission for drafting the Administrative Code. He is also Chair of the 'Law and administration' Group of the European Group of Public Administration (since 2010). His research publications include 4 *Chapters* in international books, 4 *Books in Romanian* as single author: and 3 in collaboration, 25 p*apers in scientific journals*. Selected recent publications: 'National legal tradition – Romania', in Susana Galera (ed), *Judicial review: an analysis inside the European Legal System*, Council of Europe Publishing, 2010; with Neamtu, B. Veliscu, R., 'Judicial Review in Romania between Tradition and dialogue', in R. Caranta, A. Gerbrandy, *Traditions and Change in European Administrative Law*, Europa Law Publishing, Groeningen-Utrecht, 2011; TRANSPARENCY IN PUBLIC ADMINISTRATION, Accent Publishing House, Cluj Napoca, 150 pages (Romanian and English), 2008; JUDICIAL REVIEW OF ADMINISTRATIVE DECISIONS – A COMMENTARY, C.H. BECK, 2005, (in Romanian); 2nd edition, 2009; ADMINISTRATIVE INTERNAL APPEALS AND ADMINISTRATIVE JUSTICE, ALL-BECK Publishing House, 2001, Bucharest, (in Romanian); *'Europeanisation of Administrative Law in Romania: Current Developments in Jurisprudence and Legislation',* with Bogdana Neamtu, in 'Review of European Administrative Law', no. 1/2009, Europa Law Publishing; *'Reforming local public administration in Romania: trends and obstacles',* with Bogdana Neamtu, 'International Review of Administrative Sciences', no. 40, 2007; B. Thompson, D. Dragos and B. Neamtu (editors), *Transylvanian Review of Administrative Sciences, Special Issue LAW and PUBLIC ADMINISTRATION*, no.28/E/2099.

Bogdana Neamtu is Lecturer, PhD, with the Public Administration Department at Babes-Bolyai University, Romania. MPA from Babes-Bolyai University (joint degree in Management of Public Services and European Law), MA in Urban Planning from Michigan State University, US, and a PhD in sociology from Babes-Bolyai University. She is currently a post-doc scholar, focusing on urban affairs and public participation. Her research publications include 3 *chapters* in international books, 1 *book in Romanian* in collaboration, 18 p*apers in scientific journals*; member of the editorial board for Transylvanian Review of Administrative Sciences as well as guest editor in 2010. Relevant publications in the field are mentioned above (with D. Dragos). In the field of public procurement she is mostly interested by the role played by sustainability considerations in the process of awarding PP contracts by the local public authorities.

Raluca Veliscu is Teaching Assistant since 2009, PhD student with the Faculty of Economics and Business Administration. She teaches EU Law for the undergraduate level. MPA from Babes-Bolyai University (joint degree in Management of Public Services with the Institute for Public Policy and Social Research from Michigan State University). Her research publications include 2 chapters in international books, 1 book in Romanian in collaboration, 6 papers in scientific journals (most of them with D. Dragos and B. Neamtu).

Martin Trybus is Professor of European Law and Policy and Director of the Institute of European Law at the University of Birmingham, United Kingdom. Moreover, he currently serves on the Public Procurement Review Board of the European Space Agency in Paris. His numerous publications on public procurement law include 'European Defence Procurement Law' (Kluwer, 1999), 'Public Procurement: The Continuing Revolution' (edited with Sue Arrowsmith, Kluwer, 2002) and the second book in this series: 'The Law of Green and Social Procurement in Europe' edited with Roberto Caranta, Djoef, 2010. Professor Trybus has been involved in many research projects on procurement for the European Commission, the European Defence Agency, and the OECD. He is particularly interested in European defence procurement.

Mario E. Comba is Professor of Public comparative law and President of the School of International Studies of the Political Sciences Faculty at the University of Torino, Italy. His more recent publications in the field of public procurement include 'L'esecuzione dei lavori pubblici. Profili comparatistici' (Giappichelli, 2011) and the first book of this series: 'The In-house providing in European Law' (edited with Steen Treumer, Djoef, 2010). He is also the author of several articles and chapters in books related to public procurement including 'Sale of contract after bankruptcy from an EU perspective', in NDS, 2011. Professor Comba is currently researching the interaction between public procurement and European structural funds.

François Lichère is Professor of public law at the University of Aix-Marseille III – France since 2008. After graduating in law at the University of Montpellier (Licence) and at the University of Aix-en-Provence in political sciences, he has passed his Ph.D (doctorat) at the University of Montpellier in 1998 and was appointed lecturer in public law (Maître de conferences) in Montpellier in 1999 and Professor of public law in 2000 in Metz at the age of 31 before being appointed Professor at Montpellier University in 2002. He teaches public contract law and administrative law and lectures regularly in other European universities in French or in English.

Professor Lichère has published numerous books or articles, mainly in the field of public contracts law, in French or English. He is the author of 'Droit des contrats publics' (Dalloz, 2005) and co-author of 'Pratique des partenariats publics privés' (Litec, 2006 and 2009) and of «Droit des marchés publics et contrats publics spéciaux» (Le Moniteur) for which he is also co-editor. Among more than 50 articles, some must be quoted: «La définition contemporaine du marché public, R.D.P. 1997; «Les contrats de partenariat: fausse nouveauté ou vraie libéralisation dans la commande publique?», RDP 2004, n° 6, 1547 à 1568; «Le droit anglais des contrats publics comme modèle?», *in* Mélanges Guibal «Contrats publics», 2005, p. 449 à 470; n° 1411; «Le contrôle du Conseil d'Etat de la publicité adaptée est-il adapté?»; Contrats et marchés publics, novembre 2005, p. 5; «La qualification de marchés publics pour les contrats de mobilier urbain», R.J.E.P./C.J.E.G. 2006, n° 628, p. 71; 'Damages for violation of E.C. public procurement law under French law', Public procurement law review, 2006, n° 4, p. 171 à 178.

Professor Lichère is also consultant for two law firms based in Paris, advising for clients in the public sector or the private sector.

Nicolas Gabayet is a teaching assistant and a PhD candidate at the University of Aix-Marseille III – France. He holds a LLB (Licence), two diplomas (Diplômes d'université) in English and American Law (University of Lyon), a Masters Degree in public law (Master 1) delivered by University of Lyon after validation of the grades obtained at Queen's University Belfast (Erasmus student exchange program) and a LLM (Master 2) in Administrative law (University of Aix-Marseille III). Since 2007, he has taught administrative law, administrative procedure in contentious matters and constitutional law tutorials at University of Aix-Marseille III.

Nicolas Gabayet has published several articles, and case comments in the field of public contracts law and administrative procedure in contentious matters in French or English: 'Damages as an effective remedy? French Perspective', in D. Fairgrieve and F. Lichère (Eds), Damages as an effective remedy?, Hart, 2011; 'Pas d'appel, pas de pourvoi', note sous CE, Sect., 3 octobre 2008, *M. Roche*, *AJDA* 2009, n° 3, p. 167; 'Vélib': la légalité de son extension par avenant aux communes limitrophes de Paris', note sous CE Sect., 11 juillet 2008, *Ville de Paris*, *CP-ACCP* 2008, n°82, p. 64; 'Estimation de la durée d'une délégation de service public dans l'avis de publicité', note sous CE, 4 février 2009, *Communauté urbaine d'Arras*, *CP-ACCP* 2009, n°89, p. 84.